PART 2 Macroeconomic Goals and Relationships

Introduction to

MACROECONOMICS

THIRD EDITION

EDWIN G. DOLAN

Ph.D. Yale University

BEST VALUE
TEXTBOOKS

Text Design and Composition: Archetype Book Composition
Cover Design: Walker Printing

ISBN: 1-932856-71-4

TABLE OF CONTENTS

PREFACE

AS THE ECONOMY changes, teaching materials must change, too. Many such changes are incorporated in these third editions of *Introduction to Macroeconomics* and *Introduction to Microeconomics* from Best Value Textbooks.

Many of the changes reflect the increased globalization of economic life. Years ago, international topics were confined to one or two chapters, usually tucked in at the end of textbooks, and usually skipped over in the rush to complete the semester. That approach is no longer suitable today. In the macroeconomics volume, discussion of the balance of payments, net exports, exchange rates, international financial flows, and related topics are fully integrated into the chapters where the related theory and policy issues are discussed. There is no separate international macro chapter at all. In the microeconomics volume, there is still a separate chapter covering international trade and trade policy, but this is no longer the first introduction to these topics. Instead, it is a capstone chapter that pulls together individual threads of international economics that have been introduced chapter by chapter, starting in Chapter 1.

The globalization of this text is not confined to discussion of the big issues, like exchange rates or comparative advantage. It is also reflected in a wide variety of small boxed cases and examples incorporated throughout the text. These are not drawn exclusively from U.S. experience, as was the case in textbooks of the past, and why should they be? Principles such as supply and demand, marginal cost, and the effects of expansionary monetary policy apply as much in Russia or Malawi as they do in Kansas or California. The inclusion of examples from many places around the world will make the presentation of economic principles more vivid both for increasingly outward-looking American students and for the large number of students from abroad who come to the United States for an education.

Other changes reflect trends in economics itself. Neoclassical models of rational choice remain the foundation of microeconomics, but they are increasingly supplemented by expanded approaches that incorporate insights of other social sciences. Users of the microeconomics volume will find these expanded approaches incorporated at many points. Similarly, recent years have seen a restoration of balance in the teaching of macroeconomics between long-run and short-run perspectives, and between the real and monetary sectors of the economy. The macroeconomics chapters of this new edition begin with an introduction to the theory of economic growth before introducing short-run business cycle considerations. Also, the chapters on money, banking, and monetary policy are moved to an earlier place in the book in keeping with their importance. The short-run "Keynesian cross" income determination model no longer receives chapter-length treatment, although it is still included in a shorter form.

As was the case with the second edition, it has been a pleasure for me to work with such an innovative publisher.

Acknowledgments

My first thanks must go to my long-time co-author, David E. Lindsey, with whom I worked on earlier editions of this text over a period of many years. During his years as Deputy Director of the Division of Monetary Affairs of the Board of Governors of the Federal Reserve System, David was able to find the ideal balance between the theory and practice of economics. Although he did not contribute to preparation of this new edition, his strong influence can still be seen in both the macroeconomic and microeconomic chapters.

Second, I thank the entire publishing and editorial staff of Best Value Textbooks for introducing me to this great new concept in college publishing. I hope you, the user, benefit as much as I have.

Finally, I would like to acknowledge the support and inspiration of Jere Calmes who encouraged me to try my hand at textbook writing more than 30 years ago. Without his energy and commitment over many years, this book would never have been written.

EDWIN G. DOLAN
Lopez Island, Washington

Features of This Edition

- *State of the art pedagogy*. An abundance of case studies introduce and illustrate the subject matter of every chapter.
- *Integrated international economics*. As the world economy itself comes closer together, international economics must be more closely integrated into the principles course. Accordingly, topics in international economic theory and

policy, ranging from balance of payments accounts to the foreign exchange operations of the Fed, are introduced in the chapters in which they occur naturally, rather than presented separately in a single chapter.

Supplements

Test Bank

The accompanying Test Bank contains over 2,000 questions in a variety of formats including multiple choice, true/false, and essay questions.

Instructor's Manual

The expanded Instructor's Manual contains material which can be easily included in lectures. The manual also includes all of its traditional elements, including instructional objectives, lecture notes, and suggestions.

Study Guide

The Study Guide has hands-on applications and self-testing programs. It is available in two versions, *Macroeconomics,* and *Microeconomics*. Students can gain an advantage by reinforcing their reading and lecture notes with the following study guide features:

- *Where You're Going*. The objectives and terms for each chapter are recapped to tie concepts together.
- *Walking Tour.* The "Walking Tour" section provides a narrative summary of the chapter and incorporates questions on key points. Answers are given in the margin.
- *Hands On*. Geographical and numerical exercises clarify concepts and better prepare students for tests and quizzes.
- *Economics in the News*. A news item illustrates how concepts covered in the chapter can appear in the real world. Questions and answers reinforce the concepts.
- *Questions for Review.* These questions and answers follow the key chapter concepts, preparing students for the self-test.
- *Self-Test*. Extra test preparation increases a student's understanding and ability to succeed.
- *Careers in Economics*. Formerly an appendix in the text, this material provides students with an understanding of where the study of economics could lead them.

Online Student Tutorial

Created to support and enhance the student's comprehension of the economic principles discussed in the textbook. The online tutorial includes chapters objectives and study questions. To access the tutorial please visit our Students section on our Web site www.htpublishing.com. Username: Economics Password: DolanLindsey

Economic PowerPoint Transparencies

This PowerPoint slide set combines graphics and text to further illustrate the economic principles discussed in the text.

About the Author

EDWIN G. DOLAN was born in Oklahoma and grew up in a small town in Oregon. He attended Earlham College and Indiana University, where he majored in Russian Studies and received the Certificate of Indiana University's famed Russian and East-European Institute. After earning a doctorate in economics from Yale University, he taught at Dartmouth College, the University of Chicago, George Mason University and Gettysburg College. In 1990, he began teaching in Moscow, Russia, where he and his wife founded the American Institute of Business and Economics, an independent, not-for-profit MBA program. Since retiring as President of that institution in 2001, he has taught global macroeconomics, managerial economics and public policy in Latvia, Hungary, Croatia, Bulgaria, and the Czech Republic. When not lecturing abroad, he makes his home in Washington's San Juan Islands.

PART 1

Introduction to Economics

CHAPTER 1

Economics—The Science of Choice and Exchange

After reading this chapter, you will understand:

1. The subject matter of economics
2. Four fundamental economic choices:
   – What an economy will produce
   – How goods and services will be produced
   – Who will produce which goods and services
   – For whom goods will be produced
3. How economic choices are coordinated.
4. How economists use theory, graphs, and data in their work.

2006 WAS a tough year for General Motors, the world's largest carmaker. Struggling to recover from a $10.5 billion loss in 2005, the company was hoping for an increase in sales, especially of the large SUVs that are its most profitable models. However, after sales fell 8.3 percent through November, GM announced that it would close three big SUV plants for the first two weeks of 2007, to cut excess inventories. Meanwhile, sales of fuel-efficient hybrids made by Toyota and Honda were booming. The cause of all this turmoil? Soaring gasoline prices and record-high world prices for the crude oil from which gasoline is refined.

Scarcity

A situation in which there is not enough of a resource to meet all of everyone's wants.

Rising gasoline prices and falling SUV sales are illustrations of **scarcity** and the choices people make because there is not enough of something to meet all of their wants. In this case the scarce resource is oil. American consumers want to use a lot of the world's scarce oil resources to run the large cars they love so much. But consumers in rapidly growing China and India want oil too, to build a lifestyle based on refrigerators, air conditioners, and cars of their own. There is not enough oil in the world to satisfy all wants at once, so choices must be made. Scarcity and the way people deal with it are the central topics of **economics**, which is commonly defined as the social science that seeks to understand the choices people make in using scarce resources to meet their wants.

Economics

The social science that seeks to understand the choices people make in using scarce resources to meet their wants.

Economics, as the definition makes clear, is a study not of things or money or wealth but of *people*. Economics is about people because scarcity itself is a human phenomenon. Deposits of crude oil lay undisturbed in the ground for millions of years before they became the object of human wants. Only at that point did they become scarce in the sense that economists understand the term.

The focus on the human dimension of scarcity and choice is part of what makes economics a social science. In addition, economics is a social science because people do not attempt to solve the problem of scarcity in isolation. Instead, they can meet their wants much more effectively by trading with one another. As they trade, each person gives up something of value to others in a way that each person gains from the exchange. Some economists think exchange is even more important than scarcity as a defining characteristic of economics.[1]

The wide range of topics covered by economics can be divided into two main branches. The example of gasoline prices and vehicle choices are applications from **microeconomics**. The prefix *micro*, meaning "small," indicates that this branch of economics deals with the choices of small economic units such as households, firms, and government agencies. Although microeconomics studies individual behavior, its scope can be worldwide, as when it focuses on global trade in goods such as cars and crude oil.

Microeconomics

The branch of economics that studies the choices of individuals, including households, business firms, and government agencies

Macroeconomics

The branch of economics that studies large-scale economic phenomena, particularly inflation, unemployment, and economic growth..

Economics also has another branch, known as **macroeconomics**. The prefix *macro*, meaning "large," indicates that this branch deals with larger-scale economic phenomena. Typical problems in macroeconomics include how to maintain conditions in which people who want jobs can find them, how to protect the economy against the distortions caused by widespread price increases (inflation), and how to provide for a continued increase in living standards over time. Choices studied by macroeconomics include those made by governments, for example, choices among alternative policies concerning taxes, expenditures, budget deficits, and the financial system. However, because macroeconomic phenomena like inflation represent the end result of millions of individual choices regarding the prices of particular goods and services, macroeconomics ultimately rests on a microeconomic foundation.

Whether one is dealing with microeconomics or macroeconomics, and whether with domestic or international economic relationships, all economic analysis comes down to a special way of thinking about how people interact with one another as they choose how to use scarce resources.

WHAT? HOW? WHO? FOR WHOM?

Among the most important economic choices people make are those of what goods will be produced, how they will be produced, who will do which jobs, and for whom the results of production will be available. Each of these choices is made necessary because of scarcity, and each can be used to introduce a key element of the economic way of thinking.

Deciding What to Produce: Opportunity Cost

Factors of production

The basic inputs of labor, capital, and natural resources used in producing all goods and services.

Labor

The contributions to production made by people working with their minds and muscles.

Capital

All means of production that are created by people, including tools, industrial equipment, and structures.

Natural resources

Anything that can be used as a productive input in its natural state, such as farmland, building sites, forests, and mineral deposits.

Opportunity cost

The cost of a good or service measured in terms of the forgone opportunity to pursue the best possible alternative activity with the same time or resources.

The first choice is that of what goods to produce. Although the number of goods and services that could be produced is immense, the choice of what goods to produce can be illustrated using an economy in which there are just two alternative goods.Suppose these goods are cars and education. For many students, going without a car (or driving a used car instead of a new one) is a sacrifice that must be made in order to get a college education. The same trade-off faced by an individual student is also faced by the economy as a whole: Not enough cars and education can be produced to satisfy everyone's wants. Somehow it must be decided how much of each good to produce.

The impossibility of producing as much of everything as people want reflects a scarcity of the productive resources that are used to make all goods. Many scarce productive resources must be combined to make even the simplest of goods. For example, making a table requires lumber, nails, glue, a hammer, a saw, and the labor of a woodworker. For convenience, all the various productive resources can be grouped into three basic categories, called **factors of production**: labor, capital, and natural resources. **Labor** includes all of the productive contributions made by people working with their minds and muscles. **Capital** includes all the productive inputs created by people, including tools, machinery, buildings, and intangible items, such as computer software. **Natural resources** include anything that can be used as a productive input in its natural state—for example, farmland, building sites, forests, and mineral deposits.

Productive resources that are used to satisfy one want cannot be used to satisfy another at the same time. Steel, concrete, and building sites used for automobile factories cannot also be used for classrooms. People who are employed as teachers cannot spend the same time working on an automobile assembly line. Even the time students spend in class and studying for tests represents use of a factor of production that could otherwise be used as labor in an auto plant. Whenever the inputs to production have more than one possible use, producing one good means forgoing the opportunity to produce something else instead. Economists express this basic truth by saying that everything has an **opportunity cost**. The opportunity cost of a good or service is its cost in terms of the forgone opportunity to pursue the best possible alternative activity with the same time or resources.

In our two-good economy, the opportunity cost of producing a college graduate can be stated in terms of the number of cars that could have been produced by using the same labor, capital, and natural resources. Suppose that the opportunity cost of educating a college graduate is four Toyota Camrys. Such a ratio (graduates per car or cars per graduate) is a useful way to express opportunity cost when only two goods are involved. More typically, though, we deal with situations in which there are many goods. Having more of one means giving up a little bit of many others.

In an economy with many goods, opportunity costs can be expressed in terms of a common unit of measurement, money. For example, rather than saying that a college education is worth four Camrys or that a Camry is worth one-fourth of a college education, we could say that the opportunity cost of a car is $20,000 and that of a college education is $80,000.

Useful as it is to have a common unit of measurement, great care must be taken when opportunity costs are expressed in terms of money, because not all out-of-pocket money expenditures represent the sacrifice of opportunities to do something else. At the same time, not all sacrificed opportunities take the form of money spent. *Applying Economic Ideas 1.1*, which analyzes both the out-of-pocket expenditures and the opportunity costs of a college education, shows why.

The importance of opportunity cost will be stressed again and again in this book. The habit of looking for opportunity costs is one of the distinguishing features of the economic way of thinking.

Deciding How to Produce: Efficiency and Entrepreneurship

A second basic economic choice is that of how to produce. There is more than one way to produce almost any good or service. Cars, for example, can be made in highly automated factories using a lot of capital equipment and relatively little labor, or they can be built one by one in small shops, using a lot of labor and only a few general-purpose machines. Toyota Camrys are built the first way, Ferraris the second way. The same kind of thing could be said about education. Economics can be taught in a small classroom with one teacher and a blackboard serving 20 students, or it can be taught in a large lecture hall in which the teacher uses video technology to address hundreds of students.

Economic efficiency

A state of affairs in which it is impossible to make any change that satisfies one person's wants more fully without causing some other person's wants to be satisfied less fully.

EFFICIENCY Efficiency is a key consideration in deciding how to produce. In everyday speech, efficiency means producing with a minimum of expense, effort, and waste. Economists use a more precise definition. **Economic efficiency**, they say, refers to a state of affairs in which it is impossible to make any change that satisfies one person's wants more fully without causing some other person's wants to be satisfied less fully.[2]

Although this formal definition of economic efficiency may be unfamiliar, it is actually closely related to the everyday notion of efficiency. If there is some way to make you better off without making me worse off, it is wasteful (inefficient) to pass up the opportunity. If I have a red pen that I am not using, and you need one just for a minute, it would be wasteful for you to buy a red pen of your own. It is more efficient for me to lend you my pen; it makes you better off and me no worse

APPLYING ECONOMIC IDEAS 1.1

THE OPPORTUNITY COST OF A COLLEGE EDUCATION

How much does it cost you to go to college? If you are a resident student at a typical four-year private college in the United States, you can answer this question by making up a budget like the one shown in Figure A. This can be called a budget of out-of-pocket costs, because it includes all the items—and only those items—that you or your parents must actually pay for in a year.

Your own out-of-pocket costs may be much higher or lower than those listed. Chances are, though, that these are the main categories that first come to mind when you think about the costs of college. As you begin to think more like an economist, you may find it useful to restate your college budget in terms of opportunity costs. Which of the items in Figure A represent opportunities that you have forgone in order to go to college? Are any forgone opportunities missing? To answer these questions, compare Figure A with Figure B, which shows a budget of opportunity costs.

Some items are both opportunity costs and out-of-pocket costs. The first three items in Figure A show up again in Figure B. To spend $14,000 on tuition and fees and $1,200 on books and supplies, you must give up the opportunity to buy other goods and services—to buy a car or rent a ski condo, for instance. To spend $1,100 getting to and from school, you must pass up the opportunity to travel somewhere else or to spend the money on something other than travel. Not all out-of-pocket costs are also opportunity costs, however. Consider the last two items in the out-of-pocket budget. By spending $7,000 on room, board, and personal expenses during the year, you are not really giving up the opportunity to do something else. Whether or not you were going to college, you would have to eat, live somewhere, and buy clothes. Because these are expenses that you would have in any case, they do not count as opportunity costs of going to college.

Finally, there are some items that are opportunity costs without being out-of-pocket costs. Think about what you would be doing if you were not going to college. If you were not going to college, you probably would have taken a job and started earning money soon after leaving high school. As a high-school graduate, your earnings would be about $16,000 during the nine months of the school year. (You can work during the summer even if you are attending college.) Because this potential income is something that you must forgo for the sake of college, it is an opportunity cost even though it does not involve an outlay of money.

Which budget you use depends on the kind of decision you are making. If you have already decided to go to college and are doing your financial planning, the out-of-pocket budget will tell you how much you will have to raise from savings, a job, parents' contributions, and scholarships to make ends meet. But if you are making the more basic choice between going to college or pursuing a career that does not require a college degree, the opportunity cost of college is what counts.

Figure A	Budget of Out-of-Pocket Costs	Figure B	Budget of Opportunity Costs
Tuition and fees	$14,000	Tuition and fees	$14,000
Books and supplies	1,200	Books and supplies	1,200
Transportation to and from home	1,100	Transportation to and from home	1,000
Room and board	7,000	Forgone income	16,000
Personal expenses	1,400		
Total out-of-pocket costs	**$24,700**	**Total opportunity costs**	**$32,200**

off. If there is a way to make us both better off, it would be all the more wasteful not to take advantage of the opportunity. You lend me your bicycle for the afternoon and I will lend you my volleyball. If I do not ride a bicycle very often and you do not play volleyball very often, it would be inefficient for us both to own one of each item.

Efficiency in production

A situation in which it is not possible, given available knowledge and productive resources, to produce more of one good without forgoing the opportunity to produce some of another good.

The concept of economic efficiency has a variety of applications: one such application centers on the question of *how* to produce. **Efficiency in production** refers to a situation in which it is not possible, given available productive resources and existing knowledge, to produce more of one good without forgoing the opportunity to produce some of another good. The concept of efficiency in production, like the broader concept of economic efficiency, includes the everyday notion of avoiding waste. For example, a grower of apples finds that beyond some certain quantity, using more water per tree does not increase the yield of apples. To use more than that amount would be wasteful. Better to transfer the extra water to the production of, say, peaches. That way more peaches can be grown without any reduction in the apple crop.

The economist's definition also includes more subtle possibilities for improving the efficiency of production in cases where the waste of resources is less obvious. For example, it is possible to grow apples in Georgia. It is also possible, by selecting the right tree varieties and using winter protection, to grow peaches in Vermont. Some hobbyists do grow both fruits in both states. However, doing so on a commercial scale would be inefficient even if growers in both states followed the most careful cultivation practices and avoided any obvious waste, like using too much water. To see why, suppose that initially apple and peach trees were planted in equal numbers in the two states. Then compare this with a situation in which 500 fewer struggling peach trees had been planted in Vermont, and 500 thriving apple trees had been planted instead. At the same time, suppose 500 fewer heat-stressed apple trees had been planted in Georgia, and their place had been taken by peaches. The second alternative would increase the output of both fruits without increasing the total land, labor, and capital used in fruit production. This shows that the original distribution of trees was inefficient.

HOW TO INCREASE PRODUCTION POTENTIAL Once efficiency has been achieved, more of one good can be produced only by forgoing the opportunity to produce something else, assuming that productive resources and knowledge are held constant. But over time, production potential can be expanded by accumulating more resources and finding new ways of putting them to work.

In the past, discovery of new supplies of natural resources has been an important way of increasing production potential. Population growth has always been, and still is, another way. However, as the most easily tapped supplies of natural resources are depleted and as population growth slows in most parts of the world, capital will increasingly be the factor of production that contributes most to the expansion of production potential.

Investment

The act of increasing the economy's stock of capital—that is, its supply of means of production made by people.

The act of increasing the economy's stock of capital—that is, its supply of productive inputs made by people—is known as **investment**. Investment involves a trade-off of present consumption for future consumption. To build more factories, roads, and computers, we have to divert resources from the production of bread, movies, haircuts, and other things that satisfy immediate wants. In return, we put ourselves in a better position to satisfy our future wants.

Increased availability of productive resources is not the only source of economic growth, however. Even more important are improvements in human knowledge—the invention of new technology, new forms of organization, new ways of satisfying wants. The process of looking for new possibilities—making use of new ways of doing things, being alert to new opportunities, and overcoming old limits—is called **entrepreneurship**. It is a dynamic process that breaks down the constraints imposed by existing knowledge and limited supplies of factors of production.

Entrepreneurship

The process of looking for new possibilities—making use of new ways of doing things, being alert to new opportunities, and overcoming old limits.

Entrepreneurship does not have to mean inventing something or starting a new business, although it sometimes does. It may mean finding a new market for an existing product—for example, convincing people in Germany that Japanese sushi makes a quick and tasty lunch. It may mean taking advantage of price differences between one market and another—for example, buying hay at a low price in Pennsylvania, where growing conditions have been good in the past year, and reselling it in Virginia, where the weather has been too dry.

Households can be entrepreneurs, too. They do not simply repeat the same patterns of work and leisure every day. They seek variety—new jobs, new foods, new places to visit. Each time you try something new, you are taking a step into the unknown. In this sense you are an entrepreneur.

Entrepreneurship is sometimes called the fourth factor of production. However, entrepreneurship differs from the three classical factors of production in important ways. Unlike labor, capital, and natural resources, entrepreneurship is intangible and difficult to measure. Although entrepreneurs earn incomes reflecting the value that the market places on their accomplishments, we cannot speak of a price per unit of entrepreneurship; there are no such units. Also, unlike human resources (which grow old), machines (which wear out), and natural resources (which can be used up), the inventions and discoveries of entrepreneurs are not depleted as they are used. Once a new product or concept has been invented, such as gasoline-electric hybrid power for cars, text messaging on cell phones, hedge funds as a form of financial investment, the required knowledge does not have to be created again (although, of course, it may be supplanted by even better ideas). All in all, it is more helpful to think of entrepreneurship as a process of learning better ways of using the three basic factors of production than as a separate factor of production.

Deciding Who Will Do Which Work: The Division of Labor

The questions of what will be produced and how to produce it would exist even for a person living in isolation. Even the fictional castaway Robinson Crusoe had to decide whether to fish or hunt birds, and if he decided to fish, he had to decide whether to do so with a net or with a hook and line. In contrast, the economic questions of who will do which work and for whom output will be produced exist only for people living in society—another reason economics is considered one of the social sciences.

The question of who will do which work is a matter of organizing the social division of labor. Will everyone do everything independently—be a farmer in the morning, a tailor in the afternoon, and a poet in the evening? Or will people cooperate—work together, trade goods and services, and specialize in one particular job? Economists answer these questions by pointing out that it is more efficient to cooperate. Doing so allows a given number of people to produce more than they could if each of them worked alone. Three things make cooperation worthwhile: teamwork, learning by doing, and comparative advantage.

First consider *teamwork*. In a classic paper on this subject, Armen Alchian and Harold Demsetz used the example of workers unloading bulky crates from a truck.[3] The crates are so large that one worker alone cannot move them at all without unpacking them. Two people working independently would take hours to unload the truck. If they work as a team, however, they can easily pick up the crates and stack them on the loading dock. This example shows that even when everyone is doing the same work and even when little skill is involved teamwork pays.

A second reason for cooperation applies when there are different jobs to be done and different skills to be learned. In a furniture plant, for example, some workers operate production equipment, others use office equipment, and still others buy materials. Even if all the workers start out with equal abilities, each gets better at a particular job by doing it repeatedly. *Learning by doing* thus turns workers of average productivity into specialists, thereby creating a more productive team.

A third reason for cooperation comes into play after the process of learning by doing has developed different skills and also applies when workers start out with different talents and abilities—the principle of division of labor according to *comparative advantage*. **Comparative advantage** is the ability to do a job or produce a good at a relatively lower opportunity cost than someone else.

Comparative advantage

The ability to produce a good or service at a relatively lower opportunity cost than someone else.

An example will illustrate the principle of comparative advantage. Suppose two clerical workers, Bill and Jim, are assigned the job of getting out a batch of personalized letters to clients. Jim is a whiz. He can prepare a letter in 5 minutes and stuff it into an envelope in 1 minute. Working alone, he can finish ten letters in an hour. Bill is slow and clumsy. It takes him 10 minutes to prepare a letter and 5 minutes to stuff it into the envelope. Alone, he can do only four letters an hour. In summary form:

Jim: Prepare 1 letter 5 min.
Stuff 1 envelope 1 min.

Bill: Prepare 1 letter 10 min.
Stuff 1 envelope 5 min.

Without cooperation, the two workers' limit is 14 letters per hour between them. Could they do better by cooperating? It depends on who does which job. One idea might be for Jim to prepare all the letters while Bill does all the stuffing because that way they can just keep up with each other. But at 5 minutes per letter, that kind of cooperation cuts their combined output to twelve letters per hour. It is worse than not cooperating at all.

Instead, they should divide the work according to the principle of comparative advantage. Even though Bill is slower at preparing the letters, he has a *comparative advantage* in preparation because the opportunity cost of that part of the work is lower for him: The 10 minutes he takes to prepare a letter is equal to the time he needs to stuff two envelopes. For Jim, the 5 minutes he takes to prepare a letter could be used to stuff five envelopes. For Bill, then, the opportunity cost of preparing one letter is to forgo stuffing *two* envelopes, whereas for Jim the opportunity cost of preparing one letter is to forgo stuffing *five* envelopes.

Because Bill gives up fewer stuffed envelopes per letter than Jim, the principle of comparative advantage says that Bill should spend all his time preparing letters. If he does, he can produce six letters per hour. Meanwhile Jim can spend 45 minutes of each hour preparing nine letters, and the last 15 minutes of each hour stuffing all 15 envelopes. By specializing according to comparative advantage, the two workers can increase their total output to 15 letters per hour, the best they can possible do.

In this example the principle of comparative advantage points the way toward an efficient division of labor between two people working side by side. But the principle also has broader implications. It can apply to a division of labor between individuals or business firms working far apart—even in different countries. In fact, the earliest application of the principle was to international trade (see *Who Said It? Who Did It? 1.1*). Today comparative advantage remains one of the primary motivations for mutually beneficial cooperation, whether on the scale of the workplace or on that of the world as a whole.

Whatever the context, the principle of comparative advantage is easy to apply provided one remembers that it is rooted in the concept of opportunity cost. Suppose there are two tasks, A and B, and two parties, X and Y (individuals, firms, or countries), each capable of doing both tasks, but not equally well. First ask what is the opportunity cost for X of doing a unit of task A, measured in terms of how many units of task B could be done with the same time or resources. Then ask the same question for Y. The party with the lower opportunity cost for doing a unit of task A has the comparative advantage in doing that task. To check, ask what is the opportunity cost for each party of doing a unit of task B, measured in terms how many units of task A could be done with the same time or resources. The party with the lower opportunity cost for doing a unit of task B has the comparative advantage in doing that task.

Deciding for Whom Goods will be Produced: Positive and Normative Economics

Together, the advantages of team production, learning by doing, and comparative advantage mean that people can produce more efficiently by cooperating than they

WHO SAID IT? WHO DID IT? 1.1

DAVID RICARDO AND THE THEORY OF COMPARATIVE ADVANTAGE

David Ricardo was born in London in 1772, the son of an immigrant who was a member of the London stock exchange. Ricardo's education was rather haphazard, and he entered his father's business at the age of 14. In 1793, he married and went into business on his own. These were years of war and financial turmoil. The young Ricardo developed a reputation for remarkable astuteness and quickly made a large fortune.

In 1799, Ricardo read Adam Smith's *The Wealth of Nations* and developed an interest in political economy (as economics was then called). In 1809, his first writings on economics appeared. These were a series of newspaper articles on "The High Price of Bullion," which appeared during the following year as a pamphlet. Several other short works added to his reputation in this area. In 1814, he retired from business to devote all his time to political economy.

Ricardo's major work was *Principles of Political Economy and Taxation*, first published in 1817. This work contains, among other things, a pioneering statement of the principle of comparative advantage as applied to international trade. Using a lucid numerical example, Ricardo showed why, as long as wool can be produced *comparatively* less expensively in England, it was to the advantage of both countries for England to export wool to Portugal and to import wine in return, even though both products could be produced with fewer labor hours in Portugal.

International trade is only a sideline of Ricardo's *Principles*. The book covers the whole field of economics as it then existed, beginning with value theory and progressing to a theory of economic growth and evolution. Ricardo held that the economy was growing toward a future "steady state." At that point economic growth would come to a halt and the wage rate would be reduced to the subsistence level. This gloomy view and the equally pessimistic views of Ricardo's contemporary, Thomas Malthus, gave political economy a reputation as "the dismal science."

Ricardo's book was extremely influential. For more than half a century thereafter, much of the writing on economic theory published in England consisted of expansions and commentaries on Ricardo's work. Economists as different as Karl Marx, the revolutionary socialist, and John Stuart Mill, a defender of liberal capitalism, took Ricardo's theories as their starting point. Even today there are "neo-Ricardian" and "new classical" economists who look to Ricardo's works for inspiration.

could if each worked in isolation. Cooperation, however, raises yet another issue: For whom will goods be produced? The question of the distribution of output among members of society has implications in terms of both efficiency and fairness.

EFFICIENCY IN DISTRIBUTION Consider first a situation in which production has already taken place and the supply of goods is fixed. Suppose, for example, that 30 students get on a bus to go to a football game. Bag lunches are handed out. Half the bags contain a ham sandwich and a root beer; the other half contain a tuna sandwich and a cola. What happens when the students open their bags? They do not just eat whatever they find—they start trading. Some swap sandwiches; others swap drinks. Maybe there is not enough of everything to give each person his or her first choice. Nevertheless, the trading makes at least some people better off than they were when they started. Moreover, no one ends up worse off. If some of the students do not want to trade, they can always eat what was given to them in the first place.

This example shows one sense in which the "for whom" question is partly about efficiency: Starting from any given quantity of goods, their distribution can be improved through trades that result in better satisfaction of some people's preferences. As long as it is possible to trade existing supplies of goods in a way that permits

Efficiency in distribution

A situation in which it is not possible, by redistributing existing supplies of goods, to satisfy one person's wants more fully without causing some other person's wants to be satisfied less fully.

some people to satisfy their wants more fully without making others worse off, **efficiency in distribution** can be improved even while the total quantity of goods remains fixed.

Efficiency in distribution and efficiency in production are two aspects of the general concept of economic efficiency. When both aspects are taken into account, the relationship between distribution and efficiency is not restricted to situations in which the total amount of goods is fixed in advance. That is so because the rules for distribution affect the patterns of production. For example, suppose rewards for providing nursing care are increased relative to the rewards for producing clothing. As a result, some people will switch jobs, so that more nursing care and less clothing is produced. Another reason is that rules for distribution affect incentives for entrepreneurship. If there are great rewards for discovering new ways of doing things, people will make greater efforts to improve products, methods of production, and means of distribution.

FAIRNESS IN DISTRIBUTION Efficiency is not the whole story when it comes to the question of for whom goods will be produced. One can also ask whether a given distribution is fair. Questions of fairness often dominate discussions of distribution.

One widely held view judges fairness in distribution in terms of equality. This concept of fairness is based on the idea that all people, by virtue of their shared humanity, deserve a portion of the goods and services turned out by the economy. There are many versions of this concept. Some people think that all income and wealth should be distributed equally. Others think that people have an equal right to a "safety net" level of income but that inequality in distributing any surplus beyond that level is not necessarily unfair. Still others think that certain goods, such as health care and education, should be distributed equally but that it is fair for other goods to be distributed less equally.

An alternative view, which also has many adherents, judges fairness not in terms of how much each person receives, but instead in terms of the process through which goods are distributed. In this view, fairness requires that certain rules and procedures be observed, such as respect for private property or nondiscrimination on grounds of race and gender. As long as those rules are followed, any resulting distribution of income is viewed as acceptable. In this view, equality of opportunity is emphasized more than equality of outcome.

Positive economics

The area of economics that is concerned with facts and the relationships among them.

Normative economics

The area of economics that is devoted to judgments about whether economic policies or conditions are good or bad.

POSITIVE AND NORMATIVE ECONOMICS Many economists make a sharp distinction between the question of efficiency and that of fairness. Discussions of efficiency are seen as part of **positive economics**, the area of economics that is concerned with facts and the relationships among them. Discussions of fairness, in contrast, are seen as part of **normative economics**, the area of economics that is devoted to judgments about whether particular economic policies and conditions are good or bad.

Normative economics extends beyond the question of fairness in the distribution of output. Value judgments also arise about the fairness of the other three basic choices faced by every economy. In choosing what will be produced, is it fair to permit production of alcohol and tobacco but to outlaw production of marijuana? In choosing how to produce, is it fair to allow people to work under dangerous or unhealthy conditions, or should work under such conditions be prohibited? In choosing who does which work, is it fair to limit access to specific jobs according to age, gender, race, or union membership? As you can see, normative issues extend to every corner of economics.

Positive economics, rather than offering value judgments about outcomes, focuses on understanding the processes by which the four basic economic questions are or could be answered. It analyzes the way economies operate, or would operate if certain institutions or policies were changed. It traces relationships between facts, often looking for regularities and patterns that can be measured statistically.

Most economists consider positive economics their primary area of expertise, but normative considerations influence the conduct of positive economics in several ways. The most significant of those influences is the selection of topics to investigate. An economist who sees excessive unemployment as a glaring injustice may study that problem; one who sympathizes with victims of job discrimination may take up a different line of research. Also, normative views are likely to affect the ways in which data are collected, ideas about which facts can be considered true, and so on.

At one time it was thought that a purely positive economics could be developed, untouched by normative considerations of values and fairness. Within its framework, all disputes could be resolved by reference to objective facts. Today that notion is less widely held. Nevertheless, it remains important to be aware that most major economic controversies, especially those that have to do with government policy, have normative as well as positive components, and to be aware of the way each component shapes the way we think about those controversies.

COORDINATING ECONOMIC CHOICES

To function effectively, an economy must have some way of coordinating the choices of millions of individuals regarding what to produce, how to produce it, who will do each job, and for whom the output will be produced. This section discusses how households, businesses, and the government interact in the coordination of economic choices.

A Non-economic Example

You, like almost everyone, have probably had the experience of shopping at a supermarket where there are several long checkout lines. In such a situation, you and other shoppers want to get through the checkout process as fast as possible. The store, too, would like to avoid a situation in which customers in some lines have a long wait for service while the cashiers in other lines stand idle for lack of customers. How can this be done?

One way would be for the store to follow the example of the U.S. Customs service at New York's busy Kennedy International Airport where an employee is on duty to direct arriving passengers to the agent with the shortest wait. But supermarkets do not work that way. Instead, supermarkets leave shoppers to decide for themselves which line to join based on information from their own observations. As you approach the checkout area, you first look to see which lines are the shortest. You then make allowance for the possibility that some shoppers have carts that are heaped full, while others have only a few items. Using your own judgment based on your own observations, you head for the line you think will be fastest.

The coordination system used by the Customs Service at JFK airport is an example of coordination by **hierarchy**. Hierarchy is a way of achieving coordination in which individual actions are guided by instructions from a central authority. The approach used in supermarkets is an example of coordination by **spontaneous order**. Under this system, coordination is achieved when individuals adjust their actions in response to cues received from their immediate environment. It is *orderly* because it achieves an approximately equal waiting time in each checkout line. It is *spontaneous* in that coordination is achieved without central direction. Even though no shopper has the specific goal of equalizing the lines, approximate equalization is the end result.

Hierarchy

A way of achieving coordination in which individual actions are guided by instructions from a central authority.

Spontaneous order

A way of achieving coordination in which individuals adjust their actions in response to cues from their immediate environment.

Spontaneous Order in Markets

In economics, markets are the most important example of the coordination of decisions through spontaneous order. A **market** is any arrangement people have for trading with one another. Some markets have formal rules and carry out exchanges at a single location, such as the New York Stock Exchange. Other markets are more informal, such as the word-of-mouth networks through which teenage babysitters get in touch with people who need their services. Despite the wide variety of forms that markets take, they all have one thing in common: They provide the information and incentives people need to coordinate their decisions.

Market

Any arrangement people have for trading with one another.

Just as shoppers need information about the length of checkout lines, participants in markets need information about the scarcity and opportunity costs of various goods and factors of production. Markets rely primarily on prices to transmit this information. If a good or factor of production becomes scarcer, its price is bid up. The increase in the price tells people it is worth more and signals producers to make greater efforts to increase supplies. For example, when platinum first began to be used in catalytic converters to reduce pollution from automobile exhaust, new buyers entered the market. As automakers began to compete with makers of jewelry and other traditional users, platinum became more difficult to acquire. Competition for available supplies bids up the price of platinum. This provided buyers with a cue that the value of platinum had increased and provided an incentive to be careful with its use. At the same time, producers learned that, where possible, they should increase the quantity of platinum mined.

Instead, suppose a new technology were to reduce the cost of producing platinum, for example, by allowing extraction of platinum from mine wastes that were discarded in earlier periods when platinum was less valuable. Information about the reduced cost would be transmitted by markets in the form of a lower price. People could then consider increasing the quantity of platinum they use.

In addition to knowing the best use for resources, people must also have incentives to act on that information. Markets provide incentives to sell goods and productive resources where they will bring the highest prices and to buy them where they can be obtained at the lowest prices. Profits motivate business managers to improve production methods and to design goods that match consumer needs. Workers who stay alert to opportunities and work where they are most productive receive the highest wages. Consumers are motivated to use less expensive substitutes where feasible.

Adam Smith, often considered the father of economics, saw coordination through markets as the foundation of prosperity and progress. In a famous passage in *The Wealth of Nations*, he called markets an "invisible hand" that nudges people into the economic roles they can play best (see *Who Said It? Who Did It? 1.2*). To this day, an appreciation of markets as a means of coordinating choices remains a central feature of the economic way of thinking.

The Role of Hierarchy

Important as markets are, they are not the only means of achieving economic coordination. Some decisions are guided by direct authority within organizations, that is, by the mechanism of hierarchy. Decisions made by government agencies are one important example. Government decisions are often implemented not through the spontaneous choices of individuals, but via directives issued by a central authority: pay your taxes, do not dump toxic wastes in the river, and so on. Business firms, especially large corporations, are another important example of the hierarchical form of organization. The Toyota Motor Corporation uses directives from a central authority to make many important decisions, for example, the decision to build the new hybrid version of its popular Camry in Kentucky rather than in Japan.

Although governments and corporations use hierarchical methods to make choices within their organizations, they deal with one another and with individual consumers through markets. Markets and hierarchies thus play complementary roles in achieving economic coordination. Some economies rely more on markets, others on government or corporate planning. At one extreme, the centrally-planned

WHO SAID IT? WHO DID IT? 1.2
ADAM SMITH ON THE INVISIBLE HAND

Adam Smith is considered the founder of economics as a distinct field of study, even though he wrote only one book on the subject: The Wealth of Nations, published in 1776. Smith was 53 years old at the time. His friend David Hume found the book such hard going that he doubted that many people would read it. Hume was wrong—people have been reading it for more than 200 years.

The wealth of a nation, in Smith's view, is not a result of the accumulation of gold or silver in its treasury, as many of his contemporaries believed. Rather, it is the outcome of the activities of ordinary people working and trading in free markets. To Smith, the remarkable thing about the wealth produced by a market economy is that it is not a result of any organized plan, but is rather the unintended outcome of the actions of many people, each of whom is pursuing the incentives the market offers with his or her own interests in mind. As he put it:

> It is not from the benevolence of the butcher, the brewer, or the baker that we expect our dinner, but from their regard to their own interest .... Every individual is continually exerting himself to find out the most advantageous employment for whatever capital he can command .... By directing that industry in such a manner as its produce may be of the greatest value, he intends only his own gain, and he is in this, as in many other cases, led by an invisible hand to promote an end which was no part of his intention.*

Much of the discipline of economics as it has developed over the past two centuries consists of elaborations on ideas found in Smith's work. The idea of the "invisible hand" of market incentives that channels people's efforts in directions that are beneficial to their neighbors remains the most durable of Smith's contributions to economics.

*Adam Smith, *The Wealth of Nations* (1776), Book 1, Chapter 2.

economy of North Korea places heavy emphasis on government authority. Economies, like that of the United States, make greater use of markets; but no economy uses one means of coordination to the exclusion of the other. Government regulatory agencies in the United States establish laws to control pollution or protect worker safety; on the other hand, North Korea uses small-scale markets to distribute some goods. Large corporations use commands from higher authority to make many decisions, but they also often subcontract with outsiders through the market, and they sometimes encourage their own divisions to deal with one another on a market basis.

In short, wherever one turns in economics, the question of coordination arises. Understanding economic coordination means understanding the complementary roles of markets, on the one hand, and of government and corporate hierarchies, on the other.

ECONOMIC METHOD

We have seen that economists have a distinctive way of thinking about the world based on the concepts of scarcity, choice, and exchange. They also have some distinctive methods of approaching problems and expressing the conclusions that they reach. We will conclude the chapter with a few comments about method.

Theories and Models

Theory

A representation of the way in which facts are related to one another.

Model

A synonym for theory; in economics, often applied to theories that are stated in graphical or mathematical form.

Economists try to understand the choices people make in terms of the context in which the choices are made. The relationships they propose between choices and context are called **theories** or **models**. The terms are synonyms, although economists tend to use the term theory to refer to more general statements about economic relationships and the term model to refer to more particular statements, especially those that take the form of graphs or mathematical equations.

Economics needs theories and models because facts do not speak for themselves. Take, for example, the fact that in 2005, for the first time in 25 years,US drivers logged fewer miles than the year before. The decrease was not large—only about 1 percent—but economists want to know why there was a decrease at all. They have a theory. They relate the change in driving habits to the 50 percent rise in the retail price of gasoline over the preceding two years. The relationship between the price of gasoline and driving choices is seen as a particular instance of a broader theory according to which an increase in the price of any good, other things being equal, leads consumers to seek ways to reduce their consumption of the good.

The theory as stated is a simple one. It relates driving choices to just one other fact, the price of gasoline. A more complete theory would bring in other factors that influence consumer choice, such as the prices of goods other than gasoline, consumers' incomes, changes in the social image of large SUVs versus efficient hybrids, and so on. Where does one draw the line? How much detail does it take to make a good theory?

There is no simple answer to this question, because adding detail to a theory involves a trade-off. On the one hand, if essential details are left out, the theory may fail altogether to fit the facts. On the other hand, adding too much detail defeats the purpose of understanding because key relationships may become lost in a cloud of complexity. The only real guideline is that a theory should be just detailed enough to suit the purpose for which it is intended, and no more.

By analogy, consider the models that aircraft designers use. A scaled-down wind-tunnel model made to test the aerodynamics of a new design would need to represent the shapes of the wings, fuselage, and control surfaces accurately, but it would not need to include tiny seats with tiny tables and magazine pockets. On the other hand, a full-scale model built for the purpose of training flight attendants to work on the new plane would need seats and magazine pockets, but it would not need wings.

In much the same way, the theories and models presented in this book are designed to highlight a few key economic relationships. They are helpful in understanding economics in the same way that playing a flight simulation game on a laptop computer is helpful in understanding the basics of flying. Professional economists use more detailed models, just as professional pilots train with complex flight simulators rather than with simple computer games. Nevertheless, the basic principles learned from the simple models should not contradict those that apply to the more complex ones. In the simple games, just as in the complex simulators, adjusting the rudder makes the plane turn and adjusting the elevators makes it climb or dive.

The Use of Graphs[4]

The theories introduced so far have been stated in words. Words are a powerful tool for developing understanding, but they are even more powerful when they are supplemented by pictures. Economists support their words with pictures called graphs. An example will illustrate how economists use graphs to represent theories.

THE PRODUCTION POSSIBILITY FRONTIER Recall our earlier discussion of the trade-off between education and cars. Figure 1.1 shows the trade-off in graphical form for an economy in which only those two goods are produced. The horizontal axis measures the quantity of education in terms of the number of college graduates

FIGURE 1.1 PRODUCTION POSSIBILITY FRONTIER

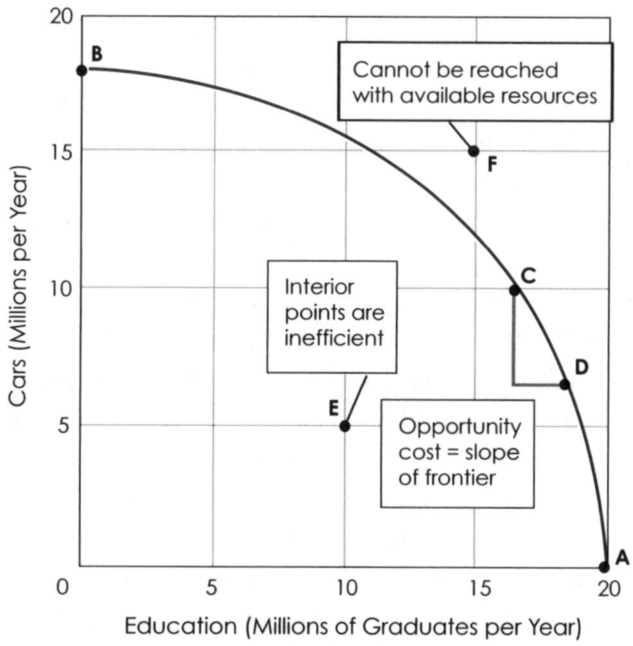

This figure shows combinations of cars and education that can be produced in a simple economy in which they are the only two products. Quantities of available factors of production and the state of existing knowledge are assumed to be fixed. If all factors are devoted to education, 20 million college graduates can be produced each year (point A). If all factors are devoted to making cars, 18 million cars can be produced each year (point B). Other combinations of the two goods that can be produced using available factors efficiently, such as those represented by points C and D, lie along a curve called a production possibility frontier. The slope of the frontier indicates the opportunity cost of education in terms of cars. Interior points, such as E, represent inefficient use of resources. Beginning from such a point, more of one good can be produced without producing less of the other. Points outside the frontier, such as F, cannot be reached using available factors of production and knowledge.

produced per year; the vertical axis measures the production of cars. Any combination of education and cars can be shown as a point in the space between the two axes. For example, production of 10 million graduates and 5 million cars in a given year would be represented by point E.

In drawing this graph, supplies of productive resources and the state of knowledge are assumed to remain constant. Even if all available resources are devoted to education, there is a limit to the number of graduates that can be produced in a year: 20 million. The extreme possibility of producing 20 million graduates and no cars is shown by point A. Likewise, the maximum number of cars that would be produced if no resources were put into education is 18 million cars, shown by point B. Between those two extremes is a whole range of possible combinations of education and cars. Those intermediate possibilities are shown by points such as C and D, which fall along a smooth curve. The curve is known as a **production possibility frontier**.

Production possibility frontier

A graph that shows possible combinations of goods that can be produced by an economy given available knowledge and factors of production.

EFFICIENCY AND ECONOMIC GROWTH The production possibility frontier is a boundary between the combinations of education and cars that can be produced and those that cannot, using given knowledge and productive resources. As such, it serves nicely to illustrate the concept of efficiency in production. Points inside the frontier, such as point E, represent inefficient production. Beginning from such a point, more cars can be made without cutting the output of education (shown by a vertical move toward the frontier); more education can be produced without cutting the output of cars (a horizontal move toward the frontier); or the output of both goods can be increased (a move up and to the right toward the frontier).

Points such as A, B, C, and D that are on the frontier represent efficient production. Starting from any of those points, it is not possible to produce more of one good without producing less of the other. For example, in moving from C to D, output of education is increased but output of cars falls. Points such as F that lie outside the frontier cannot be reached even when the currently available knowledge and factors of production are used efficiently.

Over time, however, economic growth can stretch the production possibility frontier outward so that points such as F become possible. As mentioned earlier, the discovery of new ways of using available factors of production is one source of growth. So are additions to the total stock of factors of production—for example, through growth of the labor force. Over time, the educational process itself improves the quality of the labor force, thus making a given number of people capable of producing more.

OPPORTUNITY COST AND COMPARATIVE ADVANTAGE The production possibility frontier can also be used to represent the concept of opportunity cost. As we have seen, once the economy is producing efficiently at a point on the frontier, choosing to make more of one good means making less of the other. For example, suppose we start at point C, where 16 million students graduate each year and 10 million cars are being made. If we want to increase the output of graduates to 18 million per year, we must give up some cars and use the labor, capital, and natural resources freed in this way to build and staff classrooms. In moving from point C to point D, we trade off production of 4 million cars for the extra 2 million graduates. Over that range of the frontier, the opportunity cost of each extra graduate is about two cars. The opportunity cost of graduates, measured in terms of cars, is shown by the slope of the frontier.

As more graduates are produced, and the economy moves down and to the right along the frontier, the frontier becomes steeper and the opportunity cost of producing graduates increases. A major reason is that not all factors of production—especially not all workers—are alike. Suppose we start all the way up at point B, where no education is produced, and transfer enough resources to education to open one small college. The first people we would pull off the assembly line to staff the classrooms would be those who have a comparative advantage in teaching. By the time enough resources have been transferred to education from the auto industry to reach point D, the most suitable recruits for academic life have already been used. Increasingly, to produce still more education we have to take some of the best production workers with no assurance that they will be good teachers. The opportunity cost of increasing the output of education (shown by the slope of the frontier) is correspondingly greater.

Theory and Evidence

Theories are of no use in explaining relationships among facts unless they fit those facts. Theory building is a matter of constantly comparing proposed explanations with evidence gleaned from observations of the actual choices people make—that is, with empirical evidence. When **empirical** evidence is consistent with the relationships proposed in a theory, confidence in the validity of the theory is increased. When evidence is not consistent with the theory, the theory needs to be reexamined. The relationships proposed in it may be invalid, or they may be valid only under circumstances different from those that prevailed when the observations were made. The theory then needs to be modified by changing the proposed relationships or adding detail.

Empirical

Based on experience or observation.

Government agencies and private firms generate mountains of empirical data on economic activity. Economists constantly examine those data in an effort to confirm theories or find inconsistencies that point the way to better theories. Statistical analysis of empirical economic data is known as **econometrics**— the science of economic measurement.

Econometrics

The statistical analysis of empirical economic data.

Theories and Forecasts

Economic theories can help us understand things that happened in the past—trends in gasoline consumption since the 1970s, the effects of the information revolution of the 1990s, and so on. But understanding the past is not always enough. People also want forecasts of future economic events.

Within limits, economic theory can be useful here, too. Any theory that purports to explain a relationship between past events provides a basis for predicting what will happen under similar circumstances in the future. To put it more precisely, economic theory can be used to make **conditional forecasts** of the form "If A, then B, other things being equal." Thus, an economist might say, "If gasoline prices rise, and if at the same time consumer incomes and the prices of other goods do not change, purchases of low-mileage vehicles will fall."

Conditional forecast

A prediction of future economic events in the form "If A, then B, other things being equal."

Thousands of economists make a living from forecasting. Decision-makers in business and government use economic forecasts extensively. Forecasts are not perfect, however, and forecasters sometimes make conspicuous mistakes. There are at least three reasons for the mistakes.

First, insufficient attention is sometimes paid to the conditional nature of forecasts. The news might report, for example, that "economists predict a drop in SUV sales," yet people keep right on buying big vehicles. In such a case the news report may have failed to note the forecasters' precautionary comments. The forecasters may have said that SUV sales would drop in response to a gas price increase if consumer incomes and technology remained the same, but consumers got richer and new technology made SUVs less gas-hungry, so SUV sales did not fall after all.

Second, a forecast may be invalid because the theory on which it is based is incorrect or incomplete. Economists do not always agree on what theory best fits the facts. Some theories give more weight to one fact, others to different facts. The competing theories may imply conflicting forecasts under some conditions. At least one of the forecasts will then turn out to be wrong. Finding out which theories yield better forecasts than others is an important part of the process through which valid theories are distinguished from inadequate ones.

Third, economic forecasts can go wrong because some of the things that business managers and government officials most want to know are among the hardest to predict. For example, a competent economist could produce a fairly accurate forecast of vehicle sales based on certain assumptions about incomes and the prices of gasoline and other goods. However, what the marketing people at General Motors would like to know is what will happen to the social image of SUVs—will they continue to be a symbol of high status, or will they become an embarrassment in a more environmentally conscious society? Social attitudes are not among the variables that economists can forecast accurately.

Despite these limitations, most economists take the view that well-founded conditional forecasts, for all their limitations, are a better basis for business and public policy decisions than whims and guesswork. Still, they caution against relying too heavily on forecasts.

Theory and Policy

Economists are often asked to use their theories to analyze the effects of public policies and forecast the effects of policy changes. The government may, for example, be considering new measures to aid unemployed workers, new approaches to improving air quality, or new measures to regulate international trade. How will the effects of such policies be spread through the economy? How will they affect people's lives?

Economists have their own characteristic way of thinking about public policy, just as they have their own way of thinking about other topics. In particular, economists are concerned with identifying both the direct and indirect effects of policy, as well as any indirect or unintended consequences. They are also constantly alert to both the long-run and short-term effects of policy. For example:

- Unemployment compensation has the intended effect of aiding unemployed workers, but it also has the unintended effect of increasing the number of workers who are unemployed, because workers receiving compensation can afford to take their time finding just the right new job. Many observers see generous unemployment compensation in Germany and other European countries as one reason unemployment rates there are higher than in the United States.
- Regulations intended to improve the fuel efficiency of automobiles encourage production of cars that weigh less, but the lighter cars are somewhat less safe. Increased highway deaths among drivers of the lighter cars may thus be an unintended consequence of efforts to save fuel.
- After widespread banking failures in the 1980s, U.S. regulators made rule changes intended to strengthen the balance sheets of commercial banks. Those regulations also raised the cost of bank loans relative to loans from other sources outside the banking system. As an unintended consequence, banks lost their most credit-worthy customers to other lenders and ended up with balance sheets that held higher percentages of risky loans than before.

While policies may have unintended consequences, it would be wrong to conclude that the government should never act simply because its actions may do some harm as well as some good. Sometimes the harm may outweigh the good, and sometimes not. What is important, economists say, is that policy makers look at the whole picture, not just part of it, before they make a decision. As Henry Hazlitt once put it, the whole of economics can be reduced to a single lesson:

> *The art of economics consists in looking not merely at the immediate but at the longer effects of any act or policy; it consists in tracing the consequences of that policy not merely for one group but for all groups.*[5]

As you progress through your study of economics—both the macro and micro branches—you will encounter repeated examples of the way economic theory can help understand the choices people make and the complex effects of policies intended to regulate those choices.

SUMMARY

1. **What is the subject matter of economics?** Economics is a social science that seeks to understand the choices people make in using scarce resources to meet their wants. Scarcity is a situation in which there is not enough of something to meet everyone's wants. *Microeconomics* is the branch of economics that studies choices that involve individual households, firms, and markets. *Macroeconomics* is the branch of economics that deals with large-scale economic phenomena, such as inflation, unemployment, and economic growth.

2. **What considerations underlie the choice of what an economy will produce?** Producing more of one good requires producing less of something else because productive resources that are used to produce one good cannot be used to produce another at the same time. Productive resources are traditionally classified into three groups, called *factors of production. Labor* consists of the productive contributions made by people working with their hands and minds. *Capital* consists of all the productive inputs created by people. *Natural resources* include anything that can be used as a productive input in its natural state. The *opportunity cost* of a good or service is its cost in terms of the forgone opportunity to pursue the best possible alternative activity with the same time or resources.

3. **What considerations underlie the choice of how to produce?** Goods and services can be produced in many different ways, some of which are more efficient than others. *Economic efficiency* refers to a state of affairs in which it is impossible to make any change that satisfies one person's wants more fully without causing some other person's wants to be satisfied less fully. *Efficiency in production* refers to a situation in which it is not possible, given the available productive resources and existing knowledge, to produce more of one good or service without forgoing the opportunity to produce some of another good or service. Once efficiency has been achieved, production potential can be expanded by increasing the availability of resources or by improving knowledge. The process of increasing the economy's stock of capital is known as *investment*. The process of looking for new possibilities—making use of new ways of doing things, being alert to new opportunities, and overcoming old limits—is known as *entrepreneurship*.

4. **What considerations underlie the choice of who will do which work?** Economic efficiency is greatly enhanced by cooperation with others. Three things make cooperation worthwhile: teamwork, learning by doing, and comparative advantage. Teamwork can enhance productivity even when there is no specialization. Learning by doing improves productivity even when all workers start with equal talents and abilities. Comparative advantage comes into play when people have different innate abilities or, after learning by doing, have developed specialized skills. Having a *comparative advantage* in producing a particular good or service means being able to produce it at a relatively lower opportunity cost than someone else.

5. **What considerations underlie the choice of for whom goods will be produced?** In part, deciding for whom goods will be produced revolves around issues of efficiency. *Efficiency in distribution* refers to a state of affairs in which, with a given quantity of goods and services, it is impossible to satisfy one person's wants more fully without satisfying someone else's less fully. Efficiency is part of *positive economics*, the area of economics that is concerned with facts and the relationships among them. *Normative economics* is the area of economics that is devoted to judgments about which economic conditions and policies are good or bad.

6. **What mechanisms are used to coordinate economic choices?** The two principle methods of coordinating choices are *hierarchy* and *spontaneous order.* Markets are the most important example of spontaneous order. The internal decisions made by large corporations and units of government are the most important examples of hierarchy.

7. **How do economists use theory, graphs, and evidence in their work?** A *theory* or *model* is a representation of the ways in which facts are related to one another. Economists use graphs to display data and make visual representations of theories and models. For example, a *production possibility frontier* is a graph that shows the boundary between combinations of goods that can be produced and those that cannot, using available factors of production and knowledge. Economists refine theories in the light of *empirical* evidence, that is, evidence gleaned from observation of actual economic decisions. The economic analysis of empirical evidence is known as *econometrics*. Economic models are often used to make *conditional forecasts* of the form "If A, then B, other things being equal."

KEY TERMS

Scarcity
Economics
Microeconomics
Macroeconomics
Factors of production
Labor
Capital
Natural resources
Opportunity cost
Economic efficiency
Efficiency in production
Investment
Entrepreneurship
Comparative advantage
Efficiency in distribution
Positive economics
Normative economics
Spontaneous order
Hierarchy
Market
Theory
Model
Production possibility frontier
Empirical
Econometrics
Conditional forecast

PROBLEMS AND TOPICS FOR DISCUSSION

1. **Opportunity cost.** Gasoline, insurance, depreciation, and repairs are all costs of owning a car. Which of these can be considered opportunity costs in the context of each of the following decisions?

   a. You own a car and are deciding whether to drive 100 miles for a weekend visit to a friend at another university.

   b. You do not own a car but are considering buying one so that you can get a part-time job located 5 miles from where you live.

   In general, why does the context in which you decide to do something affect the opportunity cost of doing it?

2. **Comparative advantage in international trade.** Suppose that in the United States a car can be produced with 200 labor hours while a ton of rice

requires 20 labor hours. In Japan, it takes 150 labor hours to make a car and 50 labor hours to grow a ton of rice. What is the opportunity cost of producing rice in each country, stated in terms of cars? What is the opportunity cost of cars, stated in terms of rice? Which country has a comparative advantage in cars? Which in rice?

3. **Efficiency in distribution and the food stamp program.** The federal food stamp program could have been designed so that every low-income family would receive a book of coupons containing so many bread coupons, so many milk coupons, and so on. Instead, it gives the family an allowance that can be spent on any kind of food the family prefers. For a given cost to the federal government, which plan do you think would better serve the goal of efficiency in distribution? Why?

   Now consider a program that would allow families to trade their food stamps for cash (some such trading does occur, but it is restricted by law) or one in which poor families are given cash, with which they can buy whatever they want. Compare these alternatives with the existing food stamp program in terms of both positive and normative economics.

4. **Spontaneous order in the cafeteria.** Suppose that your college cafeteria does not have enough room for all the students to sit down to eat at once, so it stays open for lunch from 11:30 a.m. to 1:30 p.m. Consider the following three methods of distributing diners over the two-hour lunch period in such a way that everyone can have a seat.

   a. The administration sets a rule: First-year stuydents must eat between 11:30 and 12:00, sophomores between 12:00 and 12:30, and so on for juniors and seniors.

   b. The lunch period is broken up into half-hour segments, with green tickets for the first shift, blue tickets for the second, and so on. An equal number of tickets of each color is printed. At the beginning of each semester an auction is held in which students bid for the ticket color of their choice.

   c. Students can come to the cafeteria whenever they want. If there are no empty seats, they have to stand in line.

   Compare the three schemes in terms of the concepts of (i) spontaneous order and hierarchy; (ii) information and incentives; and (iii) efficiency.

5. **A production possibility frontier.** Bill Schwartz has four fields spread out over a hillside. He can grow either wheat or potatoes in any of the fields, but the low fields are better for potatoes and the high ones are better for wheat. Here are some combinations of wheat and potatoes that he could produce:

Number of Fields Used for Potatoes	Total Tons of Potatoes	Total Tons of Wheat
All 4	1,000	0
Lowest 3	900	400
Lowest 2	600	700
Lowest 1	300	900
None	0	1,000

   Use these data to draw a production possibility frontier for wheat and potatoes. What is the opportunity cost of wheat, stated in terms of potatoes, when the farmer converts the highest field to wheat production? What happens to the opportunity cost of wheat as more and more fields are switched to wheat?

CASE FOR DISCUSSION

Cow Power

As natural resources go, it doesn't have much glamour; but unlike oil, the United States has plenty of it. We're talking about cow manure. The average cow puts out about 30 gallons a day. Multiply that by something like 8 million cows on the nation's 65,000 dairy farms, and you have—well, what do you have—a big problem or a big opportunity?

In the past, manure would, on balance, have been considered a problem. True, it makes good fertilizer, but with big drawbacks. Most dairy farms stored it in open lagoons before spreading it on fields. The smelly lagoons were a nuisance to neighbors. What is more, they were a big source of methane, a greenhouse gas that, pound for pound, contributes 10 times more to global warming than carbon dioxide.

Methane burns, and that's where cow manure becomes an opportunity. If farmers pump it into an anaerobic digester instead of into an open lagoon, it produces a purified gas that can either be burned on the farm to produce electricity or transported by pipeline to be burned elsewhere.

Marie and Earl Audet's dairy farm in Bridport, Vermont, expects to sell $200,000 worth of cow power this year to Central Vermont Public Service, the local electric utility. There are other benefits as well. The process also produces a clear liquid that can be used as fertilizer, and the farm will save another $50,000 by using the dry, odorless, fluff that is left over from the digester as bedding for the cows, in place of expensive sawdust.[6]

Cow power is not a free lunch, however. To make the economics favorable to farmers, Central Vermont Public Service pays them 12 cents per kilowatt hour, a 4-cent premium over the normal rate. The utility makes up the difference by selling premium-priced "green electricity" to customers who want to feel they are doing something for the planet. Other state and federal agencies subsidize an estimated 100 cow power digesters elsewhere in the country.

Boosters of cow power hope the need for subsidies will disappear as costs of manufacturing the digesters fall and as gas and electric prices continue to rise. "The business model of producing energy along with food will transform the economics of rural America," said Michael T. Eckhart, president of the American Council on Renewable Energy, based in Washington.[7]

QUESTIONS

1. Based on the information given in the case, do you think the out-of-pocket costs of producing electricity from cow manure are greater, less, or about the same as the cost of conventional power sources? On what information in the case do you base your answer?
2. Anaerobic digestion of cow manure reduces harm to neighbors (less smell) and harm to the environment (less greenhouse gas). How do these benefits enter into the calculation of the opportunity cost of producing cow power? Do these benefits tend to make the opportunity cost greater than, or less than, the out-of-pocket costs?
3. Based on information in the case, do you think the growth of the cow power industry is based on the principle of spontaneous order or that of hierarchy? Or is it a little bit of both? Explain your reasoning.

END NOTES

1. The Austrian economist Ludwig von Mises suggested that *catallactics*, meaning the science of exchange, be a better term than *economics*, which has the original meaning of household management. For better or worse, the term catallactics has never come into wide use.
2. Efficiency, defined this way, is sometimes called Pareto efficiency after the Italian economist Vilfredo Pareto.
3. Armen A. Alchian and Harold Demsetz, "Production, Information Cost, and Economic Organization," *American Economic Review* (December 1972): 777–795.
4. Some basic graphical concepts—axes, points and number pairs, slopes, and tangencies—are discussed in the appendix to this chapter.
5. Henry Hazlitt, *Economics in One Lesson* (New York: Arlington House, 1979), 17.
6. Martha T. Moore, "Cows Power Plan for Alternative Fuel," USA Today, Dec. 6, 2006, http://www.usatoday.com/news/nation/2006-12-03-cow-power_x.htm.
7. Claudia H. Deutsch, "Tapping Latent Power in What's Left Around the Barnyard," New York Times, July 4, 2006. http://select.nytimes.com/search/restricted/article?res=F20B13FD39540C778CDDAE0894DE404482

Appendix to Chapter 1: WORKING WITH GRAPHS

Which is smarter—a computer or the human brain? The computer certainly does some things faster and more accurately, say, dividing one twenty-digit number by another. The human brain, however, is programmed to solve other kinds of problems with speed and accuracy beyond the ability of most computers. Working with pictures is one of the areas in which the human brain excels. Three key abilities give the brain a comparative advantage where pictures are involved:

1. An ability to store and retrieve a vast number of images quickly and accurately. (Think of how many people's faces you can recognize.)
2. An ability to discard irrelevant detail while highlighting essentials. (Think of how easily you can recognize a politician's face in a political cartoon drawn with just a few lines.)
3. An ability to see key similarities between patterns that are not exactly the same. (That is why you can usually match two pictures of a person taken twenty years apart.)

Graphs are an invaluable aid in learning economics precisely because they make use of these three special abilities of the human brain. Graphs are not used to make economics harder, but to make it easier. All it takes to use graphs effectively as a learning tool is the inborn human skill in working with pictures plus knowledge of a few simple rules for extracting the information that graphs contain. This appendix outlines those rules in brief. Additional details and exercises can be found in the *Study Guide* that accompanies this textbook.

Pairs of Numbers and Points

The first thing to master is how to use points on a graph to represent pairs of numbers. The table in Figure 1A.1 presents five pairs of numbers. The two columns are labeled "x" and "y." The first number in each pair is called the *x value* and the second the *y value*. Each pair of numbers is labeled with a capital letter. Pair A has an x value of 2 and a y value of 3; pair B has an x value of 4 and a y value of 4; and so on.

The diagram in Figure 1A.1 contains two lines that meet at the lower left-hand corner; they are called *coordinate axes*. The horizontal axis is marked off into units representing the x value and the vertical axis into unit representing the y value. In the space between the axes, each pair of numbers from the table can be shown as a point. For example, point A is found by going two units to the right along the horizontal axis and then three units straight up, parallel to the vertical axis. That point represents the x value of 2 and the y value of 3. The other points are located in the same way.

The visual effect of a graph usually can be improved by connecting the points with a line or a curve. By doing so, the relationship between x values and y values can be seen at a glance: as the x value increases, the y value also increases.

Slope

For a straight line, the ratio of the change in the y value to the change in the x value between any two points on the line.

Slopes and Tangencies

The lines or curves used in graphs are described in terms of their slopes. The **slope** of a straight line between two points is defined as the ratio of the change in the y value to the

FIGURE 1A.1 NUMBER PAIRS AND POINTS

	x	y
A	2	3
B	4	4
C	6	5
D	8	6
E	10	7

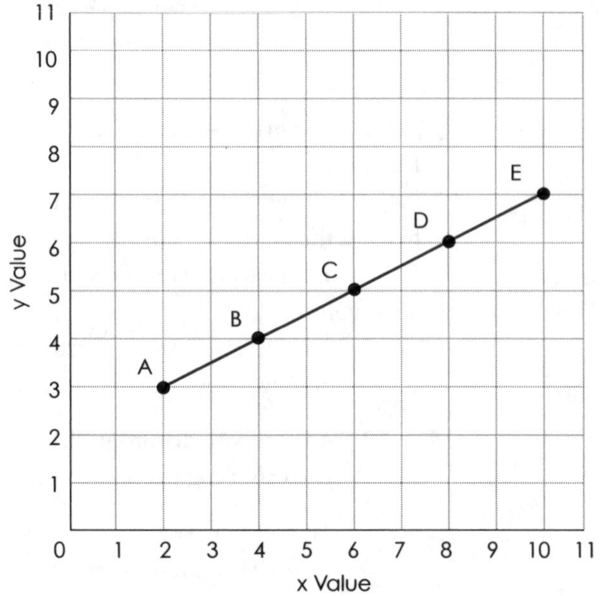

Each lettered pair of numbers in the table corresponds to a lettered point on the graph. The x value of each point corresponds to the horizontal distance of the point from the vertical axis; the y value corresponds to its vertical distance from the horizontal axis.

FIGURE 1A.2 SLOPES OF LINES

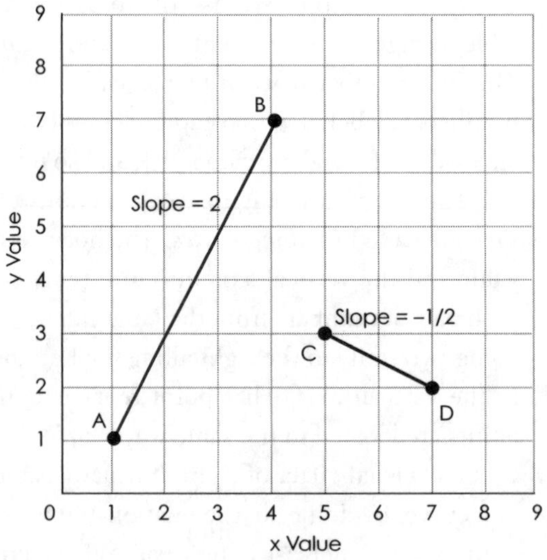

The slope of a straight line drawn between two points is defined as the ratio of the change in the y value to the change in the x value as one moves from one point to the other. For example, the line between points A and B in this Figure has a slope of +2, whereas the line between points C and D has a slope of –1/2.

change in the x value between the two points. In Figure 1A.2, for example, the slope of the line between points A and B is 2. The y value changes by six units between these two points, whereas the x value changes by only three units. The slope is the ratio 6/3 = 2.

The slope of a line between the points $(x1, y1)$ and $(x2, y2)$ can be expressed in terms of a simple formula that is derived from the definition just given:

$$\text{Slope} = (y_2 - y_1)/(x_2 - x_1)$$

Applied to the line between points A and B in Figure 1A.2, the formula gives the following result:

$$\text{Slope} = (7 - 1)/(4 - 1) = 6/3 = 2$$

Positive slope

A slope having a value greater than zero.

Direct relationship

A relationship between two variables in which an increase in the value of one variable is associated with an increase in the value of the other.

A line such as that between A and B in Figure 1A.2 is said to have a **positive slope**, because the value of its slope is a positive number. A positively sloped line represents a **direct relationship** between the variable represented on the *x* axis and that represented on the *y* axis—that is, a relationship in which an increase in one variable is associated with an increase in the other. The relationship of the age of a tree to its height is an example of a direct relationship. An example from economics is the relationship between family income and expenditures on housing.

When a line slants downward, such as the one between points C and D in Figure 1A.2, the *x* and *y* values change in opposite directions. Going from point C to point D, the y value changes by –1 (that is, decreases by one unit) and the x value changes by +2 (that is, increases by two units). The slope of this line is the ratio –1/2.

Negative slope

A slope having a value less than zero.

Inverse relationship

A relationship between two variables in which an increase in the value of one variable is associated with a decrease in the value of the other.

When the slope of a line is given by a negative number, the line is said to have a **negative slope**. Such a line represents an **inverse relationship** between the *x* variable and the *y* variable—that is, a relationship in which an increase in the value of one variable is associated with a decrease in the value of the other variable. The relationship between the temperature in the room and the time it takes the ice in your lemonade to melt is an example of an inverse relationship. To give an economic example, the relationship between the price of gasoline and the quantity that consumers purchase, other things being equal, is an inverse relationship.

Tangent

A straight line that touches a curve at a given point without intersecting it.

The concepts of positive and negative slopes, and of direct and inverse relationships, apply to curves as well as to straight lines. However, the slope of a curve, unlike that of a straight line, varies from one point to the next.[1] We cannot speak of the slope of a curve in general, but only of its slope at a given point. The slope of a curve at any given point is defined as the slope of a straight line drawn tangent to the curve at that point. (A **tangent** line is one that just touches the curve without crossing it.) In Figure 1A.3, the slope of the curve at point A is 1 and the slope at point B is –2.

Using Graphs to Display Data

Graphs are used in economics for two primary purposes: for visual display of quantitative data and for visual representation of economic relationships. Some graphs are primarily designed

[1]Economists try to be consistent, but in talking about lines and curves, they fail. They have no qualms about calling something a "curve" that is a straight line. For example, later we will encounter "demand curves" that are as straight as a stretched string. Less frequently, they may call something a line that is curved.

FIGURE 1A.3 SLOPES OF CURVES

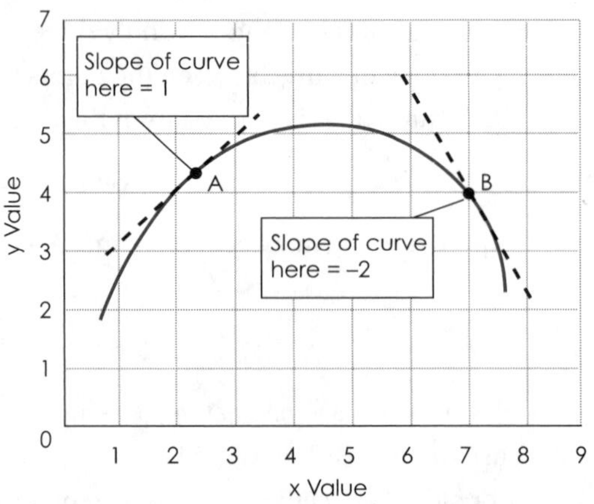

The slope of a curve at any point is defined as the slope of a straight line drawn tangent to the curve at that point. A tangent line is one that just touches the curve without crossing it. In this figure, the slope of the curve at point A is 1 and the slope at point B is –2.

to serve one purpose, some the other, and some a little of both. We begin with some common kinds of graphs whose primary purpose is to display data.

Figure 1A.4 shows three kinds of graphs often used to display data. Part (a) is *pie chart.* Pie charts are used to show the relative size of various quantities that add up to a total of 100 percent. In this case, the quantities displayed are the percentages of U.S. foreign trade accounted for by various trading partners. In the original source, the graph was drawn as part of a discussion of U.S. trade with Canada, Japan, and Western Europe. The author wanted to make the point that trade with these countries is very important. Note how the graph highlights Canadian, Japanese, and Western European trade with the U.S., and at the same time omits details not relevant to the discussion by lumping together the rest of Europe, Africa, the rest of Asia, and many other countries under the heading "rest of the world." In reading graphs, do not just look at the numbers, but ask yourself, "What point is the graph trying to make?"

Part (b) of Figure 1A.4 is a *bar chart*. Bar charts, like pie charts, are used to display numerical data (in this case, unemployment rates) in relationship to some non-numerical classification of cases (in this case, educational attainment). Bar charts are not subject to the restriction that data displayed must total 100 percent. What point do you think the author of this graph was trying to make?

Part (c) of Figure 1A.4 is an example of a data display graph very common in economics—the *time-series graph.* A time-series graph shows the values of one or more economic quantities on the vertical axis and time (years, months, or whatever) on the horizontal axis. This graph shows the ups and downs of the U.S. unemployment rate by month over the period 1980 through 2003.

Note one feature of this time-series graph: the scale on the vertical axis begins from 3 percent rather than from 0. By spreading out the data points in the range 3 to 11 percent, one can

FIGURE 1A.4 USING GRAPHS TO DISPLAY DATA

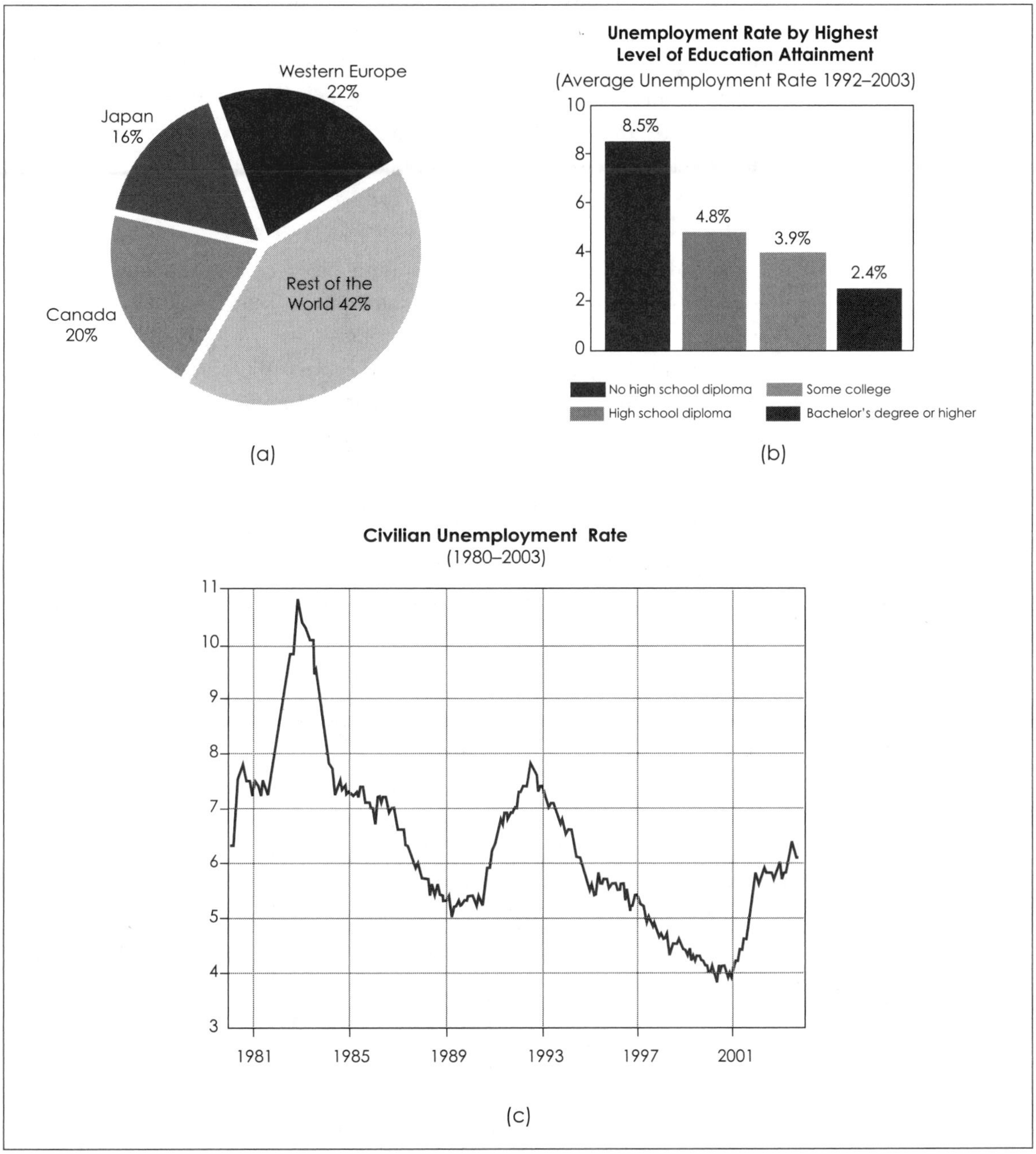

This figure shows three common kinds of data display graphs. The pie chart in part (a) is used when the data items sum to 100 percent. The bar chart in part (b), like the pie chart, is used when reporting numerical data that are associated with nonnumerical categories (in this case educational attainment). The bar chart does not require data items to sum to 100 percent. The time-series graph in part (c) shows the values of one or more economic quantities on the vertical axis and time on the horizontal axis.

Source: Part (a), U.S. Council of Economic Advisers, *Economic Report of the President* (Washington, D.C.: Government Printing Office, 2002), Table B-105, 397; part (b), Bureau of Labor Statistics, *Current Population Survey;* and part (c), Bureau of Labor Statistics, *The Employment Situation.*

show the trend of unemployment in greater detail. The advantage of greater detail has an offsetting danger, however. Careless reading of the graph could cause one to exaggerate the amount by which unemployment rises during a recession. For example, the unemployment line is more than three times higher above the horizontal axis in 2003 than in 2000. However, careful reading of the graph shows that the unemployment rate was actually only about half again as high (6% vs. 4%) in 2003 as in 2000. The moral of the story: Always examine the vertical and horizontal axes of a graph carefully.

Using Graphs to Display Relationships

Some graphs, rather than simply recording observed facts, attempt to represent theories and models—that is, to show the relationships among facts. Figure 1A.5 shows two typical graphs whose primary purpose is to display relationships.

Part (a) of Figure 1A.5 is the production possibility frontier that we encountered in Chapter 1. The graph represents the inverse relationship between the quantity of cars that can be produced and the quantity of education that can be produced, given available knowledge and productive resources.

Part (b) of Figure 1A.5 represents a relationship between the quantity of labor that a person is willing to supply (measured in worker-hours per year) and the wage rate per hour the person is paid. According to the theory portrayed by the graph, raising the wage rate will, up to a point, induce a person to work more hours. But beyond a certain point (according to the theory), a further increase in the wage will actually cause the person to work fewer hours.

FIGURE 1A.5 USING GRAPHS TO SHOW RELATIONSHIPS

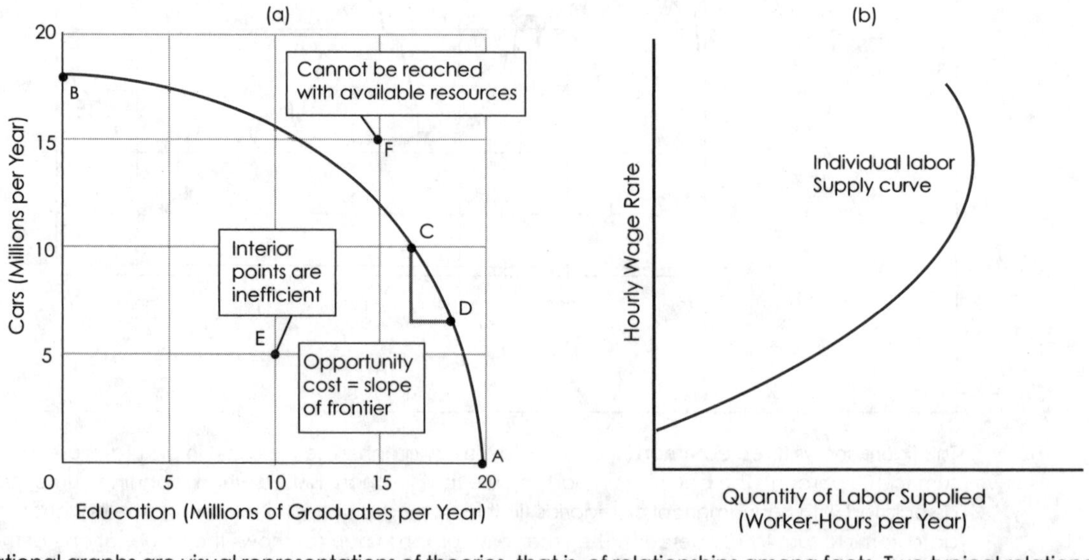

Relational graphs are visual representations of theories, that is, of relationships among facts. Two typical relational graphs are shown here. Part (a) is the production possibility frontier discussed in Chapter 1. It relates quantities of cars to quantities of education that can be produced with given factors of production and knowledge. Part (b) represents a theory of individual labor supply, according to which an increase in the hourly wage rate, after a point, will cause a person to reduce the quantity of labor supplied. Part (b) is an abstract graph in that it shows only the general nature of the relationship, with no numbers on either axis.

Why? Because the person is so well off, he or she prefers the luxury of more leisure time to the reward of more material goods.

Note one distinctive feature of this graph: There are no numbers on the axes. It is an abstract graph that represents only the qualitative relationships between the hours of labor supplied per year and the wage rate. It makes no quantitative statements regarding how much the number of hours worked will change as a result of any given change in wage rate. Abstract graphs are often used when the point to be made is a general one that applies to many cases, regardless of quantitative differences from one case to another.

Packing Three Variables into Two Dimensions

Anything drawn on a flat piece of paper is limited to two dimensions. The relationships discussed so far fit a two-dimensional framework easily, because they involve just two variables. In the case of the production possibility frontier, the two are the quantity of education (horizontal axis) and the quantity of cars (vertical axis). In the case of the labor supply, they are hours worked per year (horizontal axis) and wage rate per hour (vertical axis). But reality does not always cooperate with geometry. Often one must take three or more variables into account in order to understand relationships among facts.

A number of methods have been devised to represent relationships involving three or more variables. For example, a map of the United States might use coordinates of latitude and longitude to indicate position, contour lines to indicate altitude, and shadings of various colors to indicate vegetation. An architect might use a perspective drawing to give the illusion of three dimensions—height, width, and depth—on a flat piece of paper. This section deals with one simple method of packing three variables into two dimensions. Although the method is a favorite of economists—it will be used in dozens of graphs in this book—we will show its generality by beginning with a non-economic example.

A NONECONOMIC EXAMPLE The example concerns heart disease, the leading cause of death in the United States. The risk of heart disease is closely linked to the quantity of cholesterol in a person's blood. Studies have indicated, for example, that a 25 percent reduction in cholesterol can cut the risk of death from heart attack by nearly 50 percent. Knowing this, millions of people have had their cholesterol levels tested, and if they were found to be high, have undertaken programs of diet, exercise, or drug therapy to reduce their risk of heart disease.

Important though cholesterol is, however, just knowing your cholesterol level is not enough to tell you your risk of dying of a heart attack in the coming year. Other variables also enter into the risk of heart disease. One of the most important of these variables is age. For example, for men aged 20 with average cholesterol levels, the mortality rate from heart disease is only about 3 per 100,000. For men aged 60, the mortality rate rises to over 500 per 100,000, still assuming average cholesterol. We thus have three variables to deal with: mortality, cholesterol, and age. How can we represent these three variables using only two-dimensional graphs?

A possible approach would be to draw two separate graphs. One would show the relationship between age and heart disease for the male population as a whole, without regard to differences in cholesterol counts. The other would show the relationship between cholesterol and heart disease for the male population as a whole, without regard to age. By looking from one diagram to the other, we could get an idea of the three-variable relationship as a whole.

FIGURE 1A.6 THREE VARIABLES IN TWO DIMENSIONS

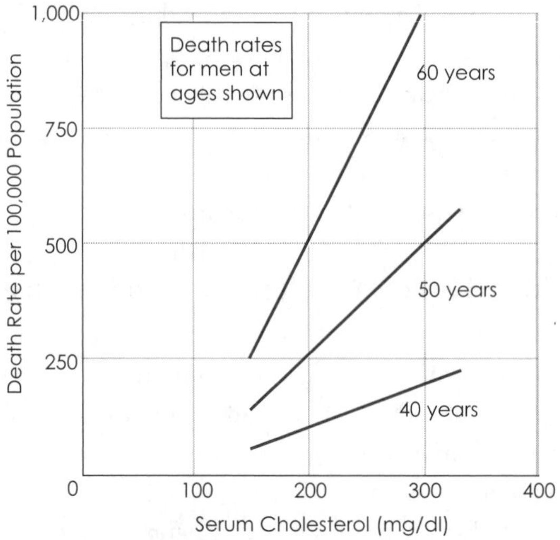

This graph shows a common way of representing a three-variable relationship on a two-dimensional graph. The three variables in this case are serum cholesterol (a measure of the amount of cholesterol in the blood), age, and death rate from heart disease for the U.S. male population. The relationship among the three variables is most easily interpreted, if all three variables are included in one graph, by drawing separate cholesterol-death rate lines for each age group. As a man ages, his cholesterol-death rate line shifts upward.

However, such a side-by-side pair of graphs would be clumsy. There must be a better way to represent the three variables in two dimensions. The better way, shown in Figure 1A.6, is to use cholesterol and mortality as the *x* and *y* axes, and to take age into account by plotting separate lines for men of various ages. That chart is far easier to interpret than the side-by-side pair would be. If you are a man and know your age and cholesterol count, you just pick out the appropriate line and read off your risk of mortality. If you do not like what you see, you go on a diet.[2]

The multi-curve graph is a lovely invention. One of the great things about it is that it works for more than three variables. For example, we could add a fourth variable, gender, to the graph by drawing a new set of lines in a different color to show mortality rates for women of various ages. Each line for women would have a positive slope similar to the men's lines, but would lie somewhat below the corresponding line for men of the same age, because women, other things being equal, experience lower mortality from heart disease.

SHIFTS IN CURVES AND MOVEMENTS ALONG CURVES Economists use three-variable, multi-curve graphs often enough that it is worth giving some attention to the termi-

[2]We could instead have started with the age-mortality chart and drawn separate lines for men with different cholesterol levels. Such a chart would show exactly the same information. We could even draw a chart with cholesterol and age on the axes, and separate contour lines to represent various levels of mortality. The choice often depends on what one wants to emphasize. Here, we emphasize the cholesterol-mortality relationship because cholesterol is something you can do something about. You cannot do anything about your age, so we give age slightly less emphasis by not placing it on one of the two axes.

nology used in discussing them. How can we best describe what happens to a man as he ages, given the relationship shown in Figure 1A.6?

One way to describe the effects of aging would be to say, "As a man ages, he moves from one curve to the next higher one on the chart." There is nothing at all wrong with saying that, but an economist would tend to phrase it a bit differently, saying "As a man ages, his cholesterol-mortality curve shifts upward." The two ways of expressing the effects of aging have exactly the same meaning. Preferring one or the other is just a matter of habit.

If we express the effects of aging in terms of a shift of the cholesterol-mortality curve, how should we express the effects of a reduction in cholesterol for a man of a given age? An economist would say it this way: "Cutting a man's cholesterol count through diet or exercise will move him down along his cholesterol-mortality curve."

Before you finish this book, you will see the phrases "shift in a curve" and "movement along a curve" a great many times. How can you keep them straight? Nothing could be easier.

- If you are talking about the effect of a change in a variable that is shown on one of the coordinate axes of the diagram, the effect will be shown as a movement along one of the curves.
- If you are talking about the effect of a change in a variable that is not shown on one of the coordinate axes of the diagram, the effect will be shown by a shift in one of the curves.

Study Hints

So much for the basic rules of graphics. Once you master them, how should you study a chapter that is full of graphs?

The first—and most important—rule is to avoid trying to memorize graphs as patterns of lines. In every economics course, at least one student comes to the instructor after failing an exam and exclaims, "But I learned every one of those graphs! What happened?" The reply is that the student should have learned economics instead of memorizing graphs. Following are some hints for working with graphs.

After reading through a chapter that contains several graphs, go back through the graphs one at a time. Cover the caption accompanying each graph, and try to express the graph's "picture" in words. If you cannot say as much about the graph as the caption does, reread the text. Once you can translate the graph into words, you have won half the battle.

Next, cover each graph and use the caption as a guide. Try to sketch the graph on a piece of scratch paper. How are the graph's axes labeled? How are the curves labeled? What are the slopes of various curves? Are there important points of intersection or tangencies? If you can go back and forth between the caption and the graph, you will find that the two together are much easier to remember than either one separately.

Finally, try going beyond the graph that is shown in the book. If the graph illustrates the effect of an increase in the price of butter, try sketching a similar diagram that shows the effect of a decrease in the price of butter. If the graph shows what happens to the economy during a period of rising unemployment, try drawing a similar graph that shows what happens during a period of falling unemployment. This is a good practice that may give you an edge on your next exam.

MAKING YOUR OWN GRAPHS For some students, the hardest test questions to answer are ones that require original graphs as part of an essay. Suppose the question is, "How does a change in the number of students attending a university affect the cost per student of providing an education?" Here are some hints for making your own graph.

1. Write down the answer to the question in words. If you cannot, you might as well skip to the next question. Underline the most important quantities in your answer, such as "The larger the *number of students* who attend a college, the lower the *cost per student* of providing them with an education, because fixed facilities, such as libraries, do not have to be duplicated."

2. Decide how you want to label the axes. In our example, the vertical axis could be labeled "cost per student" and the horizontal axis "number of students."

3. Do you have specific numbers to work with? If so, the next step is to construct a table showing what you know and use it to sketch your graph. If you have no numbers, you must draw an abstract graph. In this case, all you know is that the cost per student goes down when the number of students goes up. Your graph would thus be a negatively sloped line.

4. If your graph involves more than one relationship between quantities, repeat steps 1 through 3 for each relationship you wish to show. When constructing a graph with more than one curve, pay special attention to points at which you think the curves should intersect. (Intersections occur whenever both the x and y values of the two relationships are equal.) Also note the points at which you think two curves ought to be tangent (which requires that their slopes be equal), the points of maximum or minimum value, if any, and so on.

5. When your graph is finished, try to translate it back into words. Does it really say what you want it to?

A REMINDER As you read this book and encounter various kinds of graphs, turn back to this appendix now and then. Do not memorize graphs as patterns of lines; if you do, you will get lost. If you can alternate between graphs and words, the underlying point will be clearer than if you rely on either one alone. Keep in mind that the primary focus of economics is not graphs; it is people and the ways in which they deal with the challenge of scarcity.

CHAPTER 2

Supply and Demand: The Basics

After reading this chapter, you will understand:

1. How the price of a good or service affects the quantity demanded by buyers
2. How other market conditions affect demand
3. How the price of a good affects the quantity supplied by sellers
4. How other market conditions affect supply
5. How supply and demand interact to determine the market price of a good or service
6. Why market prices and quantities change in response to changes in market conditions
7. How price supports and price ceilings affect the operations of markets

Before reading this chapter, make sure you know the meaning of:

1. Spontaneous order
2. Markets
3. Opportunity cost
4. Law of unintended consequences

WE BEGAN THE preceding chapter with an example of the way rising gasoline prices have affected sales of gas-guzzling SUVs. Automobiles are just one category among millions of goods and services for which prices, quantities sold, and other market conditions vary from day to day and from year to year. Whether they are goods that we ourselves buy and sell, or goods that our employers, neighbors, or family members buy and sell, the changing market conditions affect our lives in m--any ways. The factors determining market prices and quantities are thus central to any discussion of economics.

Supply

The willingness and ability of sellers to provide goods for sale in a market.

Demand

The willingness and ability of buyers to purchase goods.

Economists use the term **supply** to refer to sellers' willingness and ability to provide goods for sale in a market. **Demand** refers to buyers' willingness and ability to purchase goods. This chapter will show how supply and demand work together to determine the prices of goods and services.

DEMAND

Law of demand

The principle that an inverse relationship exists between the price of a good and the quantity of that good that buyers demand, other things being equal.

According to the **law of demand**, the quantity of a good demanded tends to rise as the price falls and to fall as the price rises. We expect this to happen for two reasons. First, if the price of one good falls while the prices of other goods stay the same, people are likely to substitute the cheaper good. Second, when the price of one good falls while incomes and other prices stay the same, people feel a little richer. They use their added buying power to buy a bit more of many things, including, in most cases, a little more of the good whose price went down.

The terms *demand* and *quantity demanded*, as used in economics, are not the same as *want* or *need*. For example, I think a Porsche is a beautiful car. Sometimes when I see one on the street, I think, "Hey, I want one of those!" Alas, my income is limited. Although in the abstract I might want a Porsche, there are other things I want more. Thus, the quantity of Porsches I demand at the going price is zero.

On the other hand, I might *need* dental surgery to avoid losing my teeth. But suppose I am poor. If I cannot pay for the surgery or find someone to pay for it on my behalf, I am out of luck. The quantity of dental surgery I demand, therefore, would be zero, however great my need for that service. Demand, then, combines both willingness and ability to buy. It is not desire in the abstract, but desire backed by the intent to buy.

The Demand Curve

The law of demand states a relationship between the quantity of a good that people are willing and able to buy, other things being equal, and the price of that good. Figure 2.1 represents this one-to-one relationship for a familiar consumer good, chicken. It would be possible to discuss the demand for chicken of a single consumer, but more frequently, as in the following discussion, we focus on the total demand for the good by all buyers in the market.

Demand curve

A graphical representation of the relationship between the price of a good and the quantity of that good that buyers demand.

The figure shows the demand relationship in two different ways. First look at part (a). The first row of the table shows that when the price of chicken is \$3.00 a pound, the quantity demanded per year is 1 billion pounds. Reading down the table, we see that as the price falls, the quantity demanded rises. At \$2.50 per pound, buyers are willing and able to purchase 1.5 billion pounds per year; at \$1.50, 2.5 billion pounds; and so on.

Part (b) of Figure 2.1 presents the same information in graphical form. The graph is called a **demand curve** for chicken. Suppose we want to use the demand curve to

FIGURE 2.1 A DEMAND CURVE FOR CHICKEN

(a)

	Price of Chicken (Dollars per Pound)	Quantity of Chicken Demanded (Billions of Pounds per Year)
	$3.50	0.5
	$3.00	1
	$2.50	1.5
A	$2.00	2
	$1.50	2.5
B	$1.00	3
	$0.50	3.5

(b)

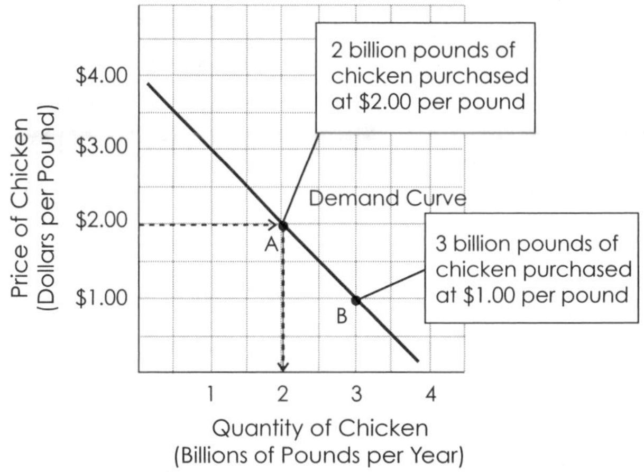

Both the table and the chart show the quantity of chicken demanded at various prices. For example, at a price of $2.00 per pound, buyers are willing and able to purchase 2 billion pounds of chicken per year. This price-quantity combination is shown by row A in part (a) and point A in part (b).

find out what quantity of chicken will be demanded at a price of $2.00 per pound. Starting at $2.00 on the vertical axis, we move across, as shown by the arrow, until we reach the demand curve at point A. Continuing to follow the arrow, we drop down to the horizontal axis. Reading from the scale on that axis, we see that the quantity demanded at a price of $2.00 per pound is 2 billion pounds per year. That is the quantity demanded in row A of the table in part (a).

The effect of a change in the price of chicken, other things being equal, can be shown as a movement from one point to another along the demand curve for chicken. Suppose that the price drops from $2.00 to $1.00 per pound. In the process, the quantity that buyers plan to buy rises. The point corresponding to the quantity demanded at the new, lower price is point B (which corresponds to row B of the table). Because of the inverse relationship between price and quantity demanded, the demand curve has a negative slope.

Change in quantity demanded

A change in the quantity of a good that buyers are willing and able to purchase that results from a change in the good's price, other things being equal; shown by a movement from one point to another along a demand curve.

Economists speak of a movement along a demand curve as a **change in quantity demanded**. Such a movement represents buyers' reaction to a change in the price of the good in question, other things being equal.

Shifts in the Demand Curve[1]

The demand curve in Figure 2.1 represents a relationship between two variables: the price of chicken and the quantity of chicken demanded. But changes in other variables can also affect people's purchases of chicken. In the case of chicken, the prices of beef and pork would affect demand. Consumer incomes are a second variable that can affect demand. Changes in expectations about the future are a third, and changes in consumer tastes, such as an increasing preference for foods with a low carbohydrate content, are a fourth. The list could go on and on—the demand for ice is affected by the weather; the demand for diapers is affected by the birthrate; the demand for baseball tickets is affected by the won-lost record of the home team; and so on.

How are all these other variables handled when drawing a demand curve? In brief, two rules apply:

1. When drawing a single demand curve for a good, such as the one in Figure 2.1, all other conditions that affect demand are considered to be fixed or constant under the "other things being equal" clause of the law of demand. As long as that clause is in force, the only two variables at work are quantity demanded (on the horizontal axis) and price (on the vertical axis). The effect of a change in price on quantity demanded thus is shown by a *movement along* the demand curve.

2. When we look beyond the "other things being equal" clause and find that there is a change in a variable that is not represented on one of the axes, such as the price of another good or the level of consumer income, the effect is shown as a *shift* in the demand curve. In its new position, the demand curve still represents a two-variable price-quantity relationship, but it is a slightly different relationship than before because one of the "other things" has changed.

These two rules for graphical representation of demand relationships are crucial to understanding the theory of supply and demand as a whole. It will be worthwhile to expand on them through a series of examples.

CHANGES IN THE PRICE OF ANOTHER GOOD We have already noted that the demand for chicken depends on what happens to the price of beef, as well as what happens to the price of chicken. Figure 2.2, which shows demand curves for both goods, provides a closer look at this relationship.

Suppose that the price of beef is initially $3.00 per pound and then increases to $4.50 per pound. The effect of this change on the quantity of beef demanded is shown in part (a) of Figure 2.2 as a movement along the beef demand curve from point A to point B. Part (b) of the figure shows the effect on the demand for chicken. With the price of beef higher than before, consumers will tend to buy more chicken *even if the price of chicken does not change*. Suppose the price of chicken is $2.00 per pound. When beef was selling at $3.00 a pound, consumers bought 2 billion pounds of chicken a year (point A' on demand curve D_1). After the price of beef goes up to $4.50 a pound, they will buy 3.5 billion pounds of chicken a year, assuming that the price of chicken does not change (point B' on demand curve D_2).

FIGURE 2.2 EFFECTS OF AN INCREASE IN THE PRICE OF BEEF ON THE DEMAND FOR CHICKEN

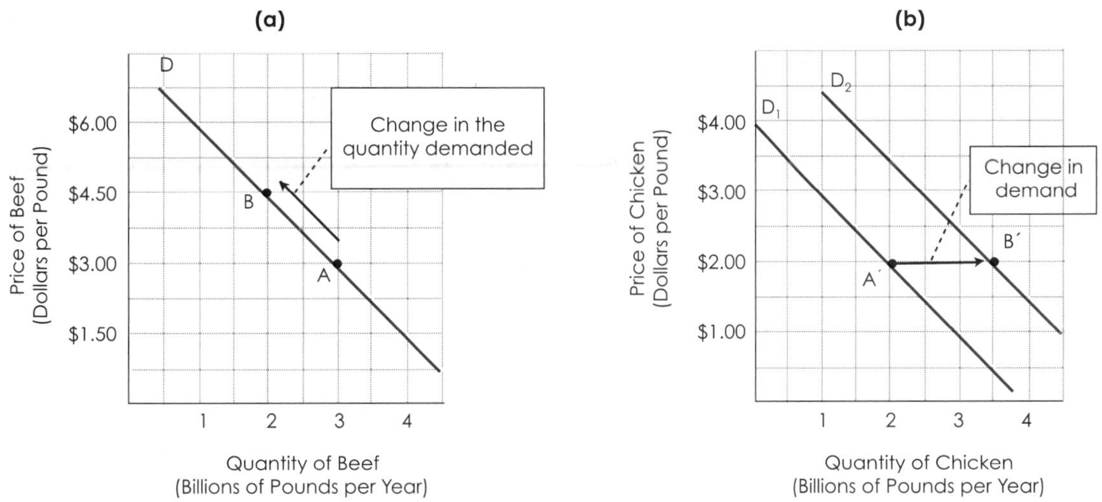

An increase in the price of beef from $3.00 to $4.50 per pound, other things being equal, causes a movement from point A to point B on the beef demand curve—a decrease in the quantity of beef demanded. With the price of chicken unchanged at $2.00 per pound, consumers will substitute chicken for beef. That will cause an increase in the demand for chicken, which is shown as a shift in the chicken demand curve from D_1 to D_2.

Change in demand

A change in the quantity of a good that buyers are willing and able to purchase that results from a change in some condition other than the price of that good; shown by a shift in the demand curve.

Substitute goods

A pair of goods for which an increase in the price of one causes an increase in demand for the other.

A rise in the price of beef would cause consumers to buy more chicken regardless of the initial price of chicken. If the price of chicken had started out at $3.00 a pound and remained there while the price of beef went up, consumers would have increased their chicken consumption from 1 billion pounds a year to 2.5 billion pounds a year. At a price of $1.00 a pound for chicken, the quantity would have risen from 3 billion pounds to 4.5 billion pounds, and so on. We see, then, that a change in the price of beef causes the entire demand curve for chicken to shift. The "other things being equal" clause of the new demand curve, D_2, incorporates a price of $4.50 a pound for beef, rather than the price of $3.00 a pound assumed in demand curve D_1.

Earlier we explained that economists refer to a movement along a demand curve as a "change in quantity demanded." The corresponding term for a shift in a demand curve is a **change in demand**. A change in quantity demanded (a movement along the curve) is caused by a change in the price of the good in question (the variable on the vertical axis). In contrast, a change in demand (a shift in the demand curve) is caused by a change in some variable other than the price of the good in question (one that does not appear on either axis).

In the example in Figure 2.2, people bought more chicken when the price of beef went up, replacing one meat with the other in their dinners. Economists call such pairs of goods **substitutes**, because an increase in the price of one causes an increase in the demand for the other—a rightward shift in the demand curve.

Consumers react differently to price changes when two goods tend to be used together. One example is cars and gasoline. When the price of gasoline goes up, people's selection of cars will be affected. In particular, they will buy fewer low-mileage, large SUVs even if there is no change in the price of those vehicles. An increase in the price of gasoline thus causes a movement upward along the gasoline demand curve and a *leftward* shift in the demand curve for SUVs. Pairs of goods that are related in this way are known as **complements**.

Complementary goods

A pair of goods for which an increase in the price of one results in a decrease in demand for the other.

Whether a given pair of goods are substitutes or complements depends on buyers' attitudes toward those goods; these terms do not refer to properties of the goods themselves. Some people might regard cheese and beef as substitute sources of protein in their diets; others, who like cheeseburgers, might regard them as complements.

One more point regarding the effects of changes in the prices of other goods is also worth noting: In stating the law of demand, it is the price of a good *relative to those of other goods* that counts. During periods of inflation, when the average level of all prices rises, distinguishing between changes in *relative prices* and changes in *nominal prices*—the number of dollars actually paid per unit of a good—is especially important. When the economy experiences inflation, a good can become relatively less expensive even though its nominal price rises, provided that the prices of other goods rise even faster.

Consider chicken, for example. Between 1950 and 2005 the average retail price of a broiler rose by almost 40 percent, from $.59 per pound to $1.05 per pound. Over the same period, however, the average price of all goods and services that consumers bought rose by about 600 percent. The relative price of chicken thus fell during the period even though its nominal price rose. The drop in the relative price of chicken had a lot to do with its growing popularity on the dinner table.

CHANGES IN CONSUMER INCOMES The demand for a good can also be affected by changes in consumer incomes. When their incomes rise, people tend to buy larger quantities of many goods, assuming that the prices of those goods do not change.

Figure 2.3 shows the effect of an increase in consumer incomes on the demand for chicken. Demand curve D_1 is the same as the curve shown in Figure 2.1. Suppose now that consumer incomes rise. With higher incomes, people become choosier about what they eat. They do not just want calories, they want high-quality calories from foods that are tasty, fashionable, and healthful. These considerations have made chicken increasingly popular as consumer incomes have risen.

More specifically, suppose that after their incomes rise, consumers are willing to buy 2.5 billion pounds of chicken instead of 1 billion pounds at a price of $3.00 per pound. The change is shown as an arrow drawn from point A to point B in Figure 2.3. If the initial price of chicken had been $2.00 per pound, even more chicken would be bought at the new, higher level of income. At the original income level and a price of $2.00, the amount purchased would be 2 billion pounds, as shown by point C. After

FIGURE 2.3 EFFECTS OF AN INCREASE IN CONSUMER INCOME ON THE DEMAND FOR CHICKEN

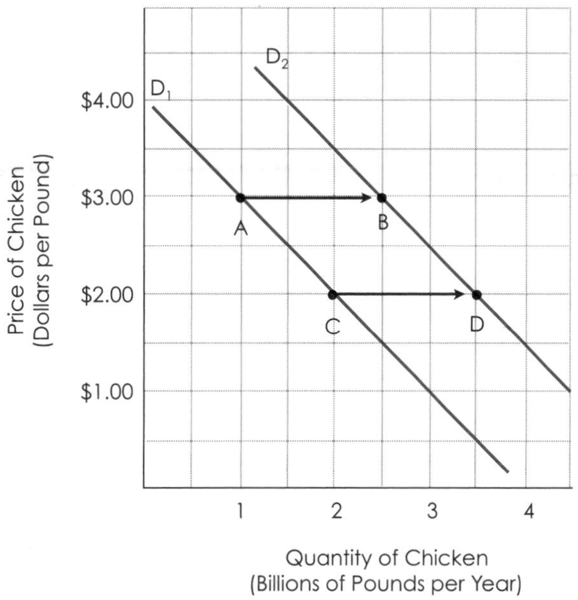

Demand curve D_1 assumes a given level of consumer income. If their incomes increase, consumers will want to buy more chicken at any given price, other things being equal. That will shift the demand curve rightward to, say, D_2. If the prevailing market price at the time of the demand shift is $3.00 per pound, the quantity demanded increases to 2.5 billion pounds (B) from 1 billion (A); if the prevailing price is $2.00 per pound, the quantity demanded will increase to 2 billion pounds (D) from 3.5 billion (C); and so on.

the increase in incomes, buyers would plan to purchase 3.5 billion pounds, shown by the arrow from point C to point D.

Whatever the initial price of chicken, the effect of an increase in consumer incomes is shown by a shift to a point on the new demand curve, D_2. The increase in demand for chicken that results from the rise in consumer incomes thus is shown as a shift in the entire demand curve. If consumer incomes remain at the new, higher level, the effects of any changes in the price of chicken will be shown as movements along the new demand curve. There is, in other words, a chicken demand curve for every possible income level. Each represents a one-to-one relationship between price and quantity demanded, given the assumed income level.

Normal good

A good for which an increase in consumer incomes results in an increase in demand.

In the example just given, we assumed that an increase in income would cause an increase in the demand for chicken. Experience shows that this is what normally happens. Economists therefore call chicken a **normal good**, meaning that when consumer incomes rise, other things being equal, people will buy more of it.

There are some goods, however, that people will buy less of when their incomes rise, other things being equal. For example, among your classmates, those with higher incomes are likely to go out for pizza more often than those with lower incomes. On nights when they eat pizza, they do not eat in the cafeteria, so the demand for cafeteria food falls as income rises. Similarly, when their incomes rise, people tend to buy less flour for baking at home and to buy more baked goods instead. People tend to buy fewer shoe repair services when their incomes rise; instead, they buy new shoes. Goods such as cafeteria food, flour, and shoe repair services are termed **inferior goods**. When consumer incomes rise, the demand curve for an inferior good shifts to the left instead of to the right. As in the case of substitutes and complements, the notions of inferiority and normality arise from consumer choices; they are not inherent properties of the goods themselves.

Inferior good
A good for which an increase in consumer incomes results in a decrease in demand.

CHANGES IN EXPECTATIONS Changes in buyers' expectations are a third factor that can shift demand curves. If people expect the price of a particular good to rise relative to the prices of other goods, or expect something other than a price increase to raise the opportunity cost of acquiring the good, they will step up their rate of purchase before the change takes place.

For example, suppose that in May, consumers rush to buy airline tickets in response to a series of news reports indicating that prices will be raised for tickets ordered after June 1. The people who buy their tickets in May will probably include many who were planning to travel late in the summer and ordinarily would have waited several more weeks before making their purchase. Thus, many more tickets will be sold in May than would have been sold at the same price if consumers had not anticipated the June price rise. We can interpret the surge in ticket sales in May as a temporary rightward shift in the demand curve.

CHANGES IN TASTES Changes in tastes are a fourth source of changes in demand. Sometimes these changes occur rapidly, as can be seen, for example, in such areas as popular music, clothing styles, and fast foods. The demand curves for these goods and services shift often. In other cases, changes in tastes take longer to occur but are more permanent. For example, in recent years consumers have been more health conscious than they were in the past. The result has been reduced demand for cigarettes and foods with high content of refined carbohydrates, along with increased demand for fish, organic vegetables, and exercise equipment.

SUPPLY

The Supply Curve

Supply curve
A graphical representation of the relationship between the price of a good and the quantity of that good that sellers are willing to supply.

We now turn from the demand side of the market to the supply side. As in the case of demand, we begin by constructing a one-to-one relationship between the price of a good and the quantity that sellers intend to offer for sale. Figure 2.4 shows such a relationship for chicken.

The positively sloped curve in Figure 2.4 is called a **supply curve** for chicken. Like demand curves, supply curves are based on an "other things being equal" condi-

FIGURE 2.4 A SUPPLY CURVE FOR CHICKEN

(a)

	Price of Chicken (Dollars per Pound)	Quantity of Chicken Demanded (Billions of Pounds per Year)
	$4.00	4
	$3.50	3.5
A	$3.00	3
	$2.50	2.5
B	$2.00	2
	$1.50	1.5
	$1.00	1

(b)

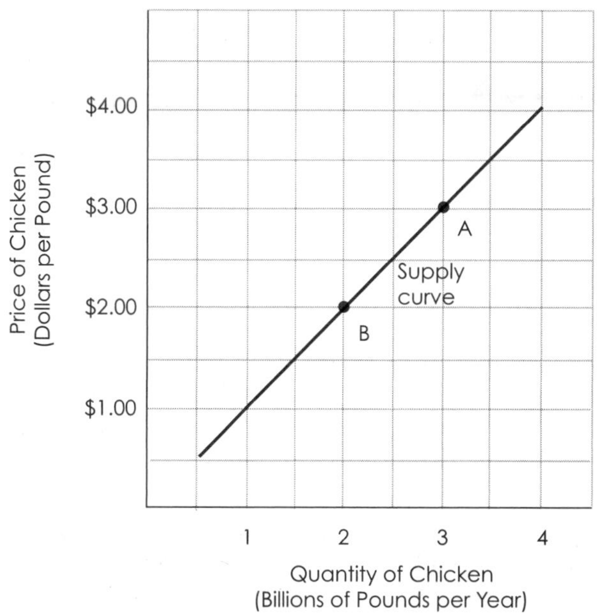

Parts (a) and (b) of this figure show the quantity of chicken supplied at various prices. As the price rises, the quantity supplied increases, other things being equal. The higher price gives farmers an incentive to raise more chickens, but the rising opportunity cost of doing so limits the supply produced in response to any given price increase.

tion. The supply curve for chicken shows how sellers change their plans in response to a change in the price of chicken, assuming that there are no changes in other conditions—the prices of other goods, production techniques, input prices, expectations, or any other relevant condition.

Why does the supply curve have a positive slope? Why do sellers, other things being equal, plan to supply more chicken when the prevailing market price is higher than they plan to supply when the price is lower? Without going too deeply into a discussion of microeconomic theory, we can consider some common-sense explanations here.

One explanation is that the positive slope of the supply curve represents *producers' response to market incentives*. When the price of chicken goes up, farmers have an incentive to devote more time and resources to raising chickens. Farmers who raise chickens as a sideline may decide to make chickens their main business. Some people may enter the market for the first time. The same reasoning applies in every market. If parents are finding it hard to get babysitters, what do they do? They offer to pay more. If a sawmill cannot buy enough timber, it raises the price it offers to loggers, and so on. Exceptions to this general rule are rare.

Another explanation is that the positive slope of the supply curve reflects *the rising cost of producing additional output in facilities of a fixed size*. A furniture factory with a fixed amount of machinery might be able to produce more chairs only by paying workers at overtime rates to run the machinery for more hours. A farmer who is trying to grow more wheat on a fixed amount of land could do so by increasing the input of fertilizer and pesticides per acre, but beyond a certain point each unit of added chemicals yields less additional output.

Finally, the positive slope of the supply curve can be explained in terms of *comparative advantage and opportunity cost*. Figure 2.5a shows a production possibility frontier for an economy in which there are only two goods, tomatoes and chicken. Farmers can choose which product they will specialize in, but some farmers have a comparative advantage in growing tomatoes, others in raising chickens. Beginning from a situation in which only tomatoes are produced, farmers with the strongest comparative advantage in raising chickens—that is, those who are able to produce chicken at relatively the lowest opportunity cost—will switch from tomatoes to

FIGURE 2.5 THE PRODUCTION POSSIBILITY CURVE AND THE SUPPLY CURVE

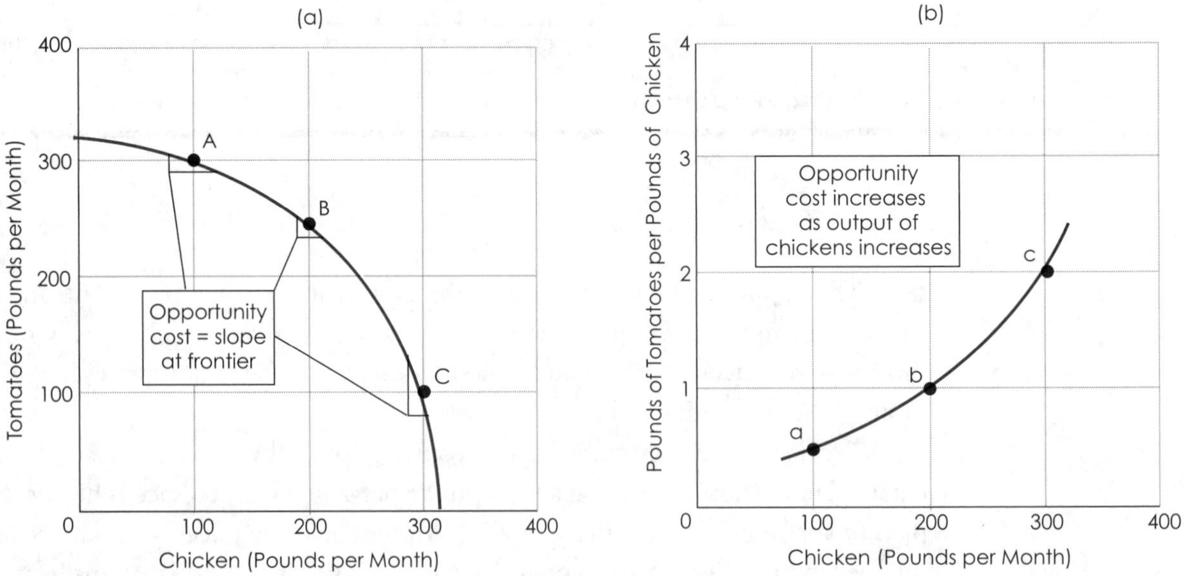

This figure offers an interpretation of the supply curve in terms of the production possibility frontier for an economy in which two goods are produced, tomatoes and chicken. Part (a) shows a production possibility frontier. The slope of the frontier at any point shows the opportunity cost of producing an additional pound of chicken measured in terms of the quantity of tomatoes that could have been produced using the same factors of production. The frontier curves because some farmers have a comparative advantage in producing tomatoes and others have a comparative advantage in producing chicken. As more chicken is produced, those with the greatest comparative advantage in producing chicken are the first to stop producing tomatoes. Because the frontier gets steeper as more chicken is produced, the opportunity cost rises, as shown in part (b). The curve in part (b) can be interpreted as a supply curve, in the sense that an incentive, in the form of a higher price, will cause factors of production to be shifted from tomatoes to chicken dspite the rising opportunity cost of producing chicken.

chicken even if the price of chicken is low. As the point of production moves along the frontier, the price of chicken must rise to induce farmers with relatively higher opportunity costs to make the switch. The slope of the frontier at any point represents the opportunity cost of producing more chicken for a farmer who finds it worthwhile to switch from tomatoes to chicken just at that point.

In Figure 2.5 the slopes at points A, B, and C in part (a) are graphed on a new set of axes in part (b). The graph can be interpreted as a supply curve if it is noted that the price of chicken must rise relative to the price of tomatoes to induce more farmers to switch to chicken as the opportunity cost rises.

Each of these common-sense explanations fits certain circumstances. Together, they provide an intuitive basis for the positive slope of the supply curve.

Shifts in the Supply Curve

As in the case of demand, the effects of a change in the price of chicken, other things being equal, can be shown as a movement along the supply curve for chicken. Such a movement is called a **change in quantity supplied**. A change in a condition other than the price of chicken can be shown as a shift in the supply curve. Such a shift is referred to as a **change in supply**. Four sources of change in supply are worth noting. Each is related to the notion that the supply curve reflects the opportunity cost of producing the good or service in question.

Change in quantity supplied

A change in the quantity of a good that suppliers are willing and able to sell that results from a change in the good's price, other things being equal; shown by a movement along a supply curve.

Change in supply

A change in the quantity of a good that suppliers are willing and able to sell that results from a change in some condition other than the good's price; shown by a shift in the supply curve.

CHANGES IN TECHNOLOGY A supply curve is drawn on the basis of a particular production technique. When entrepreneurs reduce the opportunity costs of production by introducing more efficient techniques, it becomes worthwhile to sell more of the good than before at any given price. Figure 2.6 shows how an improvement in production technology affects the supply curve for chicken.

Supply curve S_1 is the same as the one shown in Figure 2.4. It indicates that farmers will plan to supply 3 billion pounds of chicken per year at a price of $3.00 per pound (point A). Now suppose that the development of a faster-growing bird reduces the amount of feed used in raising chickens. With lower costs per unit, farmers will be willing to supply more chicken than before at any given price. They may, for example, be willing to supply 4 billion pounds of chicken at $3.00 per pound (point B). The move from A to B is part of a shift in the entire supply curve from S_1 to S_2. Once the new techniques are established, an increase or decrease in the price of chicken, other things being equal, will result in a movement along the new supply curve.

CHANGES IN INPUT PRICES Changes in input prices are a second item that can cause supply curves to shift. An increase in input prices, other things being equal, increases the opportunity cost of producing the good in question, and hence it tends to reduce the quantity of a good that producers plan to supply at a given price. Refer again to Figure 2.6. Suppose that starting from point A on supply curve S_1, the price

FIGURE 2.6 SHIFTS IN THE SUPPLY CURVE FOR CHICKEN

Several kinds of changes can cause the supply of chicken to increase or decrease. For example, a new production method that lowers costs will shift the curve to the right, from S_1 to S_2. The shift is to the right because, taking into account the new, lower cost of production per unit, producers will be willing to supply more chicken at any given price. An increase in the price of inputs, other things being equal, will shift the curve to the left, from S_1 to S_3. The shift is to the left because, taking into account the new, higher price of inputs, producers will be willing to supply less chicken at any given price. Changes in sellers' expectations or in the prices of competing goods can also cause the supply curve to shift.

of chicken feed increases and no offsetting changes occur. Now, instead of supplying 3 billion pounds of chicken at $3.00 per pound, farmers will supply, say, just 2 billion pounds at that price (point C). The move from A to C is part of a leftward shift in the supply curve, from S_1 to S_3.

If the price of feed remains at the new level, changes in the price of chicken will cause movements along the new supply curve. For example, farmers could be induced to supply the original quantity of chicken—3 billion pounds—if the price of chicken rose enough to cover the increased cost of feed. As you can see in Figure 2.6, that would require a price of $4.00 per pound for chicken (point D).

CHANGES IN THE PRICES OF OTHER GOODS Changes in the prices of other goods that could be produced using the same factors of production can also produce a shift in the chicken supply curve. In our earlier example, farmers could use available resources to produce either chickens or tomatoes. Suppose that the price of tomatoes rises while the price of chicken stays at $3.00. The rise in the price of tomatoes gives some farmers who would otherwise have produced chickens an incentive to shift the use of their labor, land, and capital to the production of tomatoes. Thus, the effect of an increase in the price of tomatoes can be shown as a leftward shift in the chicken supply curve.

CHANGES IN EXPECTATIONS Changes in expectations can cause supply curves to shift in much the same way that they cause demand curves to shift. Again, we can use farming as an example. At planting time, a farmer's selection of crops is influenced not so much by current prices as by the prices expected at harvest time. Expectations over a time horizon longer than one growing season also affect supply. Each crop requires special equipment and know-how. We have just seen that an increase in the price of tomatoes gives farmers an incentive to shift from chicken to tomatoes. The incentive will be stronger if the price of tomatoes is expected to remain at the higher level. If it is, farmers are more likely to buy the special equipment needed for that crop and to learn the necessary production techniques.

THE INTERACTION OF SUPPLY AND DEMAND

Markets transmit information, in the form of prices, to people who buy and sell goods and services. Taking these prices into account, along with other knowledge they may have, buyers and sellers make their plans.[2] As shown by the demand and supply curves, buyers and sellers plan to buy or sell certain quantities of a good at any given price.

Each market has many buyers and sellers, each making plans independently. When they meet to trade, some of them may be unable to carry out their plans on the terms they expected. Perhaps the total quantity of a good that buyers plan to purchase is greater than the total quantity that suppliers are willing to sell at the given price. In that case, some of the would-be buyers must change their plans. Or, perhaps planned sales exceed planned purchases at the given price. In that case, some would-be sellers will be unable to carry out their plans.

Market Equilibrium

Equilibrium

A condition in which buyers' and sellers' plans exactly mesh in the marketplace, so that the quantity supplied exactly equals the quantity demanded at a given price.

Sometimes no one is surprised: The total quantity of a good that buyers plan to purchase exactly matches the total quantity that producers plan to sell. When buyers' and sellers' plans mesh when they meet in the marketplace, no buyers or sellers need to change their plans. Under these conditions, the market is said to be in **equilibrium**.

Supply and demand curves, which reflect the plans of sellers and buyers, can be used to give a graphical demonstration of market equilibrium. Figure 2.7 uses the same supply and demand curves as before, but this time both curves are drawn on the

FIGURE 2.7 EQUILIBRIUM IN THE CHICKEN MARKET

(a)

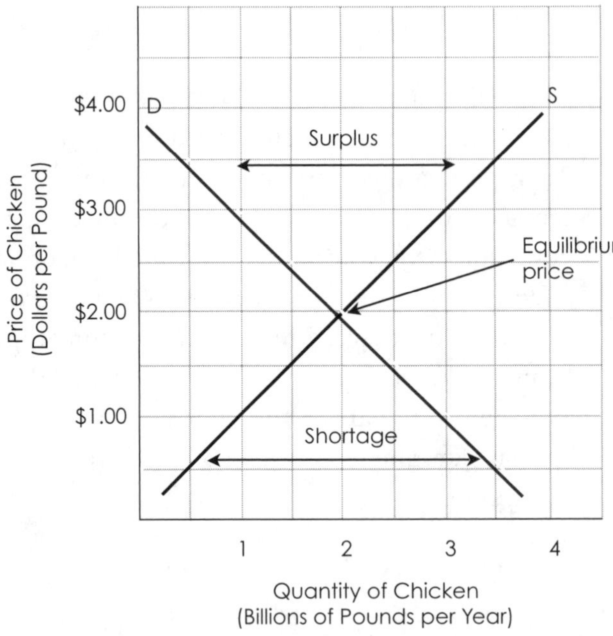

(b)

Price (per Pound)	Quantity Demanded (Billions of Pounds)	Quantity Supplied (Billions of Pounds)	Shortage (Billions of Pounds)	Surplus (Billions of Pounds)	Direction of Pressure on Price
$3.50	0.5	3.5	—	3	Downward
$3.00	1	3	—	2	Downward
$2.50	1.5	2.5	—	1	Downward
$2.00	2	2	—	—	Equilibrium
$1.50	2.5	1.5	1	—	Upward
$1.00	3	1	2	—	Upward
$0.50	3.5	0.5	3	—	Upward

This figure shows the supply and demand curves for chicken presented earlier in graphical and numerical form. The demand curve shows how much buyers plan to purchase at a given price. The supply curve shows how much producers plan to sell at a given price. At only one price—$2.00 per pound—do buyers' and sellers' plans exactly match. That is the equilibrium price. A higher price causes a surplus of chicken and puts downward pressure on price. A lower price causes a shortage and puts upward pressure on price.

same diagram. If the quantity of planned sales at each price is compared with the quantity of planned purchases at that price (either the table or the graph can be used to make this comparison), it can be seen that there is only one price at which the two sets of plans mesh. That price—$2.00 per pound—is the equilibrium price. If all buyers and sellers make their plans with the expectation of a price of $2.00, no one will be surprised and no plans will have to be changed.

Shortages

But what will happen if for some reason people base their plans for buying or selling chicken on a price other than $2.00 a pound?[3] Suppose, for example, that they base their plans on a price of $1.00. As Figure 2.7 shows, that at that price buyers will plan to purchase chicken at a rate of 3 billion pounds per year, but farmers will plan to supply only 1 billion pounds. When the quantity demanded exceeds the quantity supplied, as in this example, the difference is an **excess quantity demanded** or, more simply, a **shortage**. In Figure 2.7 the shortage is 2 billion pounds of chicken per year when the price is $1.00 per pound.

Excess quantity demanded (shortage)

A condition in which the quantity of a good demanded at a given price exceeds the quantity supplied.

Inventory

A stock of a finished good awaiting sale or use.

In most markets the first sign of a shortage is a drop in the **inventory**, that is, in the stock of the good in question that has been produced and is waiting to be sold or used. Sellers plan to hold a certain quantity of goods in inventory to allow for minor changes in demand. When they see inventories dropping below the planned level, they change their plans. Some may try to rebuild their inventories by increasing their output, if they produce the good themselves; or, if they do not make it themselves, they may order more from the producer. Some sellers may take advantage of the strong demand for their product to raise the price, knowing that buyers will be willing to pay more. Many sellers will do a little of both. If sellers do not take the initiative, buyers will—they will offer to pay more if sellers will supply more. Whatever the details, the result will be an upward movement along the supply curve as both price and quantity increase.

As the shortage puts upward pressure on price, buyers will change their plans too. Moving up and to the left along their demand curve, they will cut back on their planned purchases. As both buyers and sellers change their plans, the market will move toward equilibrium. When the price reaches $2.00 per pound, both the shortage and the pressure to change buying and selling plans will disappear.

In the markets for most goods, sellers have inventories of goods ready to be sold. There are exceptions, however. Inventories are not possible in markets for services—haircuts, tax preparation, lawn care, and the like. Also, some goods, such as custom-built houses and machine tools that are designed for a specialized need, are not held in inventories. Sellers in these markets do not begin production until they have a contract with a buyer.

In markets in which there are no inventories, the sign of a shortage is a queue of buyers. The queue may take the form of a line of people waiting to be served or a list of names in an order book. The queue is a sign that, given the prevailing price, buyers would like to purchase the good at a faster rate than that at which producers have planned to supply it. However, some plans cannot be carried out—at least not right away. Buyers are served on a first-come, first-served basis.

The formation of a queue of buyers has much the same effect on the market as a decrease in inventories. Sellers react by increasing their rate of output, raising their prices, or both. Buyers react by reducing the quantity they plan to purchase. The result is a movement up and to the right along the supply curve and, at the same time, up and to the left along the demand curve until equilibrium is reached.

Surpluses

Excess quantity supplied (surplus)

A condition in which the quantity of a good supplied at a given price exceeds the quantity demanded.

Having considered what happens when buyers and sellers initially expect a price below the equilibrium price, we now turn to the opposite case. Suppose that for some reason buyers and sellers of chicken expect a price that is higher than the equilibrium price—say, $2.50 per pound—and make their plans accordingly. Figure 2.7 shows that farmers will plan to supply 2.5 billion pounds of chicken per year at $2.50, but their customers will plan to buy only 1.5 billion pounds. When the quantity supplied exceeds the quantity demanded, there is an **excess quantity supplied**, or a **surplus**. As Figure 2.7 shows, the surplus of chicken at a price of $2.50 per pound is 1 billion pounds per year.

When there is a surplus of a product, sellers will be unable to sell all that they had hoped to sell at the planned price. As a result, their inventories will begin to grow beyond the level they had planned to hold in preparation for normal changes in demand.

Sellers will react to the inventory buildup by changing their plans. Some will cut back their output. Others will lower their prices to induce consumers to buy more and thus reduce their extra stock. Still others will do a little of both. The result of these changes in plans will be a movement down and to the left along the supply curve.

As unplanned inventory buildup puts downward pressure on the price of chicken, buyers change their plans too. Finding that chicken costs less than they had expected, they buy more of it. In graphical terms, they move down and to the right along the demand curve. As that happens, the market is restored to equilibrium.

In markets in which there are no inventories, surpluses lead to the formation of queues of sellers looking for customers. Taxi queues at airports are a case in point. At some times of the day the fare for taxi service from the airport to downtown is more than high enough to attract a number of taxis that is equal to the demand. A queue of cabs waiting for passengers then forms. In some cities drivers who are far back in the queue try to attract riders by offering cut-rate fares. Often, though, there are rules against fare cutting. The queue then grows until the next peak period, when a surge in demand shortens it.

Changes in Market Conditions

On a graph, finding the equilibrium point looks easy. In real life, though, it is a moving target. Market conditions, by which we mean all the items that lie behind the "other things being equal" clause, change frequently. When they do, both buyers and sellers revise their plans, and market prices and quantities adjust.

RESPONSE TO A SHIFT IN DEMAND We will first consider a market's response to a shift in demand. Suppose, for example, that television news broadcasts a warning that eating chicken meat might transmit a new virus. The result would be an immediate decrease in demand for chicken. Part (a) of Figure 2.8 interprets this case in terms of the supply-and-demand model.

As the figure is drawn, the chicken market is initially in equilibrium at E_1. There the price is \$3.00 per pound and the quantity produced is 2 billion pounds per year. Now the temporary change in tastes caused by the health warning shifts the demand curve to the left, from D_1 to D_2. (There is a shift in the demand curve rather than a movement along it, because a change in tastes is not one of the items represented by the axes of the diagram.) What will happen next?

At the original price of \$3.00 per pound, there will be a surplus of chicken. The supply curve shows that at that price chicken farmers will plan to produce 2 billion pounds per year. However, according to the new demand curve, D_2, consumers will no longer buy that much chicken at \$3.00 per pound. Instead, given their new tastes, they will buy only 1 billion pounds at that price.

But the price does not stay at \$3.00 for long. As soon as the demand curve begins to shift and the surplus begins to develop, chicken inventories rise above their planned levels, putting downward pressure on the price. As the price falls, producers revise their plans. They move down and to the left along their supply curve, reducing

FIGURE 2.8 EFFECTS OF CHANGING CONDITIONS IN THE CHICKEN MARKET

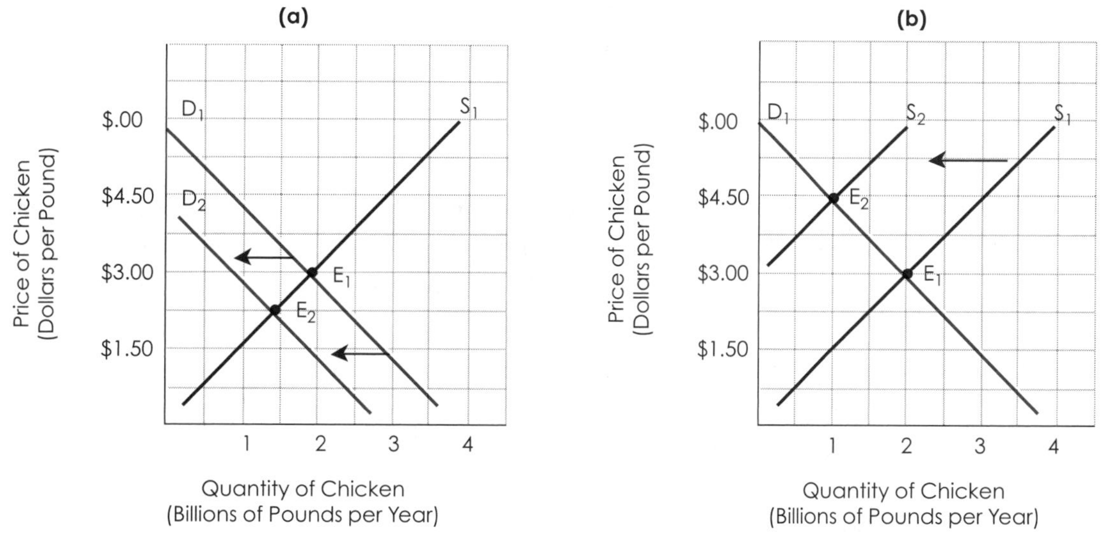

Part (a) of this figure shows the effects of a decrease in demand for chicken caused by a health warning about the safety of eating chicken. Initially the market is in equilibrium at E_1. The change in tastes causes a shift in the demand curve. At the original equilibrium price of \$3.00 per pound, there is a temporary surplus of chicken. This causes inventories to start to rise and puts downward pressure on the price. As the price falls, producers move down along their supply curve to a new equilibrium at E_2. There both the price and quantity of chicken are lower than before the shift in demand. Part (b) shows the effects of a decrease in supply caused by a drought, which raises the price of corn used to feed chicken. The shift in the supply curve causes a shortage at the initial price of \$3.00 per pound. The shortage puts upward pressure on price. As the price rises, buyers move up and to the left along the demand curve until a new equilibrium is reached at E_2. In each case, note that only one curve needs to shift to bring about the new equilibrium.

the quantity supplied. (There is a movement along the supply curve, not a shift in the curve, because the producers are responding to a change in the price of chicken, the variable shown on the vertical axis. Nothing has happened to change the "other things being equal" condition, such as technology, input prices, and so on, which could cause the supply curve to shift.)

As farmers move downward along their supply curve in the direction shown by the arrow in part (a) of Figure 2.8, they eventually reach point E_2, where their plans again mesh with those of consumers. At that point the price has fallen to \$2.25 per pound and production to 1.5 billion pounds. Although health-conscious consumers would not have bought that much chicken at the old price, they will do so at the new, lower price. E_2 thus is the new equilibrium point. Later, if the health scare proves to be baseless, the demand curve will shift back D_1 and the market price and quantity will return to their original values.

RESPONSE TO A SHIFT IN SUPPLY The original equilibrium might be disrupted by a change in supply rather than by a change in demand. For example, beginning from a condition of equilibrium, a drought in the Midwest might result in a higher price for grain used as chicken feed. That would shift the supply curve to the left while the demand curve remained unchanged, as shown in part (b) of Figure 2.8.

Given the new supply curve, there will be a shortage of chicken at the original price. Inventories will decline and the prices will rise in response. As the price increases, producers will move upward and to the right along their new supply curve, S_2, and consumers will move upward and to the left along their demand curve, D_1, which remains in its original position. A new equilibrium is established when the price reaches \$4.50 per pound.

One of the most frequent mistakes people make in learning the supply-and-demand model is to think that *both* curves always must shift in order to restore equilibrium. The examples given in Figure 2.8 show clearly that this is not the case. In part (a), after the demand curve shifts, a movement along the supply curve is enough to establish the new equilibrium. No shift in the supply curve is needed. Similarly, in part (b), after the supply curve shifts, the demand curve does not need to shift to reach the new equilibrium.

However, in the turmoil of real-world markets, cases can be found in which both curves do shift at once. This will happen when two separate changes in conditions occur at the same time, one acting on the supply curve and the other on the demand curve. *Economics in the News 2.1* provides a real-world example. It shows how beef prices were pushed upward in 2003 by two simultaneous changes in market conditions. One was a swing in consumer tastes toward beef because of the popularity of low-carbohydrate, high-protein diets. That shifted the demand curve to the right. At the same time a cutoff of beef imports from Canada shifted the supply curve to the left. Either change acting alone would have been enough to raise the price. Both changes acting together had an especially sharp impact.

ECONOMICS IN THE NEWS 2.1

BEEF PRICES UP; FAST FOOD CHAINS SWITCH TO CHICKEN

Stock up the freezer if you like steak because beef prices at the supermarket are on their way up. And they're likely to stay there for a while.

U.S. cattle prices are at a record high, say economists with the U.S. Department of Agriculture. They've increased 34% since July, and this month the benchmark price of Nebraska choice steers went from $90 to $116 per 100 pounds. A year ago, the price per 100 pounds was $64.

"We've seen increases in the last 10 days," said Jim Robb, director of the Livestock Marketing Information Center in Denver. "Choice T-bone steak and New York strip steak, those prices are double what they were three weeks ago."

"Those prices will ease off a little bit but not much," said David Kay of *Cattle Buyers Weekly*. "We look as if we're going to have even tighter cattle supplies for slaughter in 2004 and even into 2005."

Prices are up because of a set of circumstances that Robb calls "completely unprecedented." First, consumer demand for beef has increased nearly 10% since 1998 after declining for 20 years.

Recent increases in consumption may be due in part because of the increasing popularity of high-protein diets, such as this summer's blockbuster South Beach diet, and the venerable Atkins diet.

Second, as Wayne Purcell of the Research Institute on Livestock Pricing at Virginia Tech points out, the U.S. banned imports of Canadian cattle and beef five months ago. The ban was imposed because of the discovery of a case of mad cow disease there last spring and reduced cattle and meat imports to the United States by 9%.

Consumers already may be feeling the impact, whether they're eating out or at home. U.S. restaurant chains such as McDonald's and Wendy's have been hyping salads and lean chicken pieces lately, and industry observers say it's no coincidence that the switch coincides with rising beef prices. Experts expect cost-cutting by other restaurant companies to offset rising food prices.

It is not clear how long it will take for the impact of the price increases to be felt at local meat counters. Retail beef prices typically trail the price paid at the stockyard anywhere from two weeks to two months. So last week's increase will not show up at supermarkets until the first weeks of November or until Christmas.

If grocers think the price hike is temporary, they may eat the difference rather than risk aggravating customers. But if grocers do raise prices, "they'll raise their everyday prices only a little, but they will keep them up for a year or so. And we just won't see beef featured in sales very much," Kay said.

Source: Elizabeth Weise, "Beef Prices On the Way Up," USA Today, October 24, 2003.

Equilibrium as Spontaneous Order

The way that markets move toward a new equilibrium following a disturbance is an example of economic coordination through spontaneous order. In the case we have been following, the disturbance began either with a change in health consciousness among consumers or with a change in the weather. To make the adjustment to new conditions, the decisions of thousands of farmers, wholesalers, retailers, as well as that of millions of consumers, must somehow be coordinated. How can that be done?

In a market economy, no central planning agency or regulatory bureaucracy is needed. The required shift in the use of scarce resources is brought about through information and incentives transmitted in the form of changing market prices. The trend toward low-carbohydrate, high-protein diets in the early 2000s is a typical example. As demand for beef, chicken, and other high-protein foods rose, farmers responded to higher prices by raising more chickens and cattle. Labor, capital, natural resources, and entrepreneurial energy flowed into chicken and beef production without any central authority giving an order. At the same time, investments in donuts, a high-carb food that had boomed in the 1990s, slowed substantially.

The process was remarkably smooth for so vast a shift in resource use. Behind the scenes, surpluses and shortages nudged choices in the needed directions, but at no time did shortages occur in the acute form of empty meat coolers at the supermarket or lines of chicken-hungry consumers stretching down city streets. Similarly, slack demand for donuts signaled entrepreneurs to turn away from building new outlets, but it did not give rise to mountains of rotting donuts that had to be dumped into landfills.

No one *intended* this process of adjustment. Equilibrium is not a compromise that must be negotiated by a committee of consumers and producers. Just as shoppers manage to equalize the length of supermarket checkout lines without the guidance of a central authority, markets move toward equilibrium spontaneously, through the small, local adjustments that people make in their efforts to serve their own interests. As Adam Smith might have put it, we have not the benevolence of Tyson Foods or the Beef Industry Council to thank for our dinner; instead it is their self-interest that puts the right food on our table.

PRICE FLOORS AND CEILINGS: AN APPLICATION

Economics—both macro and micro—encompasses a great many applications of the concepts of supply and demand. Although each situation is unique, each to some extent draws on ideas developed in this chapter. This section, which uses the model to analyze the effects of government-imposed price floors and ceilings, provides some examples. Many more will be added in later chapters.

Price Supports: The Market for Milk

In our earlier example of the market for beef, a decrease in demand caused a surplus, which in turn caused the price to decrease until the surplus was eliminated. Markets are not always free to respond by adjusting prices, however. The market for milk is a case in point.

Figure 2.9 shows the market for milk in terms of supply and demand curves. The quantity of milk is measured in hundredweight, the unit used for bulk milk sales, equal to roughly 12 gallons. Suppose that initially the market is in equilibrium at point E_1. The wholesale price of milk is $13 per hundredweight, and 110 million hundredweight is produced per year. Then suppose that a trend in taste away from high-cholesterol foods shifts the demand curve for milk to the left. The result would be a surplus of milk at the $13 price, as shown by the arrow in Figure 2.9.

At this point a new factor comes into operation that was not present in our earlier discussion of the chicken market. In that case, chicken prices were free to fall in response to a surplus, but in the milk market they are not. Instead, an elaborate set of

FIGURE 2.9 PRICE SUPPORTS FOR MILK

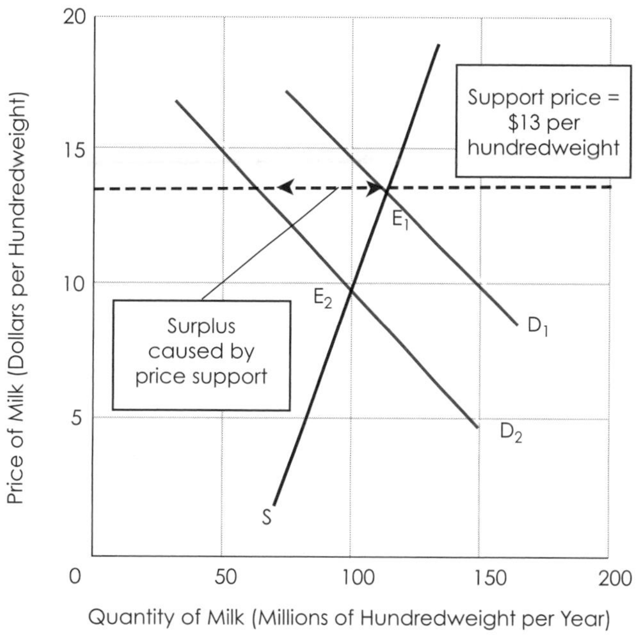

Suppose that initially the market for milk is in equilibrium at E_1. A shift in tastes away from high-cholesterol foods then shifts the demand curve to D_2. If the price were free to fall, there would be a temporary surplus that would push the price down to a new equilibrium at $10 per hundredweight. Instead, suppose that the government maintains a support price for milk at a level higher than the equilibrium price, as it did for many years ($13 per hundredweight in this example). The government would then need to buy the surplus milk and stores it in the form of powdered milk, butter and cheese to keep the price from falling.

government-imposed controls and subsidies puts a floor under the price of milk. As part of the controls, the government agrees to pay a minimum price for all milk that cannot be sold at that price on the open market. In our example, the support price is assumed to be $13.

With the demand curve in its original position D_1, there was no surplus and the government did not need to buy any milk. But with the demand curve in position D_2, there is a surplus of 40 million hundredweight per year. Under the price support law the government must buy this surplus and store it in the form of powdered milk, cheese, butter, and other products with long shelf lives.

Without price supports, the shift in demand would cause the price of milk to fall to the new equilibrium price of $10 per hundredweight. When price supports are applied to a product at a level higher than the equilibrium price, however, the result is a persistent surplus. The effects of the price support can be understood in terms of conflicting signals sent to producers and consumers. To consumers, the price of $13 says, "Milk is scarce. Its opportunity cost is high. Hold your consumption down." To producers, it says, "All is well. Incentives are unchanged. Feel free to continue using scarce resources to produce milk." Without price supports, a drop in the price to $10 would send a different set of messages. Consumers would hear: "Milk is cheaper and more abundant. Although it is not cholesterol free, give in to temptation! Drink more of it!" Producers would hear: "The milk market is not what it once was. Look at your opportunity costs. Is there perhaps some better use for your labor, capital, and natural resources?"

During the 1980s and 1990s, the government's price support was consistently higher than the equilibrium price. The program became very expensive, more than $1,000 per U.S. family by some estimates, enough to buy each family its own cow. From time to time the government has tried to eliminate the milk surplus by shifting the supply curve to the left so that it would intersect the demand curve near the support price. Under one program, for example, farmers were encouraged to sell their cows to be slaughtered for their meat, thereby reducing the size of dairy herds. Such programs, however, have failed to eliminate the milk surplus. The chief reason is the dairy farmers' entrepreneurial response to the high price of milk. The government's efforts to cut the size of herds were largely offset by increased output per cow as a result of genetic improvements and better farm management practices. The government accumulated mountains of surplus dairy products.

Then, during the early years of the 21st century, conditions in the milk market changed. By 2005, the support price had fallen below the market price and the surplus had disappeared. This, too, had unintended consequences for public policy. Under the U.S. Department of Agriculture's Commodity Supplemental Food Program, as many as 100,000 mothers, children, and elderly people had received packages of free milk powder drawn from government surpluses. Suddenly these vast stocks were threatened with exhaustion, and officials were left scrambling to find other ways to aid needy citizens. Meanwhile, across the Atlantic, the European Union continues to operate a price support system that produces an ongoing surplus of more than 30 million tons per year. The European milk market is still in a position much like that shown in Figure 2.9.

Price Ceilings: The Case of Rent Control

In the milk market, the government maintains a support price that has often been above the equilibrium price. In certain other markets, a price ceiling below the equilibrium price is imposed. An example of the latter situation is rent control in housing markets.

Rent control in one form or another has been used in several major U.S. cities, including New York, Washington, D.C., San Francisco, and Los Angeles. The controls vary from one city to another, but in all cases maximum rents, at least for some categories of apartments, are established by law. The purpose of rent control is to aid tenants by preventing landlords from charging "unreasonably high" rents. What is unreasonably high is determined by the relative political strength of landlords and tenants rather than by the forces of supply and demand.

INTENDED EFFECTS Figure 2.10 interprets the effects of rent control in terms of supply and demand. For the sake of simplicity it is assumed that the supply of rental housing consists of units of equal size and rental value. Part (a) of the figure shows the effects of rent control in the short run. Here the short run means a period that is too short to permit significant increases or decreases in the supply of rental housing. (The short-run supply curve, which is drawn as a vertical line, indicates that a change in price will not result in any change in the quantity of apartments.[4])

Under the conditions shown, the equilibrium rent per standard housing unit is $1,250 per month for each of the 200,000 units in the city. Now suppose that a rent ceiling of $500 is imposed. The result is a gain to tenants of $750 per unit per month. The total sum transferred to tenants (that is, the benefit to them from below-market rents) is $750 per unit times 200,000 units, or $150 million, in all. In graphical terms,

FIGURE 2.10 EFFECTS OF RENT CONTROL

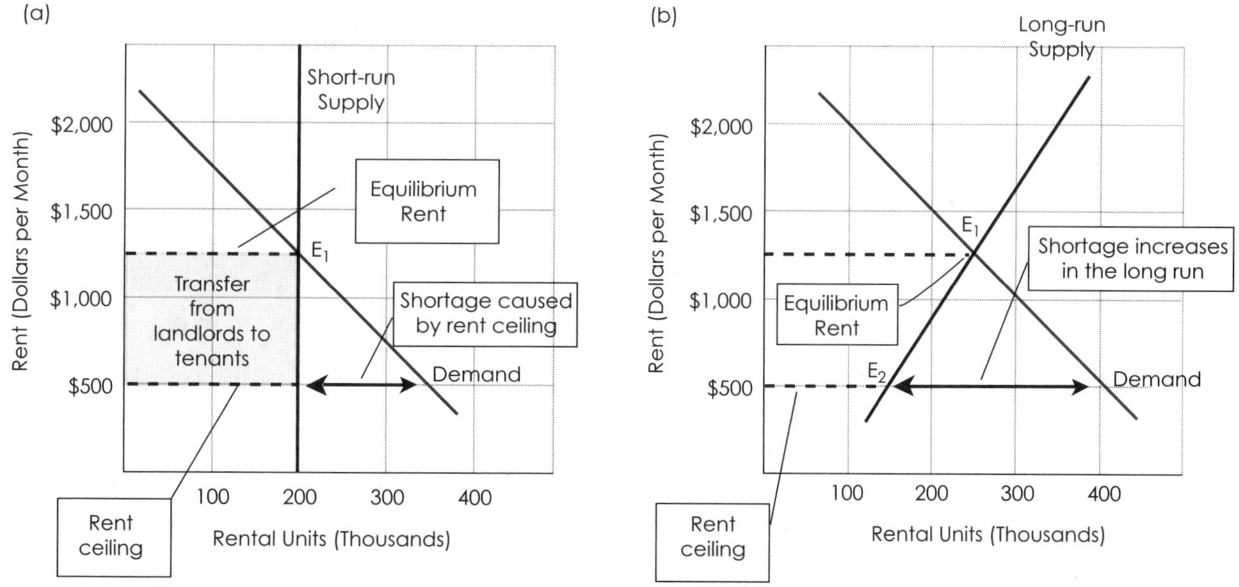

Part (a) shows the short-run effects of rent control. In the short run, the supply of rental apartments is considered to be fixed. The equilibrium rent is $1,250 per month. A rent ceiling of $500 per month is then put into effect. One possible outcome is that landlords will charge disguised rent increases, which will bring the true price back to $1,250 per month. If such disguised increases are prohibited, there will be a shortage of 350,000 units at the ceiling price. Part (b) shows the long-run effects when there is time to adjust the number of units in response to the price. If the ceiling price is enforced, landlords move down their supply curve to E2. The shortage then becomes even more severe than in the short run.

that sum is equal to the area of the shaded rectangle in Figure 2.10. The benefit to tenants at the expense of landlords is the principal intended effect of rent control.

UNINTENDED EFFECTS The policy of rent control, aims to benefit tenants at the expense of landlords and provides a classic illustration of the law of unintended consequences. In the short run, when the stock of apartments is fixed, the unintended consequences stem from the apartment shortage created by the controls. The shortage occurs because the quantity demanded is greater at the lower ceiling price than at the higher equilibrium price.

The greater quantity demanded has several sources. First, people who would otherwise own a house or condominium may now want to rent. Second, people who would otherwise live in non–rent-controlled suburbs may now seek rent-controlled units in the city. Third, each tenant may want more space, which results in a demand for more of the standardized units shown in Figure 2.10.

The shortage creates a problem for both landlords and tenants: How will the limited supply of apartments be rationed among those who want them? Both landlords and tenants devise a number of creative responses—*entrepreneurial* responses, as an economist would say.

One response on the part of landlords is to seek disguised rent increases. These may take the form of large, nonrefundable "key deposits" or security deposits. As an alternative, they may sell old, used furniture or drapes at inflated prices as a condition for renting the apartment. Finally, the costs of certain maintenance or security services that the landlord might otherwise have paid for may be transferred to tenants.

Tenants too may get into the act. When they decide to move, they may sublet their apartments to other tenants rather than give up their leases. Now it is the tenant who collects the key money or sells the old drapes to the subtenant. The original tenant may have moved to a distant city but maintains a bank account and a post office box for use in paying the rent. The subtenant is instructed to play the role of a "guest" if the landlord telephones.

Advocates of rent control view these responses as cheating and often try to outlaw them. If prohibitions are enforced, the landlord will find that there are many applicants for each vacant apartment. In that case, the landlord must decide to whom to rent the apartment. The result will often be discrimination against renters who are from minority groups, who have children, or who have unconventional lifestyles.

In the long run, rent control has other unintended effects. The long run in this case means enough time for the number of rental units to grow through construction of new units or shrink through abandonment of old ones (or their conversion to condominiums). Other things being equal, the higher the rent, the greater the rate of construction, and the lower the rent, the greater the rate of abandonment or conversion. This is reflected in the positively sloped long-run supply curve in part (b) of Figure 2.10.

If rent controls are enforced in such a way that there are no disguised charges by landlords, the number of rental units shrinks and the market moves from E_1 to E_2. At E_2, the unintended effects that appeared in the short run become more pronounced. The intensity of housing discrimination increases relative to the short-run case, because the difference between the number of units available and the number sought by renters increases. Graphically, that difference is shown by the horizontal gap between the supply and demand curves at the ceiling price. In the short run, there is a shortage of 50,000 units; in the long run, the shortage increases to 75,000 units.

Rent controls are often defended as being beneficial to the poor. But when all of the unintended effects of rent control are taken into account, one may question whether poor families really benefit. In cases in which disguised rent increases are possible, the true cost of rental housing is not really decreased. Further, it is hard to believe that landlords' tendency to discriminate against minority group members, single-parent families, and tenants with irregular work histories will benefit the poor. The most likely beneficiaries of rent control are stable, middle-class families who work at the same jobs and live in the same apartments for long periods.

Why does rent control persist as a policy, given its many seemingly perverse unintended consequences? Some economists explain the popularity of rent control in terms of the political power of the middle-class tenants who are most likely to benefit from rent controls and who see "helping the poor" as nothing more than a convenient cover for their own self-interest. Some explain their popularity in terms of the short time horizon of government officials: The adverse effect on tenants of ending rent control would appear very quickly, whereas such benefits as increased construction of new apartments would materialize only long after the next election. And some attribute the popularity of rent control to the simple fact that many voters do not give much thought to the policy's unintended consequences. Whatever the reason, it appears that very gradually rent control is weakening its hold, even in New York, long home of the strongest controls. In the past decade, some 10 percent of the 1 million or so apartments once covered by New York's rent controls have left the system, and the trend is expected to continue.

THIS CHAPTER HAS covered the basics of the supply-and-demand model and described a few applications of that model. There are many more applications in both macro- and microeconomics. In macroeconomics, the supply-and-demand model can be applied to financial markets, labor markets, and the problem of determining the rate of inflation and real output for the economy as a whole. In microeconomics, the model can be applied to product markets, markets for productive resources, and policy issues ranging from pollution to farm policy to international trade, to name just a few. As the great economist Alfred Marshall once put it, nearly all of the major problems of economics have a "kernel" that reflects the workings of supply and demand (see *Who Said It? Who Did It? 2.1*).

WHO SAID IT? WHO DID IT? 2.1

ALFRED MARSHALL ON SUPPLY AND DEMAND

Alfred Marshall, often considered to have been the greatest economist of his day, was born in London in 1842. His father was a Bank of England cashier who hoped the boy would enter the ministry. Young Marshall had other ideas, however. He turned down a theological scholarship at Oxford to study mathematics, receiving his M.A. from Cambridge in 1865.

While at Cambridge, Marshall joined a philosophical discussion group. There he became interested in promoting the broad development of the human mind. He was soon told, however, that the harsh realities of economics would prevent his ideas from being carried out. Britain's economic potential as a country, it was said, could never allow the masses sufficient leisure for education. This disillusioning episode appears to have triggered Marshall's fascination with economics.

At the time, British economics was dominated by the classical school founded by Adam Smith and David Ricardo. Marshall had great respect for the classical writers. Initially he saw his own work as simply applying his mathematical training to strengthen and systematize the classical system. Before long, however, he was breaking new ground and developing a system of his own. By 1890, when he brought out his famous *Principles of Economics*, he had laid the foundation of what we now call the neoclassical school.

In an attempt to explain the essence of his approach, Marshall included the following passage in the second edition of his *Principles*:

> *In spite of a great variety in detail, nearly all the chief problems of economics agree in that they have a kernel of the same kind. This kernel is an inquiry as to the balancing of two opposed classes of motives, the one consisting of desires to acquire certain new goods, and thus satisfy wants; while the other consists of desires to avoid certain efforts or retain certain immediate enjoyment ... in other words, it is an inquiry into the balancing of the forces of demand and supply.*

Marshall's influence on economics—at least in the English-speaking world—was enormous. His *Principles* was the leading economics text for several decades, and modern students can still learn much from it. As a professor at Cambridge, Marshall taught a great many of the next generation's leading economists. Today his neoclassical school continues to dominate the profession. It has received many challenges, but so far it has weathered them all.

When one takes a detailed look at the underpinnings of the model, it appears to fit some kinds of markets more closely than others. The fit is best for markets in which there are many producers and many customers, the goods sold by one producer are much like those sold by others, and all sellers and buyers have good information on market conditions. Markets for farm commodities, such as wheat and corn, and financial markets, such as the New York Stock Exchange, meet these standards reasonably well.

However, even in markets that do not display all of these features, the fit is often close enough so that the supply-and-demand model provides useful insights into what is going on. The rental housing market is an example: Not all rental units are, in fact, alike, even when measurement is standardized for objective characteristics such as floor space. Nevertheless, most economists would agree that valid conclusions about the effects of rent control can be arrived at by applying the supply-and-demand model to that market. Thus, the supply-and-demand model serves a precise analytical function in some markets and a broader, more metaphorical function in others. That flexibility makes the model one of the most useful items in the economist's tool kit.

SUMMARY

1. **How does the price of a good or service affect the quantity of it that buyers demand?** Economists use the term *demand* to refer to the willingness and ability of buyers to purchase goods and services. According to the *law of demand,* there is an inverse relationship between the price of a good and the quantity of it that buyers demand. The *quantity demanded* is the quantity that buyers are willing and able to pay for. The law of demand can be represented graphically by a negatively sloped *demand curve.* A change in the quantity demanded is shown by a movement along the demand curve.

2. **How do other market conditions affect demand?** A change in any of the variables covered by the "other things being equal" clause of the law of demand causes a shift in the demand curve; this is known as a *change in demand.* Examples include changes in the prices of goods that are *substitutes* or *complements* of the good in question as well as changes in consumer incomes, expectations, and tastes.

3. **How does the price of a good affect the quantity supplied by sellers?** *Supply* refers to sellers' willingness and ability to offer products for sale in a market. In most markets an increase in the price of a good will increase the quantity of the good that sellers are willing to supply. This relationship can be shown as a positively sloped *supply curve.* The higher price gives producers an incentive to supply more, but rising opportunity costs set a limit on the amount they will supply at any given price.

4. **How do changes in other market conditions affect supply?** A change in any of the items covered by the "other things being equal" clause of the supply curve will shift the curve. Examples include changes in technology, changes in the prices of inputs, changes in the prices of other goods that could be produced with the same resources, and changes in expectations.

5. **How do supply and demand interact to determine the market price of a good or service?** In a market with a positively-sloped supply curve and a negatively-sloped demand curve, there is only one price at which the quantity of a good that sellers plan to supply will exactly match the quantity that buyers plan to purchase. That is known as the *equilibrium* price. At any higher price there will be a *surplus*, and at any lower price there will be a *shortage*.

6. **Why do market prices and quantities change in response to changes in market conditions?** A change in any market condition that shifts the supply or demand curve will change the equilibrium price and quantity in a market. For example, the demand curve may shift to the right as a result of a change in consumer incomes. This causes a shortage at the old price, and the price begins to rise. As the price rises, suppliers move up along the supply curve to a new equilibrium. No shift in the supply curve is required. On the other hand, better technology may shift the supply curve to the right. In that case, there is a surplus at the old price, and the price will fall. As the price decreases, buyers will move down along their demand curve to a new equilibrium. No shift in the demand curve is required.

7. **How do price supports and price ceilings affect the operation of markets?** A price support prevents the market price from falling when the demand curve shifts to the left or the supply curve shifts to the right. The result may be a lasting surplus. A price ceiling prevents the price from rising to its equilibrium level. The result may be a permanent shortage. The total quantity supplied may then be less than the quantity that buyers would like to purchase at the ceiling price or even at the equilibrium price.

KEY TERMS

Supply
Demand
Law of demand
Demand curve
Change in quantity demanded
Change in demand
Substitute goods
Complementary goods
Normal good
Inferior good
Supply curve
Change in quantity supplied
Change in supply
Equilibrium
Excess quantity demanded (shortage)
Inventory
Excess quantity supplied (surplus)

PROBLEMS AND TOPICS FOR DISCUSSION

1. **A shifting demand curve.** A vending machine company has studied the demand for soft drinks sold in cans from machines. On a 70-degree day consumers in the firm's territory will buy about 2,000 cans at a price of $0.75. For each $.05 rise in price, the quantity sold falls by 200 cans per day; for each 5-degree rise in the temperature, the quantity sold rises by 150 cans per day. The same relationships hold for decreases in price or temperature. Using this information, draw a set of curves showing the demand for soft drinks on days when the temperature is 60, 70, and 85 degrees. Then draw a separate diagram with temperature on the vertical axis and quantity on the horizontal axis. Draw a line representing the relationship between temperature and quantity when the price is $0.75. Next draw additional temperature-quantity lines for prices of $0.50 and $1.00. Do the two diagrams give the same information? Discuss. (Note: If you have any trouble with this exercise, review the appendix to Chapter 1, "Working with Graphs," especially the section entitled "Packing Three Variables into Two Dimensions.")

2. **Demand and the relative price of motor fuel in the 1980s.** In 1979 and 1980 the nominal price of motor fuel rose much more rapidly than the general price level, pushing up the relative price of motor fuel. As we would expect, the quantity sold decreased. In 1981 and 1982 the relative price leveled off and then began to fall, but the quantity sold continued to fall. Which one or more of the following hypotheses do you think best explains the behavior of motor fuel sales in 1981 and 1982? Illustrate each hypothesis with supply and demand curves.

   a. In the 1970s the demand curve had the usual negative slope. However, in 1981 and 1982 the demand curve shifted to an unusual positively sloped position.

   b. The demand curve had a negative slope throughout the period. However, the recession of 1981 and 1982 reduced consumers' real incomes and thus shifted the demand curve.

   c. The demand curve has a negative slope at all times, but the shape depends partly on how much time consumers have to adjust to a change in prices. Over a short period, the demand curve is fairly steep because few adjustments can be made. Over the long term, it has a somewhat flatter slope because further adjustments, such as buying more fuel-efficient cars or moving closer to the job, can be made. Thus, the decreases in fuel sales in 1981 and 1982 were delayed reactions to the price increases that occurred in 1979 and 1980.

3. **Shortages, price controls, and queues.** During the late 1980s and early 1990s, economic reforms initiated by Soviet President Mikhail Gorbachev began to raise consumer incomes, but the Soviet government continued to impose price ceilings on basic goods like food, clothing,

and household goods. As a result, there were severe shortages of many goods and long lines at all kinds of stores became common. Then, in January 1992, the new Russian government, under President Boris Yeltsin, removed retail price controls on most goods. Within a month, prices more than doubled on average and lines disappeared. Analyze these events using the supply and demand model. First draw a supply and demand diagram for some common good, say, butter, showing the market in equilibrium before the beginning of the Gorbachev reforms. Next, use shifts of the appropriate curves to show why the combination of rising incomes plus price ceilings produced shortages and lines. Finally, show what happened when price controls were removed in 1992.

4. **Eliminating queues through flexible pricing.** You are a member of the Metropolitan Taxi Commission, which sets taxi fares for your city. You have been told that long lines of taxis form at the airport during off-peak hours. At peak hours, on the other hand, few taxis are available and there are long lines of passengers waiting for cabs. It is proposed that taxi fares from the airport to downtown be cut by 10 percent during off-peak hours and raised by 10 percent during peak hours. How do you think these changes would affect the queuing patterns of taxis and passengers? Do you think the proposal is a good one from the passengers' point of view? From the cabbies' point of view? From the standpoint of economic efficiency? What do you think would happen if the Taxi Commission stopped setting fares altogether and allowed passengers and drivers to negotiate any price they wanted? Discuss.

5. **Rent control.** Turn to part (b) of Figure 2.10, which shows the long-run effects of rent control. If the controls are enforced and there are no disguised rent charges, landlords move down the supply curve to E_2. Buildings are abandoned or converted because of the low rent they bring in. Now consider some alternative possibilities.

   a. Suppose that the controls are poorly enforced so that landlords, through key deposits, furniture sales, or some other means, are able to charge as much as the market will bear. What will the resulting equilibrium price and quantity be, taking both open and disguised rental charges into account?

   b. Now suppose that the controls are enforced so that landlords really cannot collect more than $500 per month. However, the controls are not enforced against tenants who sublet. What will the equilibrium quantity and price be, including both the rent paid to landlords and the disguised rental payments made by subtenants to their subleasors?

CASE FOR DISCUSSION

The hottest topic at a recent exposition for suppliers and users of off-road heavy equipment was tire shortages. Booming Chinese demand for raw materials meant that mining companies in China, Russia, and Indonesia were stocking up on new earth moving equipment and wearing tires our faster on equipment they already owned.

While demand soared, supply had a hard time keeping up. Building a new production line for large tires can take more than two years. The *Financial Times* reported that some tire makers were reactivating mothballed production lines for old-fashioned bias-ply tires. While not as good as modern radial tires, they were good enough to satisfy demand from customers who just wanted something "black and round," according to Prashant Prabhu, president of the earth-mover and industrial tire business of Michelin, the French tire maker. Prabhu also said his company was revising its pricing for large tires to take the shortage into account.

According to *Light and Medium Truck Magazine*, the shortages of huge off-road tires were spilling over into the market for heavy-duty truck tires. In addition to sharply increased demand, it blamed rising prices for materials, including both natural and synthetic rubber. The magazine predicted that the shortage would last two years or more.

Expectations, based on past experience, were a significant factor slowing the adjustment of supply to the shortage. In 2000–2003, demand for heavy-duty tires from equipment makers had dropped by more than 50%, leaving some tire makers with serious overcapacity. The fear that recent high demand might not last was leading some manufacturers to take a "wait-and-see" attitude.

Sources: *Financial Times*, Materials squeeze leads to tyre shortage, By James Mackintosh Published: April 28 2005 03:00; *Light and Medium Truck Magazine*, May 2005, http://www.ttnews.com/lmt/May05/tire.asp (May 22, 2005); and *Rental Management Online*, http://www.rentalmanagementmag.com/newsart.asp?ARTID=1776, May 22, 2005.

QUESTIONS

1. Beginning from a position of equilibrium, use supply and demand curves to show how the tire market is affected by an increase in demand for earth-moving equipment. Does the supply curve shift? The demand curve? Both? Explain.
2. Using a scheme similar to Figure 2.10, distinguish between long-run and short-run supply in the tire market. What do you expect to happen to the price and quantity of tires in the short run? The long run?
3. Why are expectations a factor determining the position of the supply curve? How would the path of price and quantity over time differ with and without the element of supplier caution based on the experience of 2000–2003?

END NOTES

1. Before continuing, the reader may want to review the Chapter 1 appendix "Working with Graphs," especially the section entitled "Packing Three Variables into Two Dimensions."
2. The "plans" referred to need not be formal or thought out in detail, and are subject to change. A consumer might, for example, make out a shopping list for the supermarket based on the usual prices for various foods, but then revise it to take into account unexpected price increases or sales on certain items. On specific occasions, consumer decisions may even be completely impulsive, with little basis in rational calculation. The model of supply and demand does not require that every decision be based on precise analysis, but only that consumer intentions, on the average, are influenced by prices and other economic considerations.
3. Why might buyers and sellers enter the market expecting a price other than the one that permits equilibrium? It may be, for example, that market conditions have caused the supply or demand curve to shift unexpectedly, so that a price that formerly permitted equilibrium no longer does so. It may be that buyers or sellers expect conditions to change, but they do not change after all. Or, it may be that government policy has established a legal maximum or minimum price that differs from the equilibrium price. Later sections of the chapter will explore some of these possibilities.
4. This is a fairly restrictive assumption. In practice, a small number of housing units can move into or out of the rental market quickly in response to changing conditions. "Mother-in-law apartments" in private homes are an example. If conditions in the rental market are unfavorable, the owners of such units may simply leave them vacant. Allowing for such fast-reaction units means that the short-run supply curve, while still quite steep, would not be vertical. However, a vertical short-run curve simplifies the geometry while capturing the essential features of the situation.

CHAPTER 3

Supply, Demand, and Elasticity

After reading this chapter, you will understand:

1. How the responsiveness of quantity demanded to a price change can be expressed in terms of elasticity.
2. How elasticity of demand is related to revenue.
3. How elasticity applies to changes in market conditions other than price.
4. How elasticity is useful in interpreting issues of taxation and other public policies.

Before reading this chapter, make sure you know the meaning of:

1. Supply and demand
2. Demand, quantity demanded
3. Supply, quantity supplied
4. Substitutes and complements
5. Normal and inferior goods

HOW MUCH DID you pay for this textbook? Was it more expensive or less expensive than the books you buy for other courses? As a student, you probably have a strong desire to pay less for your books if you can. Have you ever wondered why your professors sometimes choose books that are so expensive?

This chapter will help you understand the effect of price on choices that people make among alternative goods, like different textbooks, different foods, or different modes of transportation. It will focus on the concept of *elasticity*, a word economists use to say how sensitive such choices are to price. As a student, your choice of textbook is probably very sensitive to price—your demand is *elastic*, to use the economist's term. However, your professor, who does not pay for the books, cares less about how much they cost. Your professor's demand may be *inelastic*. In the following pages you will learn how to define, measure, and apply the important concept of elasticity.

ELASTICITY

The responsiveness of quantity demanded to a change in price can be expressed in many ways, depending on the units of measurement that are chosen. Consider the demand for chicken, an example used in the preceding chapter. A study of the budget of a single American household might find that an increase of ten cents per pound would decrease consumption by 1 pound per week. A study done in France might find that a price increase of 1 euro per kilogram decreased consumption of all consumers in the city of Lille by 25,000 kilos per month. Are the findings of these studies similar? It is hard to tell, because the units used are different. It would require more information, and some calculations, to know whether the sensitivity of demand to price as measured in different countries using different currencies, are the same. The same would be true of two studies in one country if one measured price in dollars per ton and tons per year, while the other used dollars per pound and pounds per week.

To avoid confusion arising from the choice of different units of measurement, it is useful to standardize. One common way of doing so is to express all changes as percentages. Suppose, for example, that the studies of both American and French consumers found that a 20 percent increase in price was associated with a 10 percent decrease in quantity demanded. These percentages would stay the same regardless of whether the original data were stated in dollars per pound, euros per kilo, or any other measurement.

Elasticity

A measure of the response of one variable to a change in another, stated as a ratio of the percentage change in one variable to the associated percentage change in another variable.

The use of percentages to express the response of one variable to a change in another is widespread in economics. The term **elasticity** is used to refer to relationships expressed in percentages. Like equilibrium, elasticity is a metaphor borrowed from physics. Much as equilibrium calls to mind a pendulum that has come to rest hanging straight down, elasticity conjures up the image of a rubber band that stretches by a certain percentage of its length when the force applied to it is increased by a given percentage. This chapter introduces several applications of elasticity in economics.

Price Elasticity of Demand

Price elasticity of demand

The ratio of the percentage change in the quantity of a good demanded to a given percentage change in its price, other things being equal.

We begin with the relationship between price and quantity demanded. The **price elasticity of demand** is the ratio of the percentage change in the quantity of a good demanded to a given percentage change in its price. Figure 3.1 presents five demand curves showing different degrees of price elasticity of demand. In part (a), the quantity demanded is strongly responsive to a change in price. In this case, a decrease in price from \$5 to \$3 causes the quantity demanded to increase from three units to six.

FIGURE 3.1 PRICE ELASTICITY OF DEMAND

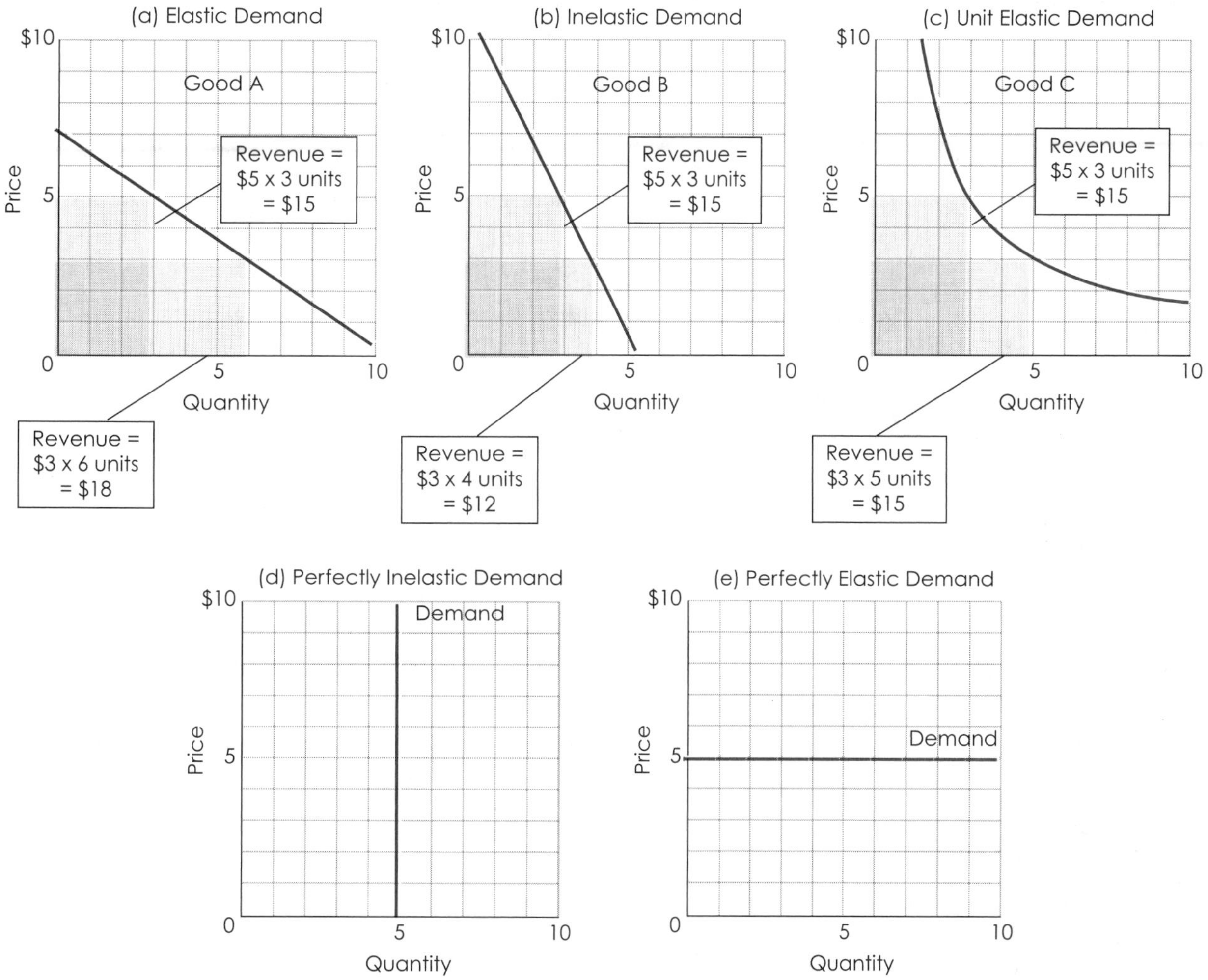

This figure shows five examples of demand curves with various degrees of elasticity over the indicated range of variation of price and quantity. The examples illustrate elastic, inelastic, unit elastic, perfectly inelastic, and perfectly elastic demand. For the first three cases, the revenue change associated with a change in price is shown. When demand is elastic, a price decrease causes revenue to increase. When demand is inelastic, a price decrease causes revenue to decrease. When demand is unit elastic, revenue does not change when price changes.

Revenue
Price times quantity sold.

Changes in price and quantity are reflected in the **revenue** earned from sale of the product. Revenue means the price times the quantity sold. In part (a) of Figure 3.1, the percentage change in quantity demanded is greater than the percentage change in price, so the drop in price causes total revenue from sales of the good to increase. On a supply-and-demand diagram, revenue can be shown as the area of a rectangle drawn under the demand curve, with a height equal to price and a width equal to quantity demanded. In this case comparison of the shaded rectangles representing revenue before the price reduction ($5 per unit x 3 units = $15) and afterward ($3 per unit x 6

Elastic demand

A situation in which quantity demanded changes by a larger percentage than price, so that total revenue increases as price decreases.

Inelastic demand

A situation in which quantity demanded changes by a smaller percentage than price, so that total revenue decreases as price decreases.

Unit elastic demand

A situation in which price and quantity demanded change by the same percentage, so that total revenue remains unchanged as price changes.

Perfectly inelastic demand

A situation in which the demand curve is a vertical line.

Perfectly elastic demand

A situation in which the demand curve is a horizontal line.

units = $18) shows that revenue is greater after the price has been reduced. When the quantity demanded changes by a greater percentage than price, so that a price decrease causes total revenue to increase, demand is said to be **elastic**.

Part (b) of Figure 3.1 shows a case in which the quantity demanded is only weakly responsive to a change in price. Here, a $2 decrease in price, from $5 to $3 per unit, causes the quantity demanded to increase by just one unit—from three to four. This time the percentage change in quantity demanded is less than that in price. As a result, the decrease in price causes total revenue to fall (again note the shaded rectangles). In such a case demand is said to be **inelastic**.

Part (c) shows a case in which a change in price causes an exactly proportional change in quantity demanded, so that total revenue does not change at all. When the percentage change in quantity demanded equals the percentage change in price, demand is said to be **unit elastic**.

The final two parts of Figure 3.1 show two extreme cases. Part (d) shows a vertical demand curve. Regardless of the price, the quantity demanded is five units—no more, no less. Such a demand curve is said to be **perfectly inelastic**. Part (e) shows a demand curve that is perfectly horizontal. Above a price of $5, no units of the good can be sold; but as soon as the price drops to $5, there is no limit on how much can be sold. A horizontal demand curve like this one is described as **perfectly elastic**. The law of demand, which describes an inverse relationship between price and quantity, does not encompass the cases of perfectly elastic and inelastic demand, and we do not expect market demand curves for ordinary goods and services to fit these extremes. Nevertheless, we will see that perfectly elastic and inelastic curves sometimes provide useful reference points for theory building, even though they do not resemble real-world market demand curves.

Calculating Elasticity of Demand

In speaking of elasticity of demand, it is sometimes enough to say that demand is elastic or inelastic, without being more precise. At other times, it is useful to give a numerical value for elasticity. This section introduces the most common method used to calculate a numerical value for elasticity of demand.

The first step in turning the general definition of elasticity into a numerical formula is to develop a way to measure percentage changes. The everyday method for calculating a percentage change is to use the initial value of the variable as the denominator and the change in the value as the numerator. For example, if the quantity of California lettuce demanded in the national market is initially 10,000 tons per week and then decreases by 2,500 tons per week, we say that there has been a 25 percent decrease (2,500/10,000 = .25). The trouble with this convention is that the same change in the opposite direction gives a different percentage. By everyday reasoning, an increase in the quantity of lettuce demanded from 7,500 tons per week to 10,000 tons per week is a 33 percent increase (2,500/7,500 = .33).

Decades ago the mathematical economist R. G. D. Allen proposed an unambiguous measure of percentage changes that uses the midpoint of the range over which change takes place as the denominator. Allen's formula is not the only possible one, but it caught on and remains the most popular.

To find the midpoint of the range over which a change takes place, we take the sum of the initial value and the final value and divide by 2. In our example, the midpoint of the quantity range is (7,500 + 10,000)/2 = 8,750. When this is used as the denominator, a change of 2,500 units becomes (approximately) a 28.6 percent change (2,500/8,750 = .286). Using Q_1 to represent the quantity before the change and Q_2 to represent the quantity after the change, the midpoint formula for the percentage change in quantity is

$$\text{Percentage change in quantity} = \frac{Q_2 - Q_1}{(Q_1 + Q_2)/2}$$

The same approach can be used to define the percentage change in price. In our case, the price of lettuce increased from about $250 per ton to about $1,000 per ton. Using the midpoint of the range, or $625, as the denominator [($250 + $1,000)/2 = $625], we conclude that the $750 increase in price is a 120 percent increase ($750/$625 = 1.2). The midpoint formula for the percentage change in price is

$$\text{Percentage change in price} = \frac{P_2 - P_1}{(P_1 + P_2)/2}$$

THE MIDPOINT FORMULA FOR ELASTICITY Defining percentage changes in this way allows us to write a useful formula for calculating elasticities. With P_1 and Q_1 representing price and quantity before a change, and P_2 and Q_2 representing price and quantity after the change, the midpoint formula for elasticity is

$$\text{Price elasticity of demand} = \frac{(Q_2 - Q_1)/(Q_1 + Q_2)}{(P_2 - P_1)/(P_1 + P_2)} = \frac{\text{Percentage change in quantity}}{\text{Percentage change in price}}$$

Here is the complete calculation for the elasticity of demand for lettuce when an increase in price from $250 per ton to $1,000 per ton causes the quantity demanded to fall from 10,000 tons per day to 7,500 tons per day:

P_1 = price before change = $250
P_2 = price after change = $1,000
Q_1 = quantity before change = 10,000
Q_2 = quantity after change = 7,500

$$\text{Elasticity} = \frac{(7{,}500 - 10{,}000)/(7{,}500 + 10{,}000)}{(\$1{,}000 - \$250)/(\$1{,}000 + \$250)}$$

$$= \frac{-2{,}500/17{,}500}{\$750/\$1{,}250}$$

$$= \frac{-.142}{.6}$$

$$= -.24$$

Because demand curves have negative slopes, this formula yields a negative value for elasticity. The reason is that the quantity demanded changes in the direction opposite to that of the price change. When the price decreases, $(P_2 - P_1)$, which appears in the denominator of the formula, is negative, whereas $(Q_2 - Q_1)$, which appears in the numerator, is positive. When the price increases, the numerator is negative and the denominator is positive. However, in this book we follow the widely used practice of dropping the minus sign when discussing price elasticity of demand. Thus, the elasticity of demand for lettuce would be stated as approximately .24 over the range studied.

A numerical elasticity value such as .24 can be related to the basic definition of elasticity in a simple way. That definition stated that price elasticity of demand as the ratio of the percentage change in quantity demanded to a given percentage change in price. Thus, an elasticity of .24 means that the quantity demanded will increase by .24 percent for each 1 percent change in price. An elasticity of 3 would mean that quantity demanded would change by 3 percent for each 1 percent change in price, and so on.[1]

ELASTICITY VALUES AND TERMINOLOGY Earlier in the chapter we defined *elastic, inelastic, unit elastic, perfectly elastic,* and *perfectly inelastic* demand. Each of these terms corresponds to a numerical value or range of values of elasticity. A perfectly inelastic demand curve has a numerical value of 0, since any change in price produces no change in quantity demanded. The term *inelastic* (but not perfectly inelastic) *demand* applies to numerical values from 0 up to, but not including, 1. *Unit elasticity,* as the name implies, means a numerical value of exactly 1. *Elastic demand* means any value for elasticity that is greater than 1. *Perfectly elastic* demand, represented by a horizontal demand curve, is not defined numerically; as the demand curve becomes horizontal, the denominator of the elasticity formula approaches 0 and the numerical value of elasticity increases without limit.

Varying- and Constant-Elasticity Demand Curves

The midpoint formula shows elasticity of demand over a certain range of prices and quantities. Measured over some other range, the elasticity of demand for the same good may be the same or different, depending on the shape of the demand curve, as shown in Figure 3.2.

Part (a) of Figure 3.2 shows a demand curve that, like most of those in this book, is a straight line. The elasticity of demand is not constant for all ranges of price and quantity along this curve. For example, when measured over the price range \$8 to \$9, the elasticity of demand is 5.66; when measured over the range \$2 to \$3, it is .33. (The calculations are shown in the figure.)

The calculations illustrate the general rule that elasticity declines as one moves downward along a straight-line demand curve. It is easy to see why. With such a demand curve, a \$1 reduction in price always causes the same absolute increase in quantity demanded. At the upper end of the demand curve, a \$1 change is a small percentage of the relatively high price, while the change in quantity is a large percentage of the relatively low quantity demanded at that price. At the lower end of the curve, however, the situation is reversed: A \$1 change is now a large percentage of the relatively low price, while the increase in quantity is smaller in relation to the relatively larger quantity demanded. Because it is percentages, not absolute amounts, that matter in elasticity calculations, a linear demand curve is less elastic near the bottom than near the top.

If the demand curve is not a straight line, other results are possible. There is an important special case in which the demand curve has just the curvature needed to keep elasticity constant over its entire length. Such a curve is shown in part (b) of Figure 3.2. As can be seen from the calculations in the figure, elasticity is 1.0 at every

FIGURE 3.2 ELASTICITY AT VARIOUS POINTS ALONG A DEMAND CURVE

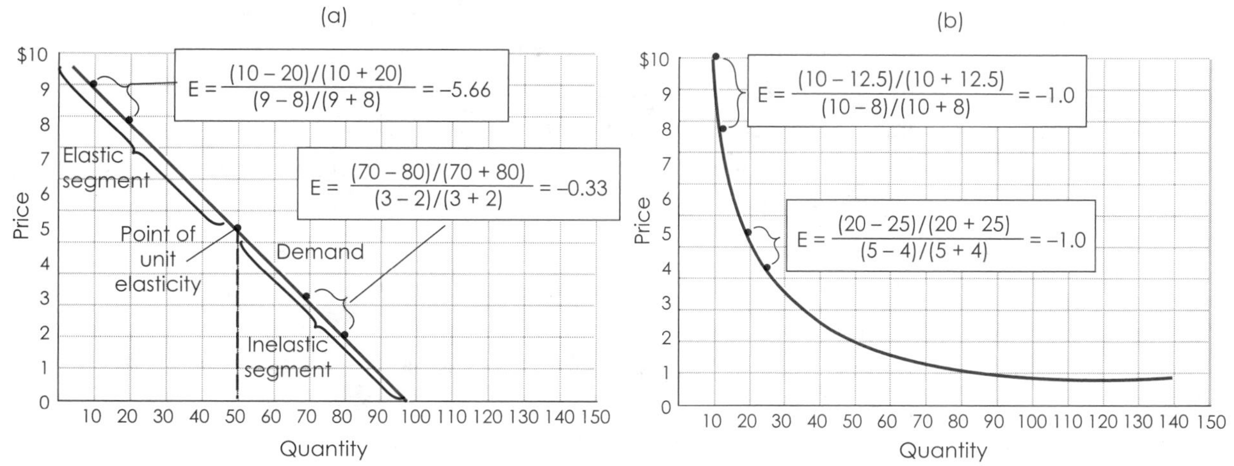

Elasticity varies along a straight-line demand curve, as part (a) of this figure illustrates. At the upper end of the curve, where the price is relatively high, a \$1 change in price is a relatively small percentage change, and, because the quantity demanded is low, the corresponding change in quantity is relatively large in percentage terms. Demand is thus elastic near the top of the demand curve. At the lower end of the curve, the situation is reversed: a \$1 change in price is now a relatively large change in percentage terms, whereas the corresponding change in quantity is smaller in percentage terms. Thus demand is inelastic. As part (b) shows, a curved demand curve can be drawn such that elasticity is constant for all ranges of price and quantity change.

point on that curve. It is possible to construct demand curves with constant elasticities of any value. Econometric studies of demand elasticity often look for the constant-elasticity demand curve that most closely approximates buyers' average sensitivity to price changes as revealed by market data over time.

Determinants of Elasticity of Demand

The fact that elasticity often varies along the demand curve means that care must be taken in making statements about the elasticity of demand for a good. In practice, what such statements usually refer to is the elasticity, measured by the midpoint formula or some alternative method, over the range of price variation that is commonly observed in the market for that good. With this understanding, we can make some generalizations about what makes the demand for some goods elastic and the demand for others inelastic.

SUBSTITUTES, COMPLEMENTS, AND ELASTICITY One important determinant of elasticity of demand is the availability of substitutes. When a good has close substitutes, the demand for that good tends to be elastic, because people willingly switch to the substitutes when the price of the good goes up. Thus, for example, the demand for corn oil is elastic because other cooking oils can usually be substituted for it. On the other hand, the demand for cigarettes is inelastic because for a habitual smoker there is no good substitute.

This principle has two corollaries. One is that the demand for a good tends to be more elastic the more narrowly the good is defined. For example, the demand for lettuce in the numerical example given earlier was inelastic. This could be because many people are in the habit of eating a salad with dinner and do not think of spinach or coleslaw as completely satisfactory substitutes. At the same time, however, it could be that the demand for any particular variety of lettuce is elastic. If the price of Boston lettuce rises while the prices of iceberg, romaine, and red-leaf lettuce remain unchanged, many people will readily switch to one of the other varieties, which they see as close substitutes.

The other corollary is that demand for the product of a single firm tends to be more elastic than the demand for the output of all producers operating in the market. As one example, the demand for cigarettes as a whole will be less elastic than the demand for any particular brand. The reason is that one brand can be substituted for another when the price of a brand changes.

The complements of a good can also play a role in determining its elasticity. If something is a minor complement to an important good (that is, one that accounts for a large share of consumers' budgets), demand for it tends to be inelastic. For example, the demand for motor oil tends to be inelastic because it is a complement to a more important good, gasoline. The price of gasoline has a greater effect on the amount of driving a person does than the price of motor oil.

PRICE VS. OPPORTUNITY COST Elasticity measures the responsiveness of quantity demanded to the monetary price of a good. In most cases, the price, in money, is an accurate approximation of the opportunity cost of choosing a good, but that is not always the case. We mentioned one example at the beginning of the chapter: The price of a textbook is an opportunity cost to the student who buys it, but it is not an opportunity cost to the professor who assigns it, because the students pay for the book, not the professor. As a result, publishers have traditionally assumed that professors will pay little attention to the price of the text, and demand will be highly inelastic. However, in recent years students have increasingly been making their influence felt, so that price-elasticity of demand for textbooks may be increasing.

The textbook market is a relatively small one, but there are other much more important markets where the responsibility for choice does not lie with the party who bears the opportunity cost. Medical care provides many examples. Doctors choose what drug to offer to patients, but either the patient or the patient's insurance company pays for the drug. As a result, demand for drugs is very inelastic, and doctors sometimes prescribe expensive brand-name drugs when cheaper generic drugs are available to do the same job.

Business travel is still another example of the separation of price and opportunity cost. Business travelers do not pay for their own airline tickets, hotels, and meals, so their demand for these services tends to be inelastic. When vacationers purchase the same services, they bear the full opportunity cost themselves. Not surprisingly, business travelers often choose more expensive options. In many cases airlines and hotels take advantage of the separation of price and opportunity cost by charging different rates to business and vacation travelers.

TIME HORIZON AND ELASTICITY One of the most important considerations determining the price elasticity of demand is the time horizon within which the decision to buy is made. For several reasons, demand is often less elastic in the short run than in the long run.

One reason is that full adjustment to a change in the price of a good may require changes in the kind or quantity of many other goods that a consumer buys. Gasoline provides a classic example. When the price of gasoline jumped in the early 2000s, many people's initial reaction was to cut out some nonessential driving, but the total quantity of gasoline demanded was not much affected. As time went by, though, consumers began adjust in many ways. One important adjustment, as mentioned in Chapter 1, was to buy fewer fuel-hungry SUVs and more higher-mileage cars. If this trend continues, the total amount of gasoline purchased could fall substantially.

Another reason elasticity tends to be greater in the long run than in the short run is that an increase in the price of one good encourages entrepreneurs to develop substitutes, which, as we have seen, can be an important determinant of elasticity. To take an example from history, consider the response to what has been called America's first energy crisis: a sharp increase in the price of whale oil, which was used as lamp fuel in the early nineteenth century. At first candles were the only substitute for whale-oil lamps, and not a very satisfactory one. People therefore cut their use of whale oil only a little when the price began to rise, but the high price of whale oil spurred entrepreneurs to develop a better substitute, kerosene. Once kerosene came onto the market, the quantity of whale oil demanded for use as lamp fuel dropped to zero.

A final reason for greater elasticity of demand in the long run than in the short run is the slow adjustment of consumer tastes. The case of beef and chicken, featured in the preceding chapter, provides an example. Chicken, originally the more expensive meat, achieved a price advantage over beef many years ago, but eating lots of beef was a habit. Gradually, though, chicken developed an image as a healthy, stylish, versatile food, and finally it overtook beef as the number-one meat in the United States.

Income Elasticity of Demand

Determining the response of quantity demanded to a change in price is the most common application of the concept of elasticity, but it is by no means the only one. Elasticity can also be used to express the response of demand to any of the conditions covered by the "other things being equal" assumption on which a given demand curve is based. As we saw in the preceding chapter, consumer income is one of those conditions.

Income elasticity of demand

The ratio of the percentage change in the quantity of a good demanded to a given percentage change in consumer incomes, other things being equal.

The **income elasticity of demand** for a good is defined as the ratio of the percentage change in the quantity of that good demanded to a percentage change in income. In measuring income elasticity, it is assumed that the good's price does not change. Using Q_1 and Q_2 to represent quantities before and after the change in income, and y_1 and y_2 to represent income before and after the change, the midpoint formula for income elasticity of demand can be written as follows:

$$\text{Income elasticity of demand} = \frac{(Q_2 - Q_1)/(Q_1 + Q_2)}{(y_2 - y_1)/(y_1 + y_2)} = \frac{\text{Percentage change in quantity}}{\text{Percentage change in income}}$$

For a normal good, an increase in income causes demand to rise. Because income and demand change in the same direction, the income elasticity of demand for a normal good is positive. For an inferior good, an increase in income causes demand to decrease. Because income and demand change in opposite directions, the income elasticity of demand for an inferior good is negative.

Some of the considerations that determine price elasticity also affect income elasticity. In particular, whether a good is considered to be normal or inferior depends on how narrowly it is defined and on the availability of substitutes. For example, a study by Jonq-Ying Lee, Mark G. Brown, and Brooke Schwartz of the University of Florida looked at the demand for frozen orange juice.[2] Orange juice considered as a broad category is a normal good; people tend to consume more of it as their income rises. However, when the definition is narrowed so that house-brand and national-brand frozen orange juice are treated as separate products, the house-brand product turns out to be an inferior good. As their incomes rise, consumers substitute the higher-quality national brands, which have a positive income elasticity of demand.

Cross-Elasticity of Demand

Cross-elasticity of demand

The ratio of the percentage change in the quantity of a good demanded to a given percentage change in the price of some other good, other things being equal.

Another condition that can cause a change in the demand for a good is a change in the price of some other good. The demand for chicken is affected by changes in the price of beef, the demand for SUVs by changes in the price of gasoline, and so on. The **cross-elasticity of demand** for a good is defined as the ratio of the percentage change in the quantity of that good demanded to a given percentage change in the price of another good. The midpoint formula for cross-elasticity of demand looks just like the one for price elasticity of demand, except that the numerator shows the percentage change in the quantity of one good while the denominator shows the percentage change in the price of some other good.

Cross-elasticity of demand is related to the concepts of substitutes and complements. Because lettuce and cabbage are substitutes, an increase in the price of cabbage causes an increase in the quantity of lettuce demanded; the cross-elasticity of demand is positive. Because SUVs and gasoline are complements, an increase in the price of gasoline causes a decrease in the quantity of SUVs demanded; the cross-elasticity of demand is negative. The previously mentioned study of frozen orange juice found a positive cross-elasticity of demand between house-brand and national-brand juices, indicating that the two are substitutes.

Price Elasticity of Supply

Price elasticity of supply

The ratio of the percentage change in the quantity of a good supplied to a given percentage change in its price, other things being equal.

Elasticity is not confined to demand; it can also be used to indicate the response of quantity supplied to a change in price. Formally, the **price elasticity of supply** of a good is defined as the percentage change in the quantity of the good supplied divided by the percentage change in its price. The midpoint formula for calculating price elasticity of supply looks like the one for determining price elasticity of demand, but the Qs in the numerator of the formula now refer to quantity *supplied* rather than quantity *demanded*. Because price and quantity change in the same direction along a positively sloped supply curve, the formula gives a positive value for the elasticity of supply. Figure 3.3 applies the elasticity formula to two supply curves, one with constant elasticity and the other with variable elasticity.

In later chapters we will look in detail at the considerations that determine the elasticity of supply for various products. Two of those considered are especially important, however, and deserve some discussion here.

One determinant of the elasticity of supply of a good is the mobility of the factors of production used to produce it. As used here, *mobility* means the ease with which factors can be attracted away from some other use, as well as the ease with which they can be reconverted to their original use. The trucking industry provides a classic example of mobile resources. As a crop such as lettuce or watermelons

FIGURE 3.3 CALCULATING PRICE ELASTICITY OF SUPPLY

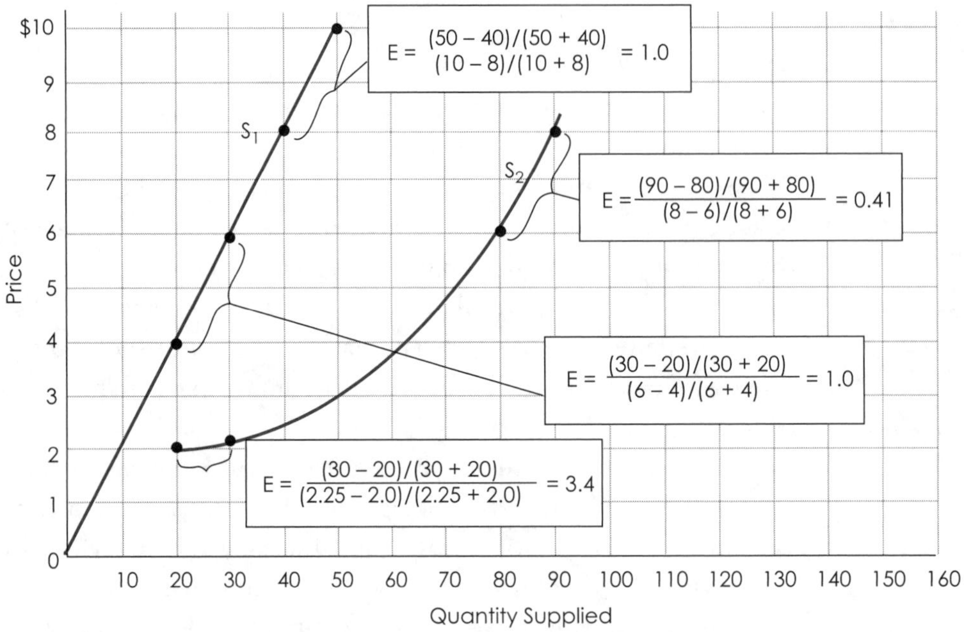

This figure gives four examples of the way price elasticity of supply is calculated. Price elasticity of supply is shown for two ranges on each of the two supply curves. Supply curve S_1 which is a straight line passing through the origin, has a constant elasticity of 1.0. Supply curve S_2, which is curved, is elastic for small quantities and inelastic for larger ones.

comes to harvest in a particular region of a country, hundreds of trucks are needed to haul it to market. Shippers compete for available trucks, driving up the price paid to truckers in the local market. Independent truckers throughout the country learn—from their own experience, from trucking brokers, and from Internet sites—where they can earn the best rates for hauling produce. It takes only a modest rise in the price for hauling a load of Georgia watermelons to attract enough truckers to Georgia to haul the crop to market. When the harvest is over, the truckers will move elsewhere to haul peaches, tomatoes, or whatever.

In contrast, other products are produced with resources that are not so mobile. Petroleum provides a good example. When oil prices rise, producers have an incentive to drill more wells. However, given limited numbers of drilling rigs and other highly specialized equipment, not to mention limited numbers of sites worth exploring, even a doubling of oil prices has only a small effect on oil output. Factor mobility in this industry is limited in the other direction, too. Once a well has been drilled, the investment cannot be converted to a different use. Thus, when world demand falls, as it did in 1998, prices fall sharply but the quantity of oil produced falls by much less than price.

A second determinant of elasticity of supply is time. As in the case of demand, price elasticity of supply tends to be greater in the long run than in the short run. In part, the reason for this is connected with mobility of resources. In the short run, the output of many products can be increased by using more of the most flexible inputs—for example, by adding workers at a plant or extending the hours of work. Such short-run measures often mean higher costs per unit for the added output, however, because workers added without comparable additions in other inputs (such as equipment) tend to be less productive. If a firm expects market conditions to warrant an increase of supply in the long run, it will be worthwhile to invest in additional quantities of less mobile inputs such as specialized plants and equipment. Once those investments have been made, the firm will find it worthwhile to supply the greater quantity of output at a lower price than in the short-run case because its costs per unit supplied will be lower. The Case for Discussion at the end of Chapter 2, which discussed the market for heavy-duty tires, provides an example of the difference between short-run and long-run elasticity of supply.

APPLICATIONS OF ELASTICITY

Elasticity has many applications in both macro- and microeconomics. In macroeconomics, it can be applied to money markets, to the aggregate supply and demand for all goods and services, and to foreign-exchange markets, to name just a few. In microeconomics, elasticity plays a role in discussions of consumer behavior, the profit-maximizing behavior of business firms, governments' regulatory and labor policies, and many other areas. To further illustrate elasticity, we conclude this chapter with applications featuring the problems of tax incidence and drug policy.

Elasticity and Tax Incidence

Who pays taxes? One way to answer this question is in terms of *assessments*—the issue of who bears the legal responsibility to make tax payments to the government. A study of assessments would show that property owners pay property taxes, gasoline retailers pay gasoline taxes, and so on. However, looking at assessments does not always settle the issue of who bears the economic burden of a tax—or, to use the economist's term, the issue of **tax incidence**.

Tax incidence

The distribution of the economic burden of a tax.

The incidence of a tax does not always coincide with the way the tax is assessed, because the economic burden of the tax, in whole or in part, often can be passed along to someone else. The degree to which the burden of a tax may be passed along depends on the elasticities of supply and demand. Let's consider some examples.

INCIDENCE OF A GASOLINE TAX First consider the familiar example of a gasoline tax. Specifically, suppose that the state of Virginia decides to impose a tax of

\$1 per gallon on gasoline beginning from a situation in which there is no tax. The tax is assessed against sellers of gasoline, who add the tax into the price paid by consumers at the pump.

Figure 3.4 uses the supply-and-demand model to show the effects of the tax. Initially, the demand curve intersects supply curve S_1 at E_1, resulting in a price of \$2 per gallon. The supply curve is elastic in the region of the initial equilibrium. The elasticity of supply reflects the fact that we are dealing with the gasoline market in just one state; only a slight rise in the price in Virginia is needed to divert additional quantities of gasoline from elsewhere in the nation, because of the wide geographic reach of the wholesale gasoline market. The retail gasoline market is more local. If the price in Virginia rises, some consumers living near the border may cross a state line to fill up in Maryland or North Carolina, but most people will continue to fill up in Virginia. In the short run, they have only limited ways to save gas, such as cutting back on nonessential trips. As a result, demand for gasoline is less elastic than the supply in the region of the initial equilibrium.

The effect of the tax is to shift the supply curve to the left until each point on the new supply curve is exactly \$1 higher than the point for the corresponding quantity

FIGURE 3.4 INCIDENCE OF A TAX ON GASOLINE

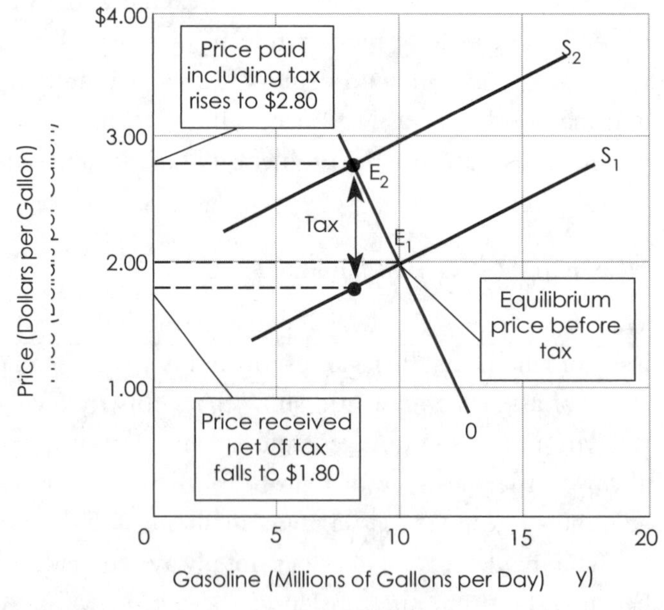

S_1 and D are the supply and demand curves before imposition of the tax. The initial equilibrium price is \$2 per gallon. A tax of \$1 per gallon shifts the supply curve to S_2. To induce sellers to supply the same quantity as before, the price would have to rise to \$3. However, as the price rises, buyers reduce the quantity demanded, moving up and to the left along the demand curve. In the new equilibrium at E_2, the price rises only to \$2.80. After the tax is paid, sellers receive only \$1,80 per gallon. Thus, buyers bear \$.80 of the tax on each gallon and sellers the remaining \$.20. Buyers bear the larger share of the tax because demand, in this case, is less elastic than supply.

on the old supply curve. (We could instead say that the supply curve shifts *upward* by \$1.) Because sellers must now turn over \$1 to the state government for each gallon of gas sold, they would have to get \$3 per gallon to be willing to sell the same quantity (10 million gallons per day) as initially. However, when sellers attempt to pass the tax on to motorists, motorists respond by reducing the amount of gas they buy. As the quantity sold falls, sellers move down and to the left along supply curve S_2 to a new equilibrium at E_2.

In the new equilibrium, the price is \$2.80 per gallon—just \$.80 higher than the original price. The new price includes the \$1 tax, which sellers add to their net price of \$1.80 per gallon—a net price that is \$.20 less than before. The amount of the tax—\$1 per gallon—is shown by the vertical gap between the supply and demand curves. The economic burden of the tax is divided between buyers and sellers, but in this case it falls more heavily on the buyers.

INCIDENCE OF A TAX ON APARTMENT RENTS In the preceding example, the incidence of the gasoline tax falls more heavily on buyers than on sellers because demand is less elastic than supply. If the elasticities are reversed, the results will also be reversed, as can be seen in the case of a tax on apartment rents.

In Figure 3.5, the market for rental apartments in Ogden, Utah (a small city) is initially in equilibrium at \$500 per month. The supply of rental apartments is inelastic. An increase in rents will cause a few new apartments to be built, whereas a reduction will cause a few to be torn down, but in either case the response will be moderate. On the other hand, demand is fairly elastic, because potential renters consider houses or condominiums a fairly close substitute for rental apartments.

Given this situation, suppose that the local government decides to impose a tax of \$250 per month on all apartments rented in Ogden. This tax, like the gasoline tax, is assessed against landlords, who include the tax payment in the monthly rental they charge to tenants. As in the previous example, the tax shifts the supply curve to the left until each point on the new supply curve lies above the corresponding point on the old supply curve by the amount of the tax. (Again, we could instead say the supply curve shifts upward by the amount of the tax.) After the shift, the market reaches a new equilibrium at E_2. There the rental price paid by tenants rises to only \$550 per month, as indicated by the intersection of the new supply and demand curves. Landlords succeed in passing only \$50 of the \$250 monthly tax along to tenants. Their net rental income, after turning over the tax receipts to the town government, is now just \$300, down from \$500 before imposition of the tax. In this case, because supply is inelastic and demand is elastic, suppliers bear most of the incidence of the tax and buyers only a little.

INCIDENCE AND TAX REVENUE When the government considers imposing a tax on gasoline, cigarettes, apartments, or any other item, the price elasticity of demand and supply is important not only for how the burden is shared between buyers

FIGURE 3.5 INCIDENCE OF A TAX ON APARTMENT RENTS

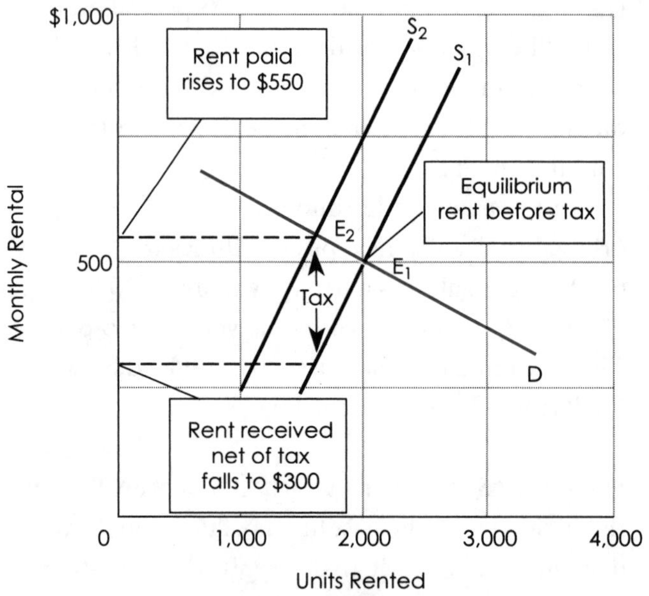

This figure shows the incidence of a tax imposed in a market in which supply is less elastic than demand. Initially, the equilibrium rent is $500 per month. A $250-per-month tax on apartment rents shifts the supply curve to S_2. The new equilibrium is at E_2. Landlords end up absorbing all but $50 of the tax. If they tried to pass more of the tax on to renters, more renters would switch to owner-occupied housing, and the vacancy rate on rental apartments would rise.

and sellers, but also for how much tax revenue the government collects. When buyers or sellers are more responsive to changes in price (when demand or supply is more elastic), a tax will generate less revenue for the government.

Figure 3.6 compares the markets for two items: milk and pork. The elasticities of supply are similar, but the price elasticities of demand differ. Pork has many obvious substitutes—beef, chicken, turkey, and other meats. Milk has few substitutes, so its demand is more inelastic. The markets for milk and pork are shown in Figure 3.6. The equilibrium price of milk is $0.50 per gallon and 12 million gallons are sold each year at this price. The milk market equilibrium is point E_1 on the left panel of Figure 3.6. The equilibrium (shown by the point E_1 on the right panel of Figure 3.6) is $0.75 per pound and 12 million pounds are sold each year.

Suppose now that the government imposes a $1.00 tax on each product. In the milk market, where demand is inelastic, the tax leads to a small decrease in the quantity, from 12 to 10 million gallons. The government collects $1.00 on each gallon of milk sold, for tax revenue of $10 million on the 10 million gallons sold after the tax. In the market for pork, the tax leads to a larger reduction in the quantity people buy, from 12 to 6 million pounds. The government will collect a total of $6 million from

FIGURE 3.6

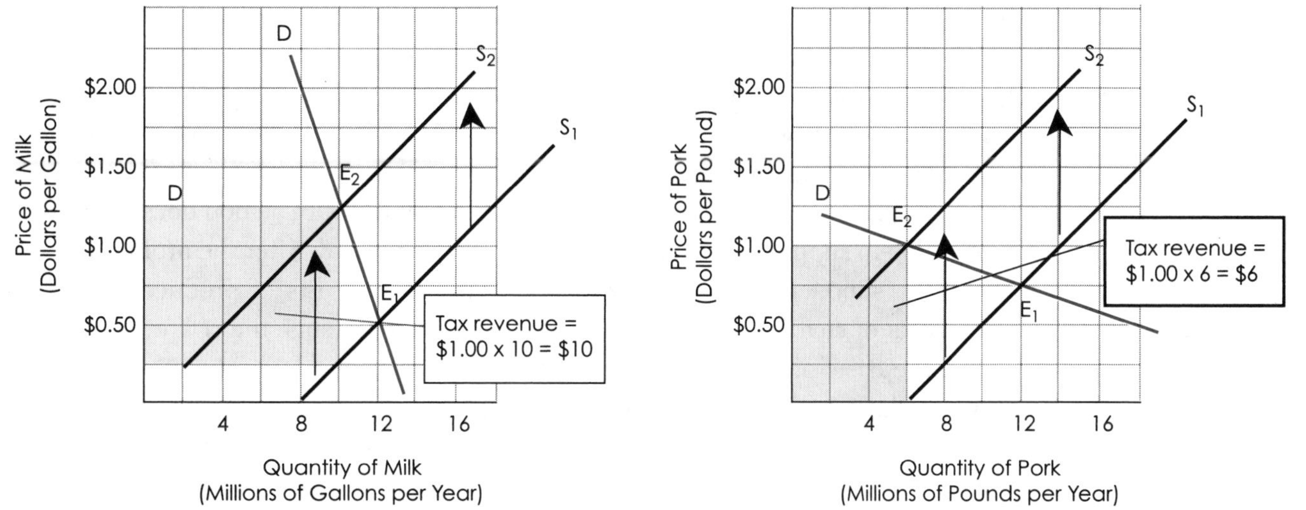

A tax imposed on a good that has an inelastic demand will generate more tax revenue than a tax on a good with elastic demand, assuming similar supply conditions. The diagrams above compare the effects of a $1.00 tax on the markets for milk (inelastic demand) and pork (elastic demand). In the market for milk, the tax reduces the equilibrium quantity by 2 million gallons, from point E_1 (12 million gallons) to E_2 (10 million gallons). Therefore, the government collects a total of $10 million from the milk tax. The same $1.00 tax on pork causes a large reduction in the quantity sold, from 12 million pounds (point E_1) to 6 million pounds (point E_2). This means the government will only collect $6 million, as only 6 million pounds of pork are sold at the new equilibrium.

the tax on pork, collecting $1.00 on each of the 6 million pounds sold. When comparing the two taxes, the government collects more revenue from the tax on milk. Today, governments rely for most of their revenue on broad-based taxes like income taxes, sales taxes, and value-added taxes. In past centuries, however, taxes on individual goods were more important than they are now. In those days, taxes on goods with highly inelastic demand—like salt, tobacco, and matches—were especially popular.

Elasticity and Prohibition

In the case of gasoline and apartment rents, a tax led to a reduction in the quantity consumed, which we characterized as an unintended consequence of the tax. In a few cases, the reduction in quantity consumed may be an *intended* consequence of the tax. Modern taxes on tobacco products are one example: because tobacco is regarded as harmful, a reduction in quantity consumed is seen as desirable. Taxes on environmentally harmful products, such as the chemicals responsible for ozone depletion, are another example.

Prohibition is a more extreme policy aimed at reducing the quantity of a product consumed. Alcoholic beverages were subject to prohibition in the United States during the 1920s, and drugs like marijuana, heroin, and cocaine are subject to prohibition today. Prohibition is a common method of environmental regulation as well. For example, use of the pesticide DDT and lead additives for gasoline are completely prohibited in the United States.

On the surface, a policy of prohibition may seem very different from a tax, since unlike a tax, prohibition raises no tax revenue for the government. However, if we use economic analysis to look below the surface, we see some similarities as well as differences between taxation and prohibition.

First, passage of a law prohibiting production and sale of a good does not make it impossible to supply the good, but simply more expensive. After the prohibition is in effect, the supplier must consider not only the direct costs of production, but the extra costs of covert transportation and distribution systems, the risk of fines or jail terms, the costs of hiring armed gangsters to protect illegal laboratories, and so on. From the law-breaking supplier's point of view, these costs can be seen as an implicit tax. If the price rises by enough to cover them, the good will still be supplied. Thus, the effect of prohibition of a good is to shift its supply curve to the left until each point on the new supply curve lies above the corresponding point on the old curve by a distance equal to the extra costs associated with evading the prohibition.

Second, the effects of the prohibition, like those of a tax, depend on the elasticities of demand and supply. This is illustrated in Figure 3.7, which compares the effects of prohibition on the U.S. markets for DDT and cocaine. The demand for DDT is shown as elastic because effective substitutes are available at a price only a little higher than the banned pesticide. The demand for cocaine is shown as inelastic, in part because once people become addicted, they will be very reluctant to curtail their use of the drug even if its price rises sharply.

In the case of elastic demand for DDT (Figure 3.7a), even a weakly enforced prohibition, which raises costs of illegal supply only a little, will sharply reduce the quantity sold. Such a weak prohibition, represented by a shift in the supply curve from S_1 to S_2, is already enough to reduce the total revenue (price times quantity sold) earned by producers from $14,000 per week to $8,500 per week. A more vigorously enforced prohibition, as represented by supply curve S_3, raises the cost of supply by enough to eliminate use of the product altogether.

In the case of cocaine, with its inelastic demand, even a strongly enforced prohibition has a small effect on quantity sold. This case is represented in Figure 3.7b by a shift in the supply curve to S_2. Because quantity demanded is not much affected by the price increase, total revenue from the sale of cocaine rises sharply, from $130,000 per week at equilibrium E_1 to $300,000 per week at equilibrium E_2. As long as demand is inelastic, increasing strictness of enforcement, which drives the supply curve still higher, will make the sales revenue of drug suppliers increase still further.

Elasticity of demand is important in understanding the intended and unintended consequences of prohibition. The intended consequence, of course, is to reduce or eliminate use of the product. As we see, the more elastic the demand for the product, the more successful is the policy of prohibition in achieving its intended effects. The unintended effects of prohibition are those associated with

FIGURE 3.7 ELASTICITY AND THE EFFECTS OF PROHIBITION

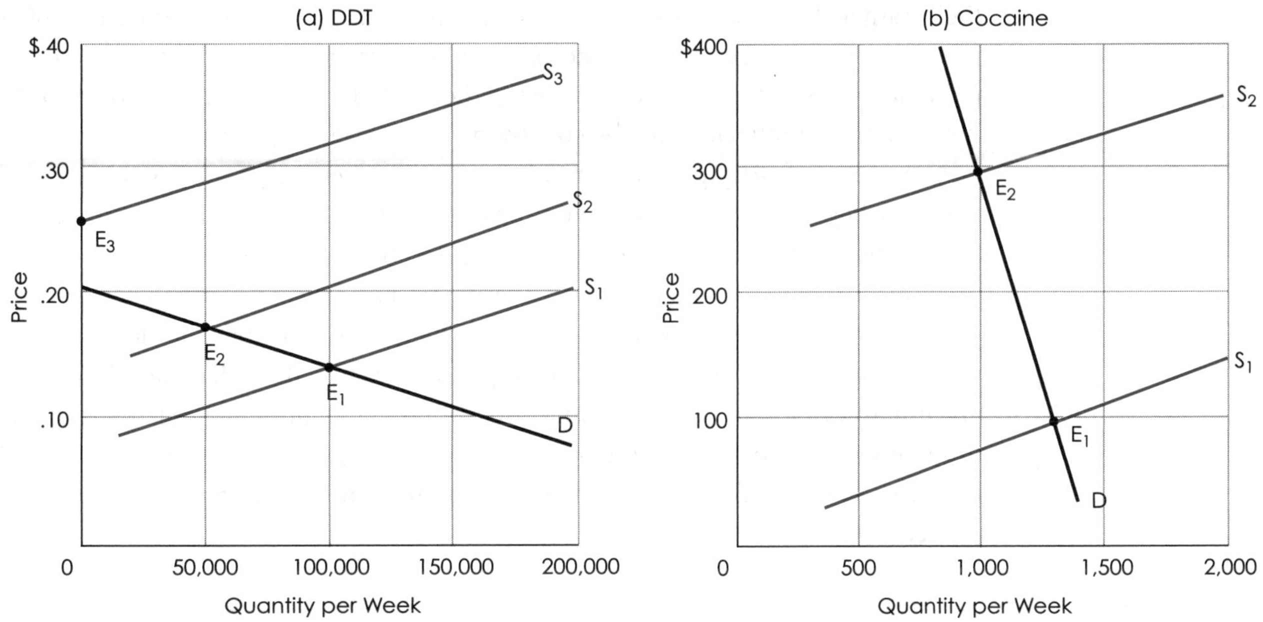

A law prohibiting production and sale of a good, like a tax on the good, shifts its supply curve to the left. The new supply curve will lie above the old supply curve at any given quantity by a distance equal to the cost of evading the prohibition. The effects on price, quantity, and revenue depend on the elasticity of demand. Part (a) uses DDT to illustrate prohibition of a good with elastic demand. A weakly enforced prohibition (S_2) raises the price, reduces the quantity, and reduces total revenue earned by producers from sale of the product. A strongly enforced prohibition reduces quantity and revenue to zero (S_3). Part (b) uses cocaine to illustrate prohibition of a good with inelastic demand. In this case, even strong efforts to enforce prohibition do not reduce quantity sold to zero. Because quantity sold increases by a smaller percentage than price increases, there is an increased total revenue and expenditure on the good.

the change in revenue that the policy produces. These are very different in the case of elastic and inelastic demand.

Where demand is elastic, there is a moderate loss of revenue to DDT producers and a small rise in the cost of growing crops as farmers switch to more expensive pesticides. Neither has major social consequences. The loss of revenue from producing DDT will be offset by increased revenue from production of substitutes, very likely by the same companies. And the increased cost of growing crops is offset by the benefits of a cleaner environment.

On the other hand, where demand is inelastic, the intended consequences are smaller and the unintended consequences greater. With inelastic demand, prohibition increases total expenditure on the banned product. The social consequences may be severe. First, users of cocaine must spend more to sustain their habit. At best this means impoverishing themselves and their families; at worst it means an increase in muggings and armed robberies by users desperate for cash. Second, the impact of the prohibition on suppliers must be considered as well. For suppliers, the increase in revenue does not just mean an increase in profit (although profits may increase), but also an increase in expenditures devoted to evading prohibition. In part, the result is simply wasteful, as when drug suppliers buy an airplane to make a single one-way flight rather than using normal transportation methods. Worse, another part of suppliers' increased expenditures take the form of hiring armies of thugs to battle the police and other suppliers, further raising the level of violence on city streets, or bribing government officials, thereby corrupting the quality of government.

The issue of drug prohibition, of course, involves many normative issues that reach far beyond the concept of elasticity. One such issue is whether people have a right to harm themselves through consumption of substances like tobacco, alcohol, or cocaine, or whether, instead, the government has a duty to act paternalistically to prevent such harm. Another concerns the relative emphasis that should be placed on prohibition versus treatment in allocating resources to reduce drug use. The analysis given here cannot answer such questions. However, it does suggest that the law of unintended consequences applies in the area of drug policy as elsewhere, and that elasticity of demand is important in determining the nature and severity of those consequences.

SUMMARY

1. **How can the responsiveness of quantity demanded to a price change be expressed in terms of elasticity?** *Elasticity* is the responsiveness of quantity demanded or supplied to changes in the price of a good (or changes in other factors), measured as a ratio of the percentage change in quantity to the percentage change in price (or other factor causing the change in quantity). The *price elasticity of demand* between two points on a demand curve is the percentage change in quantity demanded divided by the percentage change in the good's price.

2. **How is the elasticity of demand for a good related to the revenue earned by its seller?** If the demand for a good is elastic, a decrease in its price will increase total revenue. If it is inelastic, an increase in its price will increase total revenue. When the demand for a good is unit elastic, revenue will remain constant as the price varies.

3. **How can elasticity be applied to changes in market conditions other than price?** The concept of elasticity can be applied to many situations besides movements along demand curves. The *income elasticity of demand* for a good is the ratio of the percentage change in quantity demanded to a given percentage change in income. The *cross-elasticity of demand* between goods A and B is the ratio of the percentage change in the quantity of good A demanded to a given percentage change in the price of good B. The *price elasticity of supply* is the ratio of the percentage change in the quantity of a good supplied to a given change in its price.

4. **What determines the distribution of the economic burden of a tax?** The way in which the economic burden of a tax is distributed is known as the *incidence* of the tax. The incidence depends on the relative elasticities of supply and demand. If supply is relatively more elastic than demand, buyers will bear the larger share of the tax burden. If demand is relatively more elastic than supply, the larger share of the burden will fall on sellers. If the good is subject to prohibition rather than to a tax, elasticity of demand will determine how many resources are likely to be devoted to enforcement and evasion of the prohibition.

KEY TERMS

Elasticity
Price elasticity of demand
Revenue
Elastic demand
Inelastic demand
Unit elastic demand
Perfectly inelastic demand
Perfectly elastic demand
Income elasticity of demand
Cross-elasticity of demand
Price elasticity of supply
Tax incidence

PROBLEMS AND TOPICS FOR DISCUSSION

1. **Time horizon and elasticity.** Suppose a virus infects the California lettuce crop, cutting production by half. Consider three time horizons: (a) The "very short" run means a period that is too short to allow farmers to change the amount of lettuce that has been planted. No matter what happens to the price, the quantity supplied will be the amount already planted, less the amount destroyed by the virus. (b) The "intermediate" run means a period that is long enough to allow farmers to plant more fields in lettuce, but not long enough to permit them to develop new varieties of lettuce, introduce new methods of cultivation, or acquire new specialized equipment. (c) The "long" run means a period that is long enough to allow farmers to develop new varieties of virus-resistant lettuce and improve cultivation techniques. Discuss these three time horizons in terms of the price elasticity of supply. Sketch a figure showing supply curves for each of the time horizons.

2. **Calculating elasticity.** Draw a set of coordinate axes on a piece of graph paper. Label the horizontal axis from 0 to 50 units and the vertical axis from $0 to $20 per unit. Draw a demand curve that intersects the vertical axis at $10 and the horizontal axis at 40 units. Draw a supply curve that intersects the vertical axis at $4 and has a slope of 1. Make the following calculations for these curves, using the midpoint formula:

   a. What is the price elasticity of demand over the price range $5 to $7?

   b. What is the price elasticity of demand over the price range $1 to $3?

   c. What is the price elasticity of supply over the price range $10 to $15?

   d. What is the price elasticity of supply over the price range $15 to $17?

3. **Elasticity and revenue.** Look at the demand curve given in Figure 2.1 of the preceding chapter. Make a third column in the table that gives revenue for each price-quantity combination shown. Draw a set of axes on a piece of graph paper. Label the horizontal axis as in Figure 2.1, and label the vertical axis from 0 to $5 billion of revenue in increments of $1 billion. Graph the relationship between quantity and revenue using the column you added to the table. Discuss the

relationship of your revenue graph to the demand curve, keeping in mind what you know about elasticity and revenue and about variation in elasticity along the demand curve.

4. **Elasticity of demand and revenue.** Assume that you are an officer of your campus film club. You are at a meeting at which ticket prices are being discussed. One member says, "What I hate to see most of all is empty seats in the theater. We sell out every weekend showing, but there are always empty seats on Wednesdays. If we cut our Wednesday night prices by enough to fill up the theater, we'd bring in more money." Would this tactic really bring in more revenue? What would you need to know in order to be sure? Draw diagrams to illustrate some of the possibilities.

5. **Cross-elasticity of demand.** Between 1979 and 1981 the price of heating oil rose by 104 percent. Over the same period, use of fuel oil fell slightly while use of LP gas, another heating fuel, rose. Assuming that there was no change in the price of LP gas, what does this suggest about the cross-elasticity of demand for LP gas with respect to the price of fuel oil? Draw a pair of diagrams to illustrate these events. (Suggestion: Draw upward-sloping supply curves for both fuels. Then assume that the supply curve for heating oil shifts upward while the supply curve for LP gas stays the same.)

CASE FOR DISCUSSION

VP Asks Cigarette Firms for Sacrifice

Rendi A. Witular, *The Jakarta Post,* Jakarta, Indonesia, June 1, 2005

The lower profits cigarette-makers were likely to experience when the government raises the retail price on cigarettes should be viewed as a sacrifice to the state, [Indonesian] Vice President Jusuf Kalla said on Tuesday.

"The tobacco industry is one of the most profitable sectors in [Indonesian] business. Raising the (retail) rate won't affect tobacco firms much, since they will still be able to make a profit. Remember that cigarette prices here are still the lowest in the world," Kalla said.

By increasing the retail price of cigarettes the government planned to make more money on the excise duty it charged manufacturers, which was calculated on the final retail price.

The amount of the increase has not been finalized but last week the Minister of Finance Jusuf Anwar suggested it would be in the range of 15 to 20 percent. This extra revenue would help plug the state budget deficit that has increased in line with the rising costs of the government's fuel subsidy.

PT H. M. Sampoerna, the country's second-largest cigarette maker by sales, said that more than a 10 percent increase in the cigarette prices could hurt producers as it would affect sales.

Sampoerna is 98 percent-owned by U.S. cigarette giant Philip Morris International.

"Less than a 10 percent increase in the price is likely to be OK, but more (than that) could disturb sales," Sampoerna director Angky Camaro said after meeting Kalla earlier in the day.

Angky said the industry had not yet fully recovered from the aggressive excise rate hikes in 2002 and 2003, which had resulted in declines in the volumes of cigarette produced and lower profits across the board.

Last year, local cigarette company profits rose on increased consumption spurred on by higher general economic growth and the absence of any increases in excise duty.

The Indonesian Cigarette Producer Union (Gappri) estimates that some 141 million of the country's 220 million people are smokers.

Source: Rendi A. Witular, *The Jakarta Post,* Jakarta, Indonesia, June 1, 2005 (Downloaded June 5, 2005 from http://www.thejakartapost.com/yesterdaydetail.asp?field=20050601.L04).

QUESTIONS

1. On the basis of this article, do you think that price elasticity of demand for cigarettes in Indonesia is elastic, inelastic, unit elastic, perfectly elastic, or perfectly inelastic? Cite the specific passages supporting your conclusion, and note any apparent contradictions in the article.
2. According to the article, 64 percent of the people of Indonesia, where cigarette prices are among the lowest in the world, are smokers, compared to less than 25 percent in the United States, where prices are higher. What does this suggest about the price elasticity of demand for tobacco in the long run? Why might the long-run elasticity of demand for cigarettes be greater than the short-run elasticity?
3. According to Angky Camaro of Sampoerna, a tax increase that reduced quantity sold would hurt producers. Using a diagram similar to Figure 3.4, explain why this would be true even if the percentage decrease in quantity were less than the percentage increase in price.
4. According to the article, in 2004, cigarette sales increased as income increased, while taxes were unchanged. What does this tell you about the income elasticity of demand?

END NOTES

1. As we have said, the midpoint formula (also sometimes called *arc-elasticity*) is not the only one for calculating elasticity. A drawback of this formula is that it can give misleading elasticity values if applied over too wide a variation in price or quantity. Because of this limitation, it is often suggested that the midpoint formula be used only over fairly small ranges of variation in price or quantity. Following this reasoning to its logical conclusion, there is an alternative formula for calculating elasticity for a single point on the demand curve. For a linear demand curve having the formula $q = a - bp$ (with q representing quantity demanded, p the price, and a and b being constants), the *point formula* for elasticity of demand (stated, as elsewhere, as a positive number) is

$$\text{Elasticity} = bp/(a - bp).$$

2. Jonq-Ying Lee, Mark G. Brown, and Brooke Schwartz, "The Demand for National Brand and Private Label Frozen Concentrated Orange Juice: A Switching Regression Analysis," *Western Journal of Agricultural Economics* (July 1986): 1–7.

PART 2

Macroeconomic Goals and Relationships

CHAPTER 4

In Search of Prosperity and Stability

After reading this chapter, you will understand:

1. The meaning and origins of economic growth
2. The nature of the business cycle
3. The meaning of unemployment and its importance for economic policy
4. The meaning of inflation and its impact on the economy

Before reading this chapter, make sure you know the meaning of:

1. Positive and normative economics
2. Production possibility frontier

MANY ECONOMISTS DATE the beginning of their discipline from the publication, in 1776, of Adam Smith's book *The Wealth of Nations*. (See *Who Said It? Who Did It? 1.2*) Why is it, asked Smith, that some nations prosper while others lag behind? Around the world the issue remains a central focus of macroeconomic policy. In the U.S. Congressional elections of 2006, each party claimed that it would do best at creating jobs and raising living standards. In Italy, economic stagnation was a major factor in the Belusconi government's defeat in 2006 parliamentary elections. In Russia, President Vladimir Putin made doubling national product in ten years a major goal of his presidency. In China, policy makers worried that a growth rate of nearly 10 percent per year was too fast to maintain economic and political stability. This chapter begins the exploration of macroeconomics by giving two broad perspectives on the search for prosperity and stability: A long-run perspective that emphasizes economic growth, and a short-term perspective that emphasizes the business cycle, employment, and inflation.

MACROECONOMICS IN THE LONG RUN: ECONOMIC GROWTH

No country becomes wealthy overnight. Nations that are prosperous have become so as the result of steady growth over periods of decades and even centuries. Countries that are poor rarely become so because of sudden catastrophe, but rather, due to long periods of gradual decline or slow growth that lags behind the leaders.

Figure 4.1 shows how widely growth rates have differed among major areas of the world. During the second half of the 20th century, standards of living in much of Asia rose by a factor five. Countries like Korea and Japan caught up with European and North American levels of prosperity. At the same time, average incomes in Sub-Saharan Africa increased only 20 percent, and in some countries actually decreased.

FIGURE 4.1

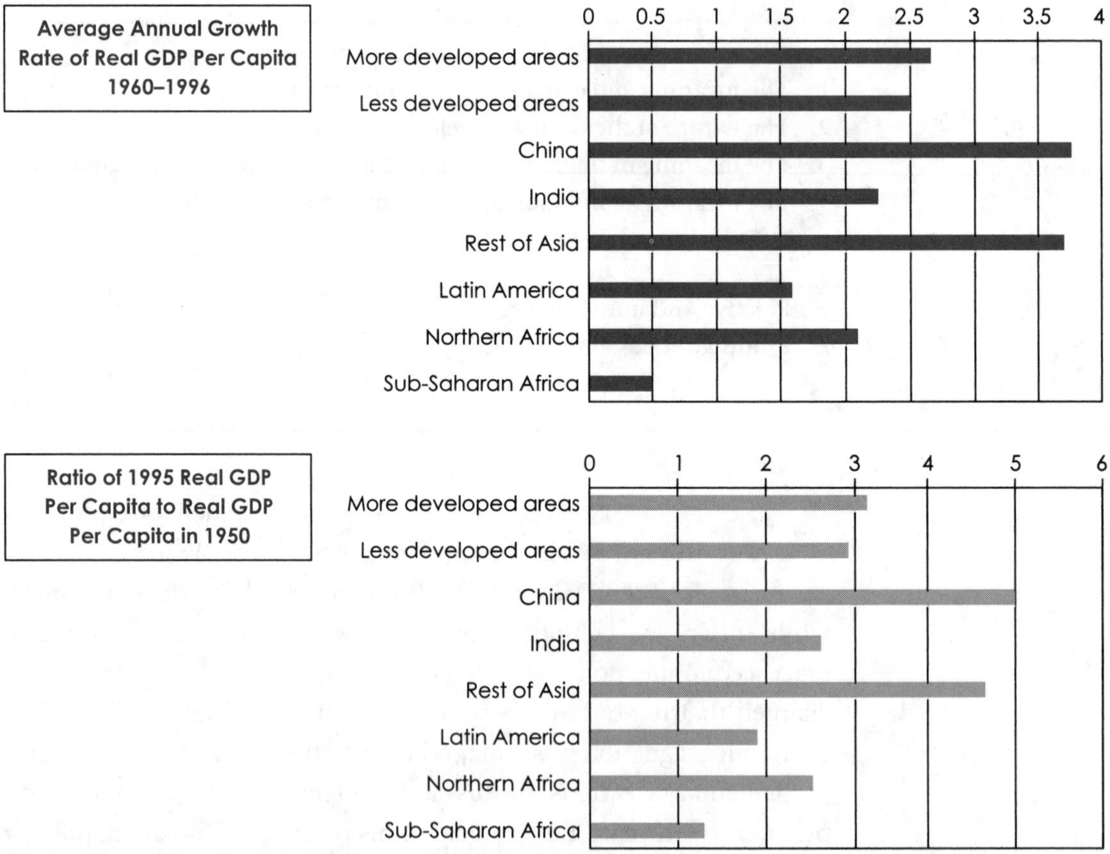

During the second half of the 20th century, growth rates of GDP per capita varied widely among regions of the world. Growth rates in China and other countries of Southeast Asia were rapid, allowing these countries to catch up with the world's most developed regions. Latin America and Africa lagged behind.

Source: Richard Easterlin, "The World Standard of Living Since 1800," Journal of Economic Perspectives, Vol 14 No 1 (Winter 2002), pp. 7-26. Data from Easterlin, Table 3; Chart by author.

Economic growth theory seeks to explain the reasons for these differences in growth over time and among countries.

Measuring Economic Growth

Economic growth is most often expressed in terms of *Gross Domestic Product* (GDP), a measure of the value of total output of goods and services produced within a nation's borders during a period of time.[1] If GDP is to provide a meaningful measure of growth over time, it, like other economic quantities, must be expressed in **real** terms; that is, it must be adjusted for the effects of changes in the average price level. For example, from 1995 to 2005 U.S. **nominal** GDP (that is, GDP measured according to prices at which goods were actually sold in the given year) grew from $7,298 billion to $12,191 billion, or 68 percent. However, part of the increase in nominal GDP can be attributed to a 20 percent rise in the average price level during the period. Adjusted for inflation and expressed in constant 1995 dollars, real GDP increased over the decade by only about 40 percent. The term **real output** is frequently used as a synonym for real gross domestic product.

Real

In economics, a term that refers to data that have been adjusted for the effects of inflation.

Nominal

In economics, a term that refers to data that have not been adjusted for the effects of inflation.

Real output

A synonym for real gross domestic product.

Sources of Economic Growth

The sources of economic growth can be divided into two main components: the growth of total labor inputs, on the one hand, and the growth of output per unit of labor, or labor productivity, on the other.

The growth of total labor inputs tends to be determined by social and demographic factors that differ from one country to another, but that do not change rapidly within any one country. One source of growth of labor inputs is population growth. Population in the United States is now growing at about 1 percent per year or less, largely thanks to immigration. Population in most other advanced countries is stable or slowly declining. Another possible source of increased labor input is increased labor force participation. In the United States, for example, from 1960 to 1989, labor force participation by women increased from 37 percent to 57 percent, more than offsetting a small decline in labor force participation among men. Since 1990, labor force participation trends of various groups have roughly balanced out, so that the total rate has not changed much. Over the same period, both population growth and increased labor force participation have been offset, in part, by a decrease in average weekly hours worked from about 39 in 1960 to about 34 today. Taking all these trends together, total hours worked in the U.S. economy have grown moderately.

In contrast to the relatively steady growth of hours worked, productivity in the United States has increased erratically over the past 50 years. From the end of World War II up to the early 1970s, productivity grew at an average rate of about 2.8 percent per year. From the mid-1970s to the early 1990s, productivity suffered a puzzling slowdown, falling to less than half its previous rate. Since the 1990s, productivity growth has recovered. In the early years of the 21st century, U.S. productivity has grown at the exceptionally rapid rate of about 4 percent per year. A later chapter will look in detail at various possible explanations for these changes in productivity growth.

Since hours worked per capita tend to fall as countries get richer, productivity growth holds the key to prosperity in the long run. What determines whether productivity grows rapidly or slowly?

According to one widely used economic model, output per labor hour can be attributed to changes in capital per worker and a catch-all category called **total factor productivity**.

Total factor productivity

A measurement of improvements in technology and organization that allow increases in the output produced by given quantities of labor and capital.

Increasing capital per worker means giving workers better tools to do their jobs. These include industrial equipment like bulldozers and assembly robots, capital used in service jobs like hospital equipment and office information systems, and infrastructure capital like roads and communications systems. Sources of total factor productivity growth include technological innovation, better education of the labor force (sometimes called "human capital,"), and improvements in political institutions that reduce productivity-sapping corruption and conflict. We will return to some of these topics in more detail in a later chapter. Meanwhile, *Applying Economic Ideas 4.1* illustrates the sources of economic growth with the case of South Korea.

The Benefits and Costs of Economic Growth

Economic growth has many benefits. First and foremost, growth provides consumers with a higher standard of living in the form of more goods and services. Growth also provides people with greater opportunities to choose between work and leisure. If more people choose to work, as has recently been the case in the United States, economic growth makes possible the capital investment needed to create jobs for them. Over a longer span of U.S. history, however, people have opted for more leisure. As the economy grew during the nineteenth and early twentieth centuries, it was possible to shorten the average workweek at the same time that material living standards were rising. Finally, economic growth is seen by many people as a necessary condition for reducing poverty and economic injustice. Whether a rising tide lifts all boats more or less automatically, as some people would have it, or whether, at least in some periods, the rich benefit more from growth than the poor remains a source of controversy. However, there is little dispute that issues of social equality are even harder to resolve in countries where the tide is going out.[2]

Despite its obvious benefits, economic growth has had its critics. More than a century ago the English economist John Stuart Mill worried that growth might cause the loss of "a great portion of the earth's pleasantries" (see *Who Said It? Who Did It? 4.1*). This sentiment is shared in our own time by environmentalists, who worry that growth is accompanied by increased pollution, destruction of wilderness areas, and the possibility of a global climate disaster.

APPLYING ECONOMIC IDEAS 4.1

DECODING KOREA'S ECONOMIC MIRACLE

South Korea's record of economic growth from 1970 to 2000 is one of the most remarkable of any country in the world. At the beginning of the period, Korea was a poor country with per capita GDP about one-seventh that of the United States. By the end of the period, its GDP per capita was half that of the United States, or about the same as middle-income European countries like Greece and Portugal. Where did this miraculous growth come from?

Economists divide the sources of economic growth into three components: Increases in labor inputs, increases in capital per worker, and improvements in technology and organization (total factor productivity). Each of these was important in Korea.

Hours worked increased largely because of an increase in the working-age population that averaged 1.9 percent per year. Adding to the effect of increases in the quantity of labor inputs were gains in education. In 1970s, only about a quarter of Korean workers had graduated from high school and fewer than 10 percent from college. By 2000, a quarter had graduated from college and about two-thirds from high school.

Growth in capital per worker was very rapid. At the peak of Korea's economic boom in the early and mid-1990s, investment in new capital averaged 36 percent of GDP, higher even than in Japan during that country's period of fastest growth, and more than double the share of investment in GDP for the United States. Much of this investment was fueled by a high domestic saving rate and some also by foreign investment.

Finally, improvements in technology and organization, known to economists as total factor productivity, contributed about 1.9 percentage points to Korea's annual growth rate. This was respectable, but not exceptional, being only about the average for the world's more developed economies.

Measured over the period 1980-2002, the final scorecard looks like this:

Source of growth	Contribution to growth	
Total Growth of real GDP		6.8%
Capital accumulation		2.0%
Growth of labor inputs		2.8%
Growth of labor force	*1.9%*	
Improved education	*0.9%*	
Total factor productivity		1.9%

Source: International Monetary Fund, "Republic of Korea: Selected Issues," IMF Country Report 03/80, March 2003.

Criticisms of economic growth have their merits. We have only to look around us to see that the economic growth we have experienced has brought costs as well as benefits. However, the critics can be faulted for often failing to distinguish between two issues: the *rate* of economic growth and its *direction*.

In Figure 4.2, a production possibility frontier is used to help separate the two issues. The diagram shows an economy in which resources can be devoted either to improving environmental quality or increasing per capita consumption of material goods. To put it even more simply, we could think of the tradeoff as one between clean air and cars. For an economy operating efficiently on its production possibility frontier, more cars will make the air dirtier; fewer cars will make possible cleaner air.

As technology is improved and more resources become available, the production possibility frontier shifts outward. If the economy follows a growth path from point A to point B, people will complain that growth has led to a deterioration of environmental quality. It is not really growth itself that is to blame, however. Instead, the problem

WHO SAID IT? WHO DID IT? 4.1
JOHN STUART MILL ON THE STATIONARY STATE

Economic growth was a major concern of the classical economists of the nineteenth century. Then, as now, most of the leading economists were inclined to view economic growth as a good thing. However, some of them feared that the pressure of growing populations on limited natural resources would sooner or later bring economic growth to a halt. Economists portrayed the "stationary state" toward which society was moving as one of poverty and overpopulation, causing one critic to dub economics the "dismal science."

John Stuart Mill thought otherwise. Mill was one of the most remarkable figures of the nineteenth century. Eldest son of the prominent economist James Mill, John Stuart Mill began studying Greek at age 3, was tutoring the younger members of his family in Latin at age 8, and first read Smith's Wealth of Nations at age 13. His Principles of Political Economy, published in 1848, was the standard text on the subject until Alfred Marshall transformed "political economy" into "economics" at the end of the century.

Mill agreed with earlier classical economists that the economy would sooner or later reach a stationary state, but he did not view the prospect as entirely gloomy:

I cannot …regard the stationary state of capital and wealth with the unaffected aversion so generally manifested towards it by political economists of the old school. I am inclined to believe that it would be, on the whole, a very considerable improvement on our present condition. I confess I am not charmed with the ideal of life held out by those who think that the normal state of human beings is that of struggling to get on; that the trampling, crushing, elbowing, and treading on each other's heels, which form the existing type of social life, are the most desirable lot of human kind, or anything but the disagreeable symptoms of one of the phases of our industrial progress…

If the earth must lose that great portion of its pleasantries which it owes to things that the unlimited increase of wealth and population would extricate from it, for the mere purpose of enabling it to support a larger, but not a better or happier population, I sincerely hope, for the sake of posterity, that they will be content to be stationary long before necessity compels them to.

Today Mill's sentiments are echoed by writers who are concerned about problems of population, pollution, and resource depletion.

lies in the *direction* of growth. Further expansion of the production possibility frontier could make possible growth along a path from point B to point C. That growth path would be possible if more effort and expense were devoted to building cars that run more cleanly, cleaning up rivers, and restoring wildlife habitats. Comparing the arrow from A to B with that from B to C, we see that growth can bring both more material output and improved environmental quality *if people choose to go that way*. As is often the case, our problems turn out to arise not from inescapable economic laws but from the choices we make.

Of these two possibilities, in which direction is the world actually headed? Many economists believe that the early stages of economic development move a country in a direction like that from A to B, and later development moves it from B to C. Among other evidence, they point to the fact that standard measures show better air and water quality in the wealthiest countries than in middle-income countries. There are also indications that measured air quality has improved in most American cities in recent decades after deteriorating through much of the 19th and early 20th centuries. Not everyone agrees with this optimistic view, however. Many environmentalists worry that in the future, poor countries will cut corners on environmental standards to attract investment, and that as old types of pollution are cleaned up, previously unknown types of toxic waste will replace them.[3]

FIGURE 4.2 ENVIRONMENTAL QUALITY AND ECONOMIC GROWTH

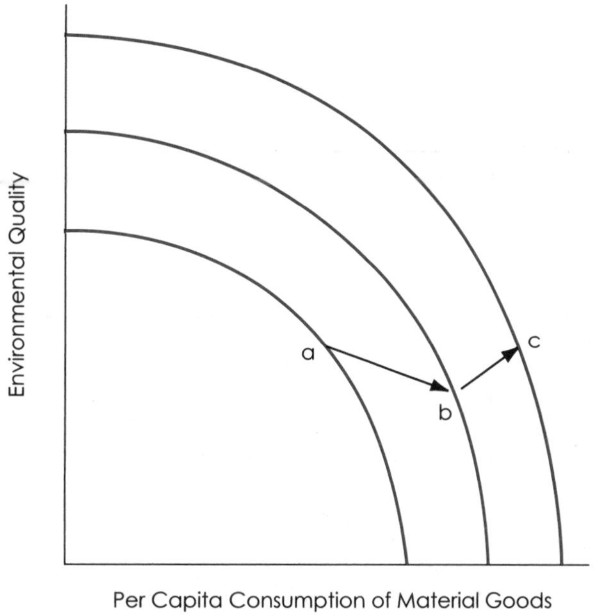

This figure shows a production possibility frontier for consumption of material goods, on the one hand, and environmental quality, on the other. At any given time there is a trade-off. For example, more cars of an unchanged kind mean dirtier air; investing more to make cars cleaner means that fewer cars can be produced. Over time, improvements in technology and the availability of additional productive resources shift the production possibility frontier outward. A choice can be made between two growth paths as the frontier expands. The path from A to B shows an increase in the output of goods and a decrease in environmental quality. The path from B to C shows growth accompanied by strong investment in pollution abatement and environmental improvements.

SHORT-RUN MACROECONOMICS AND: THE BUSINESS CYCLE

The first section of this chapter focused on prosperity—economic growth and its causes in the long run. In this section we turn to issues of stability, that is, to variations in real GDP, inflation, and unemployment that disturb the smooth operation of the economy in the short run.

Natural level of real output

The trend of real GDP growth over time, also known as potential real output.

Output gap

The economy's current level of real output minus its natural level of real output.

Figure 4.3 shows growth of the U.S. economy since 1950. Because of increasing labor inputs, capital accumulation, and technological and organizational improvements, the material standard of living has risen substantially. The straight trend line drawn in the figure represents the growth over time of the economy's **natural level of real output**, sometimes also known as *potential real output*.

As the chart shows, real GDP has moved sometimes above and sometimes below the long-term trend line. At any point in time, the difference between the current level of real output and natural real output is known as the **output gap**. The output gap is stated as a percentage of natural real output. A positive output gap indicates that real output is above its natural level; a negative output that it is

FIGURE 4.3 ECONOMIC GROWTH IN THE UNITED STATES

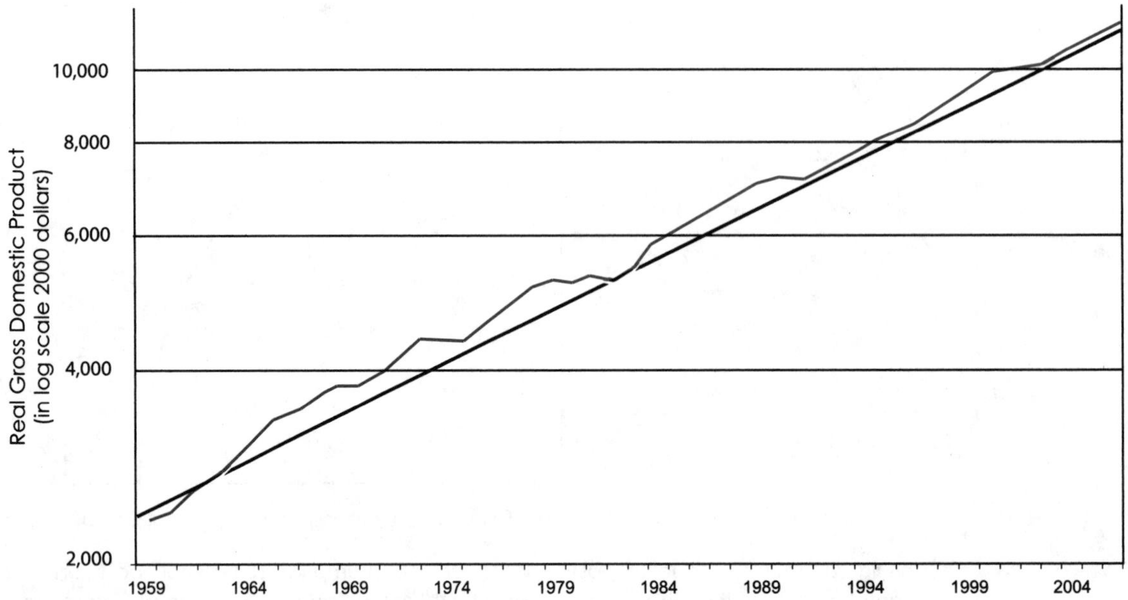

This chart shows the growth of the U.S. economy since 1960. Real Gross Domestic Product is shown for each year, along with a trend line showing average growth of about 2.5 percent per year. In some years real GDP rises above the trend and in some years it falls below it. When real output is higher than its natural level, we say there is a positive output gap. When it is below its natural level, there is a *negative output gap*.

Source: Economic Report of the President, 2007, Table B-2.

below the natural level. In some years real GDP has not just grown more slowly than the trend, but actually fallen. This pattern of irregular but repeated expansion and contraction of overall economic activity about its natural level is known as the **business cycle**.

Business cycle

A pattern of irregular but repeated expansion and contraction of aggregate economic activity.

Phases of the Business Cycle

An idealized business cycle is shown in Figure 4.4. The cycle can be divided into four phases. The peak of the cycle is the point at which real output reaches a maximum. At that point there is a positive output gap. The period during which real output falls is known as the *contraction* phase. At the end of the contraction, real output reaches a minimum known as the *trough* of the cycle. At that point there is a negative output gap. After the trough, real output begins to grow again and the economy enters an *expansion* that lasts until a new peak is reached.

FIGURE 4.4 AN IDEALIZED BUSINESS CYCLE

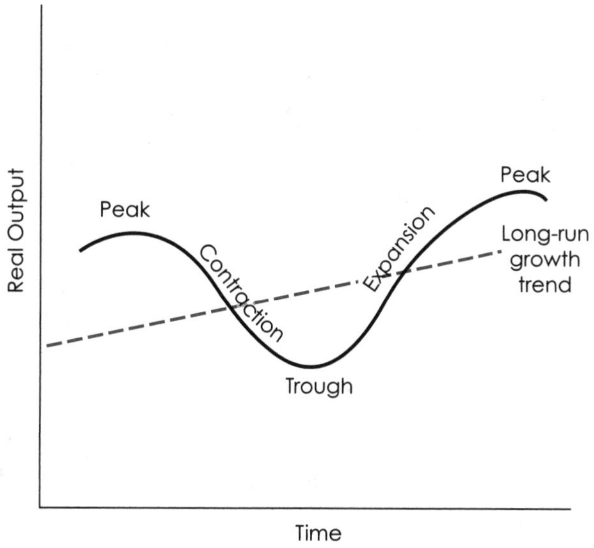

This figure shows an idealized business cycle. The cycle begins from a peak, then enters a contraction. A contraction lasting six months or more is called a recession. The low point of the cycle is known as its trough. Following the trough, the economy enters an expansion until a new peak is reached. Because real GDP varies about an upward trend, each cyclical peak tends to carry the economy to a higher level of real GDP than the previous one.

Recession

A cyclical economic contraction that lasts six months or more.

According to a commonly used (although somewhat simplified) definition, a contraction lasting six months or more is a **recession**. Several recessions, of which the most recent began in March 2001 and ended in November of the same year, can be identified in Figure 4.3.

The nineteenth and early twentieth centuries saw a number of cyclical contractions that were much more severe than any since World War II. These were called *depressions*. The most spectacular of these was the Great Depression of the 1930s, which actually consisted of two contractionary periods separated by an incomplete recovery. During this episode, real output fell by one-third, the price level fell by one-quarter, and the unemployment rate climbed to 24 percent of the labor force. Because no succeeding contraction has come close to it in severity, the term *depression* has passed out of use in all but historical contexts.

Employment and the Business Cycle

Figures 4.3 and 4.4 show the business cycle in terms of real domestic product, but real output is not the whole story. In the short run, changes in real output above or below the trend line are linked to changes in employment. These changes in employment tend to get more attention than changes in output, which is hardly surprising. Real GDP is a very abstract concept, whereas employment has a much more personal meaning. The security of your own job, and those of your relatives and close friends, have a far bigger impact on your life than a percentage-point wiggle one way or the other in real GDP.

Unemployment rate

The percentage of the labor force that is unemployed.

Employed

A term used to refer to a person who is working at least 1 hour a week for pay or at least 15 hours per week as an unpaid worker in a family business.

Unemployed

A term used to refer to a person who is not employed but is actively looking for work.

Labor force

The sum of all individuals who are employed and all individuals who are unemployed.

MEASURING UNEMPLOYMENT TRENDS The most widely-used measure of the employment situation is the **unemployment rate**, which is the percentage of the labor force that is unemployed at a given time. Understanding this deceptively simple statistic requires some definitions of related terms and a discussion of measurement technique.

The U.S. Bureau of Labor Statistics, in conjunction with the Bureau of the Census, obtains the data used in calculating unemployment from a monthly sample of about 50,000 randomly selected households. Field agents go to those households and ask a series of questions about the job status of each member of the household. The questions include such things as: Did anyone work last week? Did anyone look for work? How long has the person been looking for work? How did the person go about looking?

On the basis of their answers to these questions, people are counted as employed or unemployed. A person is considered to be **employed** if he or she works at least 1 hour per week for pay or at least 15 hours per week as an unpaid worker in a family business. A person who is not currently employed but is actively looking for work is said to be **unemployed**. The employed plus the unemployed—that is, those who are either working or looking for work—constitute the **labor force**. The unemployment rate is the percentage of the labor force that is unemployed.

If people are neither employed nor actively looking for work, they are not counted as members of the labor force. People out of the labor force include many people who could work but choose not to for one reason or another. For example, they may be full-time students or retired, or they may work full time, but without pay, at home. Two groups are automatically considered to be outside the labor force: children under 16 years of age and people who are confined to prisons and certain other institutions. The most commonly reported data for the labor force (the *civilian labor force)* and employment also exclude members of the armed forces.

Figure 4.5 presents unemployment data for the United States since 1950. The shaded band labeled "low to moderate unemployment" reflects a range of views about reasonable economic performance. During the 1950s and 1960s, the unemployment rate generally stayed within this range. In the 1970s and early 1980s, the unemployment rate took a turn for the worse. It jumped to 8.3 percent in 1975 and fell into the moderate range in only 2 of the next 12 years. Only in 1989, just before the onset of a new recession, did it again reach the levels achieved in the early 1970s.

GRAY AREAS IN THE MEASUREMENT OF UNEMPLOYMENT There are many gray areas in the measurement of unemployment. The official unemployment rate can be criticized for both understating and overstating the "true" number of unem-

FIGURE 4.5 UNEMPLOYMENT IN THE UNITED STATES SINCE 1960

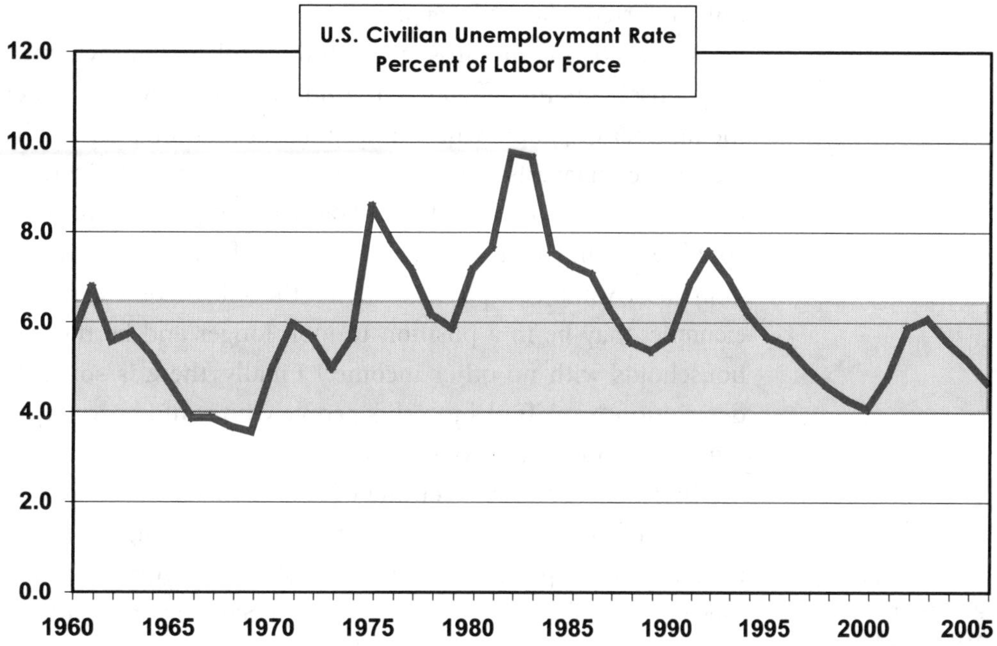

There is no one level of unemployment that is universally accepted as best for the economy. Some unemployment is always present as people change jobs or they enter the labor force in a normally functioning economy. This figure highlights a range of 4 to 6.5 percent unemployment that can be considered "low to moderate." Until 1975, unemployment stayed within that range, for the most part. The mid-1970s and early 1980s saw much higher rates. During the 1990s, unemployment returned to the moderate range.

Source: Economic Report of the President, 2007, Table B-42

ployed adults. One way to understand these gray areas better is to compare the official definition of unemployment with two common-sense definitions, namely, "not working" and "can't find a job."

The official definitions of employment and unemployment differ greatly from the simple definitions of "working" and "not working." On the one hand, there are many people who work but are not officially employed. By far the largest such group consists of people who work full time at housekeeping and child care. These occupations are counted as employment if they are performed for pay, but much of such work is done without pay. Also, children under 16 working without pay for a family farm or business also are not counted as employed.

On the other hand, not everyone who does not work is counted as unemployed. There are millions of people who are not looking for work and therefore are not counted in the labor force. There are also those who are absent from their jobs because of illness, bad weather, or labor disputes. All of these are counted as employed. Finally, there are those who work part time and are counted as employed but are actively seeking full-time employment. People in this last situation are sometimes referred to as *underemployed*.

The second common-sense definition of unemployment, "can't find a job," also only loosely fits the official definition. In some ways, the official definition overstates the number of people who cannot find jobs. Some people who are counted as unemployed are on layoffs from jobs to which they expect to be recalled, or have found jobs that they expect to start within 30 days. Other people who are counted as unemployed could easily find a job of some kind but prefer to take their time and find just the kind of job they want. (People who are not the sole income earners in their households, for example, may be in a position to look longer and be more selective than people in households with no other income.) Finally, there is some doubt as to whether the description "can't find a job" fits people who could have stayed on at their last job but quit to look for a better one.

Discouraged worker

A person who would work if a suitable job were available but has given up looking for such a job.

In other ways, however, the official definition of unemployment understates the number of people who cannot find jobs. For example, it does not include **discouraged workers**—people who are not looking for work because they believe no suitable jobs are available. The Bureau of Labor Statistics officially counts as a discouraged worker anyone who has looked for work within the last six months but is no longer actively looking. The description "can't find a job" could also be applied to the underemployed—those who have part-time jobs but would take full-time jobs if they could find them.

Natural rate of unemployment

The sum of frictional and structural unemployment; the rate of unemployment that persists when the economy is experiencing neither accelerating nor decelerating inflation.

THE NATURAL RATE OF UNEMPLOYMENT Figure 4.5 emphasized short-term swings in the unemployment rate associated with the business cycle. For a longer-term perspective, it is useful to look at trends in what economists call the **natural rate of unemployment**.[4] This is the level of unemployment reached by the economy when real GDP is at its natural level, that is, the unemployment rate associated with the trend line for GDP that was shown in Figure 4.3. Another way to express it is to say that unemployment is at its natural rate when there is a zero output gap.

Figure 4.6 shows the trend of the natural rate of unemployment in the United States, with comparison to that in major economies of European Union. As the figure shows, the natural rate of unemployment has fallen gradually in the United States since the 1980s. It is now lower than that in the largest European economies. Similar data for the United Kingdom and Ireland, whose labor markets are structurally more similar to that of the United States than to those of Continental Europe, would show a healthier unemployment trend than the two largest Continental European economies, France or Germany.

This divergence of unemployment trends has been a huge source of controversy within the European Union. Some economists argue that the trends show a clear superiority of the so-called "Anglo-American" model of flexible labor markets, with relatively few restrictions on hiring and firing workers, and a relatively modest social

FIGURE 4.6 UNEMPLOYMENT TRENDS IN THE UNITED STATES AND EUROPE

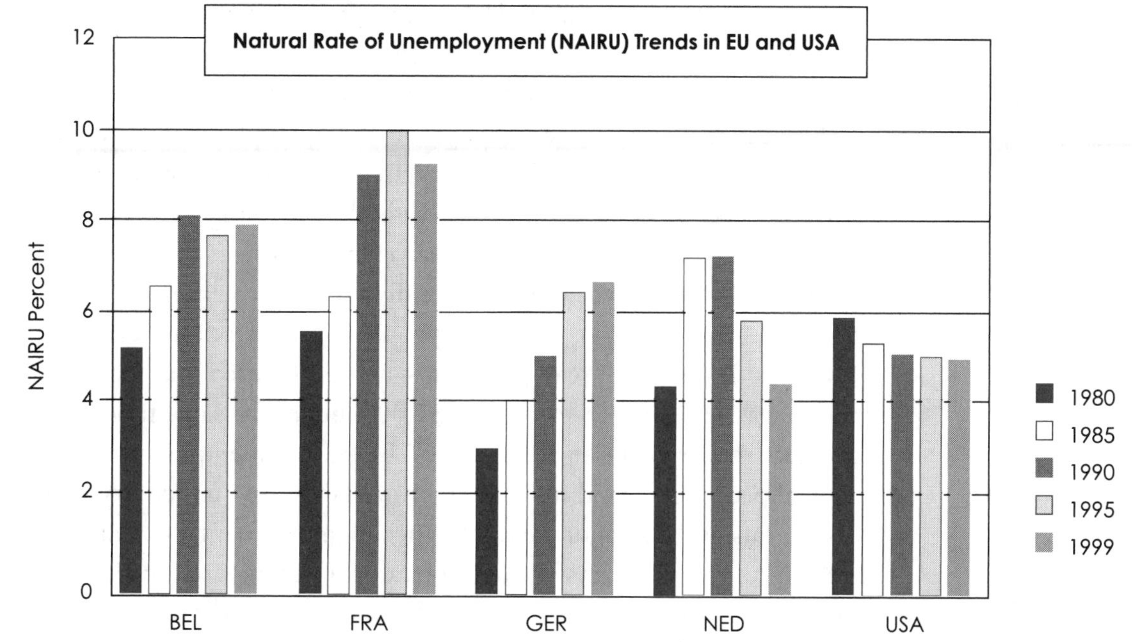

This figure shows trends in the natural rate of unemployment for the United States and several European economies. While the natural rate of unemployment has fallen gradually in the United States since 1980, it has risen in France and Germany, Europe's largest economies. Unemployment rates, which were once much lower in France and Germany than in the United States are now higher.

Source: Achim Kemmerling et. al, Regional Input: Labor Markets, Eurozoneplus Working Paper 6a, Jean Monnet Center of Excellence, Freie Univertaet Berlin, Sept. 2002, Chart 1

safety net for the unemployed. By comparison, according to these thinkers, the "Franco-German" model is fundamentally flawed. Although it intends to protect jobs by making layoffs difficult and making life easy for the unemployed, it has the unintended effect of providing too few incentives for employers to hire and workers to seek jobs. In reply, thinkers aligned with Europe's tradition of social democracy see the Anglo-American model as harsh and uncaring. Many social democratic thinkers in France and Germany believe their labor markets can be reformed without sacrificing their countries' traditional emphasis on generous social protection of workers.

OTHER MEASURES OF UNEMPLOYMENT The unemployment rate is not the only measure of the state of the labor market. Quite aside from the problems of definition just discussed, the unemployment rate may give a misleading picture of what is happening in the labor market because it is sensitive both to changes in its numerator (the number of unemployed) and its denominator (the size of the labor force). During the early stages of recovery from a recession, the labor force often grows at the same time that the number of employed people grows, and the unemployment rate remains unchanged. This happens because news of possible new jobs draws discouraged workers back into the labor force, but the new workers do not immediately find work. Once a recovery is underway, the size of the labor force stabilizes and the unemployment rate may fall even though just a few new jobs are created.

Because month-to-month changes in the unemployment rate may send misleading signals, news reports of short-term labor market developments often focus instead on the number of new payroll jobs created in a given month. The monthly figure for change in payroll jobs is based on a survey of employers that is entirely separate from the household survey used to calculate the unemployment rate. The sample size of the employer survey is larger, and some people consider it more reliable. For example, in November 2006, the Bureau of Labor Statistics reported that the number of new jobs created was a larger-than-expected 132,000, but at the same time, that the unemployment rate rose from 4.4 to 4.5 percent. The reason unemployment rose was that thousands of people streamed into the labor market to find temporary jobs for the holiday season, raising the denominator of the unemployment ratio at the same time the 132,000 new jobs increased the numerator. Press reports on the day the November 2006 figures were released mostly had an optimistic tone, focusing on rapid job growth rather than the slight upturn in the unemployment rate.

Employment-population ratio

The percentage of the noninstitutional adult population that is employed.

Still another job statistic that helps complete the picture of the labor market is the **employment-population ratio**. This ratio is the percentage of the noninstitutional adult population that is employed. The denominator of the employment-population ratio, which is governed by such demographic factors as birthrates and death rates, changes slowly and predictably. Hence, this ratio is less likely than the unemployment rate to stand still while the economy moves ahead, or to give other misleading signals. In particular, during the early stages of an economic recovery when firms first start hiring new workers, the employment-population ratio will rise even though the unemployment rate may temporarily not change because of the return of discouraged workers to the labor force.[5]

Frictional unemployment

The portion of unemployment that is accounted for by the short periods of unemployment needed for matching jobs with job seekers.

FRICTIONAL, STRUCTURAL, AND CYCLICAL UNEMPLOYMENT Still another way to look at unemployment is to ask how long people remain unemployed. Figure 4.7 shows that as of 2006, more than a third of unemployed workers were out of a job for 5 weeks or less. The term **frictional unemployment** is used to refer to short-term, largely voluntary unemployment spells needed to match jobs and workers. It represents people who quit old jobs to look for new ones, people who take a week or so to move or go on vacation before starting a newly found job, and people who enter occupations, such as construction work, in which temporary layoffs are frequent but year-round earnings are good. Economists view a certain level of frictional unemployment as necessary in a labor market in which information is incomplete and the costs of job search are often high.

FIGURE 4.7 U.S. UNEMPLOYMENT BY DURATION

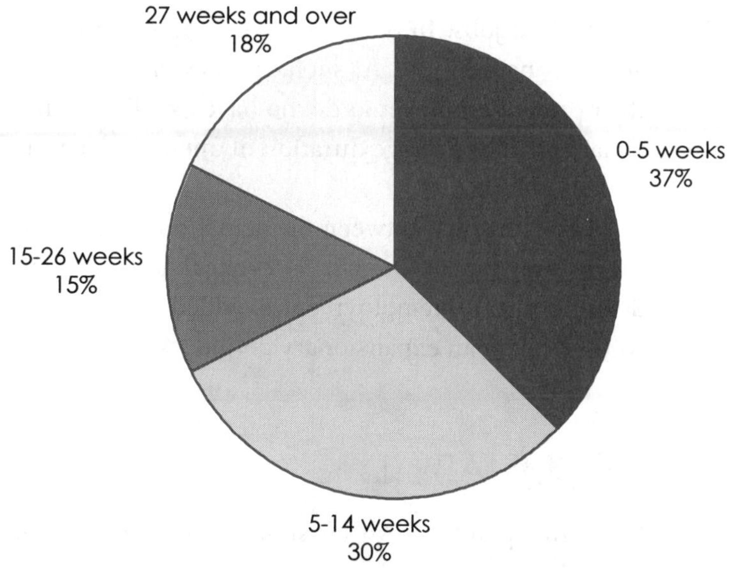

As this chart shows, there is considerable variation in the length of time people are unemployed. As of 2006, more than a third of unemployed workers spent less than five weeks out of work, while just over a quarter were out of work for six months or more.

Source: *Economic Report of the President*, 2007, Table B-44.

Structural unemployment
The portion of unemployment that is accounted for by people who are out of work for long periods because their skills do not match those required for available jobs.

The term **structural unemployment** refers to people who spend long periods out of work, often with little prospect of finding adequate jobs. Figure 4.7 shows that as of 2006, just over a quarter of unemployed workers were out of a job for half a year or more. This prolonged joblessness occurs partly because the shifting structure of the economy has made their skills obsolete. This category of workers also includes people with few skills and little work experience. Teenagers and some minority groups are particularly affected by this type of unemployment.

For these people, structural unemployment is not merely a problem of lack of jobs. Certain types of jobs—hospital workers, fast-food work, and car washing, for example—are almost always available and require few specific skills. But structurally unemployed workers who do take such jobs often work at them only for short periods before quitting to look for something better. Working for brief periods at dead-end jobs tends to build up a pattern of poor work habits and absenteeism that makes many structurally unemployed workers unattractive to potential employers.

Frictional and structural unemployment are present in good years as well as bad ones. Together, they constitute the natural rate of unemployment. But unemployment is not always at its natural level. In some years, a vigorous economic expansion makes jobs so easy to find that the duration of unemployment falls below normal, reducing the number of unemployed below the number normally unemployed for frictional and structural reasons. Even many of the hard-core structurally unemployed find jobs. In other years, business contractions cause unemployment to rise above its natural rate. At such times even workers who have worked a long time for their present employer and who have excellent skills may find themselves temporarily laid off. The average duration of unemployment rises above normal frictional plus structural levels.

The difference between the actual unemployment rate in a particular month and the natural rate is known as **cyclical unemployment**. When the economy slows down, cyclical unemployment is added to frictional and structural unemployment. At the peak of an expansionary period, cyclical unemployment is negative.

Cyclical unemployment

The difference between the observed rate of unemployment at a given point in the business cycle and the natural rate of unemployment.

PRICE STABILITY

Up to this point, our discussion has focused on real variables—real output and the level of employment. But changes in the prices at which goods and services are sold are also important. **Inflation**, which means a sustained increase in the average level of prices of all goods and services, is a potential disruptive force in the economic life of nations and individuals. **Price stability**—a situation in which the rate of inflation is low enough so that it is not a significant factor in business and individual decision making—can be considered another of the major goals of macroeconomic policy.

Inflation

A sustained increase in the average level of prices of all goods and services.

Price stability

A situation in which the rate of inflation is low enough so that it is not a significant factor in business and individual decision making.

Figure 4.8 shows inflation trends in the U.S. economy and around the world. Before the 1970s, U.S.inflation was low. In fact, for the entire century from the Civil War to the mid-1960s, the U.S. peacetime inflation rate averaged only about 2 percent per year. Beginning in the 1970s, however, inflation rose and became highly variable. The struggle against inflation was a dominant theme in economic policy throughout the 1980s. By the late 1980s, inflation was again brought under control, and has remained low since.

Figure 4.8b shows that the rise of inflation in the 1970s and its decline since the 1990s was part of a world-wide phenomenon. It also shows that the U.S. inflation experience was moderate by comparison with the average for other countries

Short-Run Costs of Inflation

Figure 4.8 shows that the rate of inflation varies over the business cycle. As the cycle approaches its peak, inflation accelerates. During recessions, inflation shows again. As inflation rises and falls over the business cycle, its costs are distributed unevenly across the population.

Most people receive the bulk of their income in the form of wages and salaries. Wage and salary earners often feel that they are badly hurt by inflation. They compare what their paychecks can buy each month at ever-higher prices with what they would be able to buy with the same paychecks if prices remained stable. However, measured over a

FIGURE 4.8 INFLATION IN THE UNITED STATES AND AROUND THE WORLD

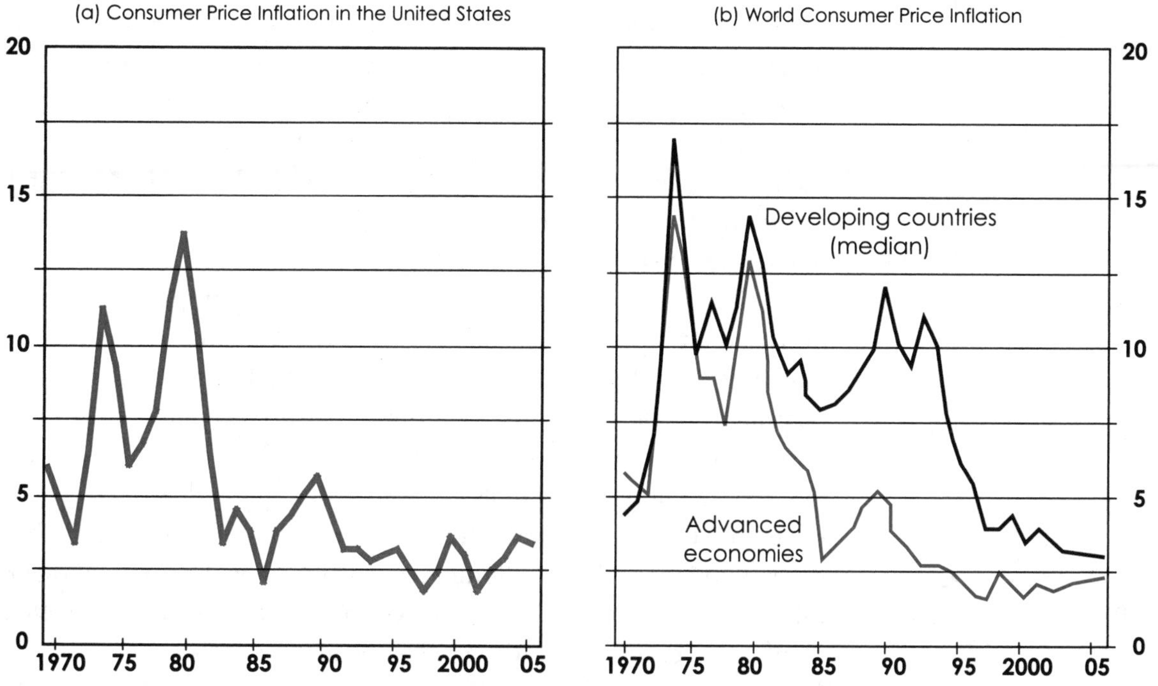

Part a of this figure shows the trend of inflation in the United States since 1970, as measured by the annual percentage change in the Consumer Price Index. The 1970s and early 1980s were years of high and variable inflation. More recently, inflation has once again been brought under control. Part b shows that the U.S. experienced was shared by both developing and advanced economies around the world.

Source: Figure 4.8a, Economic Report of the President, 2007, Table B-64. Figure 4.8b, IMF, World Economic Outlook 2003, Figure 1.1

period of several years, nominal wages and salaries tend to adjust to inflation. Real wage and salary earnings in the United States rose during the inflationary 1970s and 1980s and also during the low-inflation 1960s and 1990s. People who receive income in the form of social security, other government **transfer payments**, and some private annuities are protected from inflation by automatic adjustments that compensate for changes in consumer prices. Such automatic adjustments are called **indexation**.

Transfer payments

Payments to individuals that are not made in return for work they currently perform.

Indexation

A policy of automatically adjusting a value or payment in proportion to changes in the average price level.

Inflation also affects the income of creditors, who receive interest from mortgage loans, corporate bonds, and the like, and that of debtors, who pay interest. The traditional view is that inflation injures creditors and aids debtors. Suppose, for example, that I borrow $100 from you today, promising to repay the $100 of principal plus $5 interest, or $105 in all, at the end of a year. If there is no inflation during the year, I get the use of the funds for the year and you get $5 of real income in the form of the interest on the loan. But suppose that during the year the price level goes up by 10 percent. In that case I get the use of the funds for the year, and what is more, I pay you back in depreciated dollars. The $105 I give you at the end of the year will buy only about as much then as $95 will buy today. Your real income is negative, because the real value of $105 a year from now is less than the real value today of the $100 that I borrow. I, the debtor, benefit from inflation, and you, the creditor, are hurt.

However, this view of the effects of inflation is incomplete in that it does not distinguish between *unexpected* and *expected* inflation. The example just given implicitly assumes that neither I, the borrower, nor you, the lender, expected any inflation at the time the loan was made. Suppose instead that we both had expected a 10 percent increase in the price level between the time the loan was made and the time it was repaid. In that case, you would not have loaned me the $100 in return for a promise to repay just $105 at the end of the year. Instead, you would have insisted on a repayment of $115—the $100 principal, plus $10 to compensate you for the decline in purchasing power of the principal plus $5 of real interest income. I, in turn, would have agreed to those terms, knowing that the $115 payment under conditions of 10 percent inflation would be no more burdensome than the $105 payment I would have agreed to if no inflation had been expected.

Nominal interest rate

The interest rate expressed in the usual way: in terms of current dollars without adjustment for inflation.

Real interest rate

The nominal interest rate minus the rate of inflation.

This example shows that we need to distinguish between two interest concepts: the **nominal interest rate**, which is the interest rate expressed in the ordinary way, in current dollars, and the **real interest rate**, which is the nominal rate minus the rate of inflation. In the example, a 15 percent nominal interest rate, given a 10 percent rate of inflation, corresponds to a 5 percent real interest rate.

The distinction between nominal and real interest rates helps us to understand the impact of expected and unexpected inflation on debtors and creditors. Expected inflation, it turns out, is neutral between debtors and creditors, because the parties will adjust the nominal interest rate to take the expected inflation into account. If they would agree to a 5 percent nominal interest rate given no expected inflation, they would agree to a 15 percent nominal rate given 10 percent expected inflation, a 20 percent nominal rate given 15 percent expected inflation, and so on. All of these adjusted rates correspond to a 5 percent real rate. Unexpected inflation is not neutral, however. Unexpected inflation harms creditors and benefits debtors. If you lend me $100 at a 5 percent nominal rate of interest, and the price level unexpectedly rises by 10 percent over the year before I repay the loan, the real rate of interest that you receive is minus 5 percent.

Long-Run Costs of Inflation

In the short run, unexpected inflation helps some people while it hurts others. In the long run, however, inflation, whether expected or unexpected, has other costs that places a burden on the economy as a whole without producing offsetting benefits for anyone.

One problem arises from the way inflation upsets economic calculations. When the rate of inflation is high and variable, as it was in the United States in the 1970s and early 1980s, business planning becomes difficult. The outcomes of investment projects that require firms to incur costs now in the hope of making profits later come to depend less on manufacturing and marketing skills than on the ups and downs of wages, interest rates, and the prices of key raw materials. As the investment environment becomes riskier, firms may avoid projects with long-term payoffs and gamble instead on strategies that promise short-term financial gains. Similarly, households, facing more uncertainty about future price trends, may reduce their long-term saving in favor of increased current consumption. These effects are hard to measure, but many economists think that they are substantial.

Another set of costs arise from the effort to rid the economy of inflation once it has become established. The experiences of many countries in many periods suggest that bringing inflation under control often causes serious economic disruption during a transition period. For example, the slowdown in inflation in the United States in the early 1980s coincided with back-to-back recessions during which the unemployment rate which reached a peak of more than 10 percent, the worst in half a century.

International comparisons suggest that the adverse effect of inflation on the growth of real incomes is quite pronounced. Figure 4.9 shows data on the relationship between growth and inflation from a sample of 103 countries over a 30-year period. There is a clear tendency for inflation to undermine economic growth. Countries that experienced inflation of more than 100 percent per year (that is, a doubling or more of the price level each year) on average experienced decreases in real GDP.

However, Figure 4.9 also suggests that moderate inflation does not necessarily have negative effects on economic growth. The sample on which this figure was based did not include many very low-inflation counties, but other studies suggest

FIGURE 4.9 INFLATION AND ECONOMIC GROWTH

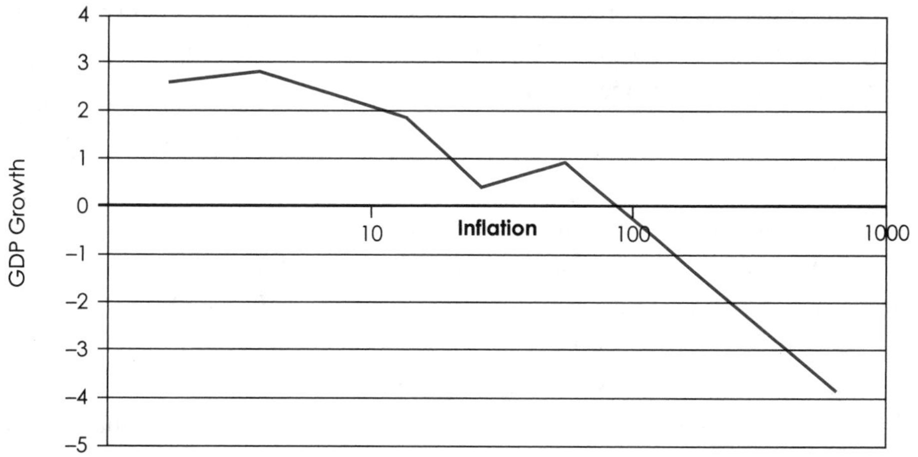

On average, inflation higher than a very moderate rate is harmful to economic growth. This chart, based on a sample of 103 countries over a period of 30 years, shows a clear inverse relationship between growth and inflation. Countries with inflation over 100 percent per year tend to have negative economic growth.

Source: Based on data from Atish Gosh and Steven Phillips, Inflation, Disinflation, and Growth, IMF Working Paper 98/68, May 1998

that complete price stability is not necessarily the best of all possible worlds. Policy makers in most countries aim not for zero inflation but rather, for a steady, moderate increase of prices of something like 2 to 4 percent per year. We will return to the issue of choosing the best target rate of inflation in a later chapter.

SUMMARY

1. **What trend has economic growth followed in the United States?** Economic growth is most commonly expressed in terms of the rate of growth of *Gross Domestic Product (GDP)*, a measure of the value of the economy's total output of goods and services during a given period of time. To avoid distortions caused by inflation, gross domestic product is expressed in real terms. Real gross domestic product has grown at an average rate of about 2–3 percent since 1950, although that growth has not been steady. Economic growth is widely seen as beneficial, in that it makes possible higher living standards, jobs for those who want them, and more leisure for those who want it. Some people criticize growth as damaging to the environment. In evaluating such damage, the composition of real domestic product as it grows must be considered as well as its rate of growth.

2. **What is the business cycle?** Over time, the economy undergoes a pattern of irregular but repeated expansion and contraction of aggregate economic activity that is known as the *business cycle*. The point at which output reaches a maximum is known as the peak of the cycle. This is followed by a contraction, a trough, an expansion, and a new peak. A contraction lasting six months or more is known as a recession. Over the course of the business cycle, the economy sometimes rises above its *natural level of real output*, resulting in a positive *output gap*, and sometimes falls below the natural level, resulting in a negative output gap.

3. **What is unemployment and why is it important for economic policy?** A person who works at least 1 hour a week for pay or 15 hours per week as an unpaid worker in a family business is considered to be *employed*. A person who is not currently employed but is actively looking for work is *unemployed*. The *unemployment rate* is the percentage of the *labor force* that is not employed. Unemployment may be classified as *frictional*, *structural*, or *cyclical*, depending on its cause. Structural plus frictional unemployment is known as the *natural rate of unemployment*. The *employment-population ratio* is the percentage of the adult non-institutional population that is employed.

4. **What is inflation and what impact does it have on the economy?** *Inflation* is a sustained increase in the average level of prices of all goods and services. *Price stability* is a situation in which the rate of inflation is low enough so that it is not a significant factor in business and individual decision making. Inflation is frequently measured in terms of the rate of change in the *consumer price index*. In measuring economic quantities, a distinction must be made between *real* values, or values adjusted for inflation, and *nominal* values, or values expressed in the ordinary way, in current dollars. Applying these concepts to interest rates, we can say that the *real interest rate* is equal to the *nominal*

interest rate minus the rate of inflation. Inflation disrupts the economy in two ways. First, it harms or benefits individuals according to their source of income; second, it disrupts economic calculation, thereby discouraging saving and investment. In addition, the effort to stop inflation once it has begun often entails substantial costs.

KEY TERMS

Real	Natural rate of unemployment
Nominal	Employment-population ratio
Real output	Frictional unemployment
Total factor productivity	Structural unemployment
Natural level of real output	Cyclical unemployment
Output gap	Inflation
Business cycle	Price stability
Recession	Transfer payments
Unemployment rate	Indexation
Employed	Nominal interest rate
Unemployed	Real interest rate
Labor force	
Discouraged worker	

PROBLEMS AND TOPICS FOR DISCUSSION

1. **Your personal labor force status.** What is your current labor force status? Are you a member of the labor force? Are you employed? Unemployed? Explain the basis for your answers. When was the last time your labor force status changed? Do you expect it to change soon? Give details.

2. **Employment hardship.** It has been suggested that the unemployment rate should be replaced with an "employment hardship index" that tries to measure the percentage of people who suffer hardship because of their labor force status. What kinds of people who are not now counted as unemployed might fit into this category? What kinds of people who are now counted as unemployed would not suffer hardship? Discuss.

3. **Real and nominal interest rates.** Check with your local bank to find out what interest rates currently apply to (a) one-year savings certificates and (b) three-year automobile loans. Compare these nominal interest rates with the current rate of inflation as measured by the most recently announced rate of change in the consumer price index. (You can get this statistic from the web site of the Bureau of Labor Statistics, www.bls.gov.) If the current rate of inflation were to continue unchanged, what real rate of interest would you earn on the saving certificate? What real rate of interest would you pay on the loan?

4. **Economic growth and the environment.** The pace of economic growth varies from one area of the United States to another. Some regions are growing rapidly, with people moving in, much new construction, rising incomes, and so on. Other areas are stagnant or declining, with little new construction and people moving away. Which type of area do you live in? Can you identify any environmental problems in your area that seem to be caused by economic growth? Can you identify any environmental problems that seem to be caused by economic decline? What policies could you suggest that would permit growth in your area to take place with less environmental disruption?

5. **The current state of the business cycle.** Unemployment and inflation data are announced monthly, and data on economic growth are announced on a quarterly basis. Watch your local newspaper, The *Wall Street Journal*, or business magazines such as Business Week for discussions of the most recent

data. What changes have there been? What is happening to the employment rate? Are the employment and unemployment rates moving in the same direction or in opposite directions? What is the current rate of inflation? Is it increasing, decreasing, or staying the same? Judging from available data, in which phase of the business cycle does the economy appear to be at the moment?

CASE FOR DISCUSSION

Unemployment and Politics

What did the elections of Presidents Truman, Johnson, Nixon, and Clinton have in common? Those of Presidents Kennedy and Reagan? The answer, for the first four, is that they all won as incumbent presidents in election years when the unemployment rate was falling. The other two were successful challengers in years when the unemployment rate was stagnant or rising.

The election of 1982, in which incumbent President George H. W. Bush faced challenger Bill Clinton, provides a particularly interesting example. In the spring of that year, the economy was just beginning recovery from a recession although its end had not yet been officially announced. But although the economy was growing, it was doing so at a rate of only about 2 percent per year. That was well below the average rate of growth of 4.6 percent per year for the six post–World War II elections in which the incumbent party retained power. In June, employers slashed 117,000 jobs from their payrolls and the unemployment rate hit an 8-year high. The jobs data made every news broadcast, and the news was bad.

Moreover, although the first President Bush could hope for good news between early summer and election time, history suggests that such news would be too little, too late. Economists like Ray Fair of Yale, who have studied the economics-politics link in detail, say that last-minute improvements are not enough. The economy's performance during the spring and summer is more important in an election year.

As it turns out, the economic numbers did improve later in the year. Unemployment fell again. An early estimate of the rate of economic growth in the third quarter, announced just before the election, turned out to be 2.7 percent, higher than forecasters had anticipated. Three weeks after the election, this was revised upward to 3.9 percent. But the third-quarter improvement was indeed too little, too late. Challenger Clinton sailed through the election by a wide margin. What is more, by the time of the next presidential election in 1996, the economy was moving strongly forward again. Thanks in part to the favorable economic climate, Clinton was re-elected for a second term.

QUESTIONS

1. If the economy was growing at a rate of 2 percent or better in mid-1992, how is it possible that the unemployment rate was rising?
2. The unemployment rate rose by only 2.7 percentage points from its low of 5.1 percent in March 1989, to its peak in June 1992. A loss of 2.7 percent of voters would not have been nearly enough to defeat the incumbent president. However, his actual vote total fell far more than that. This implies that a rise in unemployment affects the voting behavior not just of those who are actually unemployed, but of many more people as well. Why do you think this is the case?
3. Use your Internet research talents to compare the role of employment as an issue in the 1992 presidential election with that in the 2004 election. How long a period elapsed between the end of the previous recession and the presidential election? How strong were data on job growth and unemployment in the first half of 2004? On balance, do you think employment was an issue that helped George W. Bush win re-election that year,

or did he win re-election despite a jobs situation that favored the Democrats?

END NOTES

1. Chapter 7 will give a formal definition of GDP and explain the methods used to measure it.
2. Chapter 18 in the companion volume, *Introduction to Microeconomics,* explores the issues of poverty and equality in the United States and around the world in detail.
3. For a thorough discussion of these issues, see Susmita Dasgupta et al., "Confronting the Environmental Kuznets Curve," *Journal of Economic Literature,* Vol. 16 No. 1 (Winter 2002), pp. 147-168.
4. The natural rate of unemployment tends to be associated with periods during which the rate of inflation is neither accelerating nor decelerating. For that reason, another name for it is the *non-accelerating-inflation rate of unemployment,* or NAIRU. The relationship between inflation and changes in real output and unemployment will be explored in detail in later chapters.
5. All three measures of the U.S. labor market situation can be obtained from the Employment Situation Summary released monthly by the Bureau of Labor Statistics, available on line at www.bls.gov.

CHAPTER 5

The Circular Flow of Income and Product

After reading this chapter, you will understand:	1. How households and firms are linked by incomes and expenditures 2. How expenditure is divided into consumption, investment, government purchases, and net exports 3. The relationships between injections and leakages in the circular flow 4. Why some investment is planned and other is unplanned 5. How the concept of equilibrium can be applied to the circular flow of income and expenditure 6. What the multiplier effect is and how it is related to the business cycle
Before reading this chapter, make sure you know the meaning of:	1. GDP 2. Opportunity cost 3. Equilibrium 4. Inventories 5. Gross domestic product 6. Real and nominal values 7. The business cycle

THE PREVIOUS CHAPTER took a long-term perspective on growth of GDP. Sources of output growth were broken down into growth of labor inputs, increases in capital per worker, and improvements in technology and organization. Discussions of changes in GDP in the short run typically take a different perspective. For example, in January 2007 the government reported that U.S. GDP grew at an unexpectedly rapid annual rate of 3.5 percent in the fourth quarter of the previous year. News reports said nothing about growth of population, capital, or total factor productivity. Instead, they focused on the behavior of individual components of GDP. First, they noted that although imports of goods and services produced abroad were greater than exports of goods and services produced in the United States, the gap between the two was less than expected. Consumer spending was strong, especially spending on durable goods. Government spending was also up, with increased spending for the war in Iraq leading the way. The only negative note was a slowdown in housing construction and business inventory growth. All in all, it added up to a favorable GDP picture.

This chapter will adopt the same focus on GDP components as that used in news reports. It begins by introducing the **circular flow of income and product**, dividing the economy into five major sectors, and showing important linkages among them. In the second part of the chapter, the circular flow is used to develop the important concept of planned expenditure, which serves as a first step in building a general theory of macroeconomics.

Circular flow of income and product
The flow of goods and services between households and firms, balanced by the flow of payments made in exchange for goods and services.

THE CIRCULAR FLOW

Figure 5.1 divides the economy into five main sectors: firms, households, government, financial markets, and the rest of the world. Arrows indicate flows of payments among the sectors. We can begin with the largest and most important set of flows,

FIGURE 5.1 THE CIRCULAR FLOW OF INCOME AND EXPENDITURE

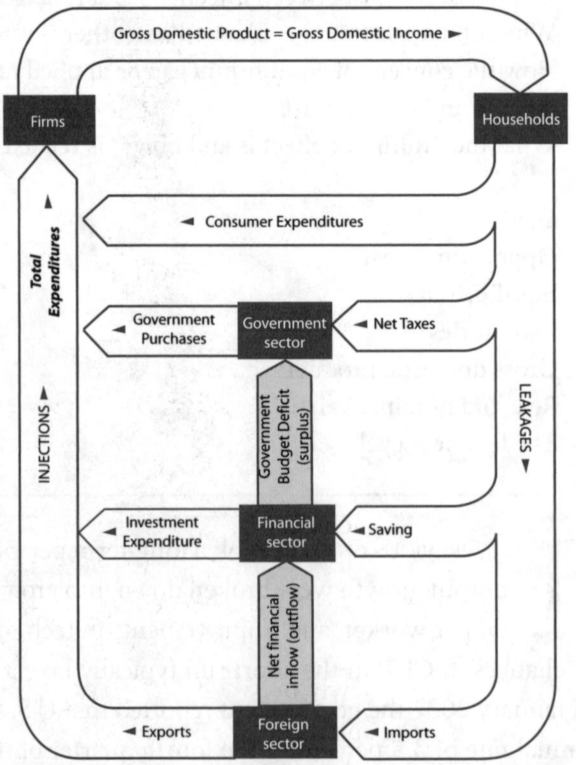

This figure shows flows of income and expenditure among five major sectors of the economy. Households receive income from firms in return for labor and other factor services used to produce gross domestic product. Most of the income goes to consumption expenditure. Some is paid to government as taxes, used to purchase imports, or saved. Government purchases, investment, and exports are additional categories of expenditure.

those representing the incomes that households receive from business firms and the expenditures they make in purchasing goods and services from those same firms.

Gross Domestic Product and Gross Domestic Income

At the very top of Figure 5.1 we encounter gross domestic product (GDP), defined in the previous chapter as a measure of a country's total output of goods and services. When these goods and services are produced, they generate income for the country's households.[1] The largest share of income is paid to households as wages and salaries in return for labor services. Some is also paid out as interest on funds that households have loaned to the firms that produce the goods and services or as rents and royalties on natural resources sold or leased to those firms. The difference between the value of goods produced by a firm and the wages, salaries, interest, rents, and other costs paid out to produce those goods is profit. Profit, which is earned by the firms' owners, is still another category of income received by households.

The sum of income received in the form of wages, rents, interest, and profit by all households is known as *gross domestic income,* or for short, simply *domestic income.* Conceptually, domestic income and domestic product are equal, since the act of producing any good or service necessarily creates income in one form or another (wages, profits, interest, or rents) for the people who produce it. The macroeconomic theories and models used in this book assume the equality of domestic income and domestic product. However, as will be explained in the next chapter, official data show a value for domestic income that is not exactly equal to GDP because of various measurement problems and accounting conventions.

Consumption

All purchases of goods and services by households for the purpose of immediate use.

Investment

The sum of fixed investment and inventory investment.

Fixed investment

Purchases of newly produced capital goods.

Inventory investment

Changes in stocks of finished goods ready for sale, raw materials, and partially completed goods in process of production.

Components of GDP

In building a model of the macroeconomy, it is useful to break GDP down into four components: consumption expenditures, investment expenditures, government purchases, and net exports. In equation form

$$Q = C + I + G + (Ex - Im)$$

Consumption includes all purchases of goods and services by households for the purpose of immediate use. In principle, purchases of long-lasting consumer goods can be counted as a form of investment rather than consumption expenditure, but for practical purposes, the national income accounts usually do not make this distinction. Purchases of newly built housing are the only important category of household purchase that is counted as investment rather than consumption.

Investment, as the term is understood in macroeconomics, is made up of two components. The first, **fixed investment**, means purchases of newly produced capital goods—machinery, office equipment, software, farm equipment, construction of buildings used for business purposes, and so on. The second component, **inventory**

investment, means changes in stocks of finished goods ready for sale, stocks of raw materials, and stocks of partially completed goods in process of production. Inventory investment has a negative value if stocks are decreasing in a given period.

The term *investment* as used in macroeconomic models is sometimes called *economic investment* to emphasize that it means expenditures on real productive assets and inventories. Economic investment should not be confused with *financial investment*, which means purchases of corporate stocks, bonds, and other securities. The latter are not included in GDP because they do not represent new production, but rather, changes in ownership claims on assets that already exist. When the term *investment* is used without modifier, either in this book or in the daily economic news, it is usually clear from context whether economic or financial investment is meant.

Government purchases of goods and services (government purchases)
Purchases of goods by all levels of government plus purchases of services from contractors and wages of government employees.

Government expenditures
Government purchases of goods and services plus transfer payments.

Transfer payments
Payments by government to individuals not made in return for services currently performed, for example, unemployment compensation and pensions.

Tax revenue
The total value of all taxes collected by government.

Net taxes
Tax revenue minus transfer payments.

Net exports
Exports minus imports of goods and services.

Injections
The government purchase, investment, and net export components of the circular flow.

The next element, **government purchases of goods and services (government purchases**, for short) includes all purchases of goods made by all levels of government (national, regional, and local) plus services purchased from contractors and the wages paid to all government employees. It is important to distinguish between government purchases and **government expenditures**. The latter include not only purchases of goods and services but also **transfer payments**. Transfer payments are payments by government to individuals that are not made in return for services currently performed for the government. Pensions, disability payments, and unemployment compensation are examples of transfers.

On the revenue side of the government's budget, we refer to the total value of taxes collected by government as **tax revenue**. The value of the government's tax revenues minus transfer payments is known as **net taxes**.

The final component of GDP is **net exports**, which means exports of goods and services minus imports. Often the term *net exports* is instead called the *trade surplus* (or the *trade deficit* if imports exceed exports).[2] Because some goods included in the consumption, investment, and government purchases components of GDP are not produced in the home country, the equation for GDP must use net exports rather than total exports. If not, there would be a problem of double counting, and the sum of GDP components would overstate the value of goods and services produced in the country.

Injections and Leakages

Government purchases, investment expenditures, and exports are known as **injections**. If the flows of income and consumption expenditures shown at the top of Figure 5.1 are thought of as the "basic" circular flow, then government purchases, investment expenditures, and export expenditures can be thought of as extra components "injected" into the basic circular flow. By the same reasoning, net taxes, saving, and imports are known as **leakages**. Total injections must be equal to total leakages:

$$S + T + Im = I + G + Ex$$

Leakages

The saving, net tax, and import components of the circular flow.

Saving

The part of household income that is not used to buy goods and services or to pay taxes.

The reason injections must equal leakages arises from the way economists define **saving**, by which they mean the part of domestic income that is not devoted to purchase of domestically produced consumer goods, payment of taxes, or purchase of imports. Note that this definition differs slightly from the everyday notion of savings as "money put in the bank." In particular, from the economic point of view, the part of one's income that is used to repay debts counts as saving, as does money used to purchase newly built housing.

Two other additional flows shown in Figure 5.1 connect financial markets to the rest of the circular flow of income and product.[3]

The first of these is the government budget deficit. If government purchases exceed net taxes, the government budget deficit can be financed by borrowing from financial markets, shown by the arrow in Figure 5.1. Using the definitions given earlier, we can express the government deficit in either of two equivalent ways:

Deficit = Government expenditures – tax revenues
Deficit = Government purchases – net taxes

If net taxes are greater than government purchases, the government budget is in surplus. In that case, the government becomes a net supplier of funds to financial markets through the repayment of previously issued government debt or through loans to the private sector. The arrow shown in Figure 5.1 would then be reversed.

The final flow connects financial markets to the foreign sector. If a country's imports exceed its exports, the country must somehow obtain funds to pay for the extra imports. This is done either by borrowing from foreign sources or by selling assets to foreign purchasers. In that case, as shown in Figure 5.1, there is a flow of funds from the foreign sector into domestic financial markets. If exports exceed imports, then the situation is reversed. In order to buy all those exports, other countries must borrow from domestic financial markets. In that case, there is a financial outflow from the country's financial markets to the rest of the world and the arrow would be reversed.

The two flows linking the financial sector to the government and foreign sectors allow the financial sector to serve a balancing function in the circular flow. Although total leakages must equal total injections, the individual leakage-injection pairs do not have to balance: government purchases need not equal net taxes, imports need not equal exports, and saving need not equal investment.

The elements of the leakages and injections equation can be grouped in various ways to highlight important macroeconomic principles. For example, we can write the following relationship:

$$(G - T) = (S - I) + (Im - Ex)$$

This equation focuses attention on the way a country can finance a government budget deficit. The excess of government purchases relative to net taxes can be financed by domestic saving, but only to the extent that private domestic saving exceeds domestic investment. If the country has insufficient saving to finance both its investment and its budget deficit, the additional financing has to come from abroad. The financial inflow is reflected in the leakages and injection equation by net imports, the term (Im – Ex). *Applying Economic Ideas 5.1* shows how the leakages-injections equation helps to understand the U.S. trade and budget deficits of the late twentieth and early twenty-first centuries.

THE DETERMINANTS OF PLANNED EXPENDITURE

Up to now, we have focused on definitions and relationships, but economic theory is concerned with more than that. To really understand the economy, we need to be able to explain why GDP or other variables have one value rather than another and why they change over time. In order to do that, we need to look at the choices made by consumers, business managers, and other decision makers. This section provides an overview of the choices that affect the various components of GDP. The appendix to this chapter supplements the overview with an optional formal model of planned expenditures.

Planned inventory investment Changes in the level of inventory made on purpose, as part of a firm's business plan.

Unplanned inventory investment Changes in the level of inventory arising from a difference between planned and actual sales.

Planned investment The sum of fixed investment and planned inventory investment.

Planned expenditure The sum of consumption, government purchases, net exports, and planned investment.

Planned Versus Unplanned Expenditure

Earlier in the chapter, we pointed out that investment can be broken down into *fixed investment* and *inventory investment*. Inventory investment, in turn, can be divided into planned and unplanned components. Inventory investment is considered **planned** if the level of inventories is increased (or reduced) on purpose as part of a firm's business plan. For example, a retail store might increase inventories in response to growth in the number of customers it serves. Inventory investment is considered **unplanned** if goods accumulate contrary to a firm's business plan because demand is less than expected so that some goods the firm wanted to sell remain unsold. If demand is greater than expected, so that inventories unexpectedly decrease (or increase at a rate less than scheduled in the business plan), there is negative unplanned inventory investment (disinvestment).

All fixed investment is treated as planned. Total **planned investment**, then, means fixed investment plus planned inventory investment. All other types of expenditure—consumption, government purchases, and net exports—are also considered to be planned. For that reason, we use the term **planned expenditure** to mean the sum of consumption, government purchases, net exports, and planned investment. In equation form:

$$Ep = C + Ip + G + (Ex - Im)$$

We can explain the level of planned expenditure as a whole by looking at the choices that lie behind each of its components.

APPLYING ECONOMIC IDEAS 5.1

UNDERSTANDING THE TWIN DEFICITS

Over the past fifteen years, the government budget and trade deficits of the United States have inspired a great amount of comment and controversy. To understand many of the issues raised by these "twin deficits," it is helpful to interpret them in terms of the concepts of leakages and injections. The needed data are shown in the chart.

The upper part of the chart is based on a classification of leakages and injections into three components corresponding to the equation (G – T) = (S – I) + (Im – Ex). G – T represents the budget deficit, or more precisely, *net government saving,* a broad measure that takes into account state and local as well as federal budget activity. Im – Ex is the trade deficit, or net imports. The S – I component is positive if there is more than enough domestic saving to finance domestic investment, and negative if saving falls short of investment. The lower part of the chart shows saving and investment separately.

Looking at the chart, we see that net government saving swung from deficit to surplus in the 1990s and back to deficit in the early 2000s. Over the same period, the trade deficit has grown steadily, from less than 1 percent of GDP in 1991 to a record level of over 5 percent of GDP by 2005. Are the twin deficits that the United States faced going into 2007 just coincidental, or is there a causal relationship?

The leakages-injections equation tells us that the budget deficit can be financed either by an excess of private domestic saving over private investment, or by a financial inflow, the mirror image of the trade deficit. The chart shows three distinct periods in the relationships among leakages and injections.

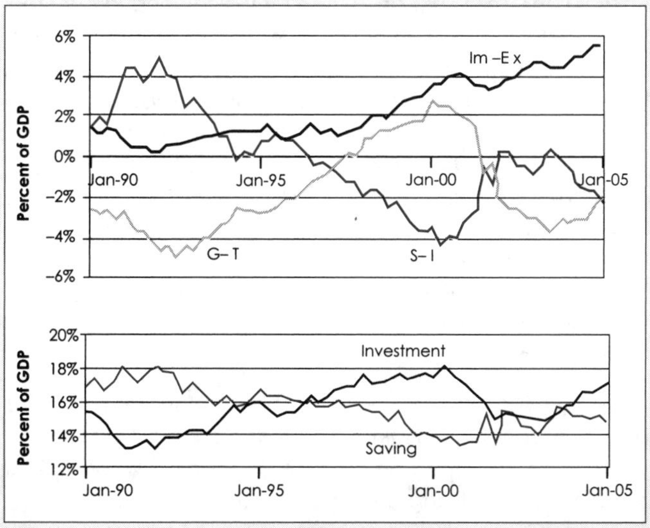

In the early 1990s, there was almost enough private saving to finance both private investment and the government deficit, so that the needed financial inflow from abroad, and the associated trade deficit, were small.

During the later 1990s, the government budget swung sharply to surplus, so that net government saving became positive. Other things being equal, this could have allowed the United States to finance all of its own investment from internal sources with some left over, and the trade balance could have moved into surplus, but this did not happen. Instead, as the lower part of the chart shows, just at this time the U.S. economy experienced a high-tech investment boom. Simultaneously, private saving fell. The government surplus helped to finance the investment boom, but was unable to do so in full, so financial inflows from abroad were still needed. In this period, it is best to think of good private investment opportunities in the United States as a magnet for foreign investment. Since inflows of foreign investment are the mirror image of the trade deficit, these inflows pushed the trade deficit higher. Some economists characterized this situation as a "healthy" trade deficit that reflects structural strength, not weakness, of the country receiving the financial inflows.

At the end of the 1990s, the high-tech investment boom collapsed. Investment being a major component of GDP, this dragged the whole economy down into recession. With incomes falling and transfer payments for unemployment compensation rising, the government budget swung into deficit. The administration of President George W. Bush, victor in the 2000 election, decided to use tax cuts to stimulate spending as a way of overcoming the recession. Perhaps in part because of the tax cuts, the recession did prove to be a short one, but economic recovery did not restore the government budget to surplus. Instead, the continued effects of tax cuts, spending to finance the war in Iraq, and other factors pushed the government budget to record levels. Where was the government to find the funds to finance its huge deficit? Not from domestic saving, which did not rise even by enough to finance the increase in domestic investment. That left just one source: the foreign sector. Once again, as in the late 1990s, financial inflows flooded into the country. This time, though, they were pulled in not by the magnet of private investment opportunities, but by the expanding sinkhole of the federal budget deficit. This gave rise to what many economists characterized as an "unhealthy" trade deficit that reflected not structural strength of the U.S. economy but structural weaknesses—an out-of-control budget deficit and weak domestic savings.

Consumption Expenditure

Choices made by consumers have a more powerful effect on the economy than those made by any other group. Consumer expenditure accounts for about two-thirds of GDP in the United States. In some other countries it is a little more, in some a little less, but everywhere consumption is the largest single component of expenditure. What determines the amount of consumer spending?

Marginal propensity to consume

The proportion of each added dollar of real disposable income that households devote to consumption.

Among the first economists to pose this question was John Maynard Keynes (*Who Said It? Who Did It? 5.1*). In his path-breaking book *The General Theory of Employment, Interest, and Money*, he put it this way: "The fundamental psychological law, upon which we are entitled to depend with great confidence . . . is that men are disposed, as a rule and on the average, to increase their consumption as their income increases, but not by as much as the increase in their income."[4] He called the amount of additional consumption resulting from a one-dollar increase in income the **marginal propensity to consume**. For example, if your marginal propensity to consume

WHO SAID IT? WHO DID IT? 5.1
JOHN MAYNARD KEYNES: THE GENERAL THEORY

John Maynard Keynes was born into economics. His father, John Neville Keynes, was a lecturer in economics and logic at Cambridge University. John Maynard Keynes began his own studies at Cambridge in mathematics and philosophy. However, his abilities so impressed Alfred Marshall that the distinguished teacher urged him to concentrate on economics. In 1908, after Keynes had finished his studies and done a brief stint in the civil service, Marshall offered him a lectureship in economics at Cambridge; Keynes accepted.

Keynes is best remembered for his 1936 work, *The General Theory of Employment, Interest, and Money*, a book that many still see as the foundation of what is today called macroeconomics. Although this was by no means Keynes's first major work, it was the basis for his reputation as the outstanding economist of his generation. Its major features are a bold theory based on broad macroeconomic aggregates and a strong argument for activist and interventionist policies.

Keynes was interested in more than economics. He was an honored member not only of Britain's academic upper class, but also of the nation's highest financial, political, diplomatic, administrative, and even artistic circles. He had close ties to the colorful "Bloomsbury set" of London's literary world. He was a friend of Virginia Woolf, E. M. Forster, and Lytton Strachey, and in 1925 he married ballerina Lydia Lopokovia. He was a dazzling success at whatever he turned his hand to, from mountain climbing to financial speculation. As a speculator, he made a huge fortune for himself, and as bursar of Kings College, he built an endowment of 30,000 pounds into one of over 380,000 pounds.

In *The General Theory*, Keynes wrote:

> *The idea of economists and political philosophers, both when they are right and when they are wrong, are more powerful than is commonly understood. Indeed the world is ruled by little else. Practical men, who believe themselves to be quite exempt from any intellectual influences, are usually the slaves of some defunct economist. Madmen in authority, who hear voices in the air, are distilling their frenzy from some academic scribbler of a few years back. . . . There are not many who are influenced by new theories after they are twenty-five or thirty years of age, so that the ideas which civil servants and politicians and even agitators apply to current events are not likely to be the newest.*

Was Keynes issuing a warning here? Whether or not he had any such thing in mind, his words are ironic because he himself has become one of those economists whose ideas remain influential long after they were first articulated.

is .75, you will tend to increase your spending by $750 if your income goes up by $1,000.

Disposable income

Income minus taxes.

This "psychological law" regarding consumption needs a few qualifications if it is to be stated exactly. First, in place of "income," we really should say **disposable income.** That means the amount of income left after taxes. If a person in one state earns $40,000 and pays $5,000 in taxes, while a person in another state earns $50,000 and pays taxes of $15,000, both would have the same disposable income of $35,000. Other things being equal, we would expect them to spend the same amount on consumption.

Second, the relationship between consumption and disposable income is properly stated in real terms. If both prices and nominal disposable income rise in exact proportion, there is no change in real income, so we would expect no change in real consumption expenditure, other things being equal.

Third, the marginal propensity to consume is not equal to the average obtained by dividing total consumption by total income. Instead, there is a minimum level of consumption that people would like to maintain even if their income were zero. Keynes called this "autonomous consumption." Intuitively, you can think of the case of a college student who has no income but maintains a minimum level of consumption by borrowing against future income, or a retired person who has no income but maintains a minimum level of consumption by drawing on past saving. The appendix to this chapter states the relationship between consumption spending and income in mathematical terms, taking into account both autonomous consumption and the marginal propensity to consume.

Although income is the principal factor that determines consumption spending, there are certain other factors that also can have an effect. Among them are:

- Changes in net taxes (either taxes paid or transfer payments received), which act by changing the amount of disposable income associated with a given total income.
- Changes in consumer wealth, that is, the accumulated value of assets a person owns, considered apart from current income. One very important example concerns the value of housing, since a home is the biggest asset for many households. In a period when housing prices rise more rapidly than income, as happened in the United States in the early 2000s, consumer spending rises more in proportion to income than it otherwise would.
- Interest rates. If interest rates fall, people can borrow more cheaply, and may buy more goods and services on credit. Also, the amount they have to pay in interest on credit cards, mortgages, and other debt decreases, leaving more to buy consumer goods.
- Consumer confidence. In periods when consumers feel secure about their jobs and expect their incomes to rise in line with general prosperity, they tend

to spend more for any given level of income. In times of pessimism and insecurity, people tend to be cautious and increase their saving as protection against the expected rainy day.

Planned Investment

The second component of planned expenditure is planned investment. It depends on two principal factors.

First, planned investment depends on interest rates (more specifically, on real interest rates, that is, interest rates adjusted for inflation, as explained in Chapter 4). This is easiest to understand in the case of a business that needs to borrow in order to undertake an investment. Suppose you run a construction business, and you are thinking about improving the productivity of your workers by buying a new backhoe, which costs $50,000. Your banker is willing to lend you the money, but you will have to pay 6 percent per year interest, equivalent to $250 per month on the loan of $50,000. If the bank charged 12 percent interest, your monthly interest payments would rise to $500, and you would be less likely to buy the new machine. If the interest rate was just 3 percent, monthly interest payments would be only $125, and you would be more likely to make the investment.

Although it is not so obvious, interest rates also play a role in investment decisions for a company that plans to finance investment from accumulated profits. Suppose that as a result of good profits in the previous year, your construction company had put aside $100,000 in cash. You would not then have to borrow from the bank to buy the backhoe. However, using half of your cash reserves to buy the backhoe still has an opportunity cost that depends on interest rates. For example, if the rate of interest on government bonds is 6 percent, your company could earn $250 per month by using $50,000 of your cash reserves to buy bonds instead of buying the backhoe.5 That is an opportunity cost. If the interest rate were 12 percent per year, your monthly income from the bonds would be $500—a greater opportunity cost—and you would be more tempted to buy the bonds instead of the backhoe.

Interest rates influence investment decisions by consumers as well as business. Residential construction accounts for about a third of all private fixed investment in the United States. When mortgage interest rates are low, as they were in the early 2000s, housing construction booms.

The importance of interest rates for investment spending is one of the reasons that we will spend several chapters in this book talking about banking, financial markets, and related topics.

Interest rates are not the only factor influencing investment decisions. The psychological factor of *business confidence* is also important. By this, we mean the whole complex of expectations and hopes on which firms make their plans for the future. If you expect a boom in the housing market in your area, your construction company is more likely than otherwise to buy that backhoe. If you expect doom and gloom ahead, you'll play it safe by buying the government bonds. Keynes referred to business confidence using the colorful term "animal spirits." In doing so, he wanted to emphasize the fact that business confidence can change quickly for reasons that are hard for economists to measure exactly.

On a global scale, the decision of how much to invest in a given country depends on the country's *investment climate.* This term is used to refer to an entire range of conditions that lead businesses to expect a reliable or questionable return on investments they make. Among the conditions that make up a country's investment climate are its tax laws, the amount of "red tape" imposed by the country's bureaucracy, the likelihood that profits will be drained away by criminal gangs or corrupt officials, and the stability of macroeconomic conditions. In countries where the investment climate is good, domestic firms are willing to put profits into expansion of their operations, and international firms are willing to bring in new capital and know-how. In countries where the investment climate is bad, domestic firms send their profits abroad for safekeeping rather than investing them at home, and global business stays away. Sometimes a change of government can make an improvement in investment climate that leads to a prolonged period of prosperity. The countries of Eastern and Central Europe that changed from Communist central planning to Western market economies in the 1990s are a good example.

Government Purchases

Exogenous

Term applied to any variable that is determined by noneconomic considerations, or by economic considerations that lie outside the scope of a given model.

Endogenous

Term applied to any variable that is determined by other variables included in an economic model.

Government purchases are considered to be **exogenous** in most simple macroeconomic models, including the one outlined in the appendix to this chapter. This means that they are determined by politics or other considerations that lie outside the model rather than by any variables that are included in the model. Transfer payments and tax revenues, on the other hand, are **endogenous**, in that they depend on on the level of real GDP, a variable that is included in the model. During the expansion phase of the business cycle, tax revenues rise and transfer payments, especially for unemployment benefits, fall. During a recession, tax collections fall and transfer payments rise.

Chapter 11 will take a closer look at the determination of government purchases and net taxes.

Net Exports

The variable *net exports* is endogenous because it also depends on real GDP. As real GDP increases, both consumers and businesses spend some of their increased income on imported goods. For this reason, net exports tend to fall, and a country's trade deficit tends to rise during the expansion phase of the business cycle.

The exchange rate of a country's currency relative to the currencies of its trading partners is another factor that affects net exports. For example, during the early 2000s, the U.S. dollar weakened relative to the euro, the currency used by the country's major European trading partners. As the dollar weakened, it became easier for U.S. firms to sell their exports in Europe, and, at the same time, imports from Europe became more expensive for U.S. buyers. Consequently, net exports to Europe strengthened. Exchange rates, in turn, are influenced by many factors, including changes in real GDP, inflation, and interest rates. The complex interaction between net exports and other economic variables will be explored in several coming chapters.

EQUILIBRIUM IN THE CIRCULAR FLOW

In Chapter 2, we introduced the concept of market equilibrium. The market for any single good, say chicken, is said to be in equilibrium when the amount buyers plan to purchase equals the amount that producers supply for sale. When the market for chicken is in equilibrium, there will be no tendency for accumulation or decrease of inventories and no immediate pressure for market participants to change their plans.

The idea of equilibrium as a situation in which there is no unplanned change in inventories can be extended to the circular flow of income and expenditure. To say that total planned expenditures (consumption plus planned investment plus government purchases plus net exports) equal GDP is the same as to say that total planned purchases will equal total production. In that case there will be no unplanned inventory change for the economy as a whole. If something happens to increase total planned expenditures, the equilibrium will be disrupted. Let's see how this process works out as the economy expands and contracts over the business cycle.

An Expansion of Planned Expenditure

Suppose that the circular flow is initially in equilibrium with total planned expenditure exactly equal to GDP. Since goods are being produced at just the rate they are being sold, the level of inventories remains constant from one month to the next. Now suppose that something happens to disturb this equilibrium. For example, suppose that development of new energy-efficient technologies inspires an upturn in investment expenditure as firms replace obsolete, energy-wasting equipment.

As equipment makers increase their output of goods to satisfy the increased investment demand, they will take on more workers. The wage component of national income will increase. Profits of equipment makers are also likely to increase, further adding to the expansion of national income.

From our earlier discussion, we know that when incomes rise, households will increase their consumption expenditure. So far there has been no change in the output of consumer goods, so consumption expenditure begins to increase, the first effect will be an unplanned decrease in inventories. Only then, when makers of consumer goods see inventories falling, will they modify their production plans to meet the new demand. As they do so, they, too, will need to hire new workers, and incomes will rise further.

In this way, the original economic stimulus, which began in the industrial equipment sector, spreads through the economy. GDP and domestic income continue to rise, but not without limit. Because, according to the principle of the marginal propensity to consume people spend only a part of any increase in income on consumer goods, each round of the cycle of more-production-more-income-more-spending is smaller than the previous one. Before long, GDP reaches a new equilibrium where production and planned expenditure balance, and there are no further unplanned changes in inventories.

Recall that the whole process began with an assumed increase in planned investment. By the time the new equilibrium is reached, the total change in GDP will be greater than the original increase in planned investment because it will also include production of additional consumer goods. The principle that an initial change in planned expenditure changes equilibrium GDP by a greater amount is known as the multiplier effect. The appendix to this chapter explains the multiplier effect in more detail.

A Contraction of Planned Expenditure

The same process operates in reverse if equilibrium is disturbed by a decrease in some category of planned expenditure. For example, suppose a crisis in the Mexican economy reduces U.S. exports to that country. The first effect will be that U.S. makers of export goods will find inventories rising because Mexican importers are not buying as much as they had planned before the crisis. To bring inventories in line with reduced sales, U.S. makers of export goods cut their output. Workers are laid off or work shorter hours, and their incomes fall. As a result, they cut back on consumption expenditures, following the principle of the marginal propensity to consume. When this happens, makers of consumer goods also find that their inventories unexpectedly increase. They, too, cut back on output, and incomes of their workers fall.

As this process continues, GDP and domestic income decrease. They do not decrease without limit, however. Before long a new equilibrium is reached. In the new equilibrium, real GDP will have decreased by a greater amount than the original change in exports. This is an example of the multiplier effect operating in reverse.

The Multiplier Effect and the Business Cycle

The **multiplier effect** was one of the key ideas in Keynes' *General Theory.* Coming at the height of the Great Depression, the multiplier effect was immediately seized on as an explanation for the business cycle.

Multiplier effect

The tendency of a given exogenous change in planned expenditure to increase equilibrium GDP by a greater amount.

In a simplified, popularized form, the Keynesian explanation of the Great Depression went something like this: During the 1920s, the U.S. economy entered a boom due to the multiplier effect of huge investment expenditures, especially expansion of automobile production and road building. Then, in 1929, came the Black Friday stock market crash. The crash destroyed business confidence, and investment fell again. This time the multiplier effect operated in reverse to produce the Great Depression.

At the same time the multiplier effect seemed to give an explanation of the causes of the Great Depression, it also seemed to suggest a cure. What if the government increased its purchases of goods and services by enough to offset the drop in private investment? Wouldn't this send equilibrium GDP back to its original level? This reasoning gave rise to various attempts to spend the country back to prosperity, for example, by hiring thousands of unemployed workers for service in national parks.

Modern macroeconomics makes a place for the multiplier effect and recognizes that there is an element of truth in the simple Keynesian view of the business cycle. However, the simple multiplier theory is seriously incomplete. One shortcoming concerns how prices change over the business cycle. When producers respond to an unexpected decrease in inventories, do they increase real output without changing prices, do they raise prices to take advantage of unexpectedly strong demand, or do they do a little of both? Another problem is that the simple multiplier theory does not consider capacity constraints related to labor inputs, capital, and technology. Does real output respond in the same way to a change in planned expenditure when the economy is operating above its natural level of real output as below it? Still another limitation is that the theory pays too little attention to the role of money and the financial sector. Later chapters will deal with all of these issues in order to give a more complete picture.

SUMMARY

1. **How are households and firms linked by incomes and expenditures?** In order to produce goods and services, firms pay wages and salaries to obtain labor inputs, interest to obtain capital, and rents and royalties to obtain natural resources. If sales exceed costs, firms earn profits. The sum of wages, salaries, interest, rents, royalties, and profits constitute domestic income.
2. **How is expenditure divided into consumption, investment, government purchases, and net exports?** The largest part of domestic income is used to purchase consumer goods and services. Some also is used to buy newly produced capital goods or add to inventories (investment), to pay for goods and services purchased by government, or to buy imported goods. Some expenditure is also made by foreign buyers. The term *net exports* refers to exports minus imports.
3. **What are the relationships between injections and leakages in the circular flow?** Saving, net taxes (tax revenues minus transfer payments), and imports are leakages from the circular flow.

Investment, government purchases, and exports are injections. The total of leakages must always equal the total of injections, but the individual pairs (saving and investment, net taxes and government purchases, imports and exports) do not need to balance. Any imbalance in the individual pairs is balanced by flows of funds through capital markets.

4. **Why is some investment planned and other unplanned?** *Planned investment* means fixed investment (purchases of newly produced capital goods) plus *planned inventory investment* (changes in inventory made on purpose as part of a business plan). In addition, inventories may change unexpectedly in ways not called for by firms' business plans. These changes are called *unplanned inventory investment.*

5. **How can the concept of equilibrium be applied to the circular flow of income and expenditure?** The *circular flow of income and product* is in equilibrium when total planned expenditure equals GDP. If *planned expenditure* exceeds GDP, so that more goods and services are being bought than are being produced, there will be unplanned decreases in inventories. In reaction, firms will increase output and GDP will tend to rise. If total planned expenditure falls short of GDP, there will be unplanned increases in inventories. In response, firms will tend to decrease their output and GDP will fall.

6. **What is the multiplier effect and how is it related to the business cycle?** According to the multiplier effect, a given change in one type of expenditure (say, planned investment) will produce a larger change in equilibrium GDP. The multiplier effect helps explain how relatively small disturbances in expenditure can cause relatively larger changes in GDP over the course of the business cycle.

KEY TERMS

Circular flow of income and product
Consumption
Investment
Fixed investment
Inventory investment
Government purchases of goods and services
Government expenditures
Transfer payments
Tax revenues
Net taxes
Net exports
Injections
Leakages
Saving
Planned inventory investment
Unplanned inventory investment
Planned investment
Planned expenditure
Marginal propensity to consume
Disposable income
Exogenous
Endogenous
Multiplier effect

PROBLEMS AND TOPICS FOR DISCUSSION

1. **Your personal expenditures.** What was your income last month (or last year) from all current resources, including wages and salaries plus any interest earned or other investment income? Do not count money that you received as transfer payments, such as government benefits, gifts from family, scholarship grants, and so on. How much was your saving? Did you add to your savings or draw down on past savings? How much did you spend on consumer goods or services? Of your spending, approximately how much do you think was spent on imported goods or services purchased while on foreign travel? Identify where the answer to each of these questions appears in the circular flow diagram, Figure 5.1.

2. **Planned versus unplanned inventory changes.** Suppose your school bookstore manager learns

from the admissions office that enrollment of students will rise by 10 percent next year. What planned inventory investments would the bookstore manager make? Suppose that a storm delays the departure of 100 students from another university who have visited your campus for a hockey game. While waiting for their buses to leave, they decide to browse your school bookstore and buy some items that catch their eye. How would this affect the store's inventories?

3. **Injections and leakages in the Russian economy.** In recent years, Russia has benefited from high world prices for the large amount of oil it produces for export. As a result, Russia has had positive net exports. Because oil is partly state owned and, where privately owned, heavily taxed, government tax revenues have increased so that the Russian government budget is in surplus. How would these differences between the Russian and U.S. economies affect the direction of the arrows in the circular flow diagram of Figure 5.1? Explain any changes that would need to be made.

4. **Unplanned inventory change and disequilibrium.** Suppose that you read in the news that inventories in retail stores fell last month, to the surprise of analysts. Would interpret this as a sign of equilibrium or disequilibrium in the circular flow? Which do you think would be more likely in the coming months, an increase or a decrease in GDP? Why?

5. **Adjustment to change in planned expenditure.** Starting from a state of equilibrium, trace the effects of each of the following. What happens to inventories? How do firms react? What happens to incomes? To consumption expenditure? To GDP?

   a. Business managers, anticipating future profit opportunities in consumer electronics, increase orders for production equipment in order to prepare for the expected increase in demand.

   b. The federal government reduces income tax rates.

   c. Good harvests in Africa reduce the demand for exports of U.S. farm products.

CASE FOR DISCUSSION

Excerpts from the Annual Report of the President's Council of Economic Advisers, 2007

The expansion of the U.S economy continued for the fifth consecutive year in 2006. Economic growth was strong, with real gross domestic product (GDP) growing at 3.4 percent during the four quarters of 2006.

Consumer spending sustained its strong growth during the four quarters of 2006 (rising 3.7 percent in real terms), continuing its 15-year pattern of rising faster than disposable income. As a result, the personal saving rate fell to a negative 1.0 percent for the year as a whole—its lowest annual level during the post-World War II era. Corporate net saving rose to 3.8 percent of gross domestic income (GDI) during the first three quarters of 2006, its highest level since the 1960s.

During 2006, real business investment in equipment and software grew 5 percent, slower than the 7 percent average pace during the 3 previous years. Its fastest-growing components included computers, as well as machinery in the agricultural and service sectors. Investment in mining and oil field machinery was also strong, likely in response to elevated crude oil prices and to the need to replace Gulf of Mexico facilities damaged by the 2005 hurricanes.

Inventory investment was fairly steady during 2006, and had only a minor influence on quarter-to-quarter fluctuations. Real nonfarm inventories grew at an average $44 billion annual pace during 2006, a 3.0 percent rate of growth that is roughly in line with the pace of real GDP growth over the same period

Real Federal [purchases of goods and services] grew 2.4 percent during 2006. This was the third consecutive year of growth at roughly 2 percent. Defense spending accounted for all of the increase during the four-quarter period, while non-defense purchases fell. Nominal Federal revenues grew 15 percent in FY 2005 and 12 percent in FY 2006. These rapid growth rates exceeded growth in outlays and GDP as a whole, and the U.S. fiscal deficit as a share of GDP shrank from 3.6 percent in FY 2004 to 2.6 percent in FY 2005 to 1.9 percent in FY 2006.

The current account deficit (the excess of imports and income flows to foreigners over exports and foreign income of Americans) jumped to 7.0 percent of GDP in the fourth quarter of 2005, partly due to petroleum imports that replaced lost Gulf of Mexico production. The current account deficit then retraced some of its earlier increase in the first three quarters of 2006, when oil imports declined.

QUESTIONS

The following questions may be answered on the basis of information in the main text of the chapter. However, if you have read the appendix, use what you learned there to give additional detail to your answers.

1. Why is growth of consumer spending considered a positive factor for expansion of GDP, even when personal saving is falling to a negative level? Are the long-term and short-term effects of a negative personal saving rate both favorable to economic growth? Discussed, based on concepts from this chapter and the preceding one.
2. According to the report, inventories grew at about the same rate as the economy as a whole. Taken in isolation from other things going on in the macroeconomy, would you expect this behavior of inventories to bias the economy toward faster expansion in the near future, bias it toward a slowdown in the near future, or to be roughly neutral in its effect?
3. According to the report, exports grew faster than imports during the first part of the year. Would you expect this to have a positive or a negative effect on future economic growth? Why?
4. The government budget remained in deficit during 2006. What information given here helps understand how the deficit was financed?

END NOTES

1. Economists use the term *households* to refer to families who live together and make economic decisions together about issues of work and spending, as well as to individuals living alone who make such decisions independently.
2. The term *trade deficit* as popularly used does not always correspond exactly to our term *net exports*. The next chapter will discuss concepts related to imports, exports, and the balance of payments in more detail.
3. The economy's financial sector, including banks, securities markets, insurance companies, and other institutions will be discussed in more detail in Chapter 7.
4. John Maynard Keynes, *The General Theory of Employment, Interest, and Money* (New York: Harcourt, Brace and World, 1936), 96.
5. To understand this example, it is important to remember that buying the backhoe is a purchase of newly produced capital goods, that is, part of the fixed investment component of planned expenditure. Buying the government bond is a financial investment, a purchase of the right to receive future payments from the government. The bonds are not newly produced capital goods and do not count as part of GDP.

Appendix to Chapter 5:
THE PLANNED EXPENDITURE MODEL

The Elements of Planned Expenditure

The object of this appendix is to present a simple graphical and mathematical model that shows how the equilibrium level of planned expenditure and GDP is determined. Our starting point is the planned expenditure equation given in the chapter:

$$E_p = C + I_p + G + (E_x - I_m)$$

Our next step is to look one by one at the main components of planned expenditure. In doing so, we will in each case distinguish between two types of expenditures: Those that are a function of the level of income, and those that are not. The former can be referred to as *income-dependent* components of planned expenditure and the latter as *autonomous* components.

Consumption. The level of consumption, other things being equal, depends on the level of disposable income, that is, on the level of gross domestic income minus net taxes. In equation form

$$C = \alpha + \beta(Q - T)$$

In this equation, which is known as the *consumption function,* α represents *autonomous consumption* (that is, the part of consumption that does not depend on the level of income), β the marginal propensity to consume, and Q the level of real GDP, which, as we know, is equal to the level of domestic income.

Many kinds of taxes, for example, income and profits taxes, are income-dependent. Other taxes, known as *autonomous net taxes,* do not depend on the level of income, for example, taxes based on the value of real estate. Taking both kinds of taxes into account, the level of net taxes, T, can be represented by the following equation:

$$T = t_0 + t_1 \times Q$$

where t_0 represents autonomous net taxes and t_1 represents the share of each added dollar of real GDP that goes to net taxes. This variable is called the *marginal tax rate.*

If the tax equation is substituted into the consumption function, the latter can be restated in terms of GDP rather than in terms of disposable income:

$$C = a + b_Q$$

The parameter a, which is equal to $\alpha - \beta t_0$, is the level of autonomous consumption corresponding to zero real GDP, and the parameter b, which is equal to $\beta(1 - t_1)$ could be called the marginal propensity to consume from GDP.

Investment. As explained earlier, the main factors that determine planned investment are interest rates, which determine the cost of financing purchases of inventories and capital goods, and business confidence. For accuracy, our model must use real interest rates. (As explained in Chapter 4, The real interest rate is the nominal interest rate minus the rate of inflation. Using r to represent the real interest rate, the level of planned investment can be stated as

$$I_p = i_0 - i_1 \times r$$

where i_0 stands for business confidence and i1 represents the sensitivity of planned investment to the real interest rate. Because it is not a represented in our model as a function of the level of GDP, planned investment is considered a type of autonomous expenditure.

Government purchases and net exports. In simple macroeconomic models, government purchases are considered to be *exogenous,* that is, not determined by variables included in the model. Because government purchases are not a function of GDP, they are considered a form of autonomous expenditure.

Net exports are an endogenous variable determined in part by exchange rates and in part by the level of GDP. As mentioned earlier in the chapter, when GDP rises, consumers and businesses tend to spend more on imports. This affects the value of the parameter b, which we have called the marginal propensity to consume from GDP. In an economy open to international trade, this variable should be interpreted as referring to the consumption of domestically produced consumer goods. As a result, the value of b in an open economy is somewhat less than it would be in a closed economy, that is, one with no international trade. Export demand is not dependent on domestic GDP, so it is treated as a type of autonomous expenditure.

Putting consumption, planned investment, and government purchases together, the level of planned expenditure can be represented by the equation

$$E_p = A + bQ$$

where A stands for *autonomous expenditure,* that is, the total of autonomous consumption, planned investment, government purchases, and the autonomous component of net exports, and the parameter b is the marginal propensity to consume from GDP. The value of A must be greater than zero, and the value of b between zero and 1.

The Equilibrium Level of Real Output

As explained earlier in the chapter, the circular flow as a whole is in equilibrium when planned expenditure equals real output, that is, $E_p = Q$. Figure 5A.1 provides a graphical representation of the concept of equilibrium.

Because autonomous expenditure is positive and the value of the marginal propensity to consume from GDP is between zero and 1, the planned expenditure schedule $E_p = A + bQ$ is a line with a positive intercept and a slope less than 1. (For the diagram, the equation $E_p = 200 + .5Q$ is used.) Equilibrium occurs where this schedule intersects the line $E_p = Q$, which represents the equilibrium condition.

For any level of real output greater than the equilibrium level, planned expenditure is less than real output. That means that consumers, investors, government and exporters are plan-

FIGURE 5A.1 EQUILIBRIUM OF PLANNED EXPENDITURE AND REAL OUTPUT IN THE CIRCULAR FLOW

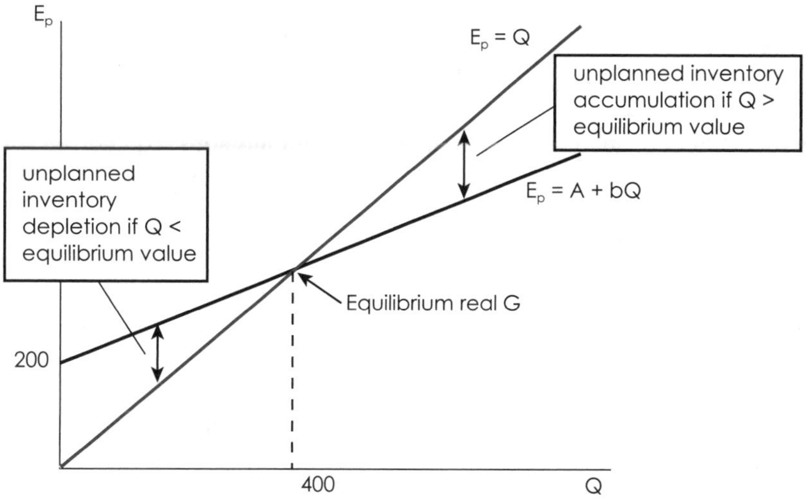

ning to buy a smaller volume of goods and services than is being produced. Goods that are produced but not purchased do not vanish into thin air. Instead, they accumulate in inventory, even though this was not part of the producers' original business plans. We can see, then, that whenever real output is greater than the equilibrium level, there must be unplanned inventory accumulation. Businesses tend to react to unplanned inventory accumulation by reducing output. When they do so, real GDP will move downward toward its equilibrium level.

Similarly, when real output is below its equilibrium level, total planned expenditure will exceed production. If more goods are being purchased than are being produced, there will be an unplanned depletion of inventories. To correct the unplanned depletion of inventories, businesses will tend to increase their level of output, and real GDP will move upward toward its equilibrium level.

We can express the same equilibrium condition in algebraic terms by substituting the planned expenditure equation $E_p = A + bQ$ into the equilibrium condition $E_p = Q$. The result is an equation for the equilibrium level of GDP:

$$Q = A \times 1/(1 - b)$$

The Multiplier Effect

The term $1/(1 - b)$ is known as the *expenditure multiplier,* because a \$1 increase in autonomous expenditure will cause equilibrium real GDP to increase by \$1 times the multiplier. For example, in Figure 5A.1, autonomous expenditure is 200 and the marginal propensity to consume from GDP is 0.5, so equilibrium GDP is 400. The value of the expenditure multiplier is 2, so a $1 increase in autonomous consumption would produce a $2 increase in the equilibrium level of real GDP.

A change for any reason in any component of autonomous expenditure can cause a change in the equilibrium level of real output. As an example, Figure 5A.2 considers the effect of a change in planned investment resulting from a change in the real interest rate. In that figure, an increase in the interest rate r from r_0 to a higher value of r_1 reduces the planned investment component of autonomous expenditure by 50 units. Graphically, this is shown as a downward shift of the planned expenditure schedule to a position where the vertical intercept is 150 rather than 200. Through the operation of the multiplier effect, the equilibrium value of real output is reduced from 400 to 300.

The value of 2 given for the expenditure multiplier in our example is arbitrary. In practice, the value of the expenditure multiplier for a given economy depends on several considerations. Other things being equal:

- The greater the marginal propensity to consume (from disposable income), the greater the multiplier.
- The greater the marginal tax rate, the lower the expenditure multiplier. The reason is that when the marginal tax rate is high, a given change in GDP will result in a smaller change in disposable income.
- The greater the share of consumption devoted to imported goods, the less the expenditure multiplier. As a result, we expect the multiplier effect to be stronger for large, relatively closed economies where most consumer goods are domestically produced than for small, open economies where more consumer goods are imported.

FIGURE 5A.2 EFFECT OF AN INCREASE IN INTEREST RATES

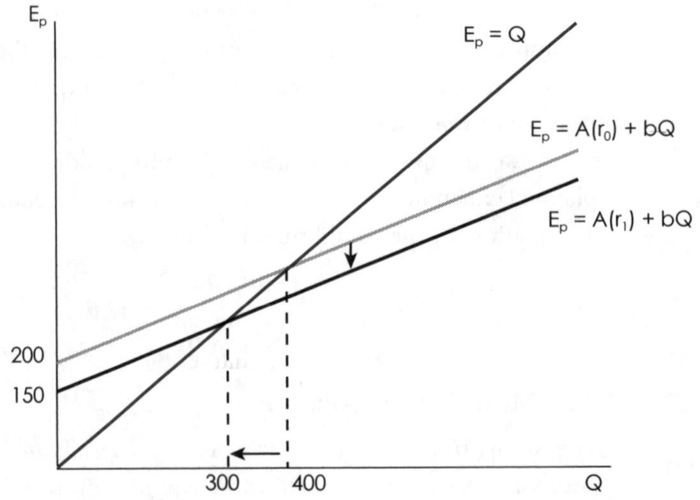

CHAPTER 6

Measuring Economic Activity

After reading this chapter, you will understand:

1. How gross domestic product is officially defined and measured
2. How the measurement of domestic income differs from the measurement of gross domestic product
3. The major types of international transactions
4. How changes in the average level of prices are measured
5. The limitations of official economic statistics

Before reading this chapter, make sure you know the meaning of:

1. Real and nominal values
2. Indexation
3. Transfer payments
4. Domestic income and product

In the internet age, government reports of GDP and related data are available, and acted on, instantly throughout the world. For example, in January 2007, when the Commerce Department reported that the U.S. trade deficit rose by more than expected in the preceding quarter, the euro immediately rose in value relative to the dollar. An index of economic expectations in Germany moved upward. Evidently, German investors thought that U.S. demand for Audis and BMWs would remain strong. But just having instant access to the numbers is not enough. To use the latest data intelligently, you must know what they mean and where they come from. That means not only knowing the theoretical relationships among GDP components, as discussed in the previous chapter, but also how they are actually measured. That is the subject of this chapter.

National income accounts

A set of official government statistics on aggregate economic activity.

Together, the data on aggregate economic activity published by the government are known as the **national income accounts.** The economists and statisticians whose job it is to make these measurements for the U.S. economy are widely held to be the best such team in the world. Yet, as this chapter will show, they face many problems. There are technical problems posed by sampling errors and survey methods. There are conceptual problems that arise when real-world institutions do not match the theoretical categories of economic models. Finally, there are problems of timeliness. Government decision-makers must sometimes work with preliminary data. For example, in January, 2007, the Commerce Department had estimated fourth-quarter, 2006, GDP growth at a strong 3.5 percent. However, after data released in February showed a higher than expected trade deficit for the quarter, analysts predicted that the GDP figure would have to be revised downward by at least .3 percentage points. The knowledge that early data are often revised makes it necessary to balance the risks of acting on an inaccurate report against those of delaying action until more information is available.

THE NATIONAL INCOME ACCOUNTS IN NOMINAL TERMS

We begin with an examination of the national income accounts in nominal terms—that is, in terms of the prices at which goods and services are actually sold. Nominal measures do not tell the whole story because they are not adjusted to reflect the effects of inflation, but they provide a starting point. Data are first collected in nominal form, and only after a set of nominal accounts have been assembled can the process of adjusting for price changes begin.

Gross Domestic Product

Gross domestic product (GDP)

The value at current market prices of all final goods and services produced annually in a given country.

Final goods and services

Goods and services that are sold to or ready for sale to parties that will use them for consumption, investment, government purchases, or export.

The most widely publicized number in the national income accounts is gross domestic product. We have mentioned this important term before; now we can give it a formal definition. **Gross domestic product (GDP)** is the value at current market prices (that is, the nominal value) of all final goods and services produced annually in a given country.

The term **final goods and services** is a key part of the definition of gross domestic product. GDP attempts to measure the sum of the economic contributions of each firm and industry without missing anything or counting anything twice. To do this, care must be taken to count only goods sold to *final users*—parties that will use them for domestic consumption, government purchases, investment, or export. *Intermediate goods*—those that are purchased for use as inputs in producing other goods or services—are excluded.

Table 6.1 shows why counting both final and intermediate goods would overstate total production. The table traces the process of producing a kitchen table with a

TABLE 6.1 VALUE ADDED AND THE USE OF FINAL PRODUCTS IN GDP

Final stage—manufacturing:		
Value of one table	$100	
Less value of lumber	−40	
Equals value added in manufacturing	60 →	$60
Next to final stage—sawmill:		
Value of lumber	$ 40	
Less value of logs	−15	
Equals value added at sawmill	25 →	25
Second to final stage—timber farming:		
Value of logs	$ 15	
Less value of fuel, equipment, etc.	−5	
Equals value added in timber farming	10 →	10
All previous stages:		
Value added in fuel, equipment, etc.	$ 5 →	5
Total value added		**$100**

This table shows why GDP must include only the value of final goods and services if it is to measure total production without double counting. The value of sales at each stage of production can be divided into the value added at that stage and the value of purchased inputs. The selling price of the final product (a $100 table, in this case) equals the sum of the values added at all stages of production.

Value added

The dollar value of an industry's sales less the value of intermediate goods purchased for use in production.

retail price of $100. The final stage of production takes place in a furniture factory, but the factory does not do $100 worth of work. Instead, it produces the table by taking $40 worth of lumber and adding $60 worth of inputs in the form of the labor of factory workers, capital in the form of woodworking machines, and other factors. The $40 worth of lumber is an intermediate good; the $60 contribution made by the manufacturer is the **value added** to the product at its final stage. (In practice, other intermediate goods, such as paint and fuel for heating the plant, are used in making the table. To simplify the example we assume that the table is made solely from lumber plus the manufacturer's effort.)

The second section of Table 6.1 shows the next-to-last stage of production: making the lumber. The sawmill buys $15 worth of logs, adds $25 worth of labor and capital, and produces lumber worth $40. The value added at the sawmill stage is thus $25.

Going still further back, we come to the stage at which the logs were produced. To produce $15 worth of logs, a forest products company bought $5 worth of fuel, equipment, and so on and added $10 in exchange for the effort involved in tending the trees and harvesting the logs. That is an additional $10 of value added.

Clearly, the process of making the table could be traced back indefinitely. The last section of the exhibit sums up the value added at all stages of production prior to timber farming—the fuel and equipment suppliers, their own suppliers, and so on. If production were traced back far enough, every penny could be attributed to the value added to the final product somewhere in the chain of production.

Now compare the first and last lines of the table. The value of the final goods turns out to be exactly equal to the sum of the values added at each stage of production. This is why only final goods are counted in GDP. Adding together the $100 value of the finished table, the $40 value of the lumber, the $15 value of the timber, and so on would far overstate the true rate of productive activity (the true total value added) in the economy.

The Expenditure Approach to Measuring GDP

In principle, GDP could be measured by adding together the value of each final good or service sold or by adding up the value added at each stage of production, as shown in Table 6.1. Instead of measuring domestic product directly, however, national income accountants make use of the equality of domestic product and total expenditure. It is easier to gather data on the total amount spent by households, investors, governments, and buyers of exports on final goods produced in the domestic economy than it is to stand at factory gates and count goods as they roll off assembly lines. This method of measuring GDP is known as the *expenditure approach*. Table 6.2 shows how it works, using 2006 data for the U.S. economy.

CONSUMPTION The first line of Table 6.2 gives total household consumption of both domestically produced and imported goods and services. The national income accounts divide consumption into three categories: durable goods, nondurable goods, and services. In principle, goods that do not wear out within a year, such as cars, furniture, and appliances, are durable, whereas goods that are used up in less than a year, such as soap, food, and gasoline, are nondurable. In practice, however, these categories are somewhat arbitrary. For example, all clothing is considered nondurable, whether the item is a pair of stockings that may last only a few weeks or a wool coat that may last many years. The remaining category—services—includes everything that is not in the form of a physical object when sold. Examples include haircuts, legal advice, financial services, and education.

All three components of consumption contain some items that do not pass through markets on their way to consumers. One such item is an estimate of the quantity of food produced and consumed on farms; another is an estimate of the rental value of owner-occupied homes. However, many non-market goods and services—for example, unpaid childcare and housework—are not captured in the national income accounts.

TABLE 6.2 NOMINAL GROSS DOMESTIC PRODUCT BY TYPE OF EXPENDITURE, 2006 (DOLLARS IN BILLIONS)

Personal consumption expenditure		$ 9,270.8
Durable goods	$ 1,071.3	
nondurable goods	2,716.0	
Services	5,483.6	
Plus gross private domestic investment		2,218.4
Fixed investment	2,165.0	
Change in private inventories	53.4	
Plus government purchases of goods and services		2,526.4
Federal	926.4	
State and local	1,600.0	
Plus net exports of goods and services		–761.8
Exports	1,466.2	
Less imports	2,228.0	
Equals gross domestic product (GDP)		$13,253.9
Less capital consumption allowance		–1,575.4
Equals net domestic product (NDP)		$11,678.5

Gross domestic product is estimated using the expenditure approach. This involves adding together the values of expenditures on newly produced final goods and services made by all economic units to get a measure of aggregate economic activity. Net domestic product is derived from gross domestic product by excluding the value of expenditures made to replace worn-out or obsolete capital equipment.

Source: *Bureau of Economic Analysis, News Release: Gross Domestic Product, Jan. 31, 2007, Table 3*

INVESTMENT The item termed *gross private domestic investment* is the sum of all purchases of newly produced capital goods (fixed investment) plus changes in business inventories (inventory investment). The fixed-investment component includes both business fixed investment—all new equipment and structures bought by firms—and the value of newly constructed residential housing. In the national income accounts, then, a homeowning household is treated like a small firm. When the house is bought, it is counted as an investment. Then, as we saw earlier, the firm's "product"—the rental value of its shelter services—is counted as part of consumption each year.

The gross private domestic investment item does not include investment in structures, software, and equipment that are made by federal, state, and local governments. These amounted to some $343 billion in 2004, adding about 17 percent to the total. From the point of view of short-run business cycle theory, it makes sense to treat government and private investment differently, since the motives for the investment are different. However, from the point of long-term growth theory, government investment, like private investment, adds to a country's stock of capital and increases future natural real GDP.

GOVERNMENT PURCHASES The item called "government purchases" in macroeconomic models is titled "Government Consumption Expenditures and Gross Investment" in the official national income accounts. As this formal term implies, the bulk of the government's contribution to GDP at the federal, state, and local levels is treated like consumption, in that the goods and factor services bought by government are considered to be "used up" as soon as they are purchased. As mentioned in the previous paragraph, about 17 percent of government purchases are investment-type expenditures. Whether consumption-like or investment-like, government purchases are valued at cost in the national income accounts. No attempt is made to measure the value added by government, because most government outputs—primary and secondary education, defense services, and police protection, to name a few—are financed by taxes and provided to the public without charge rather than sold. Transfer payments are not included in the expenditure approach to GDP, because they do not represent purchases of newly produced final goods and services.

NET EXPORTS The last item in the GDP account is *net exports*—exports minus imports. In calculating GDP, imports must be subtracted from exports to avoid double counting. Some of the goods bought by consumers, investors, and government and included in their expenditures are not produced in the domestic economy. For example, a consumer might buy a Japanese television set, an insurance company might buy Korean computers for use in its offices, and a city government might buy a Swedish-built police car. The figures for consumption, investment, and government purchases therefore overstate the final use of domestically produced goods and services to the extent that some of those goods and services were produced abroad. To correct for the overstatement in earlier lines in Table 6.2, imports are subtracted from exports at the bottom. Adding total consumption plus total investment plus total government purchases plus exports less imports yields the same sum as would be obtained by adding domestic consumption of domestically produced goods, domestic purchases of domestically produced capital goods, domestic government purchases of domestically produced goods, and total exports.

GROSS VERSUS NET DOMESTIC PRODUCT What makes gross domestic product "gross"? It is the fact that gross private domestic investment measures total additions to the nation's capital stock without adjusting for losses through wear and tear or obsolescence. For example, gross private domestic investment includes the value of new homes and factories built each year without subtracting the value of old homes and factories that are torn down. Gross private domestic investment minus an allowance for depreciation and obsolescence yields net private domestic investment, a measure of the actual net addition to the nation's capital stock each year. Only net investment adds to the capital stock, thereby helping to expand the economy's natural real output over time. The part of gross investment that covers depreciation and obsolescence is needed just to keep the capital stock from shrinking. Although depreciation and obsolescence are hard to measure accurately, national income accountants use an approximate measure called the capital consumption allowance. Gross domestic product minus the capital consumption allowance yields **net domestic product (NDP).**

Net domestic product (NDP)

Gross domestic product minus an allowance (called the *capital consumption allowance)* that represents the value of capital equipment used up in the production process.

The Income Approach to Measuring Aggregate Economic Activity

Previously, we looked at the economy in terms of a circular flow of income and product. In principle, aggregate economic activity could be measured by observing the flow at any point as it circulates. In practice, the national income accounts use two points of observation. First, as we have just seen, domestic product is measured by the expenditure approach, which is equivalent to observing the flow of aggregate economic activity at the point at which it enters product markets. Second, measurements are made of the flows of all kinds of income at the point at which they are received by households. This is known as the *income approach* to measuring aggregate economic activity. The result is shown in Table 6.3. Several items in that exhibit deserve comment.

Compensation of employees consists of wages and salaries plus certain supplements. The first supplement is employer contributions to social insurance (social security). As the social security tax law is written, employees are legally required to pay only half of the tax; employers must pay the other half. Because both halves contribute to employees' retirement benefits, however, both are counted as part of employee compensation. The supplements line also includes fringe benefits other than social insurance that employers pay for, such as health insurance, private pension plans, and some other minor forms of labor income.

Rental income of persons consists of all income in the form of rent and royalties received by property owners. *Net interest* includes interest income received by households less interest payments made by consumers.

Corporate profits encompass all income earned by the stockholders of corporations, regardless of whether they actually receive that income. Dividends are the part of corporate income that stockholders actually receive. Another part of corporate profits goes to pay taxes. Corporations keep a third part—undistributed corporate profits—for use in making investments. In measuring income, corporate profits are also adjusted for changes in inventory values and for capital consumption (depreciation). *Proprietors' income,* lumps together all forms of income earned by self-employed professionals and owners of unincorporated business. The final item includes certain items like business property taxes that are hard to categorize because

TABLE 6.3 NOMINAL DOMESTIC INCOME, 2006 (DOLLARS IN BILLIONS)

Compensation of employees		$7,493.1
Wages and salaries	$ 6,037.7	
Supplements	1,455.4	
Plus rental income of persons		76.5
Plus net interest		510.6
Plus corporate profits		1,653.3
Plus proprietors' income		1,014.8
Plus indirect business taxes, business transfers, etc.		995.3
Equals national income		11,743.6
Less receipts of factor income from rest of world		−671.9
Plus payments of factor income to rest of world		645.0
Equals domestic income		11,716.7

National and domestic income is measured using the income approach. This involves adding together the values of all forms of income earned by a country's residents. U.S. national income includes some income received in return for factors of production used abroad, and excludes payments to foreign residents for the use of factors owned by them but located in the United States. Domestic income is derived from national income by subtracting receipts of factor income from the rest of the world and adding factor income paid to the rest of the world.

Source: Bureau of Economic Analysis, Press Release: Gross Domestic Product, Jan. 31, 2007, Table 9

they are expenses to firms, but are not paid out as income to individuals. They are added to the various forms of income just discussed.

National income

The total income earned by a country's residents, including wages, rents, interest payments, and profits.

The total of these items is **national income**, the total income received by a country's residents. The term *national* is used because the income items listed in the table are those earned by a country's residents, regardless of whether their productive activities take place in the home country or another country. For example, corporate profits shown in the table would include the profits earned by capital the Ford Motor Company has invested in the UK, but they would not include profits earned by Honda Motors that is invested in a plant in the United States. In contrast, gross and net domestic product are geographical concepts that measure activity that takes place on the territory of a country, regardless of who owns the factors of production involved. We can obtain a geographical measure of income, **domestic income**, by subtracting factor income received by U.S. residents from the rest of the world and adding factor income paid to foreign residents.[1]

RECONCILING THE INCOME AND EXPENDITURE APPROACHES In the official accounts, gross and net domestic product are measured by the expenditure approach using one set of data, and domestic and national income are measured by the income approach using a different set of data. No matter how carefully the work is done, there will be some errors and omissions; therefore the two sets of figures will not quite fit together. The difference between net domestic product and domestic income is called the *statistical discrepancy.* Most of the time this error is very small—well below 1 percent of GDP. Theoretical models treat domestic income and domestic product as equal by definition.

MEASURING INTERNATIONAL LINKAGES

The item "net exports" in the national income accounts gives a glimpse of the linkage between the domestic economy and the rest of the world. These ties have grown over time. In 1960, U.S. exports amounted to only 6 percent of GDP and imports to less than 5 percent. By 2006, exports had grown to 11 percent of a much larger GDP. Imports grew even more rapidly over the same period, reaching 17 percent of GDP. In view of the growing importance of the foreign sector, then, it is worth taking a closer look at the international ties of the U.S. economy.

Any discussion of an economy's balance of international payments is complicated by the fact that thousands of different kinds of international payments are made every day. Payments for the goods and services that are exported and imported come to mind first, but there are many others. Equally important are the long- and short-term loans made to finance imports and exports and the payments made in international markets in connection with purchases or sales of assets, such as securities or real estate. In addition, governments and private individuals make many kinds of transfer payments to residents of other countries, including outright gifts, pension payments, and official foreign aid. Finally, the U.S. Federal Reserve System and foreign central banks engage in many kinds of official transactions. Table 6.4 shows a simplified version of the accounts used to keep track of these international transactions for the United States.

The Current Account

Current account

The section of a country's international accounts that consists of imports and exports of goods and services and unilateral transfers.

The first section of the international accounts shown in Table 6.4 contains what are called **current account** transactions. These include imports and exports of goods and services, payments of factor income between countries, and international transfer payments. The main items in the current account are as follows:

MERCHANDISE IMPORTS AND EXPORTS Imports and exports of merchandise (goods) are the most widely publicized items in the international accounts. During much of the nineteenth century the United States was a net importer of merchandise.

Merchandise balance

The value of a country's merchandise exports minus the value of its merchandise imports.

From 1894 to 1970 it was a net exporter. Since 1970 it has again become largely a net importer. Table 6.4 shows a negative **merchandise balance.** The negative number indicates net merchandise imports.

SERVICES In addition to trade in merchandise, the United States and other countries carry on a large trade in services. Travel expenditures, airline passenger fares, and other transportation services account for somewhat more than half of these services. Other services include insurance, royalties, and license fees. Certain transactions related to sales of military equipment are included under the heading of services. As the table shows, the United States was a net exporter of services in 2006.

FACTOR INCOME Earlier, in drawing the distinction between domestic and national product, we noted that U.S. residents receive substantial flows of factor income from U.S. assets located abroad. These are analogous to exports, and enter the current account with a positive sign. At the same time, payments of factor income are made to residents of other countries from foreign-owned assets located in the United States. These are analogous to imports, and enter the current account with a negative sign. The United States received more income from abroad than it paid in 2006.

TRANSFERS The final item on the current account consists of net transfer receipts. This typically is a negative item in the U.S. international accounts, because transfers to other countries exceed transfers received from them. This item takes into account both government transfers, such as foreign aid and social security payments to retired workers living abroad, and private transfers, such as private famine relief and church missions.

Current account balance

The value of a country's exports of goods and services minus the value of its imports of goods and services plus its net transfer receipts from foreign sources.

CURRENT ACCOUNT BALANCE When merchandise trade, services, factor income, and net transfers are combined, the result is the country's **current account balance.** Table 6.4 shows a current account deficit for the United States for 2006. The last year in which the country experienced a current account surplus was 1981.

Although the official name of this item is the current account balance, the term is not always used in news reports. Sometimes the term "balance of payments" is used and sometimes the term "balance of trade." To add to the confusion, the term "balance of trade" is sometimes used in news reports to refer to the merchandise balance. Setting aside certain methodological differences between the balance of payments accounts and the national income accounts, all in all, the current account balance is the closest thing to the item "net exports" that appears our macroeconomic models.

The Capital and Financial Account

Current account transactions are not the only ones that take place among residents of different countries. The international lending and borrowing and international sales and purchases of assets mentioned in an earlier chapter also account for an enormous

TABLE 6.4 U.S. INTERNATIONAL ACCOUNTS FOR 2006 (DOLLARS IN BILLIONS)

Current Account		
1. Merchandise balance		−835.9
2. Exports of goods	1,023.7	
3. Imports of goods	−1,859.6	
4. Services, net		70.7
5. Exports of services	413.1	
6. Imports of services	−342.4	
7. Net receipts of factor income		-7.3
8. Income receipts from abroad	622.0	
9. Income payments to the United States	−629.3	
10. Transfers, net		−84.1
11. Current account balance (lines 1 + 4 + 7 + 10)		−856.6
Capital and Financial Account		
12. Net change in U.S. assets abroad (– indicates increase in U.S. assets abroad, that is, a financial outflow)		−1,045.7
13. U.S. private assets	−1,053.3	
14. U.S. official reserve assets	2.3	
15. Other U.S. government assets	5.2	
16. Net change in foreign assets in the United States (+ indicates increase in foreign assets in the United States, that is, a financial inflow)		1,764.9
17. Foreign official assets	300.5	
18. Other foreign assets	1,464.4	
19. Capital account transactions, net		-3.9
20. Capital and financial account balance (lines 12 + 16 + 19)		715.3
21. Statistical discrepancy		141.4

This table gives details of U.S. international transactions for 2006. The first section shows current account transactions, consisting of imports and exports of goods and services, together with international flows of factor income and transfer payments. The second section shows capital and financial account transactions, consisting of international borrowing and lending, securities transactions, direct investment, and official reserve transactions. If all amounts were measured completely and accurately, the current account and financial account balances would be equal and opposite in sign. In practice, there is a statistical discrepancy indicating errors and omissions in measurement.

Source: U.S. Department of Commerce, Bureau of Economic Analysis, *U.S. International Transactions Press Release, March 14, 2007*

volume of daily transactions. A U.S. company, for example, might obtain a short-term loan from a London bank to finance the purchase of a shipload of beer for import to the United States. The Brazilian government might get a long-term loan from Citibank of New York to help finance a hydroelectric project. A U.S. millionaire might open an account in a Swiss bank. All of these transactions are recorded in the capital and financial account section of Table 6.4. In this book, we will use the shorter term "financial account" to refer to this section. Some writers, instead, use the term "capital account" as shorthand to refer to the entire capital and financial account.

Financial inflow

Purchases of domestic assets by foreign buyers and borrowing from foreign lenders ; also often called capital inflows.

Financial outflow

Purchases of foreign assets by domestic residents or loans by domestic lenders to foreign borrowers; also often called capital outflows.

Purchases of U.S. assets by foreigners and borrowing from foreign financial intermediaries by U.S. firms and individuals create flows of funds into the United States that are termed **financial inflows.** (Some writers use the term *capital inflows.*) Purchases of foreign assets by U.S. residents or loans by U.S. financial intermediaries to foreigners create flows of funds out of the United States that are termed **financial outflows.** (Some writers use the term *capital outflows.*)

Table 6.4 lists several types of capital and financial account transactions. Changes in U.S. private assets include direct investments (such as construction of foreign plants by U.S. firms) and purchases of foreign securities. Changes in U.S. official reserve assets include foreign currency and other foreign assets acquired by the Federal Reserve System and the U.S. Treasury. Changes in other U.S. government assets relate to short- and long-term credits and other assets by government agencies other than the Federal Reserve System and U.S. Treasury. Changes in official foreign assets in the United States involve purchases of U.S. government securities by foreign central banks. Direct investment in the United States and private purchases of U.S. securities by foreign buyers are included under the heading "other foreign assets in the United States." Finally, the "capital account" in the narrow sense in which the term is officially used, is a small item that refers to transactions in nonfinancial assets such as ownership of patents and copyrights, and also includes private and governmental debt forgiveness and defaults on debt.

Relationship of the Accounts

Financial account transactions are logically related to the current account surplus or deficit. If the United States runs a current account deficit, its earnings from the sales of exports will not be enough to pay for all of its imports. Additional funds for financing imports can be obtained through net financial inflows, that is, through U.S. borrowing from abroad that exceeds U.S. lending to foreigners or through sales of U.S. assets to foreigners that exceed purchases of assets abroad. This is the case for the U.S. international transactions shown in Table 6.4. On the other hand, a country with a current account surplus can use its extra import earnings to make net loans to foreign borrowers or net purchases of foreign assets. This would result in a negative balance on the financial account. Countries that are big exporters and have surpluses of funds to invest abroad are in this position. For example, in 2006, Russia and Japan had large net financial outflows.

In principle, the balances of the current and financial accounts should be equal and opposite in sign. If there is a current account surplus of $100 billion (entered with a plus sign in the accounts), there should be a net financial outflow of $100 billion (entered with a minus sign in the accounts). The reason for this symmetry is that the two account components taken together include all the sources and uses of the funds that change hands in international transactions. Every dollar used in international transactions must have a source; thus, when the sources (+) and the uses (–) are added together, the sum should be zero.

In practice, however, government statisticians always miss some items when they tally up imports, exports, and financial flows. As a result, the numbers do not quite add up. The difference between the current and financial account balances is called the *statistical discrepancy.* Much of the discrepancy is believed to reflect unrecorded financial flows, for example, investments made in the United States by residents of other countries, but never officially reported. Part of it also reflects a tendency for U.S. exports, especially to Canada, to be reported less fully than U.S. imports.

MEASURING REAL INCOME AND THE PRICE LEVEL

Between 1993 and 2006, the nominal value of U.S. gross domestic product doubled, rising from $6.6 trillion to $13.3 trillion. However, even though nominal GDP doubled over this period, the real output of goods and services that determined people's standard of living did not. A good part of the increase in the dollar value of GDP reflected an increase in the prices at which goods and services were sold; adjusted for changing prices, real GDP increased by only about 50 percent. Clearly, to understand what really happens in the economy over time, we must adjust the growth of nominal GDP and its components to account for inflation.

Real Gross Domestic Product and the Deflator

GDP deflator

A weighted average of the prices of all final goods and services produced in the economy.

To adjust nominal GDP for the effects of inflation, we need a measure of the change in the average prices of goods and services. The most broadly based measure of price changes for the U.S. economy is the **GDP deflator.** The appendix to this chapter explains how it is calculated. For now, we will simply define the GDP deflator as a weighted average of the prices of all the final goods and services that make up GDP.

Base year

The year that is chosen as a basis for comparison in calculating a price index or price level.

BASE YEAR When we speak of price changes, the first question that comes to mind is: change from what? We can answer this question by choosing a convenient **base year** as a benchmark against which to measure change. The U.S. Department of Commerce currently uses 2000 as a base year for calculating the GDP deflator. The government uses two methods of calculating the GDP deflator: fixed and chained. Here, we will focus on the first method of computing GDP using fixed, or "constant," dollars.

The base year can be used in one of two ways in stating a weighted average of prices. One way is to let the base year value equal 1.0. A statement of average prices relative to a base year value of 1.0 is called a statement of the **price level**; for example, the 2006 price level, relative to the 2000 base year, was 1.64. The other way is to let the base year value equal 100. A statement of average prices relative to a base year value of 100 is known as a **price index.** Thus, using 2000 as a base year we could say that the 2006 price index was 116.4. The price level and price index are two different ways of stating the same information. In news reports the index form is used most frequently, whereas in building economic models the price level form is more convenient.

Price level

A weighted average of the prices of goods and services expressed in relation to a base year value of 1.0.

Price index

A weighted average of the prices of goods and services expressed in relation to a base year value of 100.

To convert nominal GDP for any year to real GDP stated in constant 2000 dollars, we simply divide nominal GDP by the price level for that year. For convenience, we can refer to the year for which we are making the adjustment as the current year. In equation form, then, the rule for adjustment can be stated as follows:

Current-year real GDP = Current-year nominal GDP/Current-year price level.

For example, 2006 nominal GDP was $13,254 billion. Dividing this by the current year GDP deflator of 1.164 gives the 2006 real GDP, stated in constant 2000 dollars, of $11,386 billion. If one looks at a year earlier than the base year, the price level has a value less than one. For example, the GDP deflator for 1993, using the 2000 base year, was .88. This indicates that the price level increased substantially from 1993 to 2000. Nominal GDP in 1993 was $6,657 billion. Dividing this by .88 gives a value for 1993 real GDP of $7,564 billion.

THE CONSUMER PRICE INDEX Although the GDP deflator is the most broadly based price index for the U.S. economy, it is not the best-known one. That honor belongs to the consumer price index. Rather than taking into account the prices of all final goods and services produced in the economy, as the GDP deflator does, the **consumer price index (CPI)** considers only the goods and services that make up the "market basket" purchased by a typical urban household. For example, the CPI market basket includes cars, but not railway locomotives.

Consumer price index (CPI)

A price index based on the market basket of goods and services purchased by a typical urban household.

The CPI currently uses the period 1982–1984 rather than a single year as its base year. The appendix to this chapter explains how the CPI is calculated.

The CPI plays a key role in the economy partly because it is widely used to index wages, government transfers, and many other payments. As explained in Chapter 4, indexation of a payment means automatically adjusting it on a regular schedule for changes in the price index involved. Millions of workers whose contracts include *cost-of-living-adjustment* (COLA) clauses receive automatic raises as a result of increases in the CPI.

Producer Price Indexes

Producer price index (PPI)

A price index based on a sample of goods and services bought by business firms.

Another widely publicized set of price indexes consists of **producer price indexes.** These are price averages for three classes of goods that are traded among business firms. The most widely publicized is the producer price index for *finished goods*—investment goods sold to businesses plus other goods that are ready for final use but have not yet been sold to consumers, for example, wholesale sales of clothing to clothing stores. Other producer price indexes cover intermediate goods and crude materials ready for further processing. The producer price indexes currently use a base year of 1982. Because producer price indexes measure prices at early stages in the production process, they are often studied for hints of trends in consumer prices. They are also frequently used to index payments that firms agree to make to one another.

Table 6.5 shows data for the GDP deflator, the consumer price index, and the producer price index for finished goods. To make comparison easier, the CPI and PPI figures have been restated using the same 2000 base year as the GDP deflator. As can be seen from the table, although the indexes tend to move in the same direction, the amount of inflation recorded by the various indexes differs. This is not surprising, inasmuch as they are based on different baskets of goods and services.

How Good are the National Income Accounts?

This chapter began by stressing the importance of the national income accounts to economics while warning that they are less than perfect. Now that we have surveyed the main components of the nominal and real national income accounts, it is time to try to answer the question of how good those accounts are. We will focus on four possible problem areas: the accuracy and timeliness of the data, the underground sector of the economy, bias in price indexes, and nonmaterial aspects of the standard of living.

ACCURACY AND TIMELINESS Government decision makers pay close attention to national income accounting data to get an indication of economic trends as they unfold. Unfortunately, however, there is a trade-off between the timeliness and the accuracy of data. For example the U.S. Department of Commerce provides data on real GDP on a quarterly basis. About three weeks after the end of the quarter, for example, in late April for the January-March first quarter, it releases an "advance" estimate. . A month later, it releases a "preliminary" estimate, and a month after that, a "final" estimate. The average revision from the advance to the final estimate is about seven-tenths of a percentage point. With just an average revision, a preliminary estimate showing GDP growth of 3 percent could turn out to be only 2.3 percent or 3.7 percent when the final estimate is released. What is worse, the errors in estimating GDP tend to be larger at turning points when the economy is entering or emerg-

TABLE 6.5 U.S. PRICE INDEXES, 1980–2006

Year	GDP deflator	CPI	PPI
1980	54.0	47.9	63.8
1981	59.1	52.8	69.6
1982	62.7	56.0	72.5
1983	65.2	57.8	73.6
1984	67.7	60.3	75.1
1985	69.7	62.5	75.9
1986	71.3	63.6	74.8
1987	73.2	66.0	76.4
1988	75.7	68.7	78.3
1989	78.6	72.0	82.3
1990	81.6	75.9	86.4
1991	84.4	79.1	88.2
1992	86.4	81.5	89.3
1993	88.4	83.9	90.4
1994	90.3	86.1	90.9
1995	92.1	88.5	92.7
1996	93.9	91.1	95.1
1997	95.4	93.2	95.5
1998	96.5	94.7	94.7
1999	97.9	96.7	96.4
2000	100.0	100.0	100.0
2001	102.4	102.8	102.0
2002	104.1	104.5	100.7
2003	106.0	106.9	103.8
2004	109.0	109.7	107.6
2005	112.5	113.4	112.8
2006	116.4	117.1	116.2

This table compares the trends of the GDP deflator, the consumer price index, and the producer price index for finished goods from 1980 to 2006 for the United States. For ease of comparison, all three indexes have been restated to use the same base year, 2000.

Source: *Economic Report of the President*, 2007, Tables B-3, B-60, B-65.

ing from a recession. Lags in the availability of accurate data on GDP, inflation, and other economic quantities have major implications for policy makers' ability to fine-tune economic policy to fit events as they unfold.

THE UNDERGROUND ECONOMY The economic activity that is measured in the national income accounts constitutes the observed sector of the economy, but a considerable amount of production, consumption, and investment is never officially measured. The national income accounts try to take the unobserved sector into account when they include estimates of the rental value of owner-occupied housing and the value of food produced and consumed on farms, but those items are only the tip of the iceberg.

Some have estimated that organized crime produces some $150 billion a year in illegal goods and services in the form of drugs, gambling, pornography, and so on. If this estimate is correct, it makes organized crime the second-largest industry in the United States after the oil industry. However, organized crime is probably not the largest sector of the so-called underground economy. The unreported income of businesses and self-employed people may add as much as $250 billion. This includes cash income that goes unreported to escape payment of taxes (for example, a concert pianist failing to report income from occasional piano lessons) and barter transactions that involve no cash at all (for example, the pianist gets her teeth straightened in exchange for giving piano lessons to her orthodontist's child).

But even if the U.S. underground economy amounts to as much as 10 percent of officially measured GDP, that proportion is moderate by world standards. The French underground economy is thought to equal one-third of that country's GDP; in Italy, the figure may be 40 percent; and in many third world countries, the official GDP data bear only the haziest relationship to what is actually going on in the economy.

PRICE INDEX BIASES A third problem with the official statistics is that of price index biases. The accuracy with which changes in price levels are measured became a matter of growing concern as inflation increased in the late 1970s and indexing and automatic cost-of-living adjustments became more widespread. If the official price indexes are found to understate inflation, policy makers should perhaps make a greater effort to restore price stability. On the other hand, if price indexes overstate inflation, contracts that provide automatic adjustments for inflation may be too generous.

The problem of price index biases has been closely studied, and the results are far from reassuring. The consumer price index has been criticized for two built-in biases that have caused it to overstate inflation: substitution bias and quality bias.

Substitution Bias The first reason that the consumer price index tends to overstate the true rate of increase in the cost of living is the so-called substitution bias. As the appendix to this chapter explains, the CPI is a weighted average of the prices of goods that are typically purchased by urban consumers. Because the weights used to calculate the index remain constant, they always reflect patterns of consumption at some point in the past. However, because patterns change over time, the weights typically are not those of the most recent year being observed.

If changes in buying patterns were random, an obsolete set of weights would cause only random errors, not an upward bias, in the CPI. The bias results from the fact that consumer demand is influenced by changes in relative prices. As time passes, consumers tend to buy less of the goods whose prices have risen most and more of those whose prices have lagged behind the average or have actually fallen. Thus, the CPI tends to overstate the increase in the cost of living because it assigns unrealistically large weights to products whose prices have increased but that are consumed in relatively smaller amounts than formerly. For example, if large increases in gasoline prices lead consumers to purchase more fuel-efficient cars, and thus to consume less gasoline, the weight given to gasoline will be too high. As a result, the CPI will exaggerate the impact of gas prices on the cost of living. The market basket on which the CPI is based is periodically adjusted to reflect such changes, but the adjustments are not frequent enough to remove the bias altogether.

Quality Bias A second source of bias in the consumer price index is the failure to adjust product prices for changes in quality. It would be highly misleading, for example, to say that a 2007 model car costs three times as much as a 1987 model without considering the fact that the 2007 model can be driven longer between servicing, and is much safer than the 1984 model. In terms of dollars per unit of transportation service, the newer model clearly would be less than three times as expensive.

For automobiles, computers, and a few other major goods, the Bureau of Labor Statistics does try to make quality adjustments. As recently as the late 1960s, it cost over $1,000 to buy a desk-size electromechanical calculator that would add, subtract, multiply, and divide. Today half of that sum will buy a basic laptop computer, and a calculator equivalent to the 1960 model can be purchased for less than $5. Studies of changes in computer quality have led to significant adjustments in price indexes. However, government statisticians do not have the resources to make such detailed studies of all items that enter into GDP.

Taken together, the substitution bias and quality bias are substantial. At one time they may have added 1 to 1 1/2 percent per year to the stated rate of inflation as measured by the CPI. Recent changes in methodology are thought to have reduced the bias, but it is still probably in the range of 1/2 to 1 percent per year.

NONMATERIAL SOURCES OF WELFARE The final problem with GDP is that it measures only material sources of welfare (which, after all, is all it tries to do). Sometimes per capita GDP is used as an indication of living standards, but when one is comparing living standards over time and across countries, nonmaterial sources of welfare are important, too.

One key nonmaterial component of the standard of living is the quality of the environment. This not only varies widely from one place to another but has changed greatly over time. Problems of global warming and toxic wastes are "bads" that, in principle, should be subtracted from GDP just as "goods" are added to it. In the same spirit, Robert Repetto of the World Resources Institute in Washington, D.C., recommends that depletion of such natural resources as oil fields and tropical forests should be subtracted along with the capital consumption allowance when calculating net domestic product. For countries such as Indonesia and Brazil, which have used huge quantities of natural resources, the effect of this adjustment could cut measured rates of economic growth nearly in half.

A second nonmaterial source of welfare is the state of human health. By broad measures, especially life expectancy, standards of health in the United States appear to be improving. For example, since World War II the life expectancy of a typical 45-year-old American has increased from 72 years to 77, and a 65-year-old American can now expect to live to the age of 81. This increase clearly improves human welfare even for people who add nothing to measured GDP after they retire from their jobs. If the improvement in health could be measured, it would add to the growth of U.S. GDP. On the other hand, such an adjustment would make the economic picture look even bleaker in a country like Russia, where health indicators such as life expectancy and infant mortality have gotten worse in recent years.

The list of nonmaterial sources of welfare is endless. How important are satisfying work, friendship, social justice, economic equality, and freedom? Everyone knows of people who have been willing to give up income and wealth in pursuit of these things. Yet they must remain unmeasured.

For all of these reasons, then, GDP cannot be used as a measure of the true level of human welfare and can be used only with the greatest caution even for comparisons of material welfare in different times and places.

SUMMARY

1. **How is gross domestic product officially defined and measured?** Two domestic product concepts are featured in the official accounts of the United States. *Gross domestic product (GDP)* is defined as the value at current market prices of all *final goods and services* produced annually in a given country. *Gross national product* is the product produced by a country's factors of production, regardless of what country they are located in. *Net domestic product* is derived from GDP by subtracting a capital consumption allowance that reflects the value of capital goods worn out during the year.
2. **How does the measurement of domestic income differ from the measurement of gross domestic product?** *Domestic income* is the sum of wages and supplements, rental income of persons, corporate profits, and proprietors' income earned in a country. In principle, domestic income and gross domestic product should be equal, but in the official accounts,

they differ because of the capital consumption allowance, indirect business taxes, and a statistical discrepancy that results from the use of different data sources for income and product measurements.

3. **What are the major types of international transactions?** Many types of transactions appear in the nation's international accounts. Exports less imports of goods constitute the *merchandise balance.* Adding services yields net exports of goods and services. Adding net international transfers (normally a negative number for the United States) yields the most widely publicized balance-of-payments measure, the *current account balance.* In addition, the international accounts record financial inflows and outflows resulting from private financial transactions and official reserve transactions by the Federal Reserve and foreign central banks.

4. **How are changes in the average level of prices measured?** The *GDP deflator* is the most broadly based measure of the *price level.* It can be viewed as a weighted average of the prices of all final goods and services that go into GDP. The *consumer price index (CPI)* includes only the market basket of goods purchased by a typical urban household. The *producer price index (PPI)* is based on goods that are typically bought and sold by business firms.

5. **What are the limitations of official economic statistics?** The national income statistics of the United States are considered to be among the best in the world. However, they have some limitations. Potential problem areas include timeliness of data, the unobserved sector of the economy, price index biases, and nonmaterial aspects of the standard of living.

KEY TERMS

National income accounts
Gross domestic product (GDP)
Final goods and services
Value added
Net domestic product (NDP)
National income
Current account
Merchandise balance
Current account balance
Financial account
Financial inflow
Financial outflow
GDP deflator
Base year
Price level
Price index
Consumer price index (CPI)
Producer price index (PPI)

PROBLEMS AND TOPICS FOR DISCUSSION

1. **Updating the national income accounts.** Data on national income accounts and international transactions for the United States are available from several sources on the Internet. Two of the easiest to use are the tables attached to each year's *Economic Report of the President* (http://www.gpoaccess.gov/eop) and those given by the Commerce Department's Bureau of Economic Analysis (http://www.bea.gov) Using one of these sources, update the tables in this chapter to the most recent year or quarter. If you do not live in the United States, a search for national income accounts for your home country will very likely lead you to similar data. Be aware, however, that although the basic principles of national income accounting apply to all countries, there are often noticeable differences in terminology, presentation, and methods of data collection.

2. **Inventory in the national income accounts.** Suppose that a firm sells $10,000 worth of shoes that it has held in inventory for several years. What happens to GDP as a result? Which of its components are affected, and how?
3. **International accounts.** Following the pattern in Table 6.4, show how the international accounts might look for a year in which there was a $50 billion surplus on current account, no official reserve transactions, and no statistical discrepancy. What would the capital and financial account balance have to be?
4. **The current account deficit.** "A current account deficit is a very healthy thing. If we can get foreigners to give us real goods and services and talk them into taking pieces of paper in return, why should we want anything different?" Do you agree or disagree with this statement? Discuss.
5. **Real and nominal quantities.** In 1982 to 1984, the base period used for the consumer price index, the average earnings of construction workers were $442.74 per week. By 1989 the earnings of construction workers had reached $506.72 per week, but the consumer price index had risen to 124.0. What were construction workers' real earnings in 1989 stated in 1982–1984 dollars?
6. **Changes in prices and qualities.** Try to find a mail-order catalog that is at least ten years old; also find a recent catalog. Compare the ads for various items. By how much has the price of each item unchanged? What changes in quality have occurred? Assuming that you could buy at list price from either the new catalog or the old one, which items would you buy from the old one and which from the new one?

CASE FOR DISCUSSION

Laid-Off Steel Workers Join the Underground Economy

HOMESTEAD, PA.—A half-dozen men lounge on metal folding chairs outside a storefront on Ann Street, sweating in the muggy afternoon air and talking baseball. A pay phone rings inside, and a young man runs to answer it. Moments later, he speeds off in a long, beat-up sedan.

The man is about to cheat the government. He and the other men drive people around town for a fee, but they don't pay any taxes on the fares they receive. What's more, they don't see why they should.

Most of the men used to work at the sprawling Homestead Works a half block away. Now that the steel mill has closed, their car service allows them to make a living. "It ain't bothering anyone. It ain't stealing," says Earl Jones, who was laid off last December after 36 years at the mill. How much does he make? "Ain't saying," he replies with a smile.

The men are part of a vast underground economy made up of people who work "off the books" for cash. From the tired mill towns of the Midwest to the oil patches dotting the Southwest, the underground thrives. In communities that have suddenly lost a major employer, it helps those who were laid off make ends meet, and it helps keep towns like Homestead alive.

The number of Homestead residents with off-the-books livelihoods began to increase in the early 1980s when USX Corporation's Homestead Works, which employed about 15,000 at its peak, started to lay off workers in droves. The mill's few remaining workers lost their jobs early in 1986. For most residents here, where only half the people have their high-school diplomas, the mill was all there was.

After they were laid off, many older workers retired and some of the younger ones withdrew their savings and migrated south, chasing dreams of work in more prosperous states. But many others stayed, bound by their unmarketable homes, their families, or a strong sense of community. Unable to find legitimate jobs, they have parlayed their handyman skills underground.

One former mill worker says that half the people he knows are working off the books. For the most part, they are intensely proud people who hang the American flag from their neat front porches on holidays and respect the law, believing strongly in right and wrong. They definitely don't like the underground's seamy side—thefts and drugs. But their changed circumstances have altered the way many of them think.

"You tell me. Your kids go to bed crying at night because they're hungry. Is 'off the books' going to bother you?" asks a former steelworker.

Source: Clare Ansberry, "Laid-Off Steelworkers Find That Tax Evasion Helps Make Ends Meet," *The Wall Street Journal,* October 1, 1986, 1. Reprinted by permission of *The Wall Street Journal,* © Dow Jones & Company, Inc., 1986. All Rights Reserved Worldwide.

QUESTIONS

1. What are the advantages of working "off the books" from the viewpoint of the people involved?
2. How might the failure to measure off-the-books activity affect economic policy decisions?
3. How might off-the-books work affect the statistical discrepancy in the national income accounts?

END NOTES

1. Following the same logic, it is also possible to calculate *Gross National Product (GNP),* a measure of goods and services produced by factors of production owned by a country's residents, including factors of production physically located in another country. Until the early 1990s, U.S. accounts emphasized GNP rather than GDP, and the term GNP is sometimes still encountered in popular discussions. In practice, the difference between GDP and GNP is very small for the United States.

Appendix to Chapter 6: COMPUTATION OF PRICE INDEXES

This appendix provides further information on the GDP deflator and consumer price index. Knowing these details will make it easier to see the differences between the two indexes and to understand the source of the substitution bias, which affects each index differently.

The GDP Deflator for a Simple Economy

A much simpler economy than that of the United States will serve to illustrate the computation of price indexes. Table 6A.1 shows price and quantity data for two years for an economy in which only three goods are produced: movies, apples, and shirts. The exhibit shows that nominal GDP grew from $1,000 in 2000 to $1,700 in 2007. But what do these figures indicate? Do they mean that people really had more of the things they wanted in 2007 than in 2000? More precisely, do they mean that people had 1.7 times as much? These questions cannot be easily answered by looking at the exhibit in its present form.

A line-by-line comparison of the two years shows that the figures on nominal product do not tell the whole story. Clearly, prices went up sharply between 2000 and 2007. Movies and apples cost more than one and a half times what they used to, and shirts nearly that much. The amounts of goods produced have also changed. Twice as many movies and shirts were produced in 2007 as in 2000, but only half as many apples.

If we wish to know how much better off people were in 2007 than in 2000, we need a way to separate the quantity changes that have taken place from the price changes. One way to do this is to ask how much the total value of output would have changed from 2000 to 2007 if prices had not changed. This approach gives the results shown in Table 6A.2. There we see

TABLE 6A.1 NOMINAL GDP FOR A SIMPLE ECONOMY

2000	Quantity	Price	Value
Movies	50	$ 5.00	$ 250
Apples	1,000	.60	600
Shirts	10	15.00	150
2000 nominal GDP			$ 1,000
2007			
Movies	100	$ 8.00	$ 800
Apples	500	.80	400
Shirts	20	25.00	500
2007 nominal GDP			$1,700

In this simple economy in which only three goods are produced, nominal domestic product grew from $1,000 in 2000 to $1,700 in 2007. But because prices also went up during that time, people did not really have 1.7 times as many goods in 2007 as they did in 2000.

TABLE 6A.2 NOMINAL AND REAL GDP FOR A SIMPLE ECONOMY

Good	2007 Quantity	2007 Price	Value of 2007 Quantity at 2007 Price	2000 Price	Value of 2007 Quantity at 2000 Price
Movies	100	$8.00	800	$ 5.00	$ 500
Apples	500	.80	400	.60	300
Shirts	20	25.00	500	15.00	300
Totals			$1,700		$1,100

2007 nominal GDP = $1,700; 2007 real GDP = $1,100

This table shows how the figures from Table 6A.1 can be adjusted to take changing prices into account. The 2007 quantities are multiplied by 2000 prices to get the value of 2007 GDP that would have existed had prices not changed. The total of 2007 quantities valued at 2000 prices is a measure of real GDP for 2007 stated in constant 2000 dollars. The implicit GDP deflator for 2007, calculated as the ratio of 2007 nominal GDP to 2000 real GDP, has a value of 154.5.

that the 2007 output of 100 movies, 500 apples, and 20 shirts, which had a value of $1,700 in terms of the prices at which the goods were actually sold, would have had a value of only $1,100 in terms of the prices that prevailed in 2000. The $1,100 thus is a measure of real GDP for 2007. It is this measure that we should compare with the 2000 GDP of $1,000 if we want to know what really happened to output between the two years. Instead of having 170 percent as much output in 2007 as in 2000, as indicated by the change in nominal GDP from $1,000 to $1,700, the people in this simple economy really had only about 110 percent as much, as indicated by the change in real GDP from $1,000 to $1,000.

Now we know how to compute real and nominal GDP for 2007 directly from price and quantity data without using a price index to convert nominal values into real values. But although we have not explicitly used a price index, we have created one implicitly. This implicit index, or implicit GDP deflator, is the ratio of current-year nominal GDP to current-year real GDP times 100, as expressed in index form by the following formula:

$$\text{GDP delator} = \frac{\text{Current-year output valued at current-year prices}}{\text{Current-year output valued at base-year prices}} \times 100.$$

Applying the formula to the data in Tables 6A.1 and 6A.2 gives a value of 154.5 for the deflator.

The Consumer Price Index for a Simple Economy

The consumer price index differs from the GDP deflator in two ways. First, as mentioned in Chapter 6, it takes into account only the prices of goods and services consumed by a typical urban household. Second, it is calculated according to a formula that uses base-year rather than current-year quantities. The first difference does not matter for this simple economy in which all goods are consumer goods, but the second does, as Table 6A.3 shows.

To calculate the CPI for this economy, instead of asking how much current-year output would have cost at base-year prices, we begin by asking how much base-year output would

TABLE 6A.3 A CONSUMER PRICE INDEX FOR A SIMPLE ECONOMY

Good	2000 Quantity	2000 Price	Value of 2000 Quantity at 2000 Price	2007 Price	Value of 2000 Quantity at 2007 Price
Movies	50	$5.00	250	$ 8.00	$ 400
Apples	1,000	.60	600	.80	800
Shirts	10	15.00	150	25.00	250
Totals			$1,000		$1,450

$$\text{CPI} = \frac{\$1{,}450}{\$1{,}000} \times 100 = 145.0$$

The consumer price index can be calculated as the base-year market basket of goods valued at current-year prices divided by the base-year market basket valued at base-year prices multiplied by 100. This table shows how such an index can be calculated for a simple economy. The 2000 output cost $1,000 at the prices at which it was actually sold. Had it been sold at 2007 prices, it would have cost $1,450. Thus, the CPI for 2007 is 145.0.

have cost at current-year prices. We then calculate the index as the ratio of the two different valuations of base-year quantities:

$$\text{Consumer price index} = \frac{\text{Base-year market basket valued at current-year prices}}{\text{Base-year market basket valued at base-year prices}} \times 100.$$

The CPI is calculated using base-year quantities partly because data on current prices are easier to collect than data on current output. This index, therefore, can be announced each month with little delay.

Comparing the CPI and the GDP Deflator

As Table 6A.3 shows, the CPI for 2007 in our simple economy had a value of 145.0, whereas the GDP deflator for 2007 was 154.5. Both indexes were calculated using the same data, and both used 2000 as a base year. Which, if either, is the true measure of the change in prices between the two years?

The answer is that neither the CPI nor the GDP deflator is the only correct measure of change in the price level; instead, each answers a different question. The GDP deflator answers the question, "How much more did the 2007 output cost at the prices at which it was actually sold than it would have cost had it been sold at 2000 prices?" The CPI, in contrast, answers the question, "How much more would the 2000 output have cost had it been sold at 2007 prices instead of at 2000 prices?"

A close look at the data shows why the answers to the two questions differ. In 2000, lots of apples and few shirts were produced compared with 2007. Yet between the two years the price of apples increased 33 percent whereas the price of shirts increased 67 percent. Because the CPI uses base-year quantities, it gives a heavy weight to apples, which showed the smallest relative price increase, and a lower weight to shirts, which showed a larger price increase.

In contrast, the GDP deflator uses current-year quantities, thereby decreasing the importance of apples and increasing that of shirts.

In actuality, because people will tend to substitute purchases away from items with faster growth in prices, the CPI tends to have an upward substitution bias relative to the GDP deflator. However, that does not make the GDP deflator a true measure of change in the cost of living. It could just as easily be said that the GDP deflator has a downward substitution bias relative to the CPI or that each has an opposite bias from some "true" price index. As yet there is no foolproof way to calculate the true cost-of-living index, although some interesting attempts have been made. A discussion of these more complex types of price indexes would take us far beyond the scope of this book. However, the basic types of price indexes covered here are the ones that are most commonly used for policy-making purposes.

PART 3

Macroeconomics and Money

CHAPTER 7

Money and the Banking System

After reading this chapter, you will understand:

1. What money is and what it does
2. How the stock of money in the economy is measured
3. How the quantity of money is related to other key macroeconomic variables
4. The structure of the U.S. banking system
5. How the safety and stability of the banking system are maintained

Before reading this chapter, make sure you know the meaning of:

1. Circular flow of income and expenditure
2. Financial markets
3. Price level

IF WE THINK of the circular flow of income and expenditure as a giant system of pipes connected by pumps and valves, then we can think of money as the fluid that moves through the pipes. In this chapter, money moves to the center of the stage.

We will begin by giving a formal definition of money and explaining how it is measured. Next we will explore the banking system, which consists of several types of institutions that accept deposits from the public. Finally, we will consider the role of the central bank, which is a government agency that regulates a country's banking system and carries out monetary policy. In the United States, the central bank is called the Federal Reserve System, or simply "the Fed," for short.

MONEY: WHAT IT IS AND WHAT IT DOES

Money

An asset that serves as a means of payment, a store of purchasing power, and a unit of account.

Money is best defined in terms of what it does: It serves as a means of payment, a store of purchasing power, and a unit of account. Regardless of its name —U.S. dollars, Japanese yen, or the European euro—the monies of all countries function in all three ways.

The Functions of Money

As a means of payment, money reduces the costs of exchange, which would otherwise have to take the form of barter. Imagine a market in which farmers meet to trade produce of various kinds. Apples will get you peppers, cauliflower will get you beets, and turnips will get you garlic. But what if you want garlic and have only potatoes? What you need is a universal means of exchange—one that all sellers will accept because they know that others will also accept it; one that is in limited supply so that you know its exchange value will remain constant; and one that is easily recognized and hard to counterfeit. In times past, gold and silver coins served these purposes. In a modern economy, coins and paper currency serve for many small transactions. Larger payments are usually made by transferring funds from one bank deposit to another by check, debit card, electronic transfer, or other means.

As a store of purchasing power, money makes it possible to arrange economic activities in a convenient manner over time. Income-producing activities and spending decisions need not occur simultaneously. Instead, we can accept money as payment for our work and keep the money handy until we want to spend it. The U.S. dollar is a good store of purchasing power—so good, in fact, that billions of dollars of U.S. currency are held by citizens of other countries who trust it more than their own currencies.

Finally, as a unit of account money makes it possible to measure and record economic stocks and flows. Your own daily spending on food, transportation, and entertainment can be expressed in terms of money. So can an entire country's output of goods and services. Without money as a unit of account, private and public economic planning would be virtually impossible.

Money as a Liquid Asset

Anything of value can serve as a store of purchasing power if it can be sold and the proceeds can be used to buy something else. Money, however, has two important traits that no other asset has to the same extent. One is that money itself can be used as a means of payment without first having to be exchanged for something else. A house, a corporate bond, or a steel mill may have great value, but they cannot usually be used to buy anything without first being exchanged for an equivalent amount of money. The other trait is that money can neither gain nor lose in nominal value; this is necessarily so, because money is the unit of account in which nominal values are stated. Where a house, a bond, or a steel mill may be worth more or fewer dollars next year than this year, the nominal value of a dollar is always a dollar—no more and no less.

Liquidity
An asset's ability to be used directly as a means of payment, or to be readily converted into one, while retaining a fixed nominal value.

An asset that can be used as or readily converted into a means of payment and is protected against gain or loss in nominal value is said to be **liquid**. No other asset is as liquid as money. In fact, a comparison of the definitions of money and liquidity suggests that any perfectly liquid asset is, by definition, a form of money.

Measuring the Stock of Money

For purposes of economic theory and policy, we need to know not only what money is but also how it can be measured. Control of the money stock is an important function of government, and without measurement, control is impossible.

Currency
Coins and paper money.

Transaction deposit
A deposit from which funds can be freely withdrawn by check or electronic transfer to make payments to third parties.

CURRENCY AND TRANSACTION DEPOSITS We begin with a narrow approach to measurement that views money as consisting of just two types of assets: currency and transaction deposits. **Currency** means coins and paper money. **Transaction deposits** are deposits from which money can be withdrawn by check or electronic transfer without advance notice and used to make payments.

Unlike transaction deposits, which are provided by private banks, currency is issued by the government. In the United States, currency consists of the familiar Federal Reserve notes, which are issued in denominations of $1, $2, $5, $10, $20, $50, and $100, and of coins minted by the Department of the Treasury. Coins and paper money were formerly backed by precious metals. Until 1934, the U.S. government issued both gold coins and paper currency that could be exchanged for gold on demand; silver coins and silver-backed paper money survived until the mid-1960s. Today, coins and paper money are simply tokens whose value is based on the public's faith in their usefulness as means of paying for goods and services.

Transaction deposits are available in a number of forms. One major type of transaction deposit is the demand deposit. By law, demand deposits cannot pay interest, but banks compensate *demand-deposit* customers with various services. Until the mid-1970s, demand deposits were the only kind of transaction deposit available in the United States. They have since been joined by a variety of interest-bearing transaction deposits available to consumers through several kinds of financial institutions. In the United States, transaction deposits of all kinds are popularly known as *checking accounts*.

M1
A measure of the money supply that includes currency and transaction deposits.

The sum of currency and transaction deposits—with the small item, travelers checks, also included—is known as **M1**. Table 7.1 shows M1 and its components.

Some readers may find it odd that credit cards are not included in the monetary aggregates. After all, from the consumer's point of view, paying for a purchase with a credit card is a close substitute for paying by cash or check. *Applying Economic Ideas 7.1* discusses credit cards and explains why they do not figure in the measurement of the nation's money stock.

TABLE 7.1 COMPONENTS OF THE U.S. MONEY STOCK, FEBRUARY 2007 (BILLIONS OF DOLLARS, SEASONALLY ADJUSTED)

Currency		$751.3	
+ Travelers checks		$6.7	
+ Transactions deposits		$602.0	
Demand deposits	$298.8		
Other transaction deposits	$302.2		
= **M1**			**$1,360.0**
+ Savings deposits (including MMDAs)	$3,707.4		
+ Small-denomination time deposits	$1,168.1		
+ Retail money market fund shares	$818.2		
= **M2**			**$7,053.7**

This table breaks down the U.S. money supply into its components as of November 2002. It gives two of the most commonly used money supply measures. M1 is the total of currency and transaction deposits; M2 includes M1 plus other highly liquid assets.

Source: Board of Governors of the Federal Reserve System, H.6 Statistical Release, Feb 1, 2007.

THE BROADLY DEFINED MONEY STOCK The narrow definition of the money stock, M1, focuses on the function of money as a means of payment because almost all transactions are made with either currency or transaction deposits. However, if one chooses to focus instead on the function of money as a store of value, several other liquid assets need to be included.

Shares in money market mutual funds are one example. A *money market mutual fund* is a financial intermediary that sells shares to the public. The proceeds of these sales are used to buy short-term, fixed-interest securities such as Treasury bills. The fund passes along almost all the interest earned on those securities to its shareholders, after charging a small fee for management services. Shareholders can redeem their shares in a number of ways—by writing checks, by debit card, by electronic transfer to a merchant, or by transfer to another fund.[1] Because the proceeds from sales of shares are invested in very safe short-term assets, a money market mutual fund is able to promise its shareholders a fixed nominal value of $1 per share, although the interest paid on the shares varies with market rates. For all practical purposes, money market mutual fund balances are almost as liquid as those of ordinary transaction accounts. Money market funds grew rapidly in the late 1970s and early 1980s, when market interest rates rose while rates paid by banks were limited by federal regulations. In recent years, when interest rates have been lower, money market funds have lost some of their popularity.

Savings deposit

A deposit at a bank that can be fully redeemed at any time, but from which checks cannot be written.

Banks also offer a number of other accounts that serve as reasonably liquid stores of purchasing power. **Savings deposits** are a familiar example. Although checks cannot be written on these deposits, they are fully protected against loss in nominal value

APPLYING ECONOMIC IDEAS 7.1
"PLASTIC MONEY"

Recent innovations in banking have streamlined how people make payments and have reduced their reliance on using paper currency. For instance, instead of writing a check as a means of payment, individuals can use a debit card or a credit card. Many people wonder how this "plastic money"—the MasterCards, VISA cards, and other bank cards that so many people carry these days—relate to money as measured by M1 and M2. Just what role do these cards play in the payments system?

Credit cards, the most common type of plastic money, are not really a form of money at all. What sets credit cards apart from currency, bank deposits, and other forms of money is the fact that they are not a store of value. Instead, they are documents that make it easy for their holders to obtain a loan.

When you go into a store, present your credit card, and walk out with a can of tennis balls, you have not yet paid for your purchase. What you have done is borrow from the bank that issued the card. At the same time, you have instructed the bank to turn over the proceeds of the loan to the store. Later the bank will do so by crediting the amount to the store's account. This will pay for the tennis balls. Still later you will send money to the bank to pay off the balance on your credit card account.

Another common form of plastic money is a *debit card*. A debit card directly withdraws money from the payer's bank account and deposits these funds into the receiver's account. The funds are verified electronically, which substantially reduces the time and cost needed to clear a check. Similarly, many students in colleges today can use their student identification card as a stored-value card, or "smart card." Stored-value cards are much like debit cards except that they generally draw on funds stored with the card's administrator (such as the college/university issuing student I.D. cards) rather than in a bank account. Because stored-value and debit cards draw on funds the cardholder has deposited (in a checking or school account), the deposited funds are considered money.

Many businesses operating on the internet accept not only credit card payments but also electronic cash and electronic checks. These are much like their paper counterparts, cash and checks, except the transactions take place electronically over the internet. A downside to the use of electronic money is the possiblity for new forms of fraud. It can be difficult to verify a person's identity without photo identification or other personal information. Also, businesses using electronic money gain access to additional personal information not usually provided when using paper cash or checks.

Time deposit

A deposit at a bank or thrift institution from which funds can be withdrawn without payment of a penalty only at the end of an agreed-upon period.

M2

A measure of the money supply that includes M1 plus retail money market mutual fund shares, money market deposit accounts, and saving deposits.

and can be redeemed at any time. In addition to conventional savings deposits, since late 1982 banks have been allowed to compete with money market mutual funds by offering so-called *money market deposit accounts (MMDAs)*. These accounts have limited checking privileges and offer higher interest rates than the transaction accounts included in M1. MMDAs are included together with savings deposits in Table 7.1.

Banks also offer **time deposits.** In the case of small-denomination time deposits (up to $100,000), funds typically must be left on deposit for a fixed period, ranging from less than a month to many years, in order to earn the full interest rate, and they normally cannot be transferred to another person before maturity. This feature makes them less liquid than savings deposits or MMDAs, but in return they usually pay a higher interest rate. They, too, are protected against loss of nominal value.

Retail money market mutual fund shares, savings deposits (including MMDAs), and small-denomination time deposits are added to M1 to create a measure of the money supply known as **M2.**

Central banks of countries other than the United States publish data on M1, M2, and other measures of money in their own countries. The definitions are not completely standardized, so caution must be used when comparing one country's monetary data with that of another.

Why Money Matters

In presenting alternative measures of the money stock, we might seem to have wandered rather far afield from our main macroeconomic themes of real output growth, price stability, and employment. In fact, however, these key objectives depend closely on money. It will take several chapters to show in detail why this is so, but a preliminary overview can be given here.

THE EQUATION OF EXCHANGE The relationship between money and other key variables can be stated in the form of the following equation, which is termed the **equation of exchange:**

Equation of exchange

An equation that shows the relationship among the money stock (M), the income velocity of money (V), the price level (P), and real domestic product (Q); written as MV = PQ.

$$MV = PQ$$

where M stands for a measure of the money stock, P for the price level, and Q for real GDP. The remaining variable, V, stands for **velocity** or, more fully, the **income velocity of money.** Velocity can be thought of as the average number of times each dollar of the money stock is spent each year to purchase final goods and services of the kind that enter into GDP. . It can also be thought of as the ratio of nominal GDP to the money stock.[2] For example, if a country had a money stock of $200 billion and a real GDP of $1,000 billion, velocity would be 5, indicating that each dollar of the money stock changed hands about 5 times a year for purchases of final goods and services.

Velocity (income velocity of money)

The ratio of nominal domestic income to the money stock; a measure of the average number of times each dollar of the money stock is used each year for income-producing purposes.

The equation of exchange shows that any change in the money stock must affect the price level, real output, velocity, or some combination of these variables. Thus, control over the money stock gives the government a powerful policy instrument with which to influence key macroeconomic variables. Later chapters will show in detail the means by which policymakers can influence the money stock. They will also discuss the effects of changes in the money stock on other variables.

WHICH "M" IS BEST? As we have seen, there are various measures of the money stock. All of these measures are determined by establishing a cutoff point along a range of financial assets with varying degrees of liquidity, from currency at one end to long-term securities at the other. No hard-and-fast answer can be given to the question of which M is "best" without also asking, "Best for what?"

For example, the basic idea of M1 is to measure the money stock available for use as a means of payment. However, it does not do this perfectly. On the one hand, some consumers use interest-bearing transaction accounts primarily as a store of purchasing power. This savings motive is reflected in the fact that some of these accounts have a low *turnover rate*—that is, the ratio of the volume of transactions per year to the average balance is low. On the other hand, as we have seen, money market mutual funds have features that allow them to serve as means of payment. These assets are not included in M1 partly because they have even lower turnover rates, but they are still used for some transactions. Thus, M1 is far from perfect as a measure of means-of-payment money.

Similar problems plague M2, which is intended to measure the stock of money as a short-term, highly liquid store of purchasing power. M2 includes items such as savings and small-denomination time deposits, which have fixed nominal values despite their low turnover rates. The cutoff line between M2 and still broader measures of money is arbitrary.

For purposes of macroeconomic modeling and policy, the best money stock measure would be the one with the most predictable velocity and, hence, the most predictable relationship to the variables lying on the right-hand side of the equation of exchange (real output and the price level). At one time economists considered M1 to be the best available measure in this regard. In the 1980s, as banking institutions and ways of doing business changed, M1 began to lose its close relationship to other economic variables, and M2 came to regarded as a better measure. In this book, unless we specify otherwise, the term *money* can be understood to refer to M2.

THE BANKING SYSTEM

As Table 7.1 shows, just 22 percent of U.S. M2 consists of currency issued by government and balances in money market mutual funds. Most of the other components of M2—transaction deposits, savings deposits, and small-denomination time deposits—are issued by banks. For this reason, we need to understand the structure and operations of the banking system in order to understand monetary theory and policy.

Depository institutions

Financial intermediaries, including commercial banks and thrift institutions, that accept deposits from the public.

Commercial banks

Financial intermediaries that provide a broad range of banking services, including accepting demand deposits and making commercial loans.

Types of Depository Institutions

Up to this point, we have used the term "bank" in an informal way to refer to all institutions that accept deposits from the public, make loans, and offer other familiar financial services to consumers and businesses. Looking more closely at the U.S. banking system, we can distinguish four principal types of **depository institutions** in the United States. They differ in the types of loans and deposits in which they specialize, although their operations increasingly overlap.

The largest group of depository institutions is **commercial banks.** These usually include the word *bank* in their names. One of their specialties is making commercial loans—that is, loans to businesses, frequently short term. They also make consumer loans and home mortgage loans. Until the 1970s, commercial banks were the only institutions that could offer checking accounts, and they still hold the bulk of transaction deposits. They also raise funds by offering savings and time deposits and other financial instruments. Large commercial banks provide many services, such as wire transfers and international banking facilities, to business customers.

Thrift institutions (thrifts)
A group of financial intermediaries that operate much like commercial banks; they include savings and loan associations, savings banks, and credit unions.

Three other types of depository institutions are collectively known as **thrift institutions.** The most important of these, *savings and loan associations* (also known as *savings and loans* or *S&Ls*), specialize in home mortgage lending although they also make other real estate loans, consumer loans, and a limited number of commercial loans. Household savings and time deposits have traditionally been their main source of funds, but today they also offer fully checkable deposits as well as MMDAs with limited checking privileges. Although they are not allowed to use the word *bank* in their names, some savings and loan associations shape their operations to resemble those of commercial banks as closely as regulations permit.

Mutual savings banks are a type of depository institution that emerged in the nineteenth century to serve the needs of working-class households needing a depository for their small amounts of savings. Some still have names like "Dime Savings Bank" that reflect these origins. Mutual savings banks offer the same range of deposits as savings and loan associations, but they tend to offer more diversified types of loans.

Credit unions are small financial intermediaries organized as cooperative enterprises by employee groups, union members, or certain other groups with shared work or community ties. They specialize in small consumer loans, although a few also make mortgage loans. They offer both transaction and savings deposits.

Since the mid-1970s, the traditional distinctions among these four types of institutions have eroded. Today, both from the viewpoint of the consumer and in macroeconomic terms, there is no real difference between a transaction deposit in a commercial bank and one in a thrift institution. For that reason, we will continue to use the terms *bank* and *banking system* to refer to all depository institutions except when there is a particular reason to single out one type of institution.

Balance sheet
A financial statement showing what a firm or household owns and what it owes.

Assets
All the things that the firm or household owns or to which it holds a legal claim.

Liabilities
All the legal claims against a firm by nonowners or against a household by nonmembers.

Net worth
The firm's or household's assets minus its liabilities.

The Banking Balance Sheet

The operations of a commercial bank can best be understood by reference to its balance sheet. A firm's or household's **balance sheet** is a financial statement showing what it owns and what it owes, or, to use more technical language, its *assets, liabilities,* and *net worth.* **Assets,** which are listed on the left-hand side of the balance sheet, are all the things that the firm or household owns or to which it holds a legal claim. **Liabilities,** which are listed on the right-hand side of the balance sheet, are all the legal claims against a firm by nonowners or against a household by nonmembers. **Net worth,** also listed on the right-hand side of the balance sheet, is equal to the firm's or household's assets minus its liabilities. In a business firm, net worth represents the owners' claims against the business. *Equity* is another term that is often used to refer to net worth. In banking circles net worth is often referred to as *capital.*

The balance sheet gets its name from the fact that the totals of the two sides always balance. This follows from the definition of net worth. Because net worth is defined as assets minus liabilities, liabilities plus net worth must equal assets. In equation form, this basic rule of accounting reads as follows:

Assets = Liabilities + Net worth

Table 7.2 shows a total balance sheet for U.S. commercial banks. Balance sheet items for thrift institutions would differ in amount, but the concepts involved would be the same.

Reserves

Cash in bank vaults and banks' noninterest-bearing deposits with the Federal Reserve System.

ASSETS On the assets side of the balance sheet, the first line lists the noninterest-bearing deposits that banks maintain with the Federal Reserve System, as well as vault cash, which is currency that banks keep in their own vaults. Deposits at the Fed plus vault cash constitute a bank's reserves. Banks hold **reserves** of cash or assets that can be quickly converted into cash in order to be able to serve their customers' needs promptly. In particular, banks must have liquid reserves to pay out when customers want to withdraw funds from transaction deposits, either as currency or by using checks or electronic transfers. As we have noted, an important characteristic of transaction deposits is the right of depositors to withdraw funds without advance notice to the bank. Also, banks often make arrangements that allow their customers to borrow from the bank without advance notice. These arrangements include commercial lines of credit, consumer credit card accounts, and overdraft agreements that allow both businesses and consumers to write checks for more than the current balance in their accounts. The need to make good on lines of credit is an additional reason that banks need liquidity. In Chapter 8, we will return to the subject of how banks determine the level of liquid reserves they need.

TABLE 7.2 TOTAL BALANCE SHEET FOR U.S. COMMERCIAL BANKS, FEBRUARY 2007 (BILLIONS OF DOLLARS)

Assets		Liabilities	
Reserves and cash items	$291.5	Transaction deposits	$636.8
Securities	$2,296.9	Nontransaction deposits	$5,752.9
Loans	$6,102.5	Bank borrowing	$1,946.5
Other assets	$1,069.9	Other liabilities	$589.0
Total assets	$9,760.8	Total liabilities	$8,925.2
		Net worth	$835.6
		Total liabilities plus net worth	$9,760.8

This table shows the total balance sheet for all U.S. commercial banks as of Jan. 24, 2007. Assets of banks include noninterest-bearing reserves and interest-bearing loans and securities. Liabilities include deposits of all kinds and other borrowings. Net worth equals assets minus liabilities. The balance sheets of thrift institutions would show the same categories but would differ in details.

Source: Board of Governors of the Federal Reserve System, H.8 Statistical Release, Feb. 2, 2007.

The next two items on the assets side of the balance sheet show the banks' main income-earning assets. The largest item is loans made to firms and households. In addition, commercial banks hold a substantial quantity of securities, including securities issued by federal, state, and local governments. The final item on this side includes some smaller income-earning items plus the value of the banks' buildings and equipment.

LIABILITIES The first two items on the liabilities side of the banks' balance sheet are various kinds of deposits. They are liabilities because they represent funds to which depositors hold a legal claim. Funds that banks have borrowed are also liabilities. A small portion of these are borrowed from the Federal Reserve and the rest from private sources. Because the banks' total liabilities are less than their assets, they have a positive net worth. This sum represents the claim of the banks' owners against the banks' assets.

The Central Bank

Central bank

A government agency responsible for regulating a country's banking system and carrying out monetary policy.

We have already mentioned the Federal Reserve System, or the *Fed,* as it is known in financial circles. The Fed is the central bank of the United States. Like the **central banks** of other countries, it provides banking services to private banks and to other parts of the government. It is one of the chief regulators and supervisors of the banking system. Its responsibility for monetary policy makes it a major partner with Congress and the executive branch in macroeconomic policy making.

The Fed was established in 1913 as an independent agency of the federal government and therefore is not under the direction of the executive branch. It is subordinate to Congress, but Congress does not intervene in its day-to-day decision making. The reason for making the Fed independent was to prevent the U.S. Treasury Department from using monetary policy for political purposes. In practice, however, the Fed's monetary actions are coordinated with the Treasury's fiscal actions. The chair of the Fed's Board of Governors is in frequent contact with the secretary of the Treasury, the chair of the President's Council of Economic Advisers, and the director of the Office of Management and Budget. By law, the Fed also presents a formal report on monetary policy to Congress twice a year. The report explains how its monetary policy objectives are related to economic conditions and to the economic goals set by the administration and Congress.

FEDERAL RESERVE BANKS Most countries have a single, unified central bank (the Bank of England, the Bank of Japan, and so on), but the Federal Reserve System differs in some ways from this pattern. Because regional interests played a strong political role in founding the Federal Reserve System, it is composed of 12 Federal Reserve district banks, each of which serves a particular district of the country. The cities in which Federal Reserve Banks are located are Boston, New York, Philadelphia, Cleveland, Richmond, Atlanta, Chicago, St. Louis, Minneapolis, Kansas City, Dallas, and

San Francisco. An additional 25 cities, including Seattle, Denver, Cincinnati, Miami, and others, have branches of the Federal Reserve Bank in their district. The only similar multi-part central banking system in the world is the European Central Bank, which is responsible for monetary policy in the euro area. Each of the 13 countries that share the euro as their currency also retains its own central bank, which assists the European Central Bank in carrying out monetary policy and banking supervision for the region.

Each Federal Reserve bank is a separate unit chartered by the federal government. Its stockholders are commercial banks that are members of the Federal Reserve System. Although Federal Reserve banks issue stock to their members, they are not typical private firms in that they are neither operated for profit nor ultimately controlled by their stockholders. The Federal Reserve banks earn income from their holdings of federal securities and, since 1981, from charges for services provided to banks and thrift institutions. Each year the Fed district banks return all their income, minus operating costs, to the Treasury.

Each bank is managed by a nine-member board. Six of those members are selected by the member banks; the other three are appointed by the Fed's Board of Governors. Each board sets the policies of its own bank under the supervision of the Board of Governors. The Board of Governors also approves the appointments of each Reserve bank's top officers.

The Federal Reserve banks perform a number of important functions in the banking system. These include operating a wire system for electronic funds transfers, clearing checks, handling reserve deposits, and making loans to depository institutions. They issue paper currency in the form of Federal Reserve notes and supply Treasury coins. Several of the reserve banks are known for their strong research departments. Together with other federal agencies, they play an important role in supervising the safety and soundness of private banks. Finally, they provide banking services to the Treasury.

THE BOARD OF GOVERNORS The head of the Federal Reserve System is its Board of Governors. The Board, which supervises the 12 Federal Reserve banks, is comprised of seven members who are appointed by the president and confirmed by the Senate. Each governor serves a single 14-year term, with one term expiring every other year. The president appoints one of the board members to serve as chair for a four-year term.

The Board of Governors has the power to approve changes in the interest rate on loans made to banks and thrifts by the Fed district banks. Also, as explained in the next chapter, it can set the minimum level of reserves that banks and thrifts are required to hold relative to certain deposits. The Board supervises and regulates many types of banking institutions, including state-chartered member banks, bank holding companies, and U.S. offices of foreign banks. It also approves bank mergers and implements consumer credit regulations.

THE FEDERAL OPEN MARKET COMMITTEE Authority over purchases and sales of government securities held by the Fed—its most important monetary policy tool—rests with the Federal Open Market Committee (FOMC). The FOMC is made up of the seven members of the Board of Governors plus five district bank presidents. The president of the Federal Reserve Bank of New York is a permanent member; the remaining four seats rotate among the other 11 district banks. The committee meets eight times a year (and also confers by telephone) to set a general strategy for monetary policy. Committee decisions regarding changes in the Fed's holdings of securities are carried out through the open market trading desk at the Federal Reserve Bank of New York.

MEMBER AND NONMEMBER BANKS Approximately two-fifths of the more than 8,000 commercial banks in the United States belong to the Federal Reserve System. National banks must be members; state-chartered banks may join if they meet certain requirements. The member banks serve as stockholders of their district Federal Reserve Bank. Until 1980, member banks enjoyed certain privileges and received free services from the Fed, but in return they were subject to generally stricter regulation than nonmember banks.

In 1980 Congress passed the Depository Institutions Deregulation and Monetary Control Act, which did away with many of the distinctions between member and nonmember banks and between commercial banks and thrift institutions. As a result, since 1980 member banks, nonmember commercial banks, savings and loans, savings banks, and credit unions have all been subject to more uniform reserve requirements. In return for tighter regulation of reserves, thrift institutions won the right to compete more directly with commercial banks in making certain types of loans and offering transaction accounts. Nonmember depository institutions achieved access to Fed services such as check clearing, wire transfers, and loans on the same terms as member banks. In 1982 small depository institutions were exempted from reserve requirements. Thus, as a result of the Monetary Control Act, the distinction between banks and thrift institutions became less important.

THE FED'S BALANCE SHEET Table 7.3 shows a balance sheet for the Federal Reserve System. Government securities are by far the Fed's largest asset. These security holdings play a key role in the Fed's control of the money stock. Loans to banks and thrifts are small compared with other assets, but they are listed separately because they are important for policy purposes. Normally these loans are made to depository institutions on a short-term basis to enable them to meet their reserve requirements. However, in special circumstances longer-term loans are made to banks and thrifts that are experiencing a seasonal need for funds or are having financial difficulties. Other assets include some denominated in foreign currencies; these are important in carrying out the Fed's functions in the international monetary system.

TABLE 7.3 CONSOLIDATED BALANCE SHEET OF THE FEDERAL RESERVE BANKS, JANUARY 31, 2007 (BILLIONS OF DOLLARS)

Assets		Liabilities	
Securities	$812.1	Federal reserver notes	$765.6
Loans to banks	$1.3	Bank's reserve balances	$24.2
Other assets	$56.2	Other liabilities plus net worth	$79.8
Total assets	$869.6	Total liabilities plus net worth	$869.6

The Federal Reserve banks have liabilities to the general public in the form of Federal Reserve notes and to banks and thrifts in the form of reserve deposits. The Fed's main assets are government securities. Loans to banks with which to meet reserve requirements are small, but they are a key aspect of banking and monetary policy.

Source: Board of Governors of the Federal Reserve System, H.4.1 Statistical Release, Feb. 1, 2007.

Federal Reserve notes, which account for almost all of the nation's stock of currency, are the Fed's largest liability. These are followed by the reserves deposited with the Fed by banks and thrifts. Other liabilities include deposits of the Treasury and of foreign central banks. Because the Fed's assets exceed its liabilities, it has a positive net worth.

ENSURING THE SAFETY AND STABILITY OF THE BANKING SYSTEM

Banks play a vital role in our economy, yet we often take them for granted until they experience problems. Unfortunately, parts of the U.S. banking system have experienced serious problems from time to time, most recently in the 1980s. Although there has been no system-wide threat to the U.S. banking system since that time, individual banks occasionally run into trouble. This section looks at the sources of these failures and also at the policies used by government to ensure that the problems of individual institutions do not threaten the safety and stability of the banking system as a whole.

Risks of Banking

Banks earn a profit by lending out funds that they receive as deposits or by using those funds to buy securities at interest rates higher than those they pay to depositors. Banks have been earning profits in this way for hundreds of years, but there are some well-known risks involved.

One is *credit risk,* that is, the risk of loan losses. What happens if a bank makes a loan to a customer who is unable to repay it? When a loan goes bad, the bank's net worth is reduced by an equal amount. (In balance-sheet terms, writing off the bad loan is a reduction in assets. Liabilities—that is, deposits and borrowing—do not change. Therefore, net worth, which equals assets minus liabilities, must fall.) If loan losses are too great, the bank's net worth may fall below zero. At that point the bank will no longer have enough assets to pay off all of its depositors and other creditors. A bank whose liabilities exceed its assets is said to be *insolvent* and usually must cease doing business.

A second risk that banks face is *insufficient liquidity,* that is, having insufficient liquid assets to meet withdrawals or other obligations. When a depositor withdraws funds from a bank, the bank pays partly by drawing on the reserves it holds on deposit with the Fed or as vault cash and partly by drawing on other liquid assets that it holds for this purpose. Under normal conditions, new deposits approximately offset withdrawals, and the bank does not need to draw on its less liquid assets, such as loans and long-term securities, to cover withdrawals. If an unexpected wave of withdrawals occurs, however, the bank may use up all of its liquid assets. It will then have to convert some of its less liquid assets into cash. This may not be easy, especially if the wave of withdrawals takes place when business conditions are unfavorable, requiring the bank to sell the assets at less than the value at which they are entered on the bank's books. For example, a bank might have paid $1,000,000 for bonds issued by a state government agency. Later, because of unfavorable market conditions, it might have to sell them for just $800,000. Sales of assets at less than book value have an effect on the balance sheet similar to that of loan losses: In accordance with the basic equation of accounting, the reduction in the value of assets causes an equal reduction of the bank's net worth. If net worth falls below zero, the bank becomes insolvent.

Whether the bank's troubles begin with loan losses or with insufficient liquidity, there is a danger that they may trigger a run on the bank. A *run* is a situation in which depositors begin to withdraw their funds because they fear that the bank may become insolvent. Because large withdrawals force the bank to sell assets at less than their book values, depositors' fears become self-fulfilling and the bank fails.

In the worst possible case, the whole banking system, not just one bank, could get into trouble. If many banks faced loan losses or runs at the same time, they could not help one another with temporary loans of reserves. If large banks failed, smaller banks, which keep deposits in the large ones or make other loans to them, might be brought down, too. If many banks simultaneously tried to meet deposit outflows by selling their holdings of securities, the market price of the securities might fall, adding to their losses. A general bank crisis, in which the stability of the whole system would be threatened, could ensue.

Policies to Ensure Safety and Soundness

During the nineteenth century, a number of bank crises were touched off by recessions. As a result, both state and federal governments experimented with policies designed to ensure the safety and soundness of the banking system. Out of these efforts has evolved a system that is based on three basic tools: bank supervision and regulation, loans to troubled banks, and deposit insurance.

SUPERVISION AND REGULATION Bank examinations are the oldest tool for ensuring the safety and soundness of the banking system. These examinations, conducted by state or federal officials, are intended to ensure that banks do not make unduly risky loans, that they value their assets honestly, that they maintain an adequate level of net worth, and that they have competent management. Honest bookkeeping, prudent lending, and adequate net worth help banks to survive business downturns without becoming insolvent. A variety of federal and state agencies—including the Federal Reserve, the Federal Deposit Insurance Corporation (FDIC), and the Office of the Comptroller of the Currency (part of the Treasury) or OCC for short—share responsibility for supervision and regulation.

Supervision and regulation do not always ensure sound banking practices. Examinations do not always spot danger signals. Sometimes examiners are deceived by fraudulent operators of banks and thrifts; in other cases they do no better than bank managers in spotting bad loans or other risk factors. And sometimes the standards that examiners are asked to enforce are themselves too weak. In an attempt to improve the safety and stability of the banking system, standards have been tightened in several ways since the U.S. banking crises of the 1980s.

LENDER OF LAST RESORT Bank examinations, introduced more than a century ago, were not by themselves enough to prevent banking panics. In 1907 an especially severe panic took place, eventually leading to the establishment of the Federal Reserve System in 1913. Among other duties, the Fed has the power to aid the banking system in times of trouble by acting as a lender of last resort. For example, when the stock market experienced a record 22.6 percent loss on October 19, 1987, the Fed quickly announced that it stood ready to lend extra funds to any banks that needed additional cash because of customers' stock market losses. As discussed in *Economics in the News 7.1*, the Fed played an essential role in maintaining the soundness of the U.S. banking system following the 9/11 terrorist attacks in 2001.

Loans by the Fed to troubled institutions are useful primarily as a device to help fundamentally sound and solvent banks during temporary periods of insufficient liquidity. They cannot solve the problems of banks and thrifts that have fallen into insolvency because of imprudent management practices leading to massive loan losses.

ECONOMICS IN THE NEWS 7.1

9/11: THE FED AS A LENDER OF LAST RESORT

The September 11, 2001 attacks on the World Trade Center in New York and the Pentagon in Washington, D.C. caused severe disruptions in the financial system that left banks short on funds. The Fed's actions during the crisis highlight its importance not only as a lender of last resort, but as a central authority in the payments system.

At 11:45 a.m., just three hours after the attacks, the Federal Reserve issued the following press statement: "The Federal Reserve System is open and operating. (The discount window is available to meet liquidity needs." (The discount window is a facility that banks may use to take out loans from the Fed. Once such transactions were carried out face-to-face through an actual window; today, loan disbursements are made electronically.) In addition, the Federal Reserve's staff contacted banks in the days surrounding the attacks to promote borrowing from the Fed as banks faced difficulty in honoring payments and extending lines of credit to their customers.

A series of events prevented timely payments both in the business and banking sectors. The physical damage to communications, computers, and general operations in New York slowed payments dramatically. The Federal Aviation Administration (FAA) halted air traffic, preventing the delivery of checks to banks by air. As a result, the volume of interbank transfers, essential in the bank payments system, fell 43% between September 10 and 11, 2001.

The Federal Reserve System responded by acting in its original role as a lender of last resort, providing large sums in the form of loans to the banking system. Between September 5 and September 12, Fed loans to banks increased from $195 million to $45.6 billion. As the president of the Federal Reserve Bank of St. Louis, William Poole, stated: "In the absence of Fed intervention, we would have seen a cascade of defaults as firms due funds that were not arriving would be unable to meet their obligations."

Sources: Kristin Van Gaasbeck, "Circling the Wagons: The Fed's Response to 9/11," presented at the *Western Economics Association International 78th Annual Meeting*, Denver, CO, July 12, 2003; William Poole, "The Role of Government in U.S. Capital Markets," lecture presented at the Institute of Governmental Affairs, University of California, Davis, October 18, 2001.

DEPOSIT INSURANCE Even with its power as a lender of last resort, the Fed failed to prevent a major bank panic in 1933, during the Great Depression. In 1934, in response to that crisis, Congress established the Federal Deposit Insurance Corporation (FDIC). Since the Monetary Control Act of 1980, all deposits are insured up to $100,000 per account (and even more in special cases.)

The idea of deposit insurance is to short-circuit runs on banks. If deposits are insured, depositors need not run to the bank to withdraw their funds; even if the bank fails, the government will pay them their money or arrange for the transfer of their deposits to a solvent bank. Also, if runs can be avoided, the problems of one or a few banks will not touch off a panic that threatens the whole system. Depository institutions are supposed to bear the cost of deposit insurance through premiums charged by the insurance funds. However, in recent years, premiums have fallen short of costs and taxpayers have had to cover the insurance funds' losses.

One problem with deposit insurance is that it could encourage banks to take on excessive risk since they know the government insures their depositors. The savings and loans (S&L) crisis of the 1980s offers a perfect example of this problem. Deposit insurance encouraged some banks and thrifts to take undue risks with their depositors' money; the depositors did not object, knowing that the federal government would bail them out if the institution failed. Losses at savings and loans associations were so large that the Federal Savings and Loan Insurance Corporation (FSLIC), the deposit insurance fund for S&L and mutual savings banks at the time, itself was forced into insolvency. Since 1989, the FDIC has provided deposit insurance for S&Ls and mutual savings banks.

International Banking

Bank failures in one country have severe consequences for that country's trading partners. For this reason, in 1987 several countries attempted to establish a set of standard requirements for the international banking system. The resulting Basel Accord imposed regulations to help prevent banks from declaring bankruptcy. The Basel Accord guidelines also make recommendations regarding bank balance sheet management. In practice, the accord proved difficult to enforce because of varying accounting definitions and loopholes in the agreement. At the present time, a modified set of international standards, known as Basel II, is in the process of being implemented. It is too early to know whether the new standards will prevent the recurrence of crises like those described in *Economics in the News 7.2*.

ECONOMICS IN THE NEWS 7.2
GLOBAL BANKING CRISES

The international banking system's stability has become increasingly important but it is difficult to maintain. The table below highlights recent international banking crises and reports the estimated losses attributed to bank failures. For each country, the cost as a share of the economy's Gross Domestic Product (GDP) is reported. As the table shows, the U.S. banking crises of the 1980s, although very expensive, were not the worst when their cost is measured as a percentage of GDP.

The Basel Accord of 1987, and its successor Basel II, represent one effort to prevent banking crises around the world. The IMF's ability to provide support for central banks is another weapon. However, as long as the regulatory system of some countries remains weak, and as long as some banks undertake excessive risks, it is unlikely that banking crises will disappear entirely from the international economy.

COST OF INTERNATIONAL BANKING CRISES (1980–PRESENT)

Country	Dates	Estimated Cost as a % of GDP
Argentina	1980–82	55%
Indonesia	1997–2002	50–55%
Thailand	1997–2002	42%
Cote d'Ivoire	1988–1991	25%
Mexico	1995–2002	15%
Japan	1990s	12%
Hungary	1991–1995	10%
Russia	1998–1999	5–7%
United States	1984–1991	3%
Turkey	1982–1985	2.5%
New Zealand	1987–1990	1%

Source: Daniela Klingebiel and Luc Laewan, eds., "Managing the Real and Fiscal Effects of Banking Crises," World Bank Discussion Paper No. 428 (Washington: World Bank, 2002).

As we have seen, in the U.S. banking system, the Federal Reserve acts as a lender of last resort. Most other central banks have similar powers that allow them to support their countries' private banks during times of crises. However, sometimes a country's central bank itself runs short of liquidity. In such cases, the International Monetary Fund (IMF) has the power to make emergency loans to central banks. For example, the IMF used this power to provide loans to Korea and the Philippines during the East Asian financial crisis of 1997.

SUMMARY

1. **What is money, and what does it do?** *Money* is an asset that serves as a means of payment, a store of purchasing power, and a unit of account. Because money can be used as a means of payment and has a fixed nominal value, it is said to be *liquid.*

2. **How is the stock of money in the economy measured?** A narrow measure of the money stock, *M1,* includes *currency* (coins and paper money) plus *transaction deposits* (deposits on which checks can be freely written). A broader and more widely used measure, *M2,* includes the components of M1 plus money market mutual fund shares, money market deposit accounts, *savings deposits,* small-denomination *time deposits,* and certain other liquid assets.

3. **How is the quantity of money related to other key macroeconomic variables?** The relationship between money and other economic variables can be stated as the *equation of exchange:* MV = PQ, in which M stands for the money stock, V for *velocity,* P for the price level, and Q for real domestic product.

4. **What is the structure of the U.S. banking system?** The U.S. banking system consists of four types of *depository institutions.* The most important are commercial banks, which specialize in commercial loans and transaction deposits. In addition, there are three types of *thrift institutions:* savings and loan associations, savings banks, and credit unions. The Federal Reserve System is the nation's central bank. It provides services to depository institutions, holds much of their *reserves,* and, together with other federal agencies, regulates the banking system.

5. **How are the safety and stability of the banking system maintained?** Banks fail if they become insolvent—that is, if their assets fall below the level of their liabilities. This may happen because of loan losses or because deposit withdrawals have exhausted liquid assets. The government has three principal tools for ensuring the safety and soundness of the banking system: supervision and regulation; loans to banks and thrifts experiencing liquidity problems; and deposit insurance.

KEY TERMS

Money	Depository institutions
Liquidity	Commercial banks
Currency	Thrift institutions (thrifts)
Transaction deposit	Balance sheet
M1	Assets
Savings deposit	Liabilities
Time deposit	Net worth
M2	Reserves
Equation of exchange	Central bank
Velocity (income velocity of money)	

PROBLEMS AND TOPICS FOR DISCUSSION

1. **The functions of money.** Money serves three functions: as a means of payment, a store of purchasing power, and a unit of account. How does inflation undermine each of these functions?

2. **Barter in the modern economy.** For most purposes, money lowers the cost of making transactions relative to barter—the direct exchange of one good or service for another. However, barter has not disappeared, even in an advanced economy such as that of the United States. Can you give an example of the use of barter in the U.S. economy today? Why is barter used instead of money in this case?

3. **Plastic money.** Do you use any credit cards? Does their use reduce the amount of money you need? Which forms of money do you need less of because you have a credit card? How do credit cards differ from debit cards?

4. **The banking balance sheet.** The National Information Center is a database with banking information maintained by the Federal Reserve System. You can download balance sheet information at http://www.ffiec.gov/nic/. Do an institution search for your bank or thrift and download the balance sheet information for this institution. How does this balance sheet compare with that of all commercial banks as given in Table 7.2? *Bonus question:* Obtain the balance sheets of a bank and a thrift and compare them.

5. **Current monetary data.** Every Thursday the Federal Reserve reports certain key data on money and the banking system. These reports are available from the Board of Governors of the Federal Reserve System *H.6 Statistical Release.* Obtain the most recent H.6 release online at http://www.federalreserve.gov/releases/ and answer the following questions:

   a. What items are included in M2 that are not included in M1? What was the total of such items in the most recent month for which data are reported? Which of these money measures grew most quickly in the most recent month for which data are reported?

   b. Demand and other transaction deposits at these banks account for about what percentage of M1? What percentage of M1 is held in the form of currency and travelers checks?

6. **Recent bank failures.** The FDIC maintains a list of recently failed banks online at http://www.fdic.gov/bank/. Go to this list and download the infor-

mation for a recently failed bank. Why did the institution fail? How did federal authorities respond to the failure?

CASE FOR DISCUSSION

Makeshift Money in the French Colonial Period

The following letter was written by de Meulle, governor of the French province of Quebec in September 1685:

My Lord—

I have found myself this year in great straits with regard to the subsistence of the soldiers. You did not provide for funds, My Lord, until January last. I have, notwithstanding, kept them in provisions until September, which makes eight full months. I have drawn from my own funds and from those of my friends, all I have been able to get, but at last finding them without means to render me further assistance, and not knowing to what saint to pay my vows, money being extremely scarce, having distributed considerable sums on every side for the pay of the soldiers, it occurred to me to issue, instead of money, notes on [playing] cards, which I have had cut in quarters. I send you My Lord, the three kinds, one is for four francs, another for forty sols, and the third for fifteen sols, because with these three kinds, I was able to make their exact pay for one month. I have issued an ordinance by which I have obliged all the inhabitants to receive this money in payments, and to give it circulation, at the same time pledging myself, in my own name, to redeem the said notes. No person has refused them, and so good has been the effect that by this means the troops have lived as usual. There were some merchants who, privately, had offered me money at the local rate on condition that I would repay them in money at the local rate in France, to which I could not consent as the King would have lost a third; that is, for 10,000 he would have paid 40,000 livres; thus personally, by my credit and by my management, I have saved His Majesty 13,000 livres.

[Signed] de Meulle
Quebec, 24th September, 1685

Source: From *Canadian Currency, Exchange and Finance During the French Period,* vol. 1, ed. Adam Shortt (New York: Burt Franklin, Research Source Works Series no. 235, 1968).

QUESTIONS

1. What indication do you find that the playing-card notes issued by the governor served as a means of payment? Why were they accepted as such?
2. What indicates that the notes served as a store of value? What made them acceptable as such?
3. Did the invention of playing-card money change the unit of account in the local economy?

END NOTES

1. Money market mutual funds, which compete with banks and thrifts for household savings, make every effort to make their services as convenient as those of their competitors. They provide statements, checkbooks, deposit slips, and so on that closely resemble those used by banks and thrifts. Technically, however, their liabilities are shares in the fund's portfolio of assets, not deposits. Therefore, money market mutual funds are not considered to be depository institutions. Only retail, or consumer, money market mutual funds are included in M2—those owned by corporations are not.
2. This can be demonstrated as follows: First, the right-hand side of the equation, the price level times real domestic product (PQ), can be replaced by Y, standing for nominal domestic product. Next, both sides of the equation can be divided by M to give V = Y/M.

CHAPTER 8

Central Banking and Monetary Policy

After reading this chapter, you will understand:

1. How banks create money
2. What limits the size of the money stock
3. What instruments are available to the central bank for controlling the money stock
4. The activities that the central bank undertakes in the international sphere

Before reading this chapter, make sure you know the meaning of:

1. M1, M2
2. Balance sheets
3. Central bank
4. Federal Reserve System
5. Bank reserves
6. Current account and financial account transactions in the balance of payments.

THE INFLUENCE OF the central bank on the economy is like that of the moon on the tides—powerful but largely invisible. Walter Heller, once described joining the Fed's policy-making Open Market Committee as like being inducted into the Vatican's College of Cardinals. This chapter will show how central banks influence the internal workings of a country's economy and its economic links to the rest of the world.

The chapter begins by explaining how banks create money, and what limits their ability to do so. Next we will look at the tools that the central bank uses to control the money stock for the country as a whole. Finally, we look briefly at how central banks can act to influence international financial markets.

DETERMINING THE QUANTITY MONEY

As we saw in Chapter 7, the bulk of the U.S. money stock (M2) consists of Federal Reserve currency and deposits at commercial banks and thrift institutions. Other forms of money—Coins issued by the U.S. Treasury, travelers checks, and money market mutual fund shares—form a small part of the money stock. We will leave them out of the picture altogether in this chapter.

A Balance-Sheet View of Money

Money in the form of currency and bank deposits appears on three important balance sheets, as shown in Figure 8.1. The first balance sheet is that of the Federal Reserve System, the central bank of the United States. The second balance sheet shows the total assets, liabilities, and net worth of all the country's commercial banks and thrift institutions. The third balance sheet includes the total assets, liabilities, and net worth of everyone else in the economy, that is, all households and all business firms except banks.

FIGURE 8.1

Federal Reserve System

Government securities	Monetary base
Other net assets	*includes*
	Currency
	Reserve deposits

Commercial Banks and Thrifts

Reserves	Bank Deposits
includes	Other liabilities
Reserve deposits (at Fed)	
Currency (vault cash)	
Loans	
Other assets	Net worth

Households and firms

Currency	Bank loans
Bank deposits	Other liabilities
Other assets	Net worth

Money, consisting of currency and bank deposits, appears on three balance sheets. Currency in the hands of the public is an asset of households and non-bank firms, and a liability of the Fed. Currency held as vault cash by banks is not part of the money stock. The remainder of the money stock consists of bank deposits, which are an asset of households and firms, and a liability of banks. Currency plus banks' reserve deposits constitute the monetary base.

We can begin by looking at where currency appears on these three balance sheets. As we saw in the previous chapter, currency is a liability of the Federal Reserve System, so it appears on the right-hand side of the Fed's balance sheet. Commercial banks and thrifts keep currency on hand for their tellers to hand out over the counter and to fill their ATM machines. As explained in Chapter 6, this currency held by banks—called "vault cash"—counts as part of the bank's reserves. Because vault cash is an asset, it appears on the left-hand side of the banks' balance sheet. The rest of the currency issued by the Fed appears as an asset on the balance sheets of households and firms, who use it as a means of payment and a store of value. Only this currency—called *currency in circulation*—is included in the official measures of the money stock (M1 and M2). Vault cash does not count as part of the nation's money stock.

The second component of the money stock consists of funds on deposit at the nation's commercial banks and thrift institutions. These are assets of households and firms and liabilities of banks. They are used by the public as a means of payment and a store of value.

One last item links the balance sheet of commercial banks and thrifts with that of the Fed—the reserves that banks keep on deposit with the Fed. As we saw in Chapter 7, these reserve deposits provide necessary liquidity for banks and are used in clearing checks and making electronic transfers of funds from one bank to another. The total reserves of the banking system consist of reserve deposits at the Fed plus currency held as vault cash.

The Monetary Base

Let's look more closely now at the Fed's balance sheet. In Figure 8.1, it is presented in a slightly different way than in Table 7.3 of the previous chapter. The Fed's non-monetary liabilities (for example, deposits of the U.S. Treasury), together with its net worth, do not appear on the right-hand side of this version of the balance sheet. Instead, they are subtracted from the Fed's other assets to give the item "other net assets" shown on the left-hand side of Figure 8.1. Making this adjustment leaves only the Fed's monetary liabilities—currency and the reserve deposits of commercial banks and thrifts—on the right-hand side of the balance sheet. The sum of currency and reserve deposits is called the **monetary base**. Notice that the monetary base includes both currency in circulation, shown on the balance sheet of households and firms, and vault cash, shown on the commercial bank balance sheet. As we will see, the monetary base plays a key role in central bank control of the money stock.

Monetary base

The sum of currency and reserve deposits, the monetary liabilities of the central bank.

A Closer Look at Bank Reserves

In Chapter 7, we saw that banks hold a certain quantity of liquid reserves in order to serve the needs of their customers. In this section we take a closer look at bank reserves. First we will see how banks distribute reserves between currency and reserve deposits, and then how they determine the total amount of reserves they will hold.

RESERVE DEPOSITS VS. CURRENCY From the banks' point of view, reserve deposits and currency held as vault cash are close substitutes. Both are highly liquid assets that banks use to serve the needs of their customers. Reserve deposits are used in the process of clearing checks which are written on one bank and deposited in another and for other kinds of inter-bank transactions. Currency is distributed to customers over the counter by a bank's tellers and through Automatic Teller Machines (ATMs) located at the bank or in other convenient locations.

Banks have complete flexibility in deciding how much of their reserves to hold as currency and how much as reserve deposits. Some banks, depending on their location, their customers' needs, and the time of year, tend to receive more currency each day from their customers' deposits than they supply to customers through their branches and ATMs. When that is the case, they have the right to send the excess currency to the Fed, which records the amount received as an increase in the bank's reserve deposit. Other banks may find that they are paying out more currency to their customers than they receive as deposits. To replenish their tellers' drawers and their ATM machines, they ask the Fed to send them additional currency. The Fed loads the requested amount of currency on an armored truck and sends it to the bank. As it does so, it reduces the banks' reserve deposit by the same amount.

Whether banks send excess currency to the Fed or request additional currency from it, there is no change in total bank reserves (reserve deposits plus vault cash) and no change in the monetary base (total currency plus reserve deposits). Only the relative proportion of these items held in currency or non-currency form changes.

DETERMINING THE AMOUNT OF RESERVES In addition to deciding how to divide reserves between currency and reserve deposits, banks must also decide what total quantity of reserves to hold. The quantity of reserves is most conveniently stated as a ratio of reserves to deposits, which we will call the **reserve ratio.** Two major factors influence the quantity of reserves banks choose to hold.

Reserve ratio

The ratio of a bank's reserves (reserve deposits at the central bank plus vault cash) to its own deposit liabilities.

First, there is a trade-off between liquidity and income. On the one hand, holding a greater quantity of liquid reserves makes life easier for a bank. It has greater flexibility in meeting its customers' needs, and it also avoids risk. The risk comes from the possibility that unanticipated withdrawals of funds by depositors will drain away all of its liquid assets. When that happens, the bank will either have to borrow more reserves or sell other assets like loans or bonds. If market conditions are unfavorable, it may be costly to borrow additional reserves, and the prices it gets for selling other assets may be disappointingly low. In either case, the bank will suffer a loss. In extreme cases, the bank might not be able to obtain the needed liquid reserves at any price, and would not be able to fulfill its promise that customers can withdraw funds on demand. In that case the bank would fail. On the other hand, despite the convenience and reduced risk of holding a large amount of liquid reserves, there is an opportunity cost of doing so. The opportunity cost comes from the fact that assets held in the form of currency or reserve deposits at the Fed, unlike loans and securities, earn no interest income. Banks must find a balance between the benefits and opportunity costs of holding liquid reserves.

Second, the quantity of reserves a bank holds may be subject to regulation. The degree of regulation varies. In the past, the Federal Reserve, like most other central banks, tended to regulate reserves rather strictly. It did so by setting a minimum ratio of reserves to deposits. In recent decades, central banks have tended to back away from strict regulation of reserves. In some countries, including the United Kingdom, Canada, and New Zealand, the ratio of reserves to deposits is not regulated at all. The Fed has not gone quite so far, but it has moved more cautiously in the same direction. In 1990, it eliminated reserve requirements on saving and time deposits, which constitute nearly 90 percent of all deposits. In 1992, reserve requirements on transactions deposits were cut to 10 percent. As a result, reserve requirements, as a percent of all bank deposits, are at a historically low level.

Banks must take both central bank regulations and considerations of safe banking practice into account when choosing the amount of reserves to hold. If they hold too many reserves, they will forego an opportunity to invest in more profitable assets like loans and securities. If they hold too few, they increase their liquidity risk and they may be subject to central bank penalties for insufficient reserves. We will call the minimum quantity of reserves that banks desire to hold consistent with regulations and safe banking practices the **target reserve ratio**. In the United States, the target reserve ratio is slightly greater than the minimum required by Federal Reserve regulations. The difference between the amount of reserve a bank actually holds at any given time and the minimum required by regulations are called **excess reserves**.

Target reserve ratio

The minimum amount of reserves a bank needs to hold that is consistent with regulations and safe banking practices

Excess reserves

The difference between the amount of reserve a bank actually holds and the minimum required by regulations.

HOW BANKS CREATE MONEY

Where does money come from? There is no mystery about the creation of the part of the money stock that consists of currency. Paper money is printed by the government and distributed through the banking system whenever banks ask for it, as explained in the previous section. However, the origin of the bulk of the money stock, which consists of bank deposits, is less well understood. Lending is the most important mechanism through which the deposit component of the money stock is created. A simple example will show how a bank creates new money by making a loan:

Suppose that I am a banker and you are a consumer. You have found a nice new car at a local dealer, and have agreed on a price of $25,000. You check the balance in your account at my bank, and see that you have $10,000 on deposit, more than enough for a down payment but not enough to buy the car for cash. You come into the bank and apply for a loan of $20,000. I check your credit history and approve the loan. You sign a promissory note, promising to repay the $20,000 with interest over a three-year period. I give you the $20,000 by crediting that amount to your account. The next morning, you go on line and check your account balance once again. Sure enough, you now have $30,000—the $10,000 you started with plus the $20,000 loan proceeds that the bank credited to your account. You go to the dealer, write out a check for $25,000, and drive off in your new car. You have $5,000 left over to pay your groceries and rent for the rest of the month. Later in the day, the dealership deposits the check in its account at whatever bank it does business with—maybe my bank, but more likely, another one.

T-account

A simplified version of a balance sheet that shows only items that change as a result of a given set of transactions.

Figure 8.2 shows how these transactions affect the three key players in the monetary system—the Fed, the banking system, and the rest of the private sector, consisting of firms and households. Unlike Figure 8.1, this time we do not show the complete balance sheets for the three key players. Instead, the figure shows **T-accounts**, which are simplified versions of the balance sheets that show only the items that change as a result of a given set of transactions.

First look at the T-account for the banking system. When you signed the promissory note for the loan, my bank gained a new asset worth $20,000. This is shown as an entry of +20,000 under loans. At the same time, when I credited the $20,000 of loan proceeds to your account, my bank gained a new liability. This is shown as an entry of +20,000 under deposits. Later, when you bought the car, the deposit moved from my bank to that where the car dealer does business. That transaction does not

FIGURE 8.2

Federal Reserve System

no changes		*no changes*	

Commercial Banks and Thrifts

Reserves	*no change*	Bank Deposits	+20,000
Loans	+20,000		

Households and firms

Bank deposits	+20,000	Bank loans	+20,000

This diagram shows how the money stock is affected when a bank makes a loan. Instead of complete balance sheets, T-accounts are used, which show only items that change as the result of the loan. The loan results in an increase in bank assets and consumer liabilities; at the same time, it produces an increase in bank deposits, which are consumer assets and bank liabilities.

show up on this T-account, which shows only the total balance sheet for all banks. Just moving funds from an account at one bank to an account at another does not affect total bank assets or liabilities.

Next, look at the T-account for firms and households. The increase in deposits when I credited you with the proceeds of the loan shows up on the asset side of the T-account as an entry of +20,000. Your obligation to repay the loan according to the terms of the promissory note shows up on the liability side as an entry of +20,000. Later, you used the $20,000 to pay for the car, but that part of the transaction does not show up here because this is the total balance sheet for all firms and households. Just moving the funds from your account to that of the car dealer does not affect the totals.

While all this goes on, the balance sheet of the Fed is unaffected.

Now look at the three T-accounts together to see what has happened to the money stock. No new currency has been issued, so that part of the money stock is unchanged. However, the total amount of deposits in the economy has increased by $20,000. That is a net addition to the money stock. The lesson to be learned from this example is: *Whenever a bank makes a loan, the immediate effect is to increase the money stock by the amount of the loan.*

Limits to Banks' Ability to Create Money

But wait a minute, you say. I know bankers are rich guys, but this looks *too* easy! If banks can create money whenever they want, what keeps them from creating *unlimited* amounts of money? Why don't bankers create enough to buy up everyone and everything there is?

These are good questions and they deserve a careful answer. Although banks do create money when they make loans, they can't create unlimited amounts of money. There are two principal constraints on banks' powers of money creation.

THE RESERVES CONSTRAINT The first constraint arises from the need for banks to hold reserves of liquid assets in the form of currency or reserve deposits at the central bank. As explained in the previous section, banks try to maintain a target reserve ratio, taking into account central bank regulations and safe banking practices. Banks forego too many profitable lending opportunities if reserves are above the target ratio, and they face excessive liquidity risk and possible administrative penalties if the reserve ratio falls below the target.

A close look at Figure 8.2 shows that when a bank creates new deposits by making a loan, the amount of total reserves in the banking system does not change. However, since deposits increase and reserves do not, that means the *ratio* of reserves to deposits decreases. As banks make more and more loans, at some point the reserve ratio will fall to the target level, as determined by regulations or safe banking practices. Once this minimum is reached, banks cannot safely make more loans until the banking system receives more reserves.

For the banking system as a whole, the constraint posed by the target reserve ratio must be observed fairly strictly, but it is not absolutely binding at a given moment. If the reserve ratio temporarily falls below its target, banks have a little time to adjust. The Fed enforces its reserve requirements on average over a two week period, not on a day-to-day basis. There is a little additional flexibility because banks normally hold excess reserves equal to a few percent of total reserves. But within these limits for adjustment, banks must soon begin to restore reserves to their target ratio by reducing the volume of loans. They do this mainly by allowing old loans to be repaid without making new loans to replace them. On the other hand, banks will not allow the reserve ratio to rise above its target for long. Whenever the reserve ratio is higher than the target, they will aggressively pursue new lending opportunities, lowering interest rates or easing other loan terms if that is necessary to attract borrowers.

Despite the importance of the target reserve ratio as viewed from the point of view of the whole banking system, the target ratio does not pose a strict constraint for any individual bank. At first glance, it might seem that a bank must wait until it has excess reserves before it can make new loans, but that is not really true. Suppose some bank is already operating at its target reserve ratio when a customer comes in the door with an attractive proposal to borrow several million dollars for a real estate development. The bank has several ways of obtaining the reserves it needs to make the loan while still meeting its target reserve ratio. One option is to sell some other asset, for example, short-term securities that pay less interest than the new loan will earn. Another option is to borrow reserves from some other bank that temporarily has more reserves than it needs. Still another option is to sell large certificates of deposit through a well-developed nation-wide market for that type of bank liability. There are other options as well. None of these tactics by which a single bank can get the reserves it needs changes the total reserves of the banking system. However, they do mean that any one bank does not have to wait passively for reserves to arrive before it can take advantage of new loan opportunities.

THE DEPOSIT MULTIPLIER In a simplified banking system where deposits were the only form of money, the constraint on deposit creation imposed by the reserve ratio would imply a simple relationship between the total amount of deposit-money and total reserves. We can state this relationship as follows:

$$\text{Total deposits} = \text{Total reserves} \times (1/\text{Reserve ratio})$$

The term 1/Reserve ratio on the right-hand side of this equation can be called the **deposit multiplier**. The deposit multiplier shows the amount of deposits that can be created for each dollar of total reserves in a simple banking system where deposits are the only form of money.

Deposit multiplier

The quantity of total deposits that can be created for each dollar of total reserves in a simple banking system where deposits are the only form of money, equal to 1/Reserve ratio.

THE CURRENCY CONSTRAINT The preceding examples leave out an important aspect of the monetary system—currency. In an economy where people choose to use currency for part of their transactions, the picture changes. Bank lending still causes the money stock to increase, but not by as much. A modification of our earlier example will make this clear.

Suppose that this time, instead of borrowing money to buy a car, you want to borrow $2,000 to go on vacation. As before, you come into my bank and sign the papers for a loan. The bank credits $2,000 to your account. This time, however, as soon as you verify that the funds are on deposit in your account, you go to the nearest ATM and withdraw $1,000 in currency to take along on your trip. You leave the rest on deposit to cover parts of your vacation that you plan to pay for by check or debit card.

Figure 8.3 shows the T-accounts for this set of transactions. As before, the loan appears as an increase in bank assets and an increase in household liabilities. Also as before, the loan produces an equal increase in the money stock, this time consisting of $1,000 of additional deposits and $1,000 of currency in circulation.[1] The big difference between Figure 8.3 and Figure 8.2 lies in what happens to bank reserves. When you withdraw $1,000 from the bank's ATM, the vault cash portion of the banking system's reserves decreases by $1,000, in contrast to the earlier example, where total bank reserves remained unchanged.

The fact that a predictable fraction of each increase in the money stock will be withdrawn from the banking system as currency puts an added constraint on banks' ability to make loans. Now lending not only causes deposits to increase, it also causes

FIGURE 8.3

Federal Reserve System

no changes		*no changes*	

Commercial Banks and Thrifts

Reserves (vault cash)	-1,000	Bank Deposits	+1,000
Loans	+2,000		

Households and firms

Bank deposits	+1,000	Bank loans	+2,000
Currency	+1,000		

This figure shows the T-account effects of a loan, when part of the loan proceeds are withdrawn as cash. The end result is an increase in the money stock (bank deposits plus currency in circulation) and a decrease in total bank reserves.

total reserves to fall. Starting from any given amount of reserves, the ratio of reserves to deposits will approach the target reserve ratio faster than would be the case if deposits were the only form of money. The total amount of money that banks can create is accordingly less.

THE MONEY MULTIPLIER For an economy where deposits were the only form of money, we were able to state the money stock as a multiple of bank reserves. We can do something similar for an economy that includes currency, except that now reserves are a variable, not a constant, so they no longer make a suitable reference point. Instead, the best reference point for the size of the money stock is the *monetary base*—the sum of bank reserve deposits and currency issued by the Federal Reserve. Although total bank reserves change when currency moves from banks into the hands of the public, the monetary base does not. The monetary base includes all currency, regardless of whether it is held by banks, households, or firms.

In equation form, we can state the relationship between the money stock (currency in circulation plus bank deposits) and the monetary base (total currency plus bank reserve deposits at the central bank) as follows:

$$\text{Money stock} = \text{Monetary base} \times [(1+\text{CUR})/(\text{RES}+\text{CUR})]$$

In this equation, we use the symbol RES to stand for the target reserve ratio. The symbol CUR stands for the amount of currency that the public chooses to hold per dollar of bank deposits. The expression (1+CUR)/(RES+CUR) on the right-hand side of the equation is known as the **money multiplier.** The money multiplier gives the total quantity of money that can be created for each dollar of the monetary base.[2]

Money multiplier

The total quantity of money that can be created for each dollar of the monetary base.

For example, suppose that banks want to hold \$1 in reserves for each \$10 in deposits, so that the variable RES = 0.1. (It does not matter whether banks decide to hold this quantity of reserves because it is required by central bank regulations, or whether they decide on their own that they need that quantity of reserves in order to safely serve their customers.) Suppose also that the public decides to hold \$2 in currency for each \$10 in deposits, so that the variable CUR=0.2. In that case, the money multiplier will be (1+.2)/(.1+.2) = 1.2/.3 = 4. A maximum of \$4 of money can be created for each \$1 of the monetary base.

The money multiplier differs from one country to another depending on regulations, payment habits of the public, and the degree of development of the banking system. In the United States, the money multiplier for M2 is approximately 8. (You can estimate the value of the multiplier for yourself based on the tables in Chapter 7.) By comparison, in Russia, the money multiplier is only a little over 3. The main reason for the smaller money multiplier in Russia is that currency accounts for a much larger portion of the total money stock. That, in turn, reflects the fact that the commercial banking system in Russia is less developed and less trusted by the public than in the United States.

THE INSTRUMENTS OF MONETARY POLICY

As we learned in Chapter 7, the Fed, like the central banks of other countries, has a major role in providing services to the banking system and in ensuring its safety and stability. Now we turn to an even more important function of central banks— control of the money stock. The preceding section showed how the money stock is determined as the product of the money multiplier and the monetary base. The principal means that the Fed and other central banks use to control the money stock is to adjust the size of the monetary base. In addition, central banks can, to some extent, influence the size of the money multiplier, although in practice that is much less important as an instrument of monetary policy.

Open Market Operations

The most important of the policy instruments that the Fed uses to control the money stock is to buy or sell government securities. The U.S. Treasury sells newly issued securities to the public through frequently scheduled auctions, but the Fed is not allowed to participate in those auctions. Instead, it buys and sells government securities that have been previously issued by the treasury through securities dealers that operate in public financial markets. Because the Fed buys securities in public markets that are open to traders of all kinds, rather than buying them directly from the treasury, the Fed's purchases and sales of government securities are called *open market operations.*

EFFECTS OF AN OPEN MARKET PURCHASE Figure 8.4 shows the immediate impact of an open market purchase of $1,000,000 of securities by the Fed. The purchase appears on the Fed's T-account as a $1,000,000 increase in assets. The securities dealer from whom the securities are purchased is part of the "households and firms" sector, so the asset side of that T-account shows a decrease of government securities. The Fed pays the dealer by issuing a payment order to the commercial bank where the dealer's firm maintains a deposit. When the payment order is carried out, the dealer's deposit increases by $1,000,000, as shown by an entry on the left-hand side of the firms and households T-account and a corresponding entry on the right-hand side of the banking sector's T-account. At the same time, the bank's reserve deposit account at the Fed is credited with an increase of $1,000,000. The increase in reserve deposits is shown on the left-hand side of the banking sector's T-account and the right-hand side of the Fed's T-account.

Looking at Figure 8.4 as a whole, we see that the immediate impact of the open market operation is an increase of $1,000,000 in bank reserves, bank deposits and the money stock. That is not the end of the story, however. To trace the full impact of the open market operation on the money stock, we have to look at how banks adjust their operations in response to the increase in reserves.

FIGURE 8.4 IMMEDIATE IMPACT OF AN OPEN MARKET PURCHASE

Federal Reserve System

Government securities	+1,000,000	Reserve deposits	+1,000,000

Commercial Banks and Thrifts

Reserve deposits	+1,000,000	Bank Deposits	+1,000,000

Households and firms

Bank deposits	+1,000,000		
Government securities	-1,000,000		

This figure shows the T-account effects of a $1,000,000 open market purchase of securities by the Fed. The immediate result is an increase in commercial bank reserves, bank deposits, and the money stock. Later (not shown here), banks can use the new reserves as a basis for new loans, leading to further expansion of the money stock.

Suppose that before the open market operations, banks were operating at their target reserve ratio. If so, an equal increase in total reserves and deposits, as shown in Figure 8.4, raises the ratio of total bank reserves to deposits above its target. Banks will take advantage of the new reserves to make additional loans, and the money stock will expand further, following the process illustrated earlier in Figures 8.2 and 8.3. As the banks create additional deposits through lending, the reserve ratio decreases. When borrowers withdraw part of the loan proceeds as currency, total bank reserves decrease and the reserve ratio falls further.

When the reserve ratio reaches its target, expansion of the money stock ceases. At that point, the total change in the money stock will be equal to the money multiplier times the change in the monetary base. For example, suppose the reserve ratio is .1 and the public's desired ratio of currency to deposits is .2, as in our earlier example. In that case, the money multiplier is 4, so the $1,000,000 open market purchase of securities, and the resulting $1,000,000 increase in the monetary base, will cause the total money stock to expand by $4,000,000. Part of the newly created money will be deposits, and part currency.

The example just given assumes that the Fed makes an outright purchase of securities from a dealer. In that case, the effect on the monetary base and the money stock will be permanent. Instead of buying securities outright, the Fed often buys them subject to a *repurchase agreement*. Under a repurchase agreement, the Fed agrees to sell the securities back to the dealer, for an agreed price, at some specific date in the future, often as soon as the next day. The effects of an open market purchase subject to a repurchase agreement are only temporary, because the change in the monetary base lasts only until the repurchase is completed. Repurchase agreements are routinely used by the Fed to make small, day-to-day adjustments in the monetary base.

EFFECTS OF AN OPEN MARKET SALE If the Fed sells securities instead of buying them, the entire process just described is reversed. When the Fed sells securities, the securities dealers who buy them pay by drawing on their accounts at commercial banks. Deposits, bank reserves, the monetary base, and the money stock all fall. The immediate impact on reserves and the monetary base would be shown by a set of T-accounts identical to Figure 8.4, except that all the plus and minus signs would be reversed.

The immediate impact of an open market sale by the Fed is to decrease reserves and deposits by an equal amount, so the ratio of reserves to deposits will fall below the target reserve ratio. Given the reduced quantity of reserves, the only way banks can restore the reserve ratio to its proper level is to reduce the total amount of outstanding loans, which they can do by allowing old loans to be repaid without making enough new loans to replace them. As repayments exceed new loans, total deposits and the total money stock decrease. The process will come to an end when the reserve ratio once again reaches its target level. Assuming a money multiplier of 4, a $4,000,000 decrease in the money stock would be required to restore the target reserve ratio following a $1,000,000 open market sale of securities.

The Discount Rate

As mentioned earlier, when individual banks see profitable lending opportunities, they do not need to wait passively for new reserves to arrive from the Fed. Instead, they can borrow the reserves they need. One way to do this is to borrow them from another bank. The market in which banks make short-term loans of reserves to other banks is known in the United States as the **federal funds market**. (A more general term is the *inter-bank loan market*. All countries have inter-bank loan markets, although the names of these markets differ.) The interest rate charged on such loans is called the **federal funds rate**. Transactions in this market, in which the usual loan term is overnight, total billions of dollars per day.

The borrowing and lending of reserves through the federal funds market has no effect on total bank reserves; this type of borrowing just moves reserves around from one bank to another. However, banks also have the option of borrowing funds directly from the Fed through the so-called **discount window**. Funds that banks borrow from the Fed through the discount window are a net addition to total bank

Federal funds market

A market in which banks lend reserves to one another for periods as short as 24 hours.

Federal funds rate

The interest rate on overnight loans of reserves from one bank to another.

Discount window

The department through which the Federal Reserve lends reserves to banks.

reserves. They affect the money stock in exactly the same way as do additional reserves provided through open market operations.

Banks borrow from the Fed in two kinds of situations. The most frequent kind of borrowing, called *primary credit,* is made by banks that are fundamentally healthy but which find themselves temporarily short of reserves because of unexpected withdrawals. They are charged an interest rate called the **discount rate.** To discourage banks from borrowing too often or too much through the discount window, the Fed sets the discount rate above the prevailing level of the federal funds rate at which banks can borrow from one another. Typically, the discount rate is one percentage point above the federal funds rate.

Discount rate

The interest rate charged by the Fed on loans of reserves to banks.

In addition to such lending, the Fed sometimes makes loans to troubled banks to give them time to get their affairs in order. Since these banks are less creditworthy, they must pay a higher interest rate. Typically, their interest rate is one-half of a percentage point above the discount rate charged on primary credit loans.

The discount rate gives the Fed a second policy instrument for controlling the money supply, although a less powerful one than open market operations. If the Fed wants to encourage more borrowing of reserves, it lowers the discount rate. As the discount rate falls relative to the federal funds rate, the cost of discount borrowing falls relative to the cost of borrowing from other banks and the volume of discount borrowing expands. However, because of the administrative pressures that the Fed uses to discourage excessive discount borrowing, there is a limit to how much discount borrowing banks will want to undertake. If the Fed wants to reduce borrowing from the discount window, it raises the discount rate.

Changes in Required-Reserve Ratios

Changes in required-reserve ratios are a third potential policy instrument that central banks can use to control the money stock. Earlier in the chapter we showed that the total volume of money is equal to the monetary base times the money multiplier:

$$\text{Money stock} = \text{Monetary base} \times [(1+\text{CUR})/(\text{RES}+\text{CUR})]$$

The term RES in this equation stands for the target reserve ratio, which, in the United States, is regulated by the Fed for transaction deposits. An increase in the reserve ratio required on transaction deposits will increase the term RES. Since the term RES appears in the denominator of the money multiplier, the money multiplier decreases when RES increases. That, in turn, will cause the money stock to decrease for any given level of the monetary base. Similarly, a decrease in reserve requirements will cause the money multiplier, and the money stock, to increase.

Changes in reserve requirements have never been used for day-to-day control over the money supply, but there have been times in the past when the Fed changed the ratios in order to make a strong move toward expansion or contraction of the money supply. For example, in late 1990, the Fed eliminated a 3 percent reserve requirement on nonpersonal saving and time deposits. In April 1992, it reduced the required reserve ratio on transaction deposits from 12 percent to 10 percent. These changes were made, in part, to speed recovery from the 1990–1991 recession, although they also reflected a belief that lower reserve requirements would reduce bank's cost, encourage bank lending, and strengthen the role of banks in the financial system. Since that time, the Fed has not used the reserve requirement as an instrument to control the money supply. Changes in reserve requirements pose difficulties for bank balance sheet management, and high reserve requirements make banks less competitive with other financial institutions. Occasionally the central banks of other countries use changes in required reserves as an instrument of monetary policy, but on the whole, this instrument is not of great importance. It is not available at all in countries like the UK and Canada, where central banks leave the determination of the reserve ratio up to the business judgment of individual banks.

Other Factors Affecting the Money Multiplier

We have already seen that the money multiplier is subject to change as a result of changes in reserve requirements. In addition, even if central bank policy remains unchanged, changing market conditions can cause the money multiplier to vary through effects on the currency ratio, CUR, or the target reserve ratio, RES.

The amount of currency that firms and households want to hold per dollar of deposits varies, among other reasons, according to the season of the year. During the Christmas shopping season, consumers withdraw additional money from their bank accounts to buy gifts, and retailers also stock the cash drawers in their stores with extra currency. Accordingly, the variable CUR increases and the money multiplier decreases.[3] The same thing happens during the summer vacation season, when consumers withdraw extra cash for their travels.

The target reserve ratio can also be affected by changing conditions in financial markets. When market interest rates increase, it becomes more expensive for firms to borrow liquid reserves. They tighten their liquidity management practices in order to get by with the lowest amount of reserves they can, consistent with central bank regulations and safe banking practices. Accordingly, an increase in market interest rates, other things being equal, tends to decrease the target reserve ratio and increase the money multiplier.

Such market-driven changes in the money multiplier pose a challenge to the Fed. When the money multiplier increases, the Fed must offset the increase with open market sales of securities or an increase in the discount rate. When the money multiplier decreases, the Fed must buy securities on the open market or lower the discount rate. Normally, central banks can make such adjustments smoothly enough to maintain reasonably close control over the money stock. For example, the Fed can anticipate seasonal changes in currency demand fairly accurately. Still, because the money multiplier is not a constant, central banks cannot control the money stock precisely. In extreme cases, changes in the money multiplier may cause serious problems. For example, during Japan's long period of deflation in the late 1990s and early 2000s, that country's commercial banks became very reluctant to make new loans. As banks accumulated unused reserves, the money multiplier fell to levels far below normal, and the Bank of Japan found it very difficult to provide the amount of monetary policy stimulus it needed to speed economic recovery. Chapter 13 will take a closer look at the Japanese deflation.

CENTRAL BANKING IN THE INTERNATIONAL ECONOMY

The preceding section of this chapter looked at three instruments of monetary policy—open market operations, changes in the discount rate, and changes in reserve ratios—all of which operate within the domestic economy. In this section we turn to a fourth instrument of monetary policy, operations in the foreign-exchange market. This is the market in which U.S. dollars, Japanese yen, European euros, British pounds, and the currencies of other countries are exchanged for one another. In this section, we take a preliminary look at the mechanics of the central bank activities in the **foreign-exchange market** and the relationship between those activities and domestic monetary policy. Succeeding chapters add details relating exchange rates to the balance of payments, interest rates, inflation, and economic growth.

Foreign-exchange market

A market in which the currency of one country is traded for that of another.

Like its fellow central banks in other countries, the Fed has the right to use foreign-exchange market transactions as an instrument of monetary policy. However, for a variety of reasons, the Fed has not used this instrument as actively in recent years as have central banks abroad. Keep in mind as you read this section that although foreign-exchange market operations are a minor instrument of monetary policy for the Fed, they are a major instrument, often the most important, for many other central banks.

The Structure of the Foreign-Exchange Market

As a traveler you may have had occasion to exchange U.S. dollars for Canadian dollars, Mexican pesos, or the currency of some other country. This trading in paper currencies is a small corner of the largest set of markets in the world—the foreign-exchange market—in which trillions of dollars are traded each day. Such trading reflects the fact that most international transactions in goods, services, or financial assets are accompanied by the exchange of one currency for another.

Large trades in the foreign-exchange market, like large domestic transactions, are conducted by transfers of funds among deposits in commercial banks. A key role is played by large banks in the world's money centers—London, Zurich, Tokyo, and other cities—which are known as *trading banks*. These banks have branches all over the world and accept deposits denominated in many different currencies.

Suppose that a supermarket chain in the United States needs to buy pesos that it will use to purchase a shipment of asparagus from a grower in Mexico. The supermarket will ask the commercial bank at which it maintains its accounts to take funds from its dollar-denominated account and make an increase of equal value in a peso-dominated account in Mexico. The peso account can then be used to pay the Mexican supplier. Similarly, if a Mexican pension fund wants to buy U.S. Treasury bills, it can exchange a deposit denominated in pesos for a deposit denominated in dollars and use those dollars to buy the Treasury bills. The banks charge a fee of a small fraction of one percent for these transactions, proportionately far less than the fee you would pay for currency exchange as a tourist visiting Mexico.

FIGURE 8.5 THE FOREIGN-EXCHANGE MARKET FOR DOLLARS AND MEXICAN PESOS

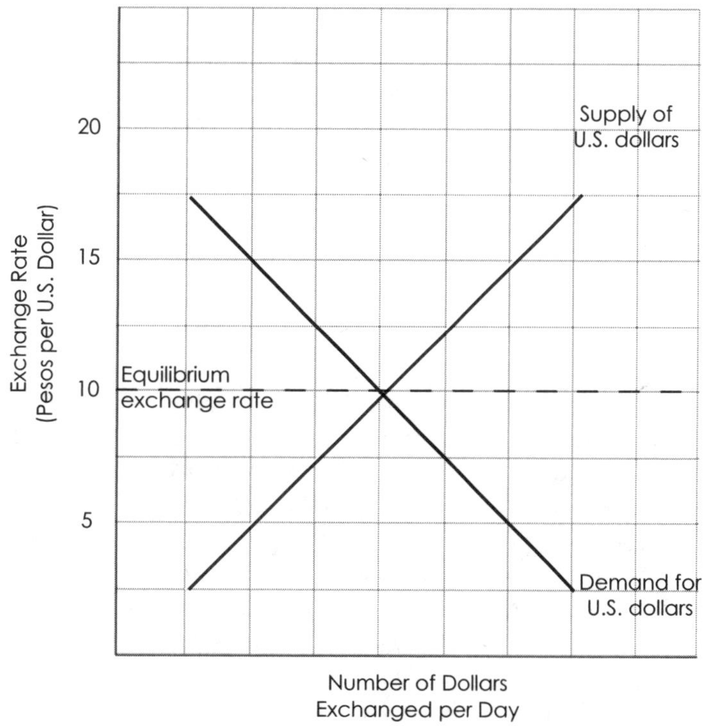

This diagram represents the foreign-exchange market in which U.S. dollars are exchanged for Mexican pesos. The exchange rate is expressed as the number of pesos needed to purchase one dollar. The supply curve of dollars reflects, in part, the activities of U.S. importers of Mexican goods and services, who sell dollars to obtain the pesos they need in order to buy Mexican asparagus, cars assembled in Mexico, and so on. It also reflects the activities of U.S. investors who need pesos in order to buy Mexican stocks, bonds, or other assets. The demand curve for dollars reflects the activities of Mexican buyers of exports from the United States. They use pesos to buy the dollars they need to buy Boeing aircraft, American wheat, and other goods. The demand curve also includes the effects of financial inflows into the United States. For example, a Mexican pension fund that wants to buy U.S. government bonds first needs to exchange pesos for dollars to use in purchasing the bonds.

Supply and Demand in the Foreign-Exchange Market

What determines the number of pesos that a customer gets in exchange for its dollars? Why, on a given day, is the exchange rate 10 pesos per dollar rather than 8 or 12? The rate depends on supply and demand as shown in Figure 8.5.

The supply curve for dollars in Figure 8.5 reflects the activities of everyone who offers dollars in exchange for pesos. These include importers, like the U.S. supermarket chain mentioned earlier that wants to buy asparagus from a Mexican grower and tourists who travel to Mexico. It also includes U.S. residents who want to invest in Mexico by buying Mexican securities or making direct investments in Mexican

FIGURE 8.6 FOREIGN-EXCHANGE RATES

Country	Monetary Unit	November, 2006	October, 2006	September, 2006	November, 2005
* Australia	dollar	0.7728	0.7544	0.7549	0.7353
Brazil	real	2.1555	2.1458	2.1679	2.2109
Canada	dollar	1.1359	1.1285	1.1161	1.1815
China, P.R.	yuan	7.8622	7.9018	7.9334	8.084
Denmark	krone	5.7858	5.908	5.8633	6.3277
* EMU Members	euro	1.2888	1.2617	1.2722	1.1789
Hong Kong	dollar	7.7816	7.7849	7.7825	7.7538
India	rupee	44.73	45.36	46.01	45.63
Japan	yen	117.32	118.61	117.21	118.45
Malaysia	ringgit	3.6413	3.6762	3.6699	3.7782
Mexico	peso	10.913	10.885	10.989	10.672
* New Zealand	dollar	0.6693	0.6621	0.6551	0.6897
Norway	krone	6.3991	6.6591	6.5008	6.6399
Singapore	dollar	1.5558	1.5775	1.5803	1.6981
South Africa	rand	7.2455	7.63	7.4465	6.6554
South Korea	won	935.41	952.64	952.29	1040.76
Sri Lanka	rupee	107.72	105.718	102.595	101.8
Sweden	krona	7.0612	7.3338	7.2844	8.1157
Switzerland	franc	1.2356	1.2602	1.2455	1.311
Taiwan	dollar	32.808	33.194	32.904	33.58
Thailand	baht	36.501	37.281	37.427	41.097
* United Kingdom	pound	1.9125	1.8765	1.8839	1.7349
Venezuela	bolivar	2144.6	2144.6	21244.6	2144.66

This table shows the exchange rate of the U.S. dollar relative to a number of foreign currencies. In most cases, the exchange rate is shown as units of foreign currency per dollar, for example, 10.9 Mexican pesos per dollar. In a few cases, marked by a star (*), the exchange rate is shown as dollars per unit of foreign currency, e.g., 1,9 dollars per British pound. Exchange rates vary according to supply and demand conditions. If a currency strengthens, it is said to appreciate. If it weakens, it is said to depreciate.

* U.S. dollars per unit of foreign currency

Source: Board of Governors of the Federal Reserve System, G.5 Statistical Release, Dec. 1, 2006.

resorts, factories, or other projects. Remittances that Mexicans working in the U.S. send home to their families are a further important supply of dollars in this market.

CHANGES IN EXCHANGE RATES Foreign-exchange rates—the prices of one currency in terms of another—change from day to day as supply and demand conditions change. Figure 8.6 shows exchange rate quotations relative to the U.S. dollar for a representative selection of currencies. Most currencies are quoted in terms of units of foreign currency per dollar, as in our supply and demand diagram. A few currencies are commonly quoted in U.S. dollars per unit of foreign currency (Australian dollar, British pound, euro), as noted in the figure.

Appreciate

A currency is said to appreciate if its value increases relative to the currency of another country.

Depreciate

A currency is said to depreciate if its value decreases relative to the currency of another country.

As supply and demand conditions change, exchange rates also change, as shown in Figure 8.6. If a currency gets stronger, it is said to **appreciate.** For example, in Figure 8.6 we see that in November 2005, one U.S. dollar would buy 6.65 South African rand, whereas in November 2006, it would buy 7.24 rand. The dollar appreciated relative to the rand over that period. If a currency gets weaker, it is said to **depreciate.** For example, in November 2005, a dollar would buy 1040 South Korean won, whereas in November 2006 it would buy only 935 won. The dollar depreciated relative to the won over this period.

A number of factors can cause an appreciation or depreciation. Look again at the market where U.S. dollars are exchanged for Mexican pesos. Suppose, for example, that a recession in the the U.S. economy decreases the demand for all sorts of goods, including goods imported from Mexico. Reduced sales of dollars by U.S. importers to acquire the pesos needed to purchase those goods would cause the supply curve for dollars to shift to the left, as shown in Part (a) of Figure 8.7. The shift of the supply curve changes the equilibrium exchange rate from 10 pesos per dollar to 15 pesos per dollar—an appreciation of the dollar and a depreciation of the peso.

These are only a few of the factors that can affect supply and demand in the foreign-exchange market. Changes in exchange rates have an important effect on patterns of international trade. As one example, *Economics in the News 8.1* discusses the effects on European shopping practices of the depreciation of the U.S. Dollar in the early 2000s.

Central Bank Intervention in the Foreign-Exchange Market

Exchange rates are not mere numbers; they have real impacts on the economy. For example, when the dollar depreciates, as it did relative to European currencies in the early 2000s, European shoppers find great bargains in New York; but U.S. consumers find European cars, travel, and fashion goods increasingly hard to afford. U.S. exporters have an easier time competing with their European rivals, but U.S. firms that depend on inputs of specialty steels, machine tools, or other items imported from Europe find it harder to compete. When the dollar appreciates relative to European currencies, as it did in the mid-1990s, these effects work the other way. No matter which way currencies move, someone wins and someone loses.

FIGURE 8.7 THE FOREIGN-EXCHANGE MARKET FOR DOLLARS AND MEXICAN PESOS

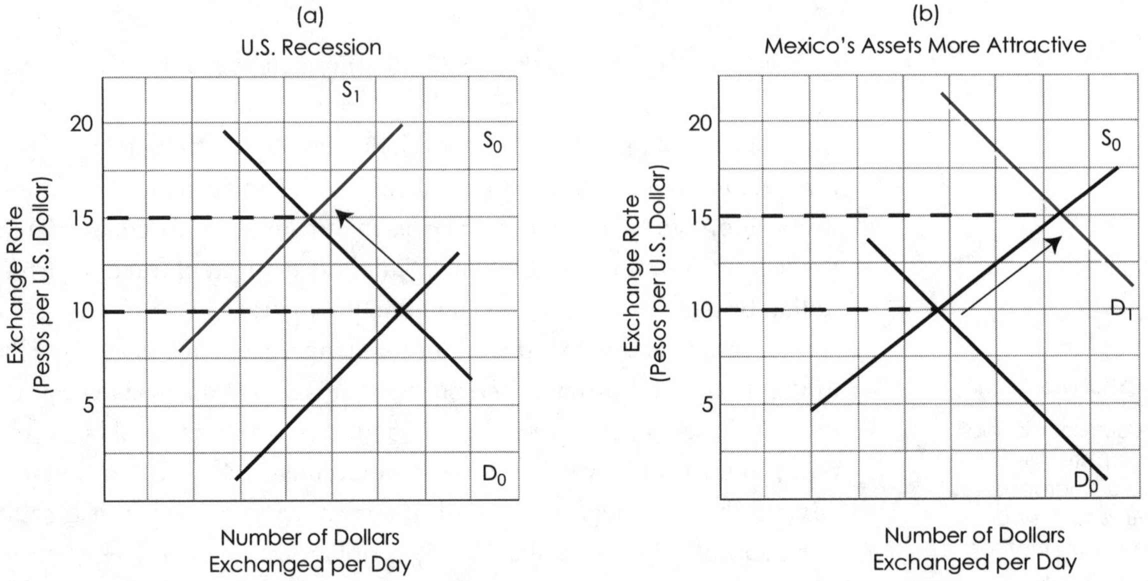

When the U.S. economy goes into a recession, U.S. importers will buy fewer goods and services from Mexican businesses. This leads to a decrease in supply of U.S. dollars because American importers do not need to exchange as many U.S. dollars for pesos. The result is an appreciation of the dollar (depreciation of the peso), as shown in part (a). Part (b) shows the result of a change in market conditions that makes U.S. assets more attractive to Mexican buyers. In that case, an increase in financial inflows to the U.S., shown as a rightward shift in the demand curve for dollars, causes the dollar to appreciate.

ECONOMICS IN THE NEWS 8.1

NEW YORK—BARGAIN CITY

Tourists arriving in New York from small-town America are often shocked by high prices—but not tourists from Europe. To them, New York is Bargain City. The cause of all the excitement? A falling dollar. At the start of 2007, a European tourist could buy a dollar for just .75 euros, a third less than five years earlier, and an 11 percent drop during 2006 alone. Combine that with the effect of U.S. sales taxes that add less to retail prices than European value added taxes, plus the operating efficiencies of large-scale American retailers, and it is not surprising that Europeans see New York prices as low, low, low.

Speaking to a reporter for The International Herald Tribune, Heather Weir of Dublin admitted to spending 1,000 euros in a bargain-hunting tear down Fifth Avenue. "I wouldn't go mad at home like I did here," she said. "You get two times as much as you get for that price at home."[i]

The New York Post described Fifth Avenue as a virtual flea market for foreign travelers. The paper reported that a Microsoft Zune Player on sale in New York for $249 would cost $442 in London, and a Panasonic mini-camcorder priced at $999 in New York would set a London buyer back $1,339. The savings on these two purchases alone would pay the lowest-cost trans-Atlantic air fare.[ii]

Just in case some shoppers might lack the initiative to find their own airline and hotel bargains, European tour operators have been busy selling "short-break" shopping trips not only to New York, but Boston, Washington D.C., and even Minnesota's Mall of the Americas. "Join us for a fantastic Christmas Shopping extravaganza ... You'll stay at Boston's Radisson Hotel with the best stores and their low, low prices just blocks away!" gushed one tour operator's ad.

[i]Neil Craven and Jennifer Sudick, "For Europeans, America is Now a Vast Shopping Mall," *International Herald Tribune*, Dec. 5, 2006.
[ii]Paul Tharp, "It's Play Money," *The New York Post*, Nov. 27, 2006.

Because exchange rates affect the welfare of consumers and firms, their level is a matter of concern for policymakers. Consequently, central banks may intervene in the foreign-exchange market in an attempt to stabilize exchange rates by offsetting market pressures that tend to change the exchange values of their currencies. As mentioned earlier, the Fed has the power to intervene in currency markets to influence the exchange rate of the dollar, but it has rarely done so in recent years. Central banks in some other countries are more active in foreign exchange markets. Some of them intervene in exchange markets on a daily basis to prevent any change at all in the exchange rate of their own currency relative to that of a chosen partner. For example, Figure 8.6 shows that the value of the Hong Kong dollar relative to the U.S. dollar hardly changes at all from month to month. The Hong Kong central bank intervenes regularly in currency markets to make sure this is the case. Other central banks intervene in an on-and-off fashion to nudge their exchange rate one way or another without maintaining a strictly fixed rate.

Figure 8.8 shows how the Mexico's central bank, Banco de Mexico, could intervene to maintain an exchange rate of 10 pesos per dollar, if it wanted to do so. (The Bank of Mexico does not currently maintain a fixed exchange rate relative to the dollar, but it has done so at times in the past.) Suppose that originally the supply and demand curves are in the positions S_0 and D_0. Then, suppose that fast growth of GDP in Mexico increases demand for imports from the United States, and shifts the demand curve for dollars rightward, to D_1. If the Bank of Mexico does nothing, the peso will depreciate to a rate of 15 pesos per dollar, as would be shown by a movement from point a to point b in the diagram. In order to hold the exchange rate at 10 pesos per dollar, the Bank of Mexico can sell dollars from its foreign exchange reserves. The sales of dollars, added to the dollars already offered for sale by private parties, would shift the supply curve rightward to S_1. Instead of moving from a to b, the market would move from a to c, and the exchange rate would remain at its target level.

MONETARY EFFECTS OF INTERVENTION Foreign-exchange market intervention as described in the preceding section has an effect on monetary conditions in the country where the intervention is carried out. In the example just given, the Bank of Mexico sells dollars in exchange for pesos. It buys the pesos either from Mexican banks or from non-bank foreign exchange dealers who pay for the dollars using their accounts at Mexican banks. Either way, a sale of dollars by the central bank decreases the banking system's reserves of the domestic currency (which in this case is the peso), and also decreases the monetary base. The effects are identical to those of an open market sale of domestic securities by the central bank. As reserves of the commercial banking system fall, banks slow their lending in order to bring the reserve ratio back up to its target level. The money stock contracts until it is equal to the money multiplier times the now-smaller monetary base.

These examples show that purchases and sales of foreign currencies are a powerful instrument of monetary policy. Although the Federal Reserve has rarely used this

FIGURE 8.8 EFFECTS OF INTERVENTION IN THE FOREIGN-EXCHANGE MARKET

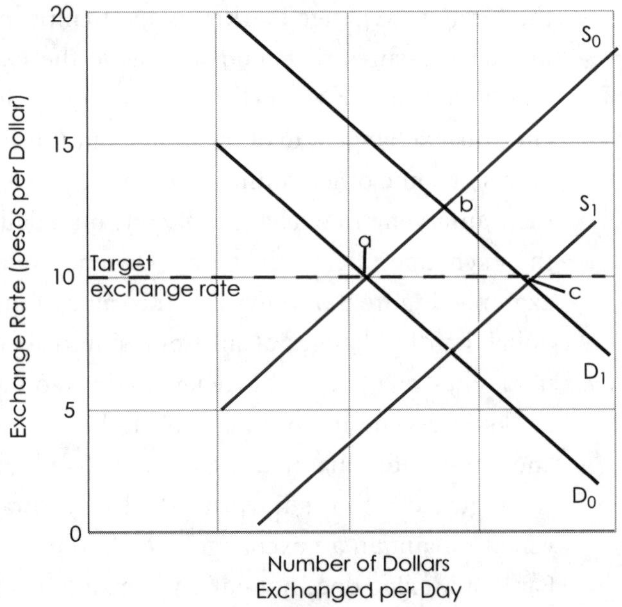

The Banco de Mexico, Mexico's central bank, could, if it wished, intervene in foreign exchange markets to hold the exchange rate at a target rate of 10 pesos per dollar. Suppose an increase in demand for dollars shifted the demand curve from D_0 to D_1. Other things being equal, the increase in demand would cause the peso to depreciate (an appreciation of the dollar). To prevent this, the Bank of Mexico could sell dollars from its foreign exchange reserves, shifting the supply curve to S_1. The exchange rate would then remain at its target value of 10 pesos per dollar.

instrument in recent years, it is the most important tool of monetary policy for many countries. For that reason, we can classify open market purchases or sales of domestic securities and purchases and sales of foreign currencies together as the two major instruments of monetary policy. Other instruments, including changes in the discount rate and changes in reserve requirements, are of relatively minor importance.

SUMMARY

1. **How do banks create money?** Banks create money, in the form of deposits, by making loans.. When a bank makes a loan, it credits the proceeds to the borrower's account. This increase in total bank deposits adds to the money stock. The borrower will probably spend the borrowed funds, rather than leaving them in the bank from which they were borrowed. As long as the funds are spent in a way that just moves them from one bank to another (for example, by writing a check on one bank that is deposited in another), lending adds to the money stock without changing the total quantity of reserves in the banking system.

2. **What limits the size of the money stock?** The reserve ratio is the bank reserves to bank deposits. When banks lend money, other things being equal, the reserve ratio falls. When it reaches the *target reserve ratio* consistent with regulations and safe banking practices, the banking system cannot further increase its total lending, and the money stock will cease growing. In addition, when banks make loans, bank customers may withdraw part of borrowed funds in the form of currency. Such withdrawals reduce the total level of bank reserves, and constitute a second limit on the ability of banks to expand the money stock by lending. Taking both limits into account, the size of the money stock is determined by the *monetary base* times the *money multiplier.*

3. **What instruments are available to the Fed for controlling the money stock?** *Open market operations,* in which the Fed affects the banking system's reserves through purchases or sales of government securities, are the Fed's principal instrument of monetary control. An open market purchase injects reserves into the banking system and allows the money stock to expand; an open market sale drains reserves and causes the money stock to contract. Changes in the discount rate charged by the Fed on loans of reserves to banks are a second instrument of monetary control. An increase in the *discount rate* reduces the quantity of reserves borrowed. This absorbs excess reserves and thus tends to cause the money stock to contract. Lowering the discount rate encourages borrowing of reserves and thus tends to allow the money stock to expand. Changes in required-reserve ratios are potentially a third means of controlling the money stock. A decrease in the required-reserve ratio creates excess reserves and allows the money stock to expand; an increase in the ratio causes the money stock to contract. In practice, the Fed no longer uses changes in reserve ratios as a policy instrument.

4. **What activities does the Fed undertake in the international sphere?** Central banks can intervene in *foreign-exchange markets* to counter-act upward or downward pressure on their currencies relative to those of other countries. For example, a central bank can resist an appreciation of its

country's currency by buying foreign currencies, and it can resist a depreciation by selling foreign currencies. A purchase or sale of foreign currencies affects bank reserves and the monetary base in exactly the same way as an open market purchase or sale of securities. A purchase of foreign currency to resist an appreciation tends, other things being equal, to increase reserves, the monetary base and the money stock. A sale of foreign currency to resist depreciation tends to decrease reserves, the monetary base and the money stock. For this reason, purchases and sales of foreign currencies are considered powerful instrument of monetary policy. The Fed has rarely intervened in foreign exchange markets in recent years, although it has the authority to do so. This instrument of monetary policy is much more important for the central banks of some other countries.

KEY TERMS

Monetary base	Federal funds rate
Reserve ratio	Discount window
Target reserve ratio	Discount rate
Excess reserves	Foreign-exchange market
T-account	Appreciate
Deposit multiplier	Depreciate
Money multiplier	
Federal funds market	

PROBLEMS AND TOPICS FOR DISCUSSION

1. **Repayment of a loan.** Suppose that you maintain a checking account at Best National Bank, and that you also have a loan from Best National. The remaining balance on the loan is $1,000. You have more than that amount in your checking account, so you write a check to the bank to pay off the loan in full. Using the T-accounts of Figure 8.2 as an example, show what happens to total bank reserves, total loans, total deposits, and the total money stock as a result of your loan repayment.

2. **Deposit of Currency.** Begin with a blank set of T-accounts for the Fed, commercial banks and thrifts, and households and firms. Now suppose that you deposit $500 of currency in your checking account at your commercial bank. Show the immediate effects of this transaction using the T-accounts. How does the deposit affect your total assets? How does it affect the monetary base? The money stock? How does it affect the total assets and total reserves of the banking system? How does it affect the ratio of reserves to deposits in the banking system? Suppose that before your deposit of currency, the banking system had reached the target reserve ratio, so that it was not able to make additional loans. Now, after your deposit, will the banking system be able to make new loans?

3. **The deposit multiplier.** What is the value of the deposit multiplier if the target reserve ratio is (a) .2? (b) .25? (c) .05? For each of these cases, what would the equilibrium quantity of deposits be, assuming total bank reserves of $1 trillion? (For this problem, assume that deposits are the only form of money in the economy.)

4. **The money multiplier.** What is the value of the money multiplier given each of the following sets of values for CUR and RES? (a) CUR=.5 and RES = .25 (b) CUR = .15 and RES = .25 (c) CUR = 1 and RES = .25. For each of these cases, what would be the equilibrium value of the total money stock assuming a monetary base of $10 trillion?

5. **Discount rate and federal funds rate.** What are the values of the federal funds and the discount

rate, according to the latest information from the Fed? You can find this information in the Fed's H.15 statistical release at http://www.federalreserve.gov/releases/ Look also at historical data for these interest rates. Have they risen or fallen over the past year? Has the difference between the rates changed, or remained constant?

6. **The foreign-exchange market.** Find the most recent foreign-exchange quotations from the Board of Governors, *G.5 Statistical Release,* available at http://www.federalreserve.gov /releases/. How has the value of the dollar changed relative to other major currencies compared with the data given in Figure 8.6?

CASE FOR DISCUSSION

Is the Chinese Yuan Too Weak?

One of the most dramatic events in the global economy in recent decades has been the rise of China as an export powerhouse. China has many advantages that have contributed to its export success. It has low wage rates and an enormous pool of workers willing to acquire industrial skills. It has a high savings rate, resulting in high investment. And it has a government that actively encourages export-oriented businesses. By 2006, these advantages had combined to bring the U.S. trade deficit with China to a level of $20 billion per month, the largest bilateral deficit with any country.

One controversial aspect of China's export push concerns the role of the Chinese central bank in regard to the Chinese currency, the yuan. The Chinese central bank intervenes aggressively to influence the value of the value of the yuan. Until mid-2005, it held the yuan closely to a value of about 8.3 yuan per dollar. Without intervention, the yuan would quickly appreciate. Such an appreciation would increase the cost of Chinese goods to U.S. buyers and would make it easier for U.S. firms to export to China.

Many U.S. politicians, eager to help exporters in their home districts, wanted to see an appreciation of the yuan. President George W. Bush spoke out in favor of such a policy change. A bill was introduced in the U.S. Congress to put pressure on China to allow the yuan to "float" to a stronger value. Finally, on July 21, 2005, China's central bank governor Zhou Xiaochuan gave into pressure and announced a change in policy. Despite the announced change, many observers were disappointed that the yuan initially appreciated by only about 2 percent, and by only an additional 4 percent or so over the next year. They took this as evidence that the Chinese central bank was still intervening behind the scenes to limit change in the exchange rate.

Some U.S. economists noted that a change in Chinese policy would not be beneficial to the U.S. economy in all ways. A stronger yen would mean higher prices for consumers of goods imported from China. Furthermore, in order to keep the yuan close to 8 to the dollar, the Chinese central bank had become a huge buyers of dollars. Its growing official reserves of dollars were invested in U.S. government bonds, helping to keep U.S. interest rates low. They warned that a change in Chinese policy might lead to a rise in U.S. interest rates that would more than offset the beneficial effect of a decrease in the trade deficit.

In the end, whether a stronger appreciation of the yuan would help or hurt the U.S. economy will be decided only when it happens. Most observers expect that to happen sooner or later, but just when is anyone's guess.

QUESTIONS

1. Explain why a weak yuan leads to large net exports from China to the United States.

2. Draw a supply and demand diagram showing yuan per dollar on the vertical axis. Draw supply and demand curves showing an initial equilibrium exchange rate of 8 yuan per dollar. Next, suppose rapid growth of the U.S. economy increases demand for imports from China. What will happen to the supply and/or demand curves?
3. In your diagram, show a rightward shift of the supply curve, tending to cause an appreciation of the yuan (fewer yuan per dollar). What could the Chinese central bank do to hold the exchange rate at 8 yuan per dollar? Would this require buying or selling dollars for its international reserves of dollars?
4. Based on your understanding of the elements of planned expenditure, what would be the effect on U.S. GDP of a decrease in net exports (Ex-Im) to China, other things being equal? What would be the effect of an increase in U.S. interest rates? Would these two effects work in the same, or opposite directions? Why?

END NOTES

1. Remember that only currency in circulation outside banks counts as part of the money stock. The $1,000 of currency that you withdraw in our example does not count as part of the money stock while it is stored in the ATM waiting for you to come by with your card. Until you withdraw it, the currency is recorded on the bank's balance sheet as vault cash, a part of bank reserves.
2. The formula for the money multiplier can be derived as follows:

   Eq1 TR = DEP*RES (TR is total reserves held by banks including reserve deposits and vault cash, DEP is total deposits held by firms and households in commercial banks, and RES is the target reserve ratio. This equation is an equilibrium condition for banks, indicating that reserves are at their target level.)

   Eq2 CC = DEP * CUR (CC is currency in circulation and CUR is the public's desired ratio of currency to deposits. This is an equilibrium condition for public distribution of money holdings between currency and deposits.)

   Eq3 B = CC + TR (B is the monetary base, which can be stated either as reserve deposits plus total currency, or as total reserves plus currency in circulation.)

   Eq4 M = CC + DEP (Definition of money stock.)

   Substitute *Eq2* into *Eq4* to get

   Eq5 M = DEP*CUR + DEP

   Simplify this to get

   Eq5a M = (1+CUR) * DEP

   Substitute *Eq1* into *Eq3* to get

   Eq6 B = CC + DEP*RES

   Substitute *Eq2* into *Eq6* to get

   Eq7 B = DEP*CUR + DEP*RES

   Solve this for DEP to get

   Eq7a DEP = B/(CUR+RES)

   Substitute *Eq7a* into *Eq5a* to get

   Eq8 M = (1+CUR)*[B/(CUR+RES)]

   Restate this to get

   Eq8a M = [(1+CUR)/(RES+CUR)]*B (The term in brackets [ ] is the money multiplier.
3. For example, suppose that initially, the currency ratio CUR is .2 and the reserve ratio is .1. As in our previous examples, the money multiplier will be (1.2)/(.3)=4. If CUR increases to .4 while RES remains at .1, the money multiplier will decrease to (1.4)/(.5) = 2.8.

CHAPTER 9

Money and Interest Rates

After reading this chapter, you will understand:

1. How nominal income and interest rates affect the demand for money
2. How the equilibrium interest rate is affected by a change in the money stock
3. How the equilibrium interest rate is affected by a change in nominal domestic income
4. How a change in monetary policy affects planned expenditure
5. The targets the Fed uses as guides for its open market operations

Before reading this chapter, make sure you know the meaning of:

1. Elasticity
2. Real and nominal interest rates
3. Stocks and flows
4. M2
5. Liquidity
6. Equation of exchange
7. Velocity
8. Federal funds market
9. Planned expenditure
10. Multiplier effect

WHILE WAITING FOR U.S. President George W. Bush, who was paying a visit to the Nissan Motor Company plant in Canton, Mississippi, a local reporter remarked to a colleague, "You never want to pass up a chance to cover the second-most powerful man in the world." And just who did the reporter have in mind as the first most powerful if the U.S. president was second?

The Chairman of the Federal Reserve Board of Governors, of course, who at that time was Alan Greenspan.[1] To understand why central bankers are considered so powerful, we need to move beyond an understanding of what money is, how it is measured, and how central banks conduct monetary policy to a discussion of how monetary policy affects interest rates and, through interest rates, how it affects real output, prices, and employment.

THE DEMAND FOR MONEY

The Demand for Money as a Stock

We begin our discussion of how money affects the economy by making use of the tools of supply and demand, first introduced in Chapter 2. There, we applied supply and demand to familiar markets like those for chicken, meat, and gasoline. In applying these tools to the monetary sector of the economy, we will find both differences and similarities with our earlier discussion.

One difference lies in the fact that money is a *stock*, not a *flow.* When we discuss the demand for chicken, we do so in terms of pounds of chicken demanded *per year.* But when we speak of the demand for money, we are talking about the quantity of money that people want to hold *at a particular point in time,* or, more precisely, the quantity they want to hold of the assets that enter into *M2:* currency, transaction deposits, savings deposits, and other M2 components.

Another difference between the demand for money and the demand for other goods lies in the fact that people do not "buy" money in the same sense that they buy other goods—at least not if we use the term "buy" to mean paying a certain price stated in money. However, people can obtain money by exchanging other assets for it, for example, by selling bonds in exchange for bank deposits or selling a car in exchange for currency. Our first job will be to examine just what are the factors that determine the quantity of money demanded.

Money Demand and Nominal Income

One well-established principle is that, other things being equal, people want to hold a stock of money that varies roughly in proportion to their income. In a feudal society, a peasant living on a subsistence income had a few copper coins in a leather bag, and the lord of the manor, with a princely income, kept stacks of gold coins in a strong room. In modern times, the average college student's stock of money may consist of a few Federal Reserve notes in her purse, whereas her parents, who are likely to earn higher incomes from full-time jobs, hold substantial balances in their bank accounts. Looking at matters from the viewpoint of the economy as a whole, the total stock of money held by all households and firms tends to vary in proportion to the level of nominal domestic income, other things being equal.

The proportionality of money demand to income arises in part from the use of money as a means of payment. Because the nominal volume of transactions made in the economy as a whole varies in proportion to nominal domestic income, other things being equal, so does the quantity of money used by households and firms to carry out those transactions. The demand for money also reflects its nature as a readily accessible liquid store of value. As the incomes of households and firms rise, so does their wealth; and they will want to hold part of that wealth in liquid forms like savings deposits, that are also included in M2.

The proportionality of demand for money to income can be expressed as the desired ratio of money to nominal domestic income, or, equivalently, as the desired ratio of nominal domestic income to money. The ratio of nominal domestic income to money is *velocity,* a term we first encountered when discussing the equation of exchange in Chapter 8. Thus, saying that people want to hold a stock of liquid assets that varies in proportion to nominal domestic income, other things being equal, is equivalent to saying that they desire to maintain a constant income velocity of money as nominal domestic income varies. For example, suppose a family with an income of $20,000 per year keeps an average balance of $2,000 in currency and bank account balances. We could call this a "family income velocity" of 10. To maintain the same family income velocity with an income of $40,000 per year, average family holdings of currency and bank balances would have to rise to $4,000.

Opportunity Cost and the Demand for Money

Let's turn now to the "other things being equal" clause in our assertion that the quantity of money demanded varies in proportion to nominal domestic income. The key item covered by the "other things being equal" clause in this statement is the *opportunity cost* of holding money. The opportunity cost arises from the fact that wealth held in the form of money could instead be held in some less liquid form that would earn a higher rate of interest.

Consider money in the sense of M2. Some of the components of M2, like currency and demand deposits, pay no interest at all. Others, like savings deposits and money market mutual fund balances, do pay interest. However, even these typically pay less interest than less liquid assets, like government or corporate bonds. In part, then, the opportunity cost of holding money is reflected in the difference between the interest rate that could be earned on nonmonetary assets and the lower interest rate earned on monetary assets.

Despite its opportunity cost, people do hold some money. They do so because the nonmonetary assets that earn higher interest have the disadvantage of lower liquidity.

They cannot be used directly as a means of payment, and their nominal value is subject to change.

Clearly, the trade-off between the advantages of holding money (its liquidity) and the disadvantages of doing so (the opportunity cost) is a matter of degree. The higher the opportunity cost, the less money people will want to hold for a given level of nominal income. The same principle can also be expressed in terms of velocity: The higher the opportunity cost of money, the higher its velocity.

The most common approach to measuring the opportunity cost of money is to select a particular nonmonetary asset as a benchmark for comparison of the interest rate on money and alternative assets. For the U.S. economy, Treasury bills with a maturity of three months are a frequently chosen benchmark. The logic of using three-month T-bills as a benchmark stems from the fact that, in terms of their degree of liquidity, they lie just outside the spectrum of assets included in M2. T-bills are, in that sense, a close substitute for money. The T-bill rate can then be compared with the M2 interest rate, or, more exactly, with a weighted average of the interest rates on the various components of M2.

The Money Demand Curve

Figure 9.1 uses a graph to show the effects of interest rates and income on the demand for money. The horizontal axis shows the quantity of money that households and firms want to hold under given conditions. The vertical axis shows the opportunity cost of holding money, measured by an appropriate nominal market interest rate like that on three-month Treasury bills rate.

Part (a) of Figure 9.1 shows a money demand curve in two positions. The curve has a negative slope, reflecting the fact that people tend to hold less money and more nonmonetary assets as market interest rates rise. As market interest rates fall, people tend to reduce their holdings of nonmonetary assets in order to gain the liquidity benefits of holding more money.

SHIFTS IN THE MONEY DEMAND CURVE The money demand curve, like other demand curves, is drawn on the basis of "other things being equal." The most important condition that is held equal for a given money demand curve is the level of nominal domestic income. As we have explained, the quantity of money people desire to hold at any given interest rate tends to vary in proportion to nominal domestic income. Thus, if there is a change in nominal domestic income, the money demand curve will shift, much as the demand for chicken will shift when consumer income changes.

Suppose, for example, that nominal domestic income doubles. This could happen because real incomes double while the price level is unchanged because prices double while real income is unchanged or as a result of a combination of both kinds of change. Whatever the cause of the doubling of nominal domestic income, every

FIGURE 9.1 A MONEY DEMAND SCHEDULE FOR A SIMPLE ECONOMY

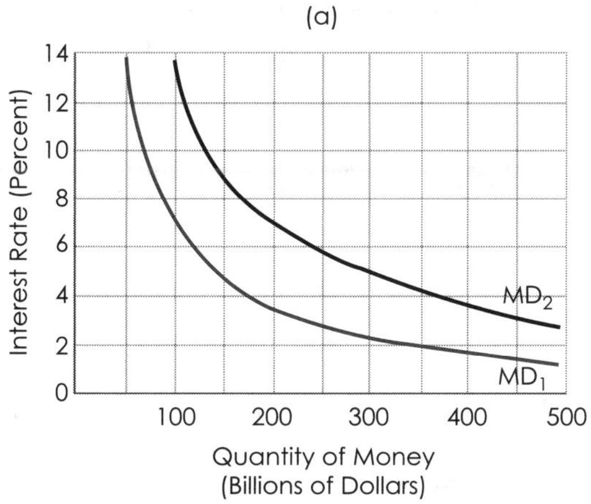

(b)

Nominal Domestic Income (Billions of Dollars)

Interest Rate (Percent)	**$200**	**$400**	**$600**	**$800**	**$1,000**	**$1,200**
2	$120	$240	$360	$480	$600	$720
3	80	160	240	320	400	480
4	60	120	180	240	300	360
6	40	80	120	160	200	240
8	30	60	90	120	150	180
10	24	48	72	96	120	144
12	20	40	60	80	100	120
14	17	34	51	68	85	102

This figure shows how the amount of money demanded varies in a simple economy as the level of nominal domestic income and the interest rate on nonmonetary assets vary. The entries in part (b) show the amount of money demanded at the interest rate corresponding to each row and the nominal domestic income corresponding to each column. Each column can be graphed to get a money demand curve for a given level of nominal domestic income. MD_1 corresponds to the fourth column ($600 billion) and MD_2 to the last column ($1,200 billion).

household and firm will, on the average, undertake twice the nominal volume of transactions as before. Other things being equal (that is, at any given level of the interest rate), they would want to hold twice as much money to facilitate these transactions. They would also tend to double the nontransactions balances they hold as a liquid store of purchasing power. Therefore, as shown in part (a) of Figure 9.1, a doubling of nominal domestic income will cause the money demand curve to shift to the right, from MD_1 to MD_2.

Part (b) of Figure 9.1 presents the same relationships in numerical form. Each column of the table represents a single money demand curve. The columns show what happens to the quantity of money demanded as the interest rate changes while nominal domestic income remains the same. Each row of the table, on the other hand, shows how the demand for money responds to a change in nominal domestic income at a given interest rate. The general principle is that when the interest rate is held constant, the quantity of money demanded is proportional to nominal domestic income.

MONEY DEMAND AND VELOCITY The data in part (b) of Figure 9.1 imply that at any given nominal interest rate there will be a certain ratio of nominal domestic income to the quantity of money demanded. For example, consider the row of the table corresponding to an interest rate of 12 percent. Reading along that row, we see that when nominal domestic income is $200 billion, the quantity of money demanded is $20 billion; when nominal domestic income is $400 billion, the quantity of money demanded is $40 billion; and so on. For an interest rate of 12 percent, then, the ratio of nominal domestic income to the quantity of money demanded—that is, the income velocity of money—is 10 for all levels of nominal domestic income. Looking at other rows in the table, we see that velocity is 5 when the interest rate is 6 percent, 2.5 when the interest rate is 3 percent, and so on.

SUPPLY, DEMAND, AND INTEREST RATES

Having looked in some detail at the demand for money, we are ready to put demand together with supply. As explained in Chapters 7 and 8, the supply of money consists of currency and bank deposits. The quantity of money supplied is controlled by the central bank by way of instruments that influence the monetary base and the money multiplier. Putting the supply and demand for money together results in a graph like that shown in Figure 9.2.

FIGURE 9.2 EQUILIBRIUM IN THE MONETARY SECTOR

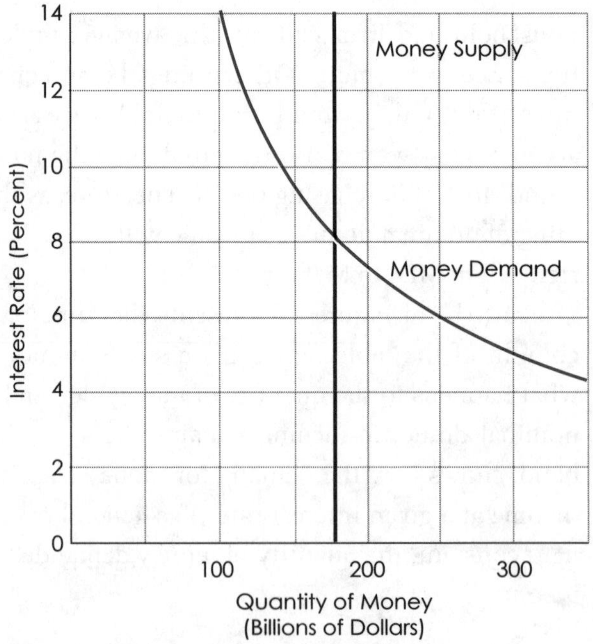

The money demand curve shown here is based on the data given in part (b) of Figure 9.1, assuming a nominal domestic income of $1,200 billion. The money supply curve assumes that the central bank sets a money supply target of $180 billion and adjusts total reserves to maintain this quantity of money regardless of what happens to interest rates. Under these conditions, the equilibrium interest rate is 8 percent.

The horizontal axis shows the money stock, measured in dollars; the vertical axis shows the market interest rate as a percentage per year. The money demand curve in Figure 9.2 shows the amount of money that people want to hold at each given interest rate assuming nominal domestic income of $1,200 billion. An increase in nominal domestic income will shift the money demand curve to the right, and a decrease will shift it to the left.

The vertical supply curve in Figure 9.2 is based on the assumption that the Fed sets a target for the money stock ($180 billion in this case) and uses open market operations to stabilize reserves so as to keep the money stock on target regardless of what happens to the interest rate.[2]

Equilibrium in the Monetary Sector

The supply and demand curves in Figure 9.2 intersect at an interest rate of 8 percent. At that rate, the amount of money supplied just equals the amount people want to hold. There is neither upward nor downward pressure on interest rates.

No other interest rate would permit such equilibrium. Suppose, for example, that the interest rate were just 4 percent. With such a low opportunity cost of money, people would want to hold more of it. They would try to obtain more money by borrowing from banks. However, as we learned in Chapter 8, the banking system as a whole cannot increase total lending unless it receives additional reserves beyond the quantity of reserves assumed when the money supply curve was drawn. Some banks may try to borrow the reserves they need from others via the federal funds market, but with no increase in total reserves, competition among banks would only drive up the federal funds rate. Other short- and long-term market interest rates, including banks' lending rates and market rates on short-term securities, tend to adjust quickly to changes in the federal funds rate. As the whole family of short-term interest rates rises, the monetary sector returns to equilibrium at 8 percent, the point where the supply and demand curves intersect in Figure 9.2. The monetary sector would then be back in equilibrium.

In Figure 9.2, a rising interest rate brings the monetary sector back into equilibrium by reducing the amount of money demanded rather than by increasing the amount of money supplied. As long as the Fed provides no more reserves to the banking system, banks cannot supply any more money. Even though any one person can add money to his or her portfolio by borrowing or by selling some other asset, this will not affect the amount of money in the banking system as a whole.

The same story can be told in reverse for the case in which the interest rate is higher than its equilibrium value. In that event, people would not be willing to hold all the money that banks want to supply. Banks cannot force people to hold deposits. They can, however, attempt to put excess reserves to work by lending them to other banks in the federal funds market. Under such circumstances, competition among banks will drive the federal funds rate down, and other interest rates will fall as a consequence. As the interest rate falls, the public becomes willing to hold the quantity of money that banks would like to supply, given the amount of reserves available to the system.

Effects of a Change in the Money Supply

The preceding section showed how supply and demand conditions in the monetary sector determine an equilibrium interest rate. Now we can use the same concepts to show the effects of shifts in the money supply curve.

Figure 9.3 shows the monetary sector in equilibrium at E_1 with a money supply of $180 billion and an interest rate of 8 percent. Starting from this point, the Fed decides to increase the money stock to $360 billion. It can do this by using open market purchases to increase the monetary base by an appropriate amount. For example, if the money multiplier is 10, an $18 billion increase in the monetary base would be needed to increase the money stock by the needed $180 billion.

The immediate impact of the open market operation is to boost banks' excess reserves. Some banks may immediately use the new reserves to make new loans. Others may put their excess reserves to work, at least initially, by lending them to other banks through the federal funds market. Their attempts to do so will drive down the federal funds rate. Soon the decline in interest rates will spread to other markets, including the markets for consumer and business loans and markets for short-term securities.

FIGURE 9.3 EFFECTS OF AN INCREASE IN THE MONEY SUPPLY

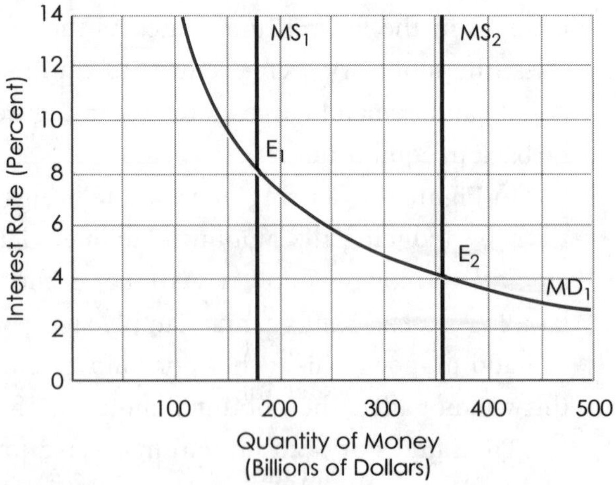

The money stock starts out at $180 billion, putting the money supply curve in the position MS_1. An open market purchase by the Fed injects new reserves into the banking system. Banks' competitive efforts to put the new reserves to work drive rates down, first in the federal funds market and then in other markets. As the money supply expands, the economy moves toward a new equilibrium, E_2, where the interest rate has fallen by enough to make people willing to hold the larger quantity of money.

As the volume of lending expands, the quantity of deposits supplied to the public increases. In Figure 9.3 this is shown as a shift in the money supply curve from MS_1 to MS_2. At the same time, falling interest rates will affect the quantity of money that households and firms want to hold. At point E_1 people were content to hold the old quantity of money, $180 billion. Now falling interest rates reduce the opportunity cost of holding money, so people become willing to absorb the increased quantity supplied by banks. This is shown in Figure 9.3 by a movement downward and to the right along the money demand curve. In time a new equilibrium is reached at point E_2, where the money stock is greater and the interest rate lower than before.

If the Fed withdraws reserves from the banking system through an open market sale, the same process operates in reverse. Banks find themselves with less than the required quantity of reserves. At first, they will try to obtain the reserves they need in the federal funds market. However, with total reserves fixed, their attempts to do so will only drive up the federal funds rate. As that happens, banks may decide to restore their balance sheets to equilibrium by reducing their holdings of securities or loans. To do so, they sell securities or raise interest rates on loans by enough to reduce the rate of new lending below that at which old loans are paid off. As interest rates rise through the economy, people become willing to hold a smaller quantity of money. A new equilibrium is reached in which the money supply is smaller and the interest rate higher than before.

Effects of an Increase in Income

In discussing the effects of a change in the money supply, we have assumed that the level of nominal domestic income remained constant. Next we can ask what happens to the monetary sector when nominal domestic income changes while the money supply curve stays put.

Figure 9.4 sets the stage. It shows the market in equilibrium at E_1 with an interest rate of 4 percent and a money supply of $180 billion. Nominal domestic income is assumed to be $600 billion, which puts the money demand curve in the position MD_2.

Now assume that nominal domestic income rises to a level of $1,200 billion. As we saw earlier in the chapter, an increase in nominal domestic income, other things being equal, shifts the money demand curve to the right. The new position of the money demand curve is MD_2.

At the new, higher income level, people will want more money with which to carry out transactions and to hold as a liquid store of value. They will attempt to obtain the additional money partly by borrowing from banks. Banks, in turn, will try to get the reserves they need to support the added loans and deposits by borrowing in the federal funds market. The federal funds market, however, only moves reserves around from one bank to another. The banking system as a whole cannot increase its total deposits given the total reserves supplied by the Fed. Competition among borrowers thus will not increase the money stock as a whole, but will

FIGURE 9.4 EFFECTS OF AN INCREASE IN NOMINAL DOMESTIC INCOME

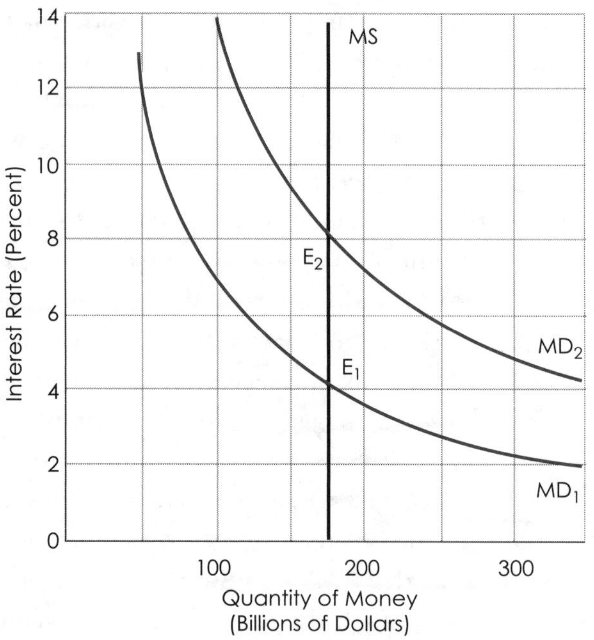

A nominal domestic income of $600 billion puts the money demand curve at MD_2. The equilibrium interest rate is 4 percent given this income and the money supply of $180 billion. If an increase in nominal income to $1,200 billion shifts the money demand curve to MD_2, there will be an excess demand for money at the initial interest rate. People will try to increase the quantity of money they hold, in part by borrowing from banks. As a result of competition among banks for reserves to meet the increased loan demand, interest rates will rise, first in the federal funds market, and then in the loan market and other markets.

instead drive up interest rates. The higher interest rates will make people willing to get along with the limited money stock available despite their higher incomes. Thus, the economy will move to a new equilibrium at E_2. There nominal domestic income and the interest rate are higher than before and the money stock has not changed.

If nominal domestic income falls, the same process will occur in reverse. With lower incomes, people will require less money. If the interest rate does not change, they will reduce their demand for deposits, in the process tending to pay off old loans without taking out an equal volume of new ones. Banks will attempt to lend the resulting excess reserves in the federal funds market, but because many banks are doing so at once, their efforts will cause the federal funds rate to fall. Other rates, including, eventually, loan rates, will be pushed down as well. When interest rates fall enough to make people content to hold the existing money stock even at a lower level of nominal domestic income, the monetary sector will be back in equilibrium. The interest rate will be lower than before; nominal domestic income will be lower; and the money stock will not have changed.

The Monetary Sector, Interest Rates, and Planned Expenditure

Having seen how supply and demand conditions in the monetary sector affect interest rates, we turn to the effect of interest rates on the economy. In Chapter 5, we introduced the concept of planned expenditure, which is the total of consumption, planned investment, government purchases, and net exports. The set of channels through which monetary policy affects planned expenditure is known as the **transmission mechanism.**

Transmission mechanism
The set of channels through which monetary policy affects planned expenditure.

Monetary policy has its most direct impact on planned expenditure via planned investment. When interest rates fall, so does the cost to firms of borrowing or the opportunity cost of using their own funds to make fixed investments in plant and equipment. Lower interest rates also decrease the opportunity cost of carrying inventories, so firms may allow stocks of raw materials and finished goods to increase. In addition to affecting business fixed investment and inventories, lower interest rates on home mortgages will stimulate the rate of housing construction, which is also a major component of planned investment. Acting via the multiplier effect, a given increase in planned investment causes a larger increase in the equilibrium level of planned expenditure as a whole.

Planned investment is central to the transmission mechanism of monetary policy, but it is not the whole story. A change in monetary policy affects planned expenditure in other ways as well, thereby adding force to the transmission mechanism.

One of these additional components of the transmission mechanism acts via exchange rates and their effects on net exports. A decrease in U.S. interest rates, other things being equal, will make U.S. assets less attractive to foreign investors and, accordingly, will decrease financial inflows. Decreased financial inflows, in turn, mean a decrease in demand for the dollar, on foreign exchange markets, which will cause the dollar to depreciate relative to foreign currencies. At the new exchange rate, U.S. exports become relatively cheaper for foreign buyers, while imports become relatively more expensive for U.S. buyers. Increased exports and lower imports both add to the net exports component of planned expenditure.

Another of the additional components of the transmission mechanism acts via consumption, which can also be stimulated by a decrease in interest rates. In part, this is because of increased demand for automobiles and other consumer durables that tend to be bought on credit. In addition, lower interest rates give homeowners a chance to refinance mortgages in a way that lowers their monthly payments. This gives them cash to spend on consumer goods and services of all kinds, both durable and nondurable.

Finally, some economists think expansionary monetary policy is transmitted to a significant degree through channels that do not involve interest rates at all, or do so only indirectly. In this view, an expansion of the highly liquid assets that make up the money stock causes people to reevaluate their strategies for investments in all kinds of assets. Some of this impact of monetary policy may spill over into the stock market. As increased demand pushes up stock prices, firms find it easier to sell new stock to finance investment. Some of the increase in demand for assets may also spill over into the housing market, adding to the stimulus that housing investment already receives from lower mortgage rates. Increasing prices on assets of all kinds—stocks, housing, and others—further stimulates consumption.

In sum, the transmission mechanism for monetary policy operates through many channels, some of central importance, and some minor significance. As we move along in our discussion of macroeconomics, sometimes we will focus on the interest-investment linkage alone, but keep in mind that in doing so, we are using a sort of short-hand to stand for the entire transmission mechanism in all its complexity.

Monetary Policy Instruments and Targets

Because monetary policy has such an important effect on inflation, output, unemployment, exchange rates, and other variables, it is prominently featured in financial news. *Economics in the News 9.1* is typical in its emphasis on the power of monetary policy. However, in light of what we have learned about monetary policy so far, there is something in this news story that does not seem quite right. The story focuses on the ability of the Fed to control interest rates, whereas, up to this point, we have emphasized the Fed's control of the money stock. In doing so, we have shown changes in interest rates only as an indirect effect of shifts in the money supply curve. So which interpretation is right—do central banks control the quantity of money, or do they control interest rates?

The answer is that there there is no contradiction between the analysis we read in the newspapers and the theory presented in this chapter. They are simply different

ECONOMICS IN THE NEWS 9.1

INVESTORS TO LISTEN FOR FED COMMENTS

WASHINGTON, D.C. (February 7, 2007) At its January 31 meeting, the Federal Reserve's Open Market Committee announced that it would keep the federal funds rate unchanged at the 5.25 percent level it has maintained since mid-2006. Stock market investors were encouraged by the news. The Dow Jones Industrial average of blue-chip stock prices surged 100 points, and other market averages also rose.

Now, just a week later, comments by Charles Plosser, president of the Federal Reserve Bank of Philadelphia, has sounded a note of caution. In Plosser's view, the long period of unchanged interest rates may come to an end later this year. Plosser's primary concern is inflation. "Additional monetary policy action may be needed to keep us moving along the path to price stability," he said.

Plosser's comments call attention to the fact that current economic data contain both good news and bad news for the economy. On the good side, the housing market seems only to be slowing and looks less likely to crash than some thought late last year. Also, wages of hourly workers are showing some gains, which should help support consumer spending.

On the bad side, both of these developments carry hidden threats. Higher wages could fuel inflation if passed through to product prices. Continued strong housing markets could keep materials prices high. Together, they make it more likely that the Fed will raise interest rates later in the year, as Plosser is warning it might do.

ways of looking at central bank actions. The economic viewpoint focuses on *policy instruments,* whereas reports in the financial press focus on *policy targets.* This next section will explain the importance of this distinction.

TARGETS AND INSTRUMENTS A *policy instrument* is any variable over which the central bank has direct administrative control. In Chapter 8, we looked at two major policy instruments and two minor ones:

Major monetary policy instruments

- Open market purchases and sales of domestic securities
- Purchases and sales of foreign currency

Minor policy instruments

- Changes in the required reserve ratio
- Changes in the discount rate

A *policy target,* on the other hand, is a variable that the central bank aims to affect by making changes in policy instruments. Interest rates are an important example of a policy target. For example, as was shown in Figure 9.3, the Fed can use an open market purchase to increase the monetary base and shift the money supply curve to the right. As banks and the nonbank public adjust their behavior to the change in money supply, market interest rates will fall.

The Fed, like the central banks of many other countries, guides day-to-day operations by setting an **operating target** in the form of a short-term market interest rate. The specific rate used by the Fed is the federal funds rate at which banks make short-term loans of reserves to one another. (In other countries, similar but differently-named short-term interest rates serve as targets.) The federal funds rate is extremely sensitive to open market operations and changes in other policy instruments. It reacts to the Fed's actions within moments of when they are taken.

Operating target

A financial variable for which the Fed sets a short-term target, which it then uses as a guide in the day-to-day conduct of open market operations.

Figure 9.5 shows how the Fed can use open market operations, its most important policy instrument, to achieve its operating target for the federal funds rate. Suppose, for example, that operating target for the federal funds rate is 1 percent, plus or minus 1/10 percent. In Figure 9.5, the target range is shown as a band around a horizontal line that is the announced target. In order to keep the interest rate within the target range, the Fed needs to use its policy instruments to move the MS curve to a position such that it intersects the MD curve no lower than .9% and no higher than 1.1%.

Holding the interest rate within its target range is not just a matter of "set it and forget it." Market conditions are constantly changing in ways that push the money supply and demand curves around. For example, the level of domestic income changes from day to day depending on the weather, the calendar, and more basic

FIGURE 9.5 AN INTEREST-RATE OPERATING TARGET

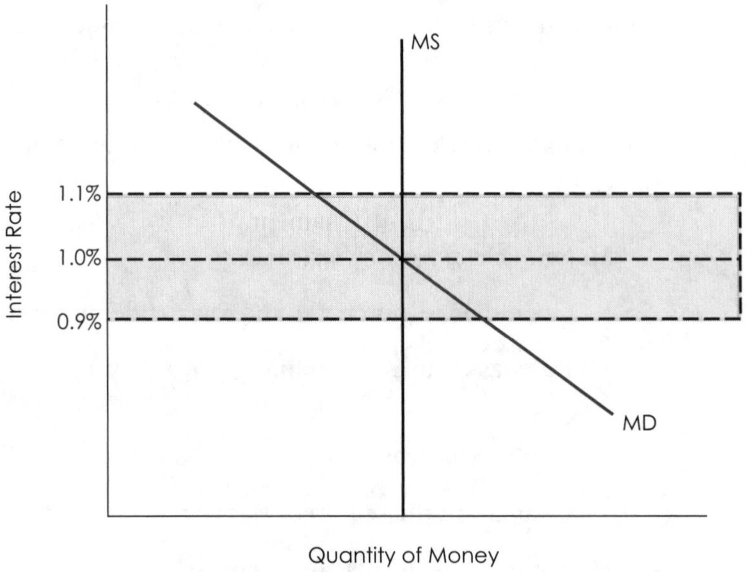

This figure shows how the Fed could set an operating target of 1 percent, plus or minus 1/10 percent, for the federal funds rate. If market forces tended to push the rate above the operating target, the Fed would use an open market purchase of securities (a policy instrument) to increase the money supply, thereby bringing the interest rate back within its target range. Similarly, an open market sale of securities would be used if the interest rate fell too low.

economic trends, thereby shifting the demand curve. Also, the money multiplier can change from day to day or week to week, for example, when people withdraw additional currency from ATM machines on holidays. Each day the Fed reviews market conditions and determines what open market purchases or sales are needed when market conditions threaten to push the interest rate above or below the target range.

Understanding how central banks use interest rates as an operating target explains the headlines. When the headline says "Fed Increases Interest Rates," it should be interpreted as journalistic shorthand for something like this: "The Fed has decided to increase its operating target for the federal funds rate. To move the rate up to its new target range, the Fed will manipulate the money stock by carrying out open market sales of securities or other actions designed to reduce reserves of the banking system and bring about the needed changes in the behavior of commercial banks and the public."

Interest rates are the key operating target of the Fed and the central banks of many countries, but they are not the only possible one. Some central banks focus their day-to-day operations not on an interest rate target, but rather, on a target value for the exchange rate of their currency relative to some other currency. We looked briefly at exchange rate policy in Chapter 8 and we will return to this topic in Chapter 13.

It is also important to emphasize that the concerns of central bankers extend beyond short-term operating targets like interest rates or exchange rates. Over a somewhat longer time horizon than day-to-day operations, they set *intermediate targets* for key economic variables like inflation, unemployment, or economic growth. Even the central bank's intermediate targets are not the whole story of monetary policy. In a broader context, the central bank is only one of a number of policy-making units within a country's government. Its job is to work together with the country's ministry of finance, its parliament, its president, and other leaders to pursue the ultimate policy goal of economic stability and prosperity for all citizens. The complex relationships among monetary policy instruments, targets, and ultimate goals will be explored further in coming chapters.

SUMMARY

1. **How do nominal income and interest rates affect the demand for money?** Other things being equal, the quantity of money people desire to hold varies in proportion to nominal domestic income. Because the components of M2 pay a lower interest rate on average than nonmonetary assets, there is an opportunity cost associated with holding money, which varies directly with market interest rates. Therefore, for a given nominal domestic income, the quantity of money demanded varies inversely with market interest rates. The demand for money can be represented by a downward-sloping curve on a graph in which the horizontal axis measures the quantity of money and the vertical axis measures the interest rate. An increase in nominal domestic income shifts the money demand curve to the right, and a decrease shifts it to the left.

2. **How is the equilibrium interest rate affected by a change in the money stock?** An expansion of the monetary base shifts the money supply curve to the right. As banks receive new reserves and expand their lending, competition drives interest rates down. This in turn increases the quantity of money that the public is willing to hold. The economy thus moves down along the money demand curve to a new equilibrium in which the interest rate is lower. A decrease in bank reserves causes a reversal of this sequence of events.

3. **How is the equilibrium interest rate affected by a change in nominal domestic income?** An increase in nominal domestic income increases the quantity of money that people would like to hold at any given interest rate, thereby shifting the money demand curve to the right. People attempt to obtain more money by borrowing more from banks, causing banks to compete for the limited available supply of reserves. This competition drives interest rates up until a new equilibrium is reached at which people are satisfied to hold the existing quantity of money at the new level of nominal domestic Income.

4. **How does a change in monetary policy affect planned expenditure?** An increase in the money stock tends to reduce interest rates. Lower interest rates, in turn, affect planned expenditure via the transmission mechanism. The most important

aspect of the transmission mechanism is the tendency for lower interest rates to stimulate planned investment. Lower interest rates can also act on planned expenditure via the exchange rate and net exports, and via consumption expenditure.

5. **What targets does the Fed use as a guide for its open market operations?** The Fed implements monetary policy by use of *policy instruments,* of which open market operations are the most important. As a guide to the conduct of open market operations, it sets an *operating target* for the federal funds rate. If market forces tend to push the interest rate above its target level, the Fed makes open market purchases of securities to boost the money stock, and if market forces tend to push interest rates below the target, the Fed makes open market sales. The operating target for interest rates is adjusted from time to time in light of intermediate policy targets and ultimate policy goals, such as price stability, full employment, and economic growth.

KEY TERMS

Transmission mechanism
Operating target

PROBLEMS AND TOPICS FOR DISCUSSION

1. **Velocity.** Using the Federal Reserve Economics Database (FRED) available on the St. Louis Fed Web site http://research.stlouisfed.org, find the values of M2, nominal GDP, and the three-month Treasury bill rate for the two most recent years reported. Calculate velocity for the two years. If the T-bill rate changed from one year to the next, did velocity change in the same direction? If the Treasury bill rate was unchanged, did velocity also remain unchanged?
2. **Money demand and the price level.** Some economists draw a different type of money demand curve from the one used in this book. They begin with a diagram that shows the quantity of money demanded on the horizontal axis and the price level on the vertical axis. Sketch these axes on a sheet of graph paper. Number the vertical axis from 0 to 10 and the horizontal axis from 0 to $500 billion. Assume a constant real domestic income of $200 billion and a constant nominal interest rate of 4 percent. Using part (b) of Figure 9.2 as a guide, draw a curve showing how the quantity of money demanded varies as the price level changes. (Remember that nominal domestic income equals real domestic income times the price level.) How does this version of the money demand curve shift if the interest rate rises from 4 to 6 percent?
3. **Effects of a decrease in money supply.** Rework the example given in Figure 9.3 for the case of a decrease in money supply from $180 billion to $120 billion.
4. **Effects of a decrease in nominal domestic income.** Rework the example given in Figure 9.4 for the case of a decrease in nominal domestic income from $600 billion to $400 billion. (Use part (b) of Figure 9.2 to draw the demand curve for a nominal domestic income of $400 billion.)
5. **Recent monetary policy.** View the statements issued from the FOMC's meetings at http://www.federalreserve.gov/fomc/. Go to the statement for the most recent meeting. Did the FOMC choose to change the federal funds rate target? What reasons did it cite for its decision?

CASE FOR DISCUSSION

Deciphering Bond Prices and Interest Rates

One of the jobs of a journalist specializing in reporting on financial markets is to interpret each day's movements in security prices and interest rates. In this job, the reporter is aided by a few fixed principles but must nevertheless rely on some creative guesswork.

One of the fixed principles is that the prices of fixed-income securities such as long-term bonds will move in the opposite direction to market interest rates. The reason for the inverse relationship between interest rates and bond prices can be made clear by an example. Suppose ABC Corporation sells a 30-year bond with $1,000 face value at a time when the market interest rates on loans and securities of such a maturity is 10 percent. The bond will consist of a promise to make a fixed payment of $100 per year to the holder of the bond for 30 years, plus a final payment of $1,000 at the end of that period. The fixed annual payment, expressed as a percentage of the bond's face value, is called the bond's coupon rate. Suppose that a year later, market conditions change. Interest rates on securities and loans of all kinds are lower. Under the new conditions ABC Corporation sells additional 30-year bonds with a coupon rate equal to the new market interest rate of 8 percent (that is, the new bonds promise the holder just $80 per year per $1,000 of face value).

Once the new bonds are issued, how much will investors be willing to pay for the old bonds? Obviously, they'll be willing to pay more than for the new ones because the old bonds pay $100 per year whereas the new ones pay just $80 per year. Specifically, an investor who would be willing to pay $1,000 for one of the new bonds would be willing to pay about $1,250 for an old bond with the same face value—a difference in price that reflects the difference in the coupon rate of the two bonds.

But the fact that bond prices are inversely related to market interest rates is only the starting point for the journalist's daily analysis of bond prices. The hard part of the job is to explain why interest rates change.

To give a specific example, in December bond prices fell moderately and interest rates rose. What new developments in world financial markets might have caused this to happen? Reporters considered the following possibilities:

- The Philadelphia branch of the Federal Reserve reported a slowdown in economic activity in the important mid-Atlantic region. A survey of attitudes of business leaders by Reuters indicated the possibility of a further slowdown.
- A report suggested that the Central Bank of China might reduce the share of its massive foreign currency reserves that it holds in U.S. dollars. The Bank of China is one of the world's largest holders of U.S. Treasury bonds, so any action to sell off these assets would have a significant impact on market prices.
- Government data released in mid-December showed that U.S. wholesale prices rose in November by 2 percent, the fastest monthly increase in several years.

Reporters characterized the first two of these developments as "bearish"—that is, as tending to push bond prices lower. On the other hand, the third development, increased inflation, was characterized as "bullish"—that is, as tending to push bond prices higher. The fact that bond prices in fact declined slightly during most of December suggested that the bearish news had more impact than the bull news.

The market was said to have "shrugged off" the inflation numbers, perhaps because the higher November wholesale prices were narrowly centered on the automotive sector of the economy and were not expected to continue.

Because each day brings some bullish and some bearish news, bond-marker journalists can almost always find some explanation of why prices and interest rates moved as they did.

QUESTIONS

1. Suppose, as in the example given, that ABC Corporation issues a 30-year bond with a 10 percent coupon rate. A year later, market interest rates have risen sharply, and ABC sells new 30-year bonds with a coupon rate of 9.5 percent. Assuming the new bonds have a market price equal to their face value of $1,000, approximately what will be the market price of the old bonds under these conditions?
2. Taking into account the factors that affect the demand for money, and assuming a fixed supply of money, explain how each of the following would affect interest rates and bond prices: (a) a decrease in exports; (b) an increase in inflation, assuming no change in real domestic income; and (c) an increase in government purchases.
3. Look for articles related to bond prices and interest rates in recent issues of *The Wall Street Journal* or in the financial pages of another national newspaper. What is the current direction of change of bond prices? Of interest rates? What "bullish" or bearish news is cited to explain these movements?

END NOTES

1. Quoted by Scott Waller, "Greenspan, Not Bush, Most Powerful Man in the World," Jackson, Mississippi, *Clarion Ledger,* June 12, 2005.
2. A vertical money supply curve is not the only possibility. In some periods in the past, the Fed has allowed the monetary base to increase as market interest rates rise. A more advanced treatment of the monetary sector would consider this alternative case, which results in a positively sloped money supply curve.

CHAPTER 10

Prices and Real Output in the Short Run

After reading this chapter, you will understand:

1. The conditions that determine the slope of the aggregate demand curve
2. The sources of shifts in the aggregate demand curve
3. The conditions that determine the slopes of short- and long-run aggregate supply curves
4. The sources of shifts in the aggregate supply curves
5. How prices, real output, and unemployment behave as the economy responds to a change in aggregate demand

Before reading this chapter, make sure you know the meaning of:

1. Supply and demand
2. Elasticity
3. Real and nominal values
4. Natural level of real output
5. Money
6. Planned expenditure
7. The multiplier effect
8. Final goods
9. Price level
10. Output gap

THIS CHAPTER RETURNS to the search for prosperity and stability, first introduced in Chapter 4. We saw there that macroeconomics is dominated by two great sets of questions. One set of questions is associated with Adam Smith's book *The Wealth of Nations:* What are the sources of economic growth in the long run? Why are some countries rich and others poor? The other set of questions is associated with John Maynard Keynes' book *The General Theory of Employment, Interest, and Money:* Why does the economy not grow steadily in the short run? Why does the economy sometimes drop below its long run trend of growth and fall into recession? Why do increases in planned expenditure sometimes cause inflation as well as, or instead of, increases in real output? What, if anything, can government do to tame the business cycle?

In Chapter 4, we were able to pose these questions but not to answer them in more than a very preliminary way. Since that time we have acquired a number of useful tools and concepts. We know how the parts of the economy fit together in the circular flow. We know how prices and real output are measured. And we know how the banking system and monetary policy work. This chapter will pull together these ideas to formulate a model of the macroeconomy for which we will find many applications in the remaining chapters of this book.

THE AGGREGATE DEMAND CURVE

Our first step will be to develop a new type of supply and demand model. We call it the aggregate supply and demand model because it shows supply and demand relationships not for individual goods, but for the economy as a whole. **Aggregate demand** means total real planned expenditure. **Aggregate supply** means total real output of final goods and services, a synonym for real GDP. The aggregate supply and demand model focuses on the relationship between aggregate demand (real planned expenditure) and aggregate supply (real output), on the one hand, and the aggregate price level, as measured by a price index like the GDP deflator.

Aggregate demand

Total real planned expenditure.

Aggregate supply

Total real output of final goods and services (real GDP).

Aggregate and Market Demand Curves

Figure 10.1 shows a typical **aggregate demand curve.** In some ways, the aggregate demand curve is similar to the demand curves for individual markets that we introduced in Chapter 2. Both kinds of curves represent inverse relationships between price and quantity variables. Both summarize the market choices made by many individual buyers. And, as we will show, both kinds of curves interact with other curves representing supply to determine equilibrium conditions. However, there are some important differences between the aggregate demand curve and market demand curves. Two of those differences concern the "other things being equal" conditions that lie behind the curves:

Aggregate demand curve

A graph showing the relationship between aggregate demand and the aggregate price level.

- The market demand curve for a good such as chicken is drawn on the assumption that the prices of all other goods remain constant as the price of chicken varies. There is no similar assumption for the aggregate demand curve. As the economy moves along the aggregate demand curve, the prices of any or all goods and services produced by the economy may change as the average level of prices changes.

FIGURE 10.1 AN AGGREGATE DEMAND CURVE

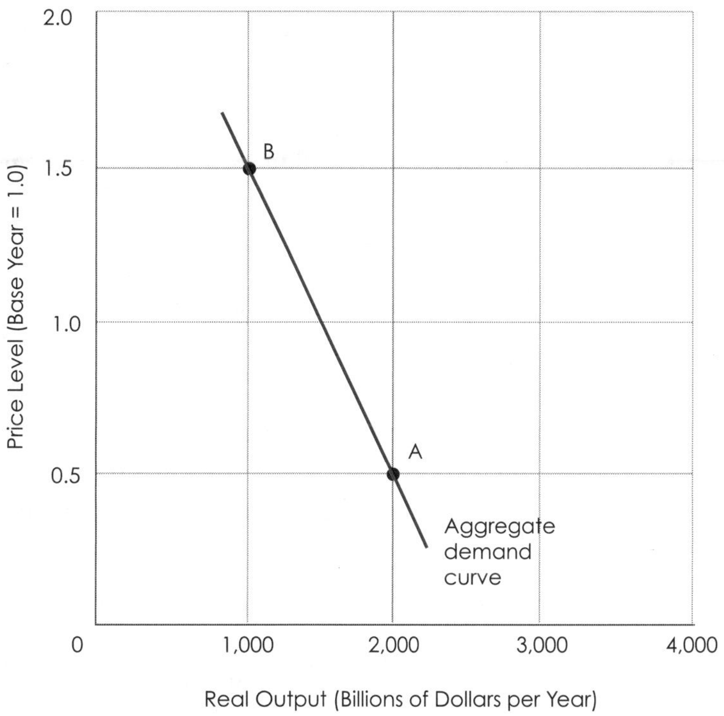

The aggregate demand curve shows the relationship between total real planned expenditure on final goods and the average price level of final goods. The curve has a negative slope because each of the major components of real aggregate demand—consumption, planned investment, government purchases, and net exports—varies inversely with the price level of final goods. Aggregate demand is relatively inelastic with respect to changes in the price level. As a result, nominal aggregate demand (real aggregate demand times the price level) increases as one moves up along the curve. For example, nominal aggregate demand is $1,000 billion at point A and $1,500 billion at point B.

- A market demand curve is drawn on the assumption that consumers' incomes remain constant at all points along the demand curve. The same is not true of total income in relation to the aggregate demand curve. In Chapter 5, we learned that within the circular flow of income and expenditure, any change in real output necessarily brings with it a change in real income. As we will see shortly, changes in the price level along the aggregate demand curve are also associated with changes in real output, and hence real domestic income.

If prices of other goods and incomes are not held constant as we move along the aggregate demand curve, what are the "other things being equal" conditions for this curve? We will discuss several of them in detail as we develop our model, but we can give a quick preview by noting that a given aggregate demand curve assumes constant values for the following:

- Expectation-related determinants of planned expenditure, for example, consumer confidence and business confidence.
- Policy-related variables, including both policies related to government purchases and net taxes, and the nominal quantity of money as determined by central bank policy.
- Economic conditions in the rest of the world, in particular, the levels of real GDP and interest rates in other countries and exchange rates of various currencies against one another.

These points should be kept in mind as we address the question of the slope of the aggregate demand curve. It is tempting to reason that the aggregate demand curve must have a negative slope simply because the individual demand curves for all the goods entering into aggregate demand have negative slopes. However, because the two kinds of demand curves involve different "other things being equal" assumptions, such a line of reasoning is invalid. A different approach must be taken instead.

The Slope of the Aggregate Demand Curve

The best approach to understanding the slope of the aggregate demand curve is to break down aggregate demand into its principal components: consumption, planned investment, government purchases, and net exports. By looking at how decisions regarding the real levels of each of these components are affected by changes in the price level, we can understand why the aggregate demand curve as a whole has a negative slope.

CONSUMPTION We begin by considering how the real demand for consumer goods is affected by an increase in the average level of prices. When the price level rises, firms' revenues from sales of a given quantity of goods and services rise by the same proportion. As those revenues are passed along to households in the form of wages, profits, and other factor payments, consumers' nominal incomes also rise. This shields them, in part, from the effects of inflation.

However, even if consumer incomes in nominal terms keep up with the increase in the price level, consumers are not protected in all respects from the effects of inflation. In particular, the money that they hold in currency and bank balances has a fixed nominal value. As the price level increases, the real purchasing power of those nominal money balances falls. For example, $100 in twenty-dollar bills might be enough to buy yourself a week's worth of groceries today; but if you hold onto those five twenties for a year while the average price level rises 15 percent, the same money will buy only enough groceries to last about six days. Because of the falling real value of nominal money balances, then, consumers become less wealthy in terms of real purchasing power when the price level rises. They will correspondingly tend to buy less real output than they would have if the price level had not risen.

Similar reasoning would apply to a period during which the price level fell. Although it has been many years since the United States has experienced a sustained drop in the price level, the effect of such a drop would be to increase the real value of consumers' nominal holdings of money. As the purchasing power of each dollar in circulation increased, real wealth would rise, real consumption would be stimulated, and real aggregate demand would increase. Taking both increases and decreases in the price level into account, then, we conclude that the real consumption expenditure tends to vary inversely with the price level. That is the first reason for the negative slope of the aggregate demand curve.

INVESTMENT Real planned investment will also be affected by changes in the price level. The reason is that a change in the price level, other things being equal, will change interest rates, and, as we know, interest rates are a key determinant of planned investment.

To understand why, we can trace the effects of an increase in the price level on the monetary sector, assuming that the central bank takes no action to shift the money supply curve. As we have seen, when prices rise, incomes tend to rise too, protecting consumers in part from the effects of inflation. A simultaneous increase in both prices and real income means an increase in nominal income.

As we saw in Chapter 9, other things being equal, an increase in nominal income will increase the demand for money. Consumers will attempt to obtain the added money they need in part by borrowing from banks. However, by assumption, the central bank has done nothing to increase the nominal quantity of bank reserves or the monetary base. With no new reserves, banks will be unable to significantly increase their volume of loans, so the increase in demand will simply drive up interest rates. Also, in part, consumers may try to get the extra money they need by selling less liquid assets, such as bonds, in exchange for money. With the demand for bonds falling, interest rates in bond markets will also rise.

As the rise in interest rates spreads through financial markets of all kinds, including markets for bonds and for bank loans, businesses are faced with an increase in the opportunity cost of investment. They cut back real planned investment in capital goods, and may also trim inventories to save carrying costs. Meanwhile, as the rise in interest rates spreads to the mortgage market, the cost of buying a new home also increases, so the housing component of planned investment also falls.

Taken together, the link from higher prices to higher interest rates to lower planned investment is the most important single reason for the negative slope of the aggregate demand curve.

GOVERNMENT PURCHASES The effect of a change in the price level on real government purchases is not the same for all budget items or for all levels of government. Many government purchase decisions are made in real terms. For example, Congress might decide to authorize the Pentagon to buy 100 jet fighters. If the price per plane goes up, more dollars will be added to the defense department budget to purchase the authorized number of planes. However, other government purchase decisions are made in nominal terms. For example, the Virginia Department of Transportation may be given a budget of $50 million for road improvements. If the price of asphalt goes up, the department, constrained by its $50 million budget, will be unable to pave as many miles of roads as it had planned. Perhaps it will be able to persuade the legislature to increase it budget next year, but in the meantime the price increase results in less spending in real terms.

Generalizing from this example, we conclude that to the extent that some elements of government budgets (federal, state, and local) are set in nominal terms, the government purchases component of aggregate demand will tend to fall in real terms as the price level rises, at least in the short run. Over a longer period, to the extent that inflation raises tax revenues, the government purchases component of planned expenditure is less sensitive to changes in the price level.

NET EXPORTS Prices can rise in one country and remain the same in others. Suppose, for example, that the United States experiences higher prices while prices in Japan stay the same. With a given exchange rate between the dollar and the Japanese yen, U.S. goods will become more expensive for Japanese buyers and Japanese goods will become relatively cheaper for U.S. buyers. As U.S. buyers switch from domestic goods to imports and U.S. exports become harder to sell abroad, the real net export component of aggregate demand falls.

Interest rate changes also come into play. We have already seen that an increase in the U.S. price level will affect interest rates. If U.S. interest rates rise while those in Japan remain the same, financial inflows from Japan to the United States will increase. Those flows will add to the total demand for dollars in foreign exchange markets, and will tend to cause an appreciation of the dollar relative to the yen. As the dollar appreciates, Japanese goods become cheaper for U.S. buyers while U.S. goods become more expensive for Japanese buyers. This provides a further reason for U.S. net exports to fall as the price level rises.

Taken together, then, the tendency of real net exports to decrease when a country's price level rises, other things being equal, is another reason for the negative slope of the aggregate demand curve.

The Elasticity of Aggregate Demand

Our examination of real values of consumption, investment, government purchases, and net exports indicates that each component of real aggregate demand varies inversely with the price level. We conclude, then, that the aggregate demand curve as a whole must have a negative slope, as shown in Figure 10.1.

We have not yet said anything about the elasticity of the aggregate demand curve. If it is unit elastic, real planned expenditure will decrease exactly in proportion to any increase in price, so that nominal planned expenditure (price times quantity) will be the same at all points on the aggregate demand curve. If it is elastic, real output will fall by a greater percentage than the percentage increase in prices, so that nominal planned expenditure will fall as we move up the aggregate demand curve. And if it is inelastic, real output will fall by a smaller percentage than the increase in the price level, so that nominal planned expenditure will rise as we move up the curve. Which is the case?

The answer can be given in terms of the equation of exchange, MV = PQ. The right-hand side of this equation, price times real output, is equal to nominal planned expenditure. The left-hand side is equal to the money stock multiplied by velocity. One of our "other things being equal" assumptions for the aggregate demand curve is that the nominal money stock does not change when the price level changes. The key to what happens to nominal planned expenditure must then lie with whether velocity increases, decreases, or remains constant as the price level rises.

As it turns out, we can be confident that velocity will increase as we move up along the aggregate demand curve. The reason is that an increase in the price level, given a constant nominal money stock, pushes up interest rates, and rising interest rates mean an increased opportunity cost of holding money. To say that the quantity of money demanded per dollar of income decreases is the same as to say that velocity increases. With M constant and V increasing, M times V, the left-hand side of the equation of exchange, must increase. The right-hand side, P times Q, or nominal planned expenditure, must therefore also increase. We conclude that the aggregate demand curve must have an elasticity less than one, that is, that it must be *inelastic*.

Consider, for example, the aggregate demand curve in Figure 10.1. This curve is inelastic along the segment from point A to point B.[1] At point A the price level is 0.5 and the quantity of real domestic product demanded is $2,000 billion. Nominal aggregate demand at point A thus is 0.5 ¥ $2,000 billion, or $1,000 billion. As we move along the curve to point B, the price level rises from 0.5 to 1.5 and the quantity of real domestic product demanded falls from $2,000 billion to $1,000 billion. As a result, nominal aggregate demand at point B is $1,500 billion. Nominal aggregate demand thus is higher at point B than at point A, as would be expected for an inelastic aggregate demand curve.

Shifts in the Aggregate Demand Curve

As in the case of individual demand curves, a change in market conditions other than the price level will cause the aggregate demand curve to shift to the left or right. However, because of differences in the "other things being equal" assumptions underlying the two kinds of demand curves, the sources of the shifts are different. Among the sources of shifts in aggregate demand curves are expectations, changes in government policy, and changes in the world economy.

EXPECTATIONS Expectation is one of the conditions that is held constant in drawing an aggregate demand curve. Chapter 5 emphasized the importance of consumer and investor confidence as determinants of planned expenditure. If consumers become more optimistic about the future, they may increase their real planned expenditures at any given price level. Similarly, an increase in firms' optimism about future profit opportunities may increase real planned investment at any given price level. In either case, the aggregate demand curve shifts to the right, as illustrated by the shift from AD_1 to AD_2 in Figure 10.2. A swing toward pessimistic expectations by consumers or firms would shift the aggregate demand curve to the left.

CHANGES IN GOVERNMENT POLICY Changes in government policy can also affect aggregate demand. An increase in government purchases, which are a component of planned expenditure, shifts the aggregate demand curve to the right, and a decrease in government purchases shifts it to the left. As explained in

FIGURE 10.2 SHIFTS IN THE AGGREGATE DEMAND CURVE

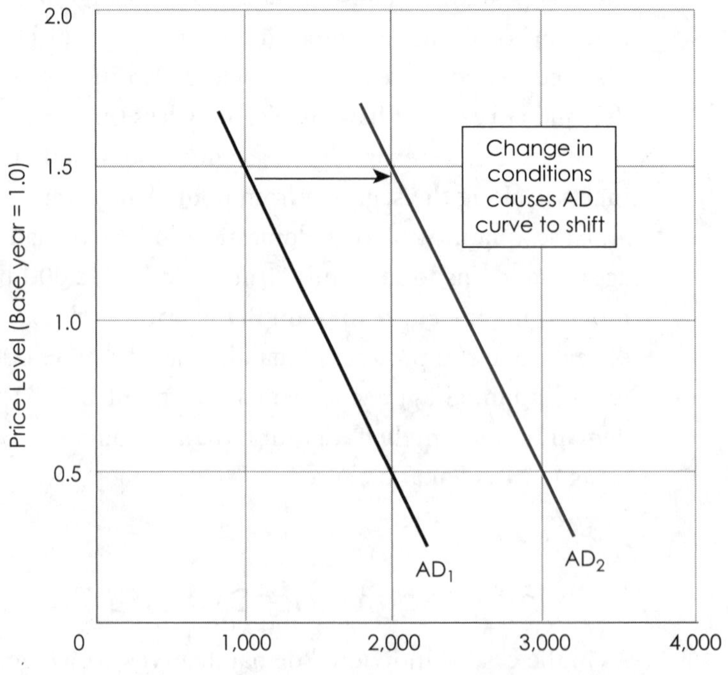

A change in the price level causes a movement along a given aggregate demand curve, other things being equal. A change in economic conditions other than the price level can cause the quantity of real planned expenditure associated with a given price level to change. In that case, the aggregate demand curve will shift, as shown in this diagram. Among the sources of shifts are changes in consumer or business expectations; changes in policies regarding government purchases, taxes, or money; and changes in the world economy.

Chapter 5, the multiplier effect operates to increase the impact of a change in government purchases on aggregate demand. For example, suppose the government of the state of Montana hires 100 previously unemployed people as maintenance workers for state parks at a total cost of $250,000 per month. When these workers receive their paychecks, they spend much of their new income on consumer goods, in accordance with the marginal propensity to consume, thereby further adding to planned expenditure. The added expenditures stimulate hiring by consumer goods producers, continuing the multiplier process. In the end, the total addition to planned expenditure is greater than the initial $250,000 addition to government purchases.

Decreases in net taxes also cause aggregate demand to increase. If marginal tax rates are reduced, consumers have more disposable income left for any given total income. They use the extra income to buy consumer goods, adding to planned expenditure. The same is true of a reduction in net taxes taking the form of an increase in transfer payments. For example, an increase in government pensions adds to demand by stimulating consumption expenditure by retired people.

Changes in monetary policy are another way that the government can increase or decrease aggregate demand. As we saw in Chapter 9, expansionary monetary policy can increase bank reserves, ease credit market conditions, and lead to lower interest rates. The expansionary monetary policy is transmitted to the economy via several channels, including increased planned investment in business equipment and housing and changes in exchange rates. In some countries (but rarely in the United States), the central bank may also stimulate aggregate demand by intervening in currency markets to bring about a depreciation of the currency, thereby stimulating net exports. Just as expansionary monetary policy can be used to shift the aggregate demand curve to the right, contractionary monetary policy can be used to shift it to the left.

Both fiscal and monetary policies play important roles in short-run stabilization of the economy. Chapter 11 will discuss fiscal policy in more detail, and Chapter 12 will offer an integrated view of monetary and fiscal policy.

CHANGES IN THE WORLD ECONOMY Events in foreign countries have an impact on aggregate demand in the United States via the net exports component of planned expenditure. For example, suppose that the rate of real economic growth in-creases in the economy of a major U.S. trading partner—say, Canada. When this happens, Canadian firms and consumers will tend to buy more imported goods, thereby boosting the real net exports component of U.S. planned expenditure and shifting the aggregate demand curve to the right. Also, changes in price levels in foreign countries will affect U.S. net exports by changing the relative prices of imported and exported goods. The effects of price-level changes may be felt, in part, through changes in the exchange rates. The whole set of variables related to events in the world economy is held equal in drawing a given aggregate demand curve.

THE AGGREGATE SUPPLY CURVE

Aggregate supply curve

A graph showing the relationship between real output (real domestic product) and the average price level of final goods.

We turn now to the supply side of our aggregate supply-and-demand model. An **aggregate supply curve** shows the quantity of real domestic product supplied by the economy at various price levels. The aggregate supply curve can be used to show how the economy's equilibrium real output and price level change when there is a shift in the aggregate demand curve.

The Importance of Input Prices

Input prices

A measure of the average prices of lab or, raw materials, and other inputs that firms use to produce goods and services.

As we did for the aggregate demand curve, we must pay careful attention to the "other things being equal" assumptions that underlie the aggregate supply curve. In Chapter 2, where we dealt with individual goods like chicken and beef, one of our key assumptions was that **input prices** remained unchanged as firms moved along the supply curve. By input prices, we mean the average prices of labor, raw materials, and other inputs that firms use to produce goods and services. For example, the input prices for a car maker would include the wages of production workers, the price of steel, rates paid for electric power, along with prices of many other inputs.

Although it is reasonable to assume that input prices for an individual firm remain unchanged as it varies prices and output along its own individual supply curve, the assumption makes less sense for aggregate supply. It is not reasonable to assume that input prices remain unchanged as *all* firms in the economy vary prices and outputs. There are two reasons for this.

The first reason is that some firms' outputs are other firms' inputs. If an electric utility increases its rates, that not only increases the cost of electricity for homeowners who consume electricity as a final good, but also for a car maker that uses electricity as an intermediate good. At the same time, the electric utility must buy cars and trucks for its own corporate fleet. An increase in output prices by the car maker is thus an increase in input prices for the electric utility. It follows that an increase in the average price level of all goods in the economy, reflected in a move along the economy's aggregate supply curve, can hardly fail to have an effect on input prices, as well.

The second reason why a change in the average price level for final goods must affect input prices has to do with the impact on wages of changes in the cost of living. Suppose there is a 10 percent increase in the average price of all final goods, including all consumer goods. If workers' nominal wages remain unchanged, they will experience a decline in their standard of living. Some workers will react by demanding raises from their bosses to make up for the higher cost of living. If their employers are getting higher prices for the goods they produce, they may well be willing to grant the wages. Other workers will react to the decline in living standards by looking for better jobs. If some employers resist demands for wage increases while others grant them, workers will move from lower-paying to higher-paying jobs. In one way or another, then, it is reasonable to expect that for the economy as a whole, an increase in output prices will be reflected in upward pressure on the wage component of input prices.

For these two reasons, the simple "other things being equal" assumption that input prices are independent of output prices will not work for the aggregate supply curve. That leaves us with another question: *How rapidly and completely* will input prices adjust when there are changes in aggregate demand and supply? The answer depends on the amount of time allowed for the economy to adjust to changed conditions.

Long-Run and Short-Run Aggregate Supply Curves

First let's take a long-run perspective. The long run, in this case, means a period of time long enough for all markets in the economy to adjust fully to changes in conditions of aggregate supply and demand. Given enough time to adjust, it is reasonable for firms to expect input prices to adjust fully in proportion to any change in output prices. For example, suppose there is a 10 percent across-the-board increase in the prices of final goods, as measured by the GDP deflator. If you are, say, a chicken farmer, you expect the price you get for a broiler to go up by 10 percent, and you expect the prices of feed, fuel to heat your buildings, and the wages of your employees to increase by 10 percent, as well.

When input and output prices change in the same proportion, your profit per unit of output, adjusted for inflation, will not change at all. As a result, you have no incentive either to increase or decrease your output. If all firms in the economy behave the same way, there will be no change in real GDP as the economy moves along its aggregate supply curve. Consequently, the long-run aggregate supply curve will a vertical line, as shown in Figure 10.3a. The intercept of the long-run aggregate supply curve with the horizontal axis coincides with the economy's natural level of real output.

Next we consider a short-run perspective. Even if we can expect input prices to move proportionately to output prices in the long run, that does not mean they do so immediately. In the short run, it is reasonable for firms to expect some, if not all, input prices to adjust only gradually when aggregate demand increases. In that case, there will be a chance for them to take advantage of strong demand to improve profits by raising prices or increasing output during the interval while costs have not increased fully in proportion to revenues. If we assume that in the short run, some firms respond to an increase in aggregate demand by increasing output, others by increasing prices, and others by doing a little of both, the economy's average price level and total output will both increase. As a result, the short-run aggregate supply curve will have a positive slope, like that shown in Figure 10.3b.

There are several reasons to expect that input prices will not adjust fully and immediately to changes in aggregate demand in the short run.

FIGURE 10.3 AGGREGATE SUPPLY CURVES

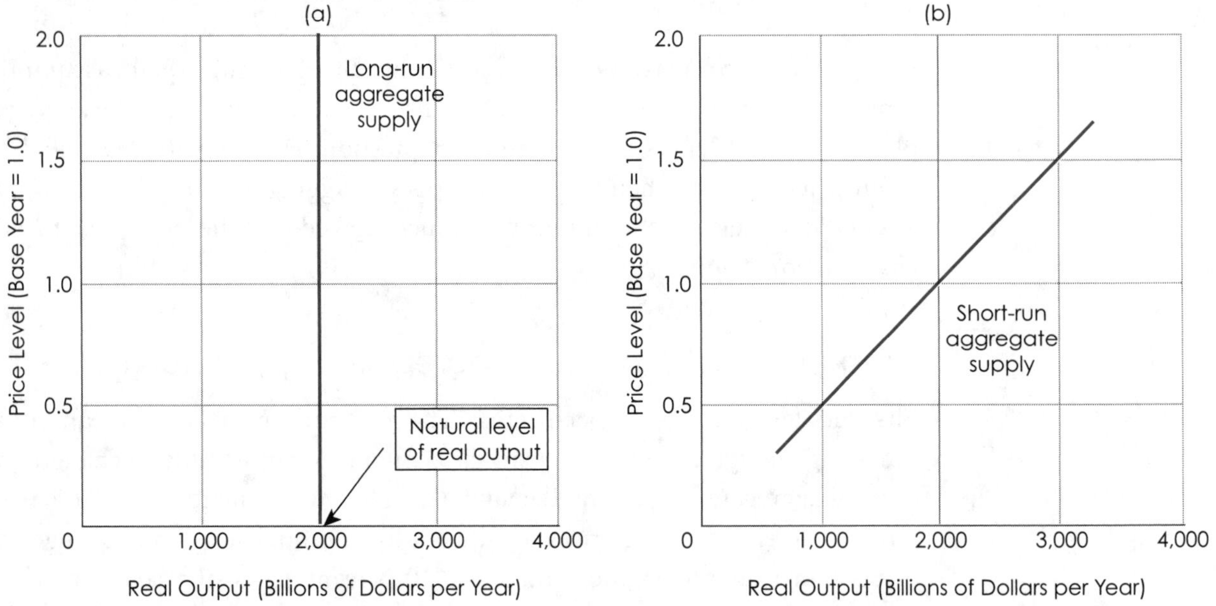

An aggregate supply curve shows the relationship between the level of final-goods prices and the level of real output (real domestic product). The slope of the aggregate supply curve depends on the way input prices are assumed to change when the prices of final goods change. In the long run, input prices can reasonably be expected to change in proportion to changes in the prices of final goods. The long-run aggregate supply curve therefore is a vertical line drawn at the economy's natural level of real output, as shown in part (a). In the short run, input prices can reasonable be assumed to adjust more slowly than the prices of final goods. Thus, the short-run aggregate supply curve has a positive slope, as shown in part (b).

1. *Long-term contracts.* The prices of some inputs are fixed by long-term contracts. Union labor contracts are one example. Some firms may also rent buildings, buy fuel, or hire transportation services under long-term contracts. When the price level of final goods rises, the prices of these inputs cannot rise until it is time to renegotiate the contracts.

2. *Inventories.* Inventories tend to have a cushioning effect on input prices. To illustrate, suppose that a bakery experiences an increase in demand for its bread. At first it may gladly bake and sell more bread, using up its inventories of flour in the process. If prices have been rising throughout the economy, the bakery may have to pay more for the next batch of flour it orders. This change in input prices will cause it to revise its output and pricing plans, but by then a certain amount of time will have passed. Economists have sometimes argued that rational managers should adjust output prices immediately to reflect the expected replacement cost of inputs used from inventory, but in fact, many firms do not follow this practice.

3. *Incomplete knowledge.* Firms may mistakenly interpret broad changes in demand as local changes affecting only their own market. For example, a bakery might think that an increased demand for bread is limited to the city it serves. Such a change would not be expected to have a perceptible effect on the price of flour, which is determined in a nationwide market. Only later will the bakery find out that the increase in demand for its bread is part of a broad increase in aggregate demand, so that it will affect the price of flour and other inputs.

4. *Cost of changing prices.* When input prices change by small amounts, some firms may find it too costly to make immediate changes in the prices of the goods they produce. For example, suppose the owner of an independent pizza restaurant visits the market one morning and finds that the price of onions has increased from $.20 per pound to $.25 per pound. That will increase the cost of producing one of her special onion pizzas by one cent. Should she reprint her menu to show a price of $2.96 for an onion pizza instead of the previous $2.95? Probably not. The cost of printing the menu is greater than the gain from fine-tuning the product price to the small change in input prices. It would take a larger and more persistent change in input prices to trigger a change in the price of pizza as stated on the menu. Many firms other than restaurants experience costs of changing prices, and therefore do not change them immediately in response to small or transitory changes in input prices. Although this phenomenon is seen far more widely than in the restaurant business alone, economists have taken to using the term menu costs to refer to them regardless of the product involved. *Applying Economic Ideas 10.1* reports a specific example of menu costs in action.

Just how short is this short run, and how gradual is the gradual adjustment of prices? There is no simple answer. In reality, the rate at which input prices adjust will depend on a variety of circumstances and will vary from one input to another. In what follows, we will make a simplifying assumption: When prices of final goods change, we will assume that firms expect the prices of all inputs to remain unchanged for a specific period of time, (for the sake of discussion, we will assume one year), and then move up or down all at once in accordance with the preceding change in the prices of final goods. This stepwise adjustment of input prices is, of course, only a convenient approximation to the more complex adjustment process that takes place in the real world.

Shifts in the Short-Run Aggregate Supply Curve

The distinctions between input and output prices and between long-run and short-run adjustments provide a basis for understanding shifts in the aggregate supply curves. We begin with shifts in the short-run curve.

APPLYING ECONOMIC IDEAS 10.1

MENU COSTS AND THE INTRODUCTION OF THE EURO

In January 2002, twelve European countries made a historic policy change. Hoping to encourage further integration of their economies, they abandoned their long-established national currencies—the French franc, the German mark, the Spanish peseta, and others—in favor of a brand new currency, the euro.

The introduction of the euro was carefully planned. Long before paper euro notes were put into circulation, the euro had already been introduced in electronic form in banking and financial markets. The ratio at which each currency was converted to the euro was exactly calculated. For example, the German mark was converted at a rate of 1.95583 marks per euro, rather than rounding off to a more convenient 2-to-1 ratio. One of the aims of the planning was to avoid any unpleasant jump in inflation when the euro went into circulation. The European Commission, which planned the change, was rightly worried that any such burst of price increases would undermine public confidence in the new currency.

By and large, the careful planning paid off. On average, prices in the twelve euro area countries increased by just twelve-hundredths of one percent in January 2002, a barely measurable amount. But in one sector there was a big surprise. Restaurant prices increased by 15 percent on average for the twelve countries. In Germany the increase was 28 percent. Consumers were angry and the European Commission was put on the defensive. What went wrong?

According to a study by economists Bart Hobijn, Frederico Ravenna, and Andrea Tambalotti, the sudden jump in restaurant prices can be explained by menu costs. In their view, menu costs interacted with the introduction of the euro in two ways.

First, introduction of the euro affected the timing of menu revisions. Without the euro, each month a few restaurants would have decided that cost increases had accumulated to the point where it was worth printing new menus. The increases would have been staggered over time, so that the average increase in restaurant prices would have been gradual, in line with the general rate of inflation for all goods and services. However, introduction of the euro meant that all restaurants knew they would have to print new menus for January 2002. Restaurants that might normally have raised their prices in, say, September would think, why bother—wait until January. Restaurants that might normally have waited until June 2002 to revise prices would decide to do so early, since they had to print new menus denominated in euros whether they raised prices or not. As a result, a higher than normal percentage of restaurants raised prices at the moment the new currency was introduced.

The other mechanism acting on menu costs has to do with the time horizon taken into account by restaurants when they print new menus. Normally, when setting prices, they would take into account cost increases that they expect to occur for many months ahead. However, restaurants that printed new menus in the last months before the end of 2001 would have had a shorter time horizon. They would have taken into account only cost increases up to January 2002, because they would have known they would have to print new menus again at that time. For that reason, part of the price increases normally expected in 2001 would be shifted forward to 2002.

Using a mathematical model that incorporates the ideas of timing and horizon effects, the authors compared the behavior of restaurant prices in the twelve countries that adopted the euro with those in other European countries, like the U.K. and Sweden, which did not do so. Their conclusion: menu costs explain most, if not all of the unusual jump in restaurant prices.

Source: Bart Hobijn, Frederico Ravenna, and Andrea Tambalotti, "Menu Costs at Work: Restaurant Prices and the Introduction of the Euro," Federal Reserve Bank of New York Staff Report No. 195, October 2004.

When the economy is in long-run equilibrium at its natural level of real output, markets for individual goods, services, and factors of production are also in equilibrium. In that situation the prices of final goods and services that firms sell and the prices of the inputs they use must be related in certain consistent ways:

1. In equilibrium, the prices of final goods must be at levels that will bring in sufficient revenue for firms to cover the costs of all inputs, given the prices of those inputs, and obtain a normal profit.

2. In equilibrium, the prices of labor inputs must be sufficient to balance supply and demand in labor markets. This means that, given the cost of living as determined by the prices of consumer goods, wages and salaries must be high enough to make it worthwhile for workers to acquire the skills they need for each kind of job and to show up for work each day. It also means that unemployment will be at its natural rate,which corresponds to the natural level of real output.

Suppose that we choose as a base year one in which the economy is in long-run equilibrium. In that year the prices of inputs and final goods will be related in the ways just described. We can assign a value of 1.0 to both the average level of input prices and the average level of prices of final goods for that year. We can then measure changes relative to those base year levels.

In graphical terms, the situation in such a base year is represented by point A in Figure 10.4. Real output is equal to its natural level, which is also its long-run equilibrium level. Point A thus is on the long-run aggregate supply curve, which is a vertical line at the natural level of real output. The short-run aggregate supply curve AS1 that passes through point A shows the way firms will react to changes in aggregate demand during the interval before they expect any change in the prevailing level of input prices, 1.0.

Over a longer period, however, firms will expect input prices to adjust in response to an increase in demand. Suppose, for example, that after a number of years, the average price level of final goods rises to 2.0 and input prices have time to adjust fully, so that they too rise to an average level of 2.0. Such a situation is shown as point B in Figure 10.4. In that situation, input prices and the prices of final goods will once again be in an equilibrium relationship. Firms will be selling their outputs for twice as much, enabling them to pay for their inputs, which also cost twice as much. Workers will be earning double the nominal wages and salaries they earned previously, which is just enough to allow them to maintain their original standard of living, given the doubled level of price level of consumer goods.

Given this new equilibrium situation, a new short-run aggregate supply curve, AS2, can be drawn through point B. This new aggregate supply curve shows how firms will react to changes in aggregate demand if they expect input prices to remain at the new level of 2.0 for the short run. The short-run aggregate supply has shifted upward because the level of input prices that firms expect to prevail when they make short-run production plans has increased.

To summarize:

1. The short-run aggregate supply curve intersects the long-run aggregate supply curve at a height corresponding to the level of input prices that firms expect to prevail in the short run. The expected level of input prices thus is the key "other things being equal" assumption underlying the short-run aggregate supply curve.

FIGURE 10.4 A SHIFT IN THE SHORT-RUN AGGREGATE SUPPLY CURVE

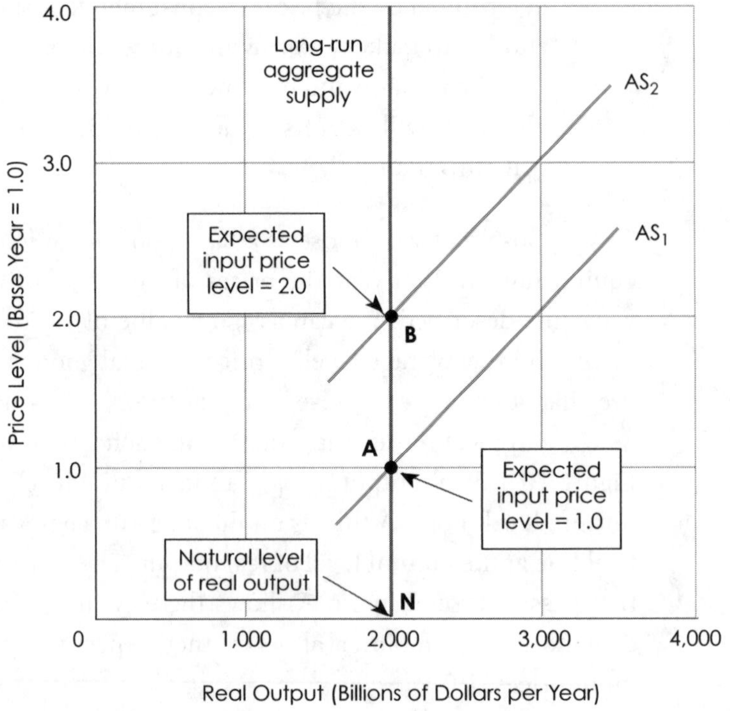

The short-run aggregate supply curve is drawn so that it intersects the long-run aggregate supply curve at the expected level of input prices. Here, the short-run aggregate supply curve AS_1, which intersects the long-run aggregate supply curve at point A, is based on an expected input price level of 1.0. If the expected level of input prices later increases to 2.0, the aggregate supply curve will shift upward to the position AS_2.

2. Over a longer period of time, a change in the expected level of input prices will cause the short-run aggregate supply curve to shift upward or downward to a new intersection with the long-run aggregate supply curve.

Shifts in the Long-Run Aggregate Supply Curve

The key "other things being equal" assumption that underlies the long-run aggregate supply curve and determines its position is the economy's natural level of real output—the level of real output that can be produced with given technology and productive resources when unemployment is at its natural rate. As we first saw in Chapter 4, over time, the economy can expand its production potential through development of new technologies, growth of the labor force, investment in new capital, and development of new natural resources. Such long-run growth was represented in Chapter 4 as an outward expansion of the economy's production possibility frontier. Using the model presented in this chapter, the same kind of expansion can be represented by a rightward shift in the long-run aggregate supply curve.

The remainder of this chapter and the next three will focus on the short run. During this part of the discussion, we will assume that the position of the economy's long-run aggregate supply curve remains fixed. Chapter 14 will return to the question of long-run growth and shifts in the long-run aggregate supply curve.

THE INTERACTION OF AGGREGATE SUPPLY AND DEMAND IN THE SHORT RUN

Now that we have reviewed the conditions that determine the slopes of the aggregate supply and demand curves and shifts in those curves, we can put the curves together to form a complete model of short-run changes in prices and real output. This model will be applied to several issues of theory and policy in coming chapters. In this section we illustrate its basic principles by showing how the economy responds to an increase in aggregate demand, beginning from a position of long-run equilibrium.

Characteristics of Short- and Long-Run Equilibrium

The story begins at point E_0 in Figure 10.5, where the economy is in a position of both short- and long-run equilibrium. This situation is characterized by the intersection of three curves: the aggregate demand curve AD_1, the short-run aggregate supply curve AS_1, and the long-run aggregate supply curve. The significance of each of the intersections is as follows:

1. Expected input prices and prices of final goods are in their long-run equilibrium relationship at the intersection of the short-run aggregate supply curve AS_1 with the long-run aggregate supply curve. *The height of the intersection of the long- and short-run aggregate supply curves indicates the expected level of input prices.*
2. The intersection of AS_1 with AD_1 indicates the level of final-goods prices and real domestic product for which aggregate supply equals aggregate demand, given the expected level of input prices used in drawing AS_1. *The intersection of the short-run aggregate supply curve with the aggregate demand curve is always the economy's point of short-run equilibrium.*
3. The intersection of AD_1 with the long-run aggregate supply curve indicates the price level at which total real planned expenditures are equal to the economy's natural level of real output. *The economy can be in long-run equilibrium only at a point where the aggregate demand curve intersects the long-run aggregate supply curve.*

FIGURE 10.5 SHORT-RUN AND LONG-RUN EQUILIBRIUM

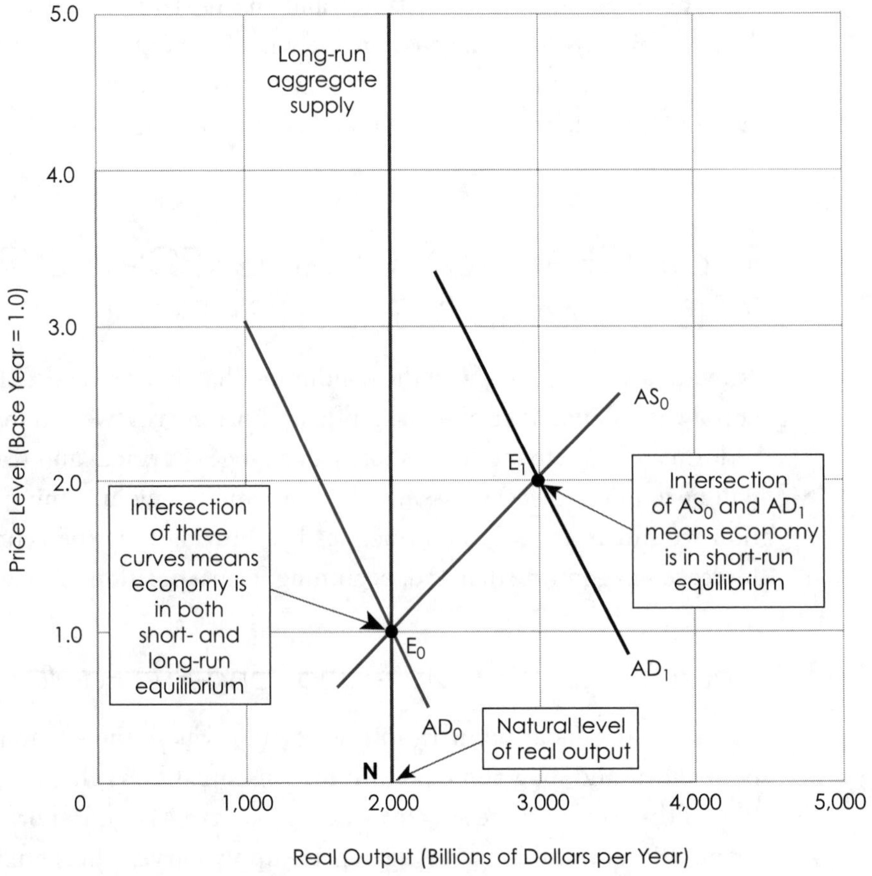

The economy is in short-run equilibrium at the point where the aggregate demand curve intersects the short-run aggregate supply curve. It can be in long-run equilibrium only at a point where the aggregate demand curve intersects the long-run aggregate supply curve. In this diagram, point E_0 is a point of both long- and short-run equilibrium, assuming that the aggregate demand curve is in the position AD_1. If the aggregate demand curve shifts to the position AD_2, the short-run equilibrium point moves to E_1, where there is a positive output gap. E_1 is not a point of long-run equilibrium because it is not on the long-run aggregate supply curve.

4. The intersection of all three curves at E_0 indicates a price level and real domestic product that meet *both* the short-run and the long-run equilibrium conditions.

These four characteristics of short- and long-run equilibrium are essential to understanding the aggregate supply and demand model. Along with an understanding of the sources of shifts in each of the curves, they provide a set of basic working rules that can be applied to solve any problem that falls within the scope of the model.

Short-Run Effects of an Increase in Aggregate Demand

Now suppose that, beginning from point E_0 in Figure 10.5, something causes an increase in total real planned expenditure so that the aggregate demand curve shifts to the right from AD_0 to AD_1. For the moment it does not matter just what causes the shift. It could be a change in government policy, a spontaneous increase in real consumption spending, an increase in real planned investment resulting from greater business confidence, a boom in demand for U.S. exports, or some combination of these factors.

Whatever the cause, the immediate effect of the increase in planned expenditure will be an unplanned decrease in inventories. Seeing that their products are being bought up faster than they can be produced, firms will alter their plans accordingly. As explained earlier, their short-run reactions to the change in demand will be based on the assumption that input prices will not immediately adjust to the change in demand for final goods. Given that assumption, firms will react to the increase in demand partly by increasing output and partly by raising prices. In graphical terms, these reactions are shown by a movement up and to the right along the short-run aggregate supply curve AS_1, which is drawn on the assumption that input prices are expected to remain at their initial level of 1.0 for the time being. As the economy moves along the aggregate supply curve, real output increases and the unemployment rate falls. Using a term introduced in Chapter 4, we can say that a *positive output gap* develops as real GDP rises above its natural level.

When the economy reaches point E_1, where AS_0 and AD_1 intersect, planned expenditure and real output will be back in balance and the unplanned inventory depletion will cease. This is a new position of short-run equilibrium for the economy that is applicable as long as the aggregate demand and short-run aggregate supply curves remain in the positions shown.

Transition to a New Long-Run Equilibrium

The point at which curves AS_0 and AD_1 intersect is a point of short-run equilibrium for the economy, but it is not a point of long-run equilibrium. Whenever there is a positive output gap, as there is at E_1, the price level of final goods will be greater than the expected level of input prices at that point. Expected input prices are still at level 1.0, shown by the intersection of AS_0 with the long-run aggregate supply curve. Prices of final goods, however, have risen to a level of 2.0 at E_1. This situation cannot be maintained indefinitely. Over time, input prices will gradually adjust to the change that has taken place in final-goods prices.

Figure 10.6 shows what happens as this adjustment takes place. Suppose that after a certain period (say, one year), input prices increase to a level of 2.0, catching up with the increase in prices of final goods that took place as the economy moved from E_0 to E_1. This new level of input prices will become the basis for business

FIGURE 10.6 SHORT-RUN AND LONG-RUN ADJUSTMENT TO AN INCREASE IN AGGREGATE DEMAND

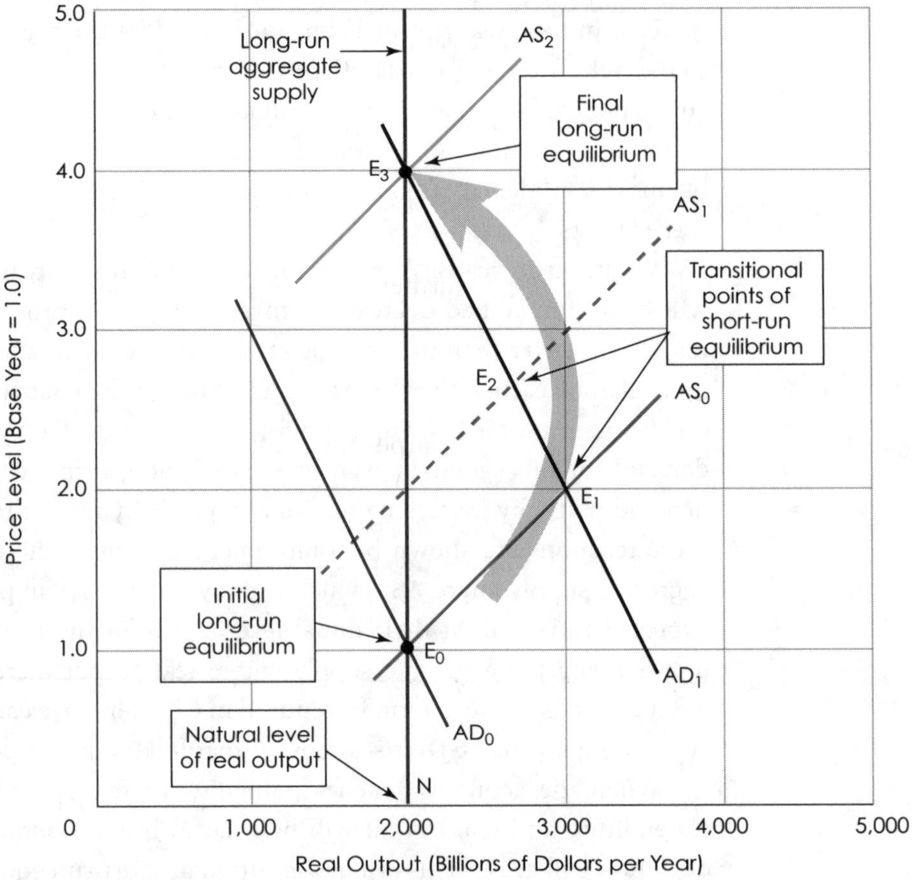

Beginning from an initial long-run equilibrium at E_0, a shift in the aggregate demand curve to AD_1 will cause the economy to move to a new short-run equilibrium at E_1. As it does so, real output will rise above its natural level, the price level of final goods will rise, a positive output gap will develop, and unemployment will fall below its natural rate. After a time, the expected level of input prices will begin to move upward in response to the increase that has taken place in the prices of final goods. As this happens, the short-run aggregate supply curve will shift upward, and the economy will move up and to the left along AD_1. Eventually it will reach a new equilibrium at E_3. As the economy moves from E_1 to E_3, the price level of final goods will continue to rise, the output gap will decrease until real output returns to its natural level, and unemployment will rise back to its natural rate.

expectations in the subsequent year. Graphically, the increase in the expected level of input prices is shown as an upward shift in the short-run aggregate supply curve, from AS_0 to AS_1. AS_1 now intersects the long-run aggregate supply curve at the new expected level of input prices, 2.0.

Assuming that no further change takes place in planned expenditures, the aggregate demand curve will remain at AD_1. Given an unchanged level of aggregate demand, firms will react to the new, higher, expected level of input prices by raising their prices and reducing their output. As they do so, the economy will move along the aggregate demand curve from E_1 to E_2, where AS_2 and AD_2 intersect. Because the output gap is decreasing, the unemployment rate begins to rise.

However, like E_1, E_2 is not a point of long-run equilibrium. In the process of moving to E_2, the prices of final goods have increased again, reaching a level of about 2.7. They are again out of balance with the expected level of input prices, which is now 2.0. Whenever the price level of final goods is above the expected level of input prices, input prices will tend to increase. Input prices thus will continue their gradual upward adjustment. As they do so, the short-run aggregate supply curve will continue to shift upward.

A succession of further intermediate positions could be shown as the aggregate supply curve shifts upward along the aggregate demand curve. To make a long story short, however, we will jump ahead to the point at which it has shifted all the way up to the position AS_2. When it reaches that position, its intersection with the aggregate demand curve AD_1 is at point E_3, which is also where AD_1 intersects the long-run aggregate supply curve. At E_3, then, all three curves again intersect at a common point. The economy is once again in both short-run and long-run equilibrium. The gradual process through which expected input prices catch up to the prices of final goods is complete. Both input prices and output prices have reached the level of 4.0 and are in a consistent relationship to one another. Real output is back to its natural level, the output gap is zero, and unemployment is back to its natural rate. If there is no further shift in aggregate demand, the economy can remain at E_3 indefinitely.

Effects of a Decrease in Aggregate Demand

After a time, events may sooner or later cause aggregate demand to change again. Beginning from the long-run equilibrium point E_3, let's see what will happen if the aggregate demand curve shifts all the way back to its initial position, AD_0. Again, it does not matter for the moment whether the decrease in demand takes the form of a decrease in consumption, planned investment, government purchases, or net exports. Nor does it matter whether the change originates with a change in government policy, or with a change in the choices made by households, firms, or buyers of exports.

Figure 10.7 shows how the firm will react to the leftward shift of the aggregate demand curve. Firms will notice a reduction in planned expenditure through an unplanned increase in their inventories. At first, they may not know whether the decrease in demand is local or is occurring throughout the economy. In any event, some will react by cutting output, some by reducing their prices, and many by doing some of both. The economy will move down and to the left along the aggregate supply curve AS_2 to a short-run equilibrium at E_4. There, the price level will have fallen to 3.0, and real output to $1,000 billion. Unemployment will also have increased and a negative output gap will have developed. The economy will have experienced a recession.

FIGURE 10.7 SHORT-RUN AND LONG-RUN ADJUSTMENT TO A DECREASE IN AGGREGATE DEMAND

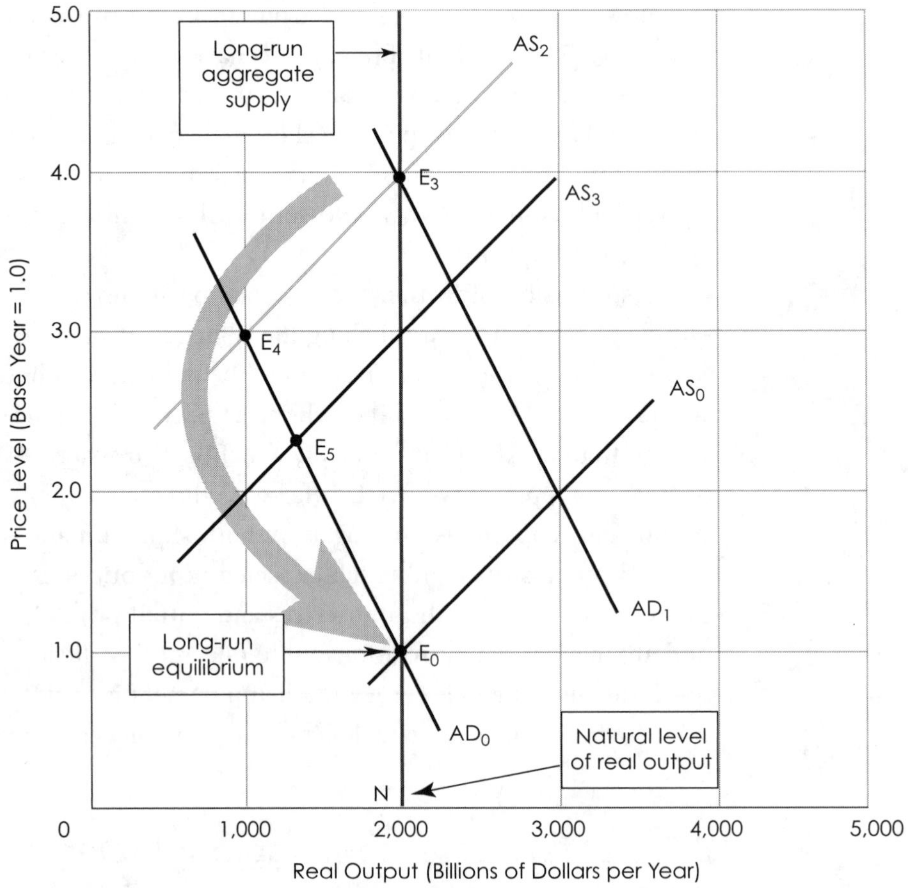

This figure begins from point E_3, the end point of the sequence of events described in Figure 10.6. From this point, aggregate demand is assumed to shift back to the position AD_0. At first, firms respond to falling demand and unexpected inventory accumulation by cutting back output and reducing prices. As the economy moves to a short-run equilibrium at E_3, the unemployment rate rises and final-goods prices fall. When expected input prices also begin to fall, the aggregate supply curve begins to shift downward. As it does so, the economy moves along AD_0, through the intermediate point E_5, and on down to E_0. If there is no further change in aggregate demand, the economy will remain in equilibrium at that point.

As in the case of an increase in aggregate demand, point E_4 is not a possible long-run equilibrium because final-goods prices are out of line with the expected level of input prices. The negative output gap will soon begin to exert a downward pull on the expected and actual levels of input prices. Firms that produce intermediate goods, such as energy and semi-finished products, will find that demand for those goods is weak, and will react by cutting prices (although perhaps only when long-term contracts are up for renewal). Unemployed workers will accept lower nominal wages in order to find some work. And even workers who have kept their jobs may be willing to accept lower nominal wages when their contracts are renewed, if they realize that lower final-goods prices mean that it costs less to maintain a given standard of living.

In response to the drop in input prices, and the expectation that they will fall still more, the aggregate supply curve shifts downward. AS_3 is an intermediate position corresponding to an expected input price level of 3.0. However, E_5, at the intersection of AD_0 and AS_3, is still not a long-run equilibrium because the level of final-goods prices there is less than 3.0. Long-run equilibrium will not be restored until the economy moves all the way back to its natural level of real output at E_0 and the negative output gap has disappeared. During the transition from E_4 to E_0, output will be increasing and unemployment decreasing, even while the price level of final goods continues to fall.

Aggregate Supply, Demand, and the Business Cycle

If we look at the entire sequence of events shown in Figures 10.6 and 10.7, we can see that the economy has traced out something that looks very much like the business cycles discussed in Chapter 4:

1. Beginning from the natural level of real output, the economy expands. A positive output gap develops as domestic product rises above its natural level, unemployment falls below its natural rate, and the price level begins to rise.
2. After a time, a peak of real output is reached after which real output, although still above its natural level, begins to decrease and unemployment begins to increase.
3. If aggregate demand shifts to the left again after real output returns to its natural level, the economy will continue to contract, a negative output gap will develop, and unemployment will rise above its natural rate. During this phase of the cycle, the price level begins to decrease.
4. Eventually real output reaches a minimum, the trough of the recession. As real output moves back toward its natural level, unemployment again decreases. In principle, the economy could come to rest at the natural level of real output. If aggregate demand increases once more, however, a new cycle will begin.

This is not yet a complete theory of the business cycle, but it is a step forward over the simple Keynesian multiplier model. One big improvement over the simple multiplier model is that we now can show clearly how a given change in nominal planned expenditure is divided, in the short run and the long run, between changes in real output and changes in the price level. The other is that we now understand the role played by monetary conditions and interest rates in determining changes in planned expenditure, and, consequently, aggregate demand. We will build further on this model in the next three chapters.

SUMMARY

1. **What are the conditions that determine the slope of the aggregate demand curve?** The *aggregate demand curve* shows the relationship between real planned expenditure on final goods and the average price level of final goods. The curve has a negative slope because each of the components of real aggregate demand—consumption, planned investment, government purchases, and net exports—varies inversely with the price level. The aggregate demand curve is inelastic. As a result, the nominal value of planned expenditure (real planned expenditure times the price level) increases as one moves up and to the left along the curve.

2. **What are some sources of shifts in the aggregate demand curve?** Movements along the aggregate demand curve are associated with changes in the price level of final goods. Changes in other conditions can cause shifts in the curve. Among the sources of shifts are changes in consumer or business expectations; changes in policy regarding government purchases, taxes, and money; and changes in the world economy. Because of the *multiplier effect*, an initial $1 change in any of the components will cause the curve to shift to the right or left by more than $1.

3. **What are the conditions that determine the slopes of the short- and long-run aggregate supply curves?** An *aggregate supply curve* shows the relationship between the quantity of real output supplied (that is, real domestic product) and the average price level of final goods. The slope of the curve depends on what assumption is made about the way firms expect input prices to be affected by changes in the prices of final goods. In the long run, it is reasonable to expect input prices to adjust proportionately to changes in the prices of final goods. In that case, firms have no incentive to increase or decrease output, so the long-run aggregate supply curve is a vertical line drawn at the economy's natural level of real output. In the short run, actual and expected input prices adjust only gradually to changes in the prices of final goods. Thus, in the short run, firms find it worthwhile to increase both output and prices in response to an increase in demand.

4. **What are the sources of shifts in the aggregate supply curves?** At the intersection of the long- and short-run aggregate supply curves, the price level of final goods and the expected level of input prices are equal. An increase (or decrease) in the expected level of input prices thus will cause the short-run aggregate supply curve to shift up (or down) along the long-run aggregate supply curve. The location of the long-run aggregate supply curve is determined by the natural level of real output. An increase in natural real output resulting from improved technology or greater availability of productive resources will cause a rightward shift in the long-run aggregate supply curve.

5. **How do prices, real output, and unemployment behave as the economy responds to a change in aggregate demand?** Beginning from a state of long-run equilibrium, an increase in real aggregate demand will, in the short run, cause the economy to move up and to the right along its short-run aggregate supply curve. As it does so, the prices of final goods will rise, a positive output gap will develop as real output rises above its natural level, and unemployment will fall below its natural rate. After a time, the expected level of input prices will begin to rise as a result of the increases that have taken place in the prices of final goods. As that happens, the economy will move up and to the left along the aggregate demand curve, assuming no further shift in that curve. The price level of final goods will continue

to rise, real output will fall back toward its natural level, and unemployment will rise back toward its natural rate. If, after the new equilibrium is reached, aggregate demand shifts to the left again, a negative output gap will develop as real output drops below its natural level, and unemployment will rise above its natural rate. The level of final goods prices will fall below the expected level of input prices. Soon, the expected level of input prices, too, will begin to fall. If there is no further change in aggregate demand, the economy will return to equilibrium at the natural level of real output.

KEY TERMS

Aggregate demand	Aggregate supply curve
Aggregate supply	Input prices
Aggregate demand curve	

PROBLEMS AND TOPICS FOR DISCUSSION

1. **Elasticity of aggregate demand.** Turn to the aggregate demand curve AD_2 in Figure 10.1. Along that curve, as the price level rises from 0.5 to 1.5, the quantity of real output demanded declines from $3,000 billion to $2,000 billion. What happens to the aggregate quantity demanded in nominal terms over this interval? Using the formula for price elasticity of demand (the ratio of the percentage change in the quantity of a good demanded to a given percentage change in its price), what is the elasticity of aggregate demand over this interval?

2. **The multiplier effect.** Suppose that a newly released popular hit by a U.S. rock group causes fans in Asia to order $50,000 worth of T-shirts with the band's picture. The T-shirts are entirely made in the United States. Other things being equal, would this tend to increase planned expenditure in the United States by exactly, more than, or less than $50,000? Would it shift the aggregate demand curve to the right, the left, or not at all? Explain in detail.

3. **Long- and short-run aggregate supply curves.** On a piece of graph paper draw a set of axes, such as those in Figure 10.4, but do not draw the supply curves shown there. Instead, draw a long-run aggregate supply curve based on the assumption that the natural level of real output is $3,000 billion. What is the slope of the curve? At what point does it intersect the horizontal axis? Next draw a short-run aggregate supply curve based on the assumption that the expected level of input prices is 1.5. Where does this short-run aggregate supply curve intersect the long-run aggregate supply curve that you drew?

4. **Final goods prices and expected input prices.** Given an aggregate demand curve and a short-run aggregate supply curve, how can you determine the short-run equilibrium price level of final goods? Given a long-run aggregate supply curve and a short-run aggregate supply curve, how can you determine the expected level of input prices? Turn to Figure 10.6. Give the short-run equilibrium price level of final goods and the expected level of input prices for each of the points E_0, E_1, E_2, and E_3.

5. **Long- and short-run equilibriums.** On a piece of graph paper draw a set of axes identical to those in Figure 10.6. Draw a long-run aggregate supply curve based on the assumption that a natural level of real output is $2,500 billion. Draw a short-run aggregate supply curve that passes through the points (2,500, 1.0) and (3,500, 2.0).

Label it AS_1. What is the expected level of input prices indicated by this supply curve? Draw an aggregate demand curve that passes through the points (2,000, 2.0) and (2,500, 1.0). Label it AD_2. Given these three curves, where is the economy's point of short-run equilibrium? Where is its point of long-run equilibrium? Now draw another aggregate demand curve that passes through the points (2,500, 4.0) and (4,000, 1.0). Label it AD_2. Given AD_2 and the aggregate supply curves on your diagram, where is the economy's point of short-run equilibrium? What is the relationship between the short-run equilibrium price level of final goods and the expected level of input prices? Is there a possible point of long-run equilibrium for the economy, given AD_2 and the long-run aggregate supply curve? If so, explain how the economy can reach that point starting from the short-run equilibrium just described.

CASE FOR DISCUSSION

We Weren't Talking Revolution; We Were Talking Jobs

Ed Paulsen's family was from South Dakota. He finished high school in 1930, as the country was sliding toward the Great Depression. He went West to pick apples in Washington state and then worked on road gangs. In 1931 he ended up in San Francisco. These are his words.

> I tried to get a job on the docks. I was a big husky athlete, but there just wasn't any work. Already by that time, if you were looking for a job at a Standard Oil service station you had to have a college degree. It was that kind of market...
>
> I'd get up at five in the morning and head for the waterfront. Outside the Spreckles Sugar Refinery, outside the gates, there would be a thousand men. You know dang well there's only three or four jobs. The guy would come out with two little Pinkerton cops: "I need two guys for the bull gang. Two guys to go into the hole." A thousand men would fight like a pack of Alaskan dogs to get through there. Only four of us would get through.
>
> These were fathers, 80 percent of them. They had held jobs and didn't want to kick society to pieces. They just wanted to go to work and they just couldn't understand. There was a mysterious thing. You watched the papers, you listened to rumors, you'd get word somebody's going to build a building.
>
> So the next morning you get up at five o'clock and you dash over there. You got a big tip. There's three thousand men there, carpenters, cement men, guys who knew machinery and everything else. These fellas always had faith that the job was going to mature somehow. More and more men were after fewer and fewer jobs....
>
> We weren't greatly agitated in terms of society. Ours was a bewilderment, not an anger. Not a sense of being particularly put upon. We weren't talking revolution; we were talking jobs.

Source: Excerpts from Studs Terkel, *Hard Times: An Oral History of the Great Depression* (New York: Pantheon Books, 1970), 29–31.

QUESTIONS

1. Economic historians most frequently cite a decrease in planned investment as one of the major causes for the Great Depression of the 1930s. Explain how a decrease in planned investment, other things being equal, would affect planned expenditure and the aggregate demand curve. How would the resulting shift in the aggregate demand curve affect real output and employment?

2. If wages and prices adjusted immediately and fully to changes in demand, what would happen to unemployment as a result of a decrease in planned investment?
3. What does the story of Ed Paulsen suggest regarding the speed of adjustment of wages and prices to a shift in aggregate demand? What might cause a gradual, rather than a rapid, adjustment?

END NOTES

1. Elasticity varies from one point to another along a straight-line demand curve. Any straight-line demand curve becomes more elastic as it approaches its intersection with the vertical axis. Strictly speaking, it would be better to draw aggregate demand curves whose slope increases toward the top of the diagram. Such curves could be drawn with a constant elasticity that is less than unity throughout their length. We use straight-line aggregate demand curves in this book because they simplify the diagrams. This will cause no difficulty as long as we focus on changes occurring along the inelastic part of the curve.

PART 4

Macroeconomic Policy

CHAPTER 11

Fiscal Policy and Economic Stability

After reading this chapter, you will understand:

1. How fiscal policy—that is, changes in government purchases and net taxes—can be used to fight recession and inflation
2. How government receipts and expenditures are affected by changing economic conditions
3. How the federal budgetary system works and the limitations of that system
4. How the federal budget deficit is measured and why it has grown
5. Whether large federal deficits are a threat to economic stability

Before reading this chapter, make sure you know the meaning of:

1. Real and nominal interest rates
2. Government purchases
3. Transfer payments
4. Net taxes
5. Expenditure multiplier
6. Output gap

Fiscal policy

Policy that is concerned with government purchases, taxes, and transfer payments.

FISCAL POLICY MEANS policy related to government spending and taxes. In the world of fiscal policy, economics and politics are tightly mixed. Spending and tax policy during the administration of U.S. President George W. Bush are a case in point. One of the first actions of U.S. President George W. Bush, after taking office in 2001, was to propose broad cuts in federal income taxes. The tax cuts were justified on the grounds that they would stimulate the economy and speed recovery of the U.S. economy from recession, but they also served the political purpose of solidifying support for Republicans among influential campaign contributors. Soon the terrorist attacks of September 11, 2001 and the outbreak of war in Afghanistan and Iraq introduced further fiscal challenges. To minimize political damage, the Bush administration chose to finance these military actions through a series of emergency appropriations rather than through the regular budget process. By 2004, the economy was expanding rapidly, but unemployment was still higher than usual for that stage of the economic recovery. To position themselves more favorably for the upcoming 2004 elections, the President and Republicans in Congress agreed to extend the 2001 tax cuts, making many of them permanent. The string of political victories built, in part, on these fiscal policies did not come to an end until the 2006 Congressional elections. The interaction of politics and fiscal policy in the U.S. in this period was not unique. A similar mixture of political and economic motivations could be illustrated with fiscal policy decisions from both Democratic and Republican administrations in the United States, and, in fact, from almost any country or time period.

In this chapter, we use the models developed earlier to explore the economics of fiscal policy, including such topics as defense spending, the federal budget deficit, and the national debt. We will also look at the political process behind fiscal policy decisions. Finally, we will look at the economic and political debate over the budget deficit and the national debt.

THE THEORY OF FISCAL POLICY

As long ago as the 1930s, John Maynard Keynes and his followers proposed increases in government purchases as an antidote to the Great Depression. The arguments given at that time for using fiscal policy to stimulate economic expansion remain relevant to the fiscal policy debate in the United States today. A discussion of how fiscal policy can be used as a tool for combating economic contractions makes a suitable starting point for the chapter.

Using Government Purchases to Combat a Negative Output Gap

Figure 11.1 uses the aggregate supply and demand model to show how fiscal policy can be used to combat an economic contraction. In that figure, there is a negative output gap at point E_1, where the aggregate supply curve, AS_1, meets aggregate demand curve AD_1. There real domestic product is \$500 billion below its natural level of \$2,000 billion, and, as a result, unemployment is above its natural rate. As explained in Chapter 10, if aggregate demand remained at this low level, the prices of final goods and inputs would gradually adjust. Real output would eventually return to its natural level as the aggregate supply curve shifted downward and the economy slid down and to the right along AD_1. But would the return to normalcy occur fast enough? Or would the reluctance of firms to lower their prices and the unwillingness

FIGURE 11.1 USING FISCAL POLICY TO COMBAT AN ECONOMIC CONTRACTION

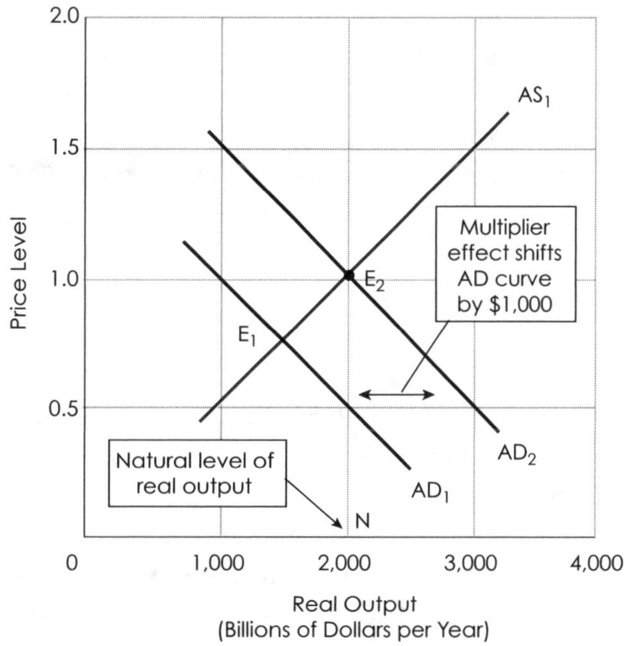

In this figure, a negative output gap has developed at E_1. To reach the natural level of real output at E_2 without waiting for a downward shift of the aggregate supply curve, the aggregate demand curve must be shifted to the right by $1,000 billion, from AD_1 to AD_2. This can be done by increasing real government purchases and taking advantage of the multiplier effect. Given an expenditure multiplier of 4, a $250 billion increase in government purchases will bring about the required $1,000 billion shift in the aggregate demand curve. However, because the price level rises, equilibrium real domestic product does not increase by the full $1,000 billion by which the aggregate demand curve shifts. The same shift can be accomplished with a cut in net taxes, but the multiplier effect of a tax cut will be smaller than that of an increase in government purchases.

of workers to accept lower nominal wages delay the downward shift of the aggregate supply curve and make the adjustment slow and painful?

As Keynes once said, "in the long run, we are all dead." Suppose that the president and Congress, impatient with the economy's natural speed of adjustment, want to do something about the recession now. The problem is insufficient aggregate demand. Given the position of the aggregate supply curve, the aggregate demand curve needs to be shifted from AD_1 to AD_2 in order to bring real output back to its natural level at E_2. How can this be done?

IDENTIFYING THE SPENDING GAP Although the gap between real domestic product and its natural level is only $500 billion, the horizontal gap between the aggregate demand curves AD_1 and AD_2 is $1,000 billion, as shown by the arrow in Figure 11.1. Policy makers need to fill the entire $1,000 billion gap between the aggregate demand curves to bring real output to its natural level.

Of course, the gap might be filled even if policy makers did nothing. Exports might pick up; business managers might become more optimistic and increase planned investment; a rise in consumer confidence might spur consumption. But instead of waiting and hoping, policy makers could turn to the element of planned expenditure that is most directly under their control: government purchases. It is not hard to think of things that the government could spend money on—a new postal sorting station here, a stretch of interstate highway there, new vehicles for park rangers somewhere else. But just how much spending for new government purchases is needed?

USING THE MULTIPLIER EFFECT To move the aggregate demand curve to the right by $1,000 billion, it is not necessary to increase government purchases by that amount. The reason is that each dollar of new government purchases is amplified by the multiplier effect. Spending $1 on a federal highway project boosts the income of construction workers, who then spend more on, say, groceries, clothing, and cars. Their spending raises the incomes of grocers, textile workers, and autoworkers, who in turn consume more. As the multiplier effect cascades through the economy, each $1 of new government purchases causes more than $1 of additional planned expenditure.

Suppose that the value of the expenditure multiplier is 4. This means that $1 of government purchases will raise the equilibrium level of planned expenditure at a given price level by $4. (This calculation takes into account both the initial increase in government purchases and the induced increases in consumption expenditure.) Therefore, it will take $250 billion of additional government purchases to shift the aggregate demand curve to the right by $1,000 billion.[1]

CHANGING PRICES AND AGGREGATE DEMAND As the aggregate demand curve shifts from AD_1 to AD_2, the economy moves up and to the right along the aggregate supply curve. In the process, the increase in prices affects real planned expenditure in ways that partially offset the multiplier effect of the original increase in government purchases. As we saw in the preceding chapter, there are four reasons why a change in the price level will affect real planned expenditure:

1. Real consumption is restrained by the fact that the real value of nominal money balances falls as the price level rises.
2. Real planned investment is moderated by the higher interest rates associated with a higher price level.
3. The parts of government budgets that are set in nominal terms will command fewer real goods and services as the price level rises.
4. Real net exports will fall because domestic prices will rise relative to prices abroad.

These effects are built into the slope of the aggregate demand curve. They do not cause the aggregate demand curve to shift away from its new position at AD_2. Instead, they cause the economy to move up to point E_2 on AD_2. There, equilibrium planned expenditure is \$2,000 billion, which is only \$500 billion greater than at E1, despite the fact that the aggregate demand curve has shifted to the right by \$1,000 billion.

In short, because a rise in the price level tends to lower every type of planned expenditure, the equilibrium level of real domestic product rises by less than the expenditure multiplier times the initial change in real government purchases.

Using a Change in Taxes or Transfer Payments to Combat a Negative Output Gap

Government purchases are only one side of the fiscal policy equation. The other side consists of net taxes. The term *net taxes* means tax revenues collected by government minus transfer payments made by government to individuals. A tax cut or an increase in transfer payments operates on the economy via its effect on consumption.

Let us return to point E_1 in Figure 11.1 and see how a change in net taxes can be used to combat the negative output gap. As before, the problem is to shift the aggregate demand curve to the right by \$1,000 billion. Suppose that in an attempt to stimulate the economy Congress votes a \$100 billion increase in real social security benefits while leaving taxes unchanged. This amounts to a \$100 billion cut in real net taxes. How does it affect aggregate demand?

To begin with, the action raises the real disposable incomes of social security recipients by \$100 billion. If the marginal propensity to consume is, say, 75, they raise their consumption by \$75 billion. The increase in consumer spending by social security recipients for groceries, cars, and the like boosts the incomes of grocers, autoworkers, and others by \$75 billion; they, in turn, increase their consumption expenditures by \$56,250,000,000; and so on.

We see, then, that a cut in net taxes, like an increase in government purchases, touches off an expansionary multiplier process. This is true whether the reduction in net taxes takes the form of a cut in taxes paid to government or an increase in transfer payments made by government. However, there is an important difference in the first-round impact of the two policy changes. A \$100 billion increase in government purchases is itself a \$100 billion *direct* addition to aggregate demand. However, a \$100 billion tax cut or increase in transfer payments is not in itself a direct addition to aggregate demand, because it does not represent a decision by government to buy any newly produced goods and services. Therefore, the only effect of the cut in net taxes is the induced increases in consumption expenditures. For that reason, a cut in net taxes has a multiplier effect that is somewhat smaller than the effect of an equal increase in planned expenditure.

Suppose, for example, that the multiplier for a reduction in net taxes is 3, rather than the multiplier of 4 for government purchases. We can now return to Figure 11.1 and see how much of a cut in real net taxes is needed to eliminate the negative output gap. The required shift in the aggregate demand curve is \$1,000 billion, so

\$333 billion in tax cuts or transfer payment increases are needed to shift the aggregate demand curve to the right by \$1,000 billion. In response to this shift, real output rises by \$500 billion, taking into account the effects of a rising price level on the various components of real planned expenditure.

An important qualification is in order, however. The preceding analysis suggests that, on a dollar-for-dollar basis, changes in net taxes are only slightly less effective than changes in government purchases in influencing the level of aggregate demand. But in reaching this conclusion, we have assumed that households will spend the same fraction of an additional dollar received through tax cuts as they will of an additional dollar in earned income. Some economists do not think that will be the case. For one thing, consumers are likely to change their consumption less in response to temporary tax changes than to permanent changes. For example, the one-time tax rebate of 1975 appears mainly to have led to an increase in saving with little impact on consumption. Even if a tax cut is announced as permanent, consumers may still be concerned that the resulting increase in government borrowing may lead to higher taxes in the future when it is time for the borrowing to be repaid. In that case, too, they would increase saving in response to expected future tax increases. Because of these two effects, the impact of a change in taxes on aggregate demand is more ambiguous than the simple multiplier model suggests.

Fiscal Policy and Inflation

In previous sections we have seen how fiscal policy can be used to speed up recovery from a contraction. Now we will see that fiscal policy can also play a part in fighting inflation or, for that matter, can cause inflation if used irresponsibly.

COUNTERACTING PROJECTED INFLATION Consider the situation shown in Figure 11.2. The economy has been in equilibrium for some time at E_1, where real output is at its natural level. As the federal budget for the coming year is being prepared, forecasters warn of the possibility of that a positive output gap will develop as a result of projected growth in the private components of aggregate demand—a surge in export demand, a boom in consumer spending, or an increase in planned investment. If something is not done, the forecasters say, the aggregate demand curve for the coming year will shift rightward to AD_2. That will cause inflation by driving the economy up and to the right along aggregate supply curve AS_1, to E_2.

The short-run result will be an increase in the price level from P_1 to P_2, but inflation will not stop there. The rise in the prices of final goods will, in time, cause firms to raise their expectations regarding wages and other input prices. As a result, the short-run aggregate supply curve will shift upward to AS_2. Inflation will continue as long as the positive output gap persists. Only when real output falls back to its natural level, will the economy reach a new long-run equilibrium at point E_3.

FIGURE 11.2 FISCAL POLICY AND INFLATION

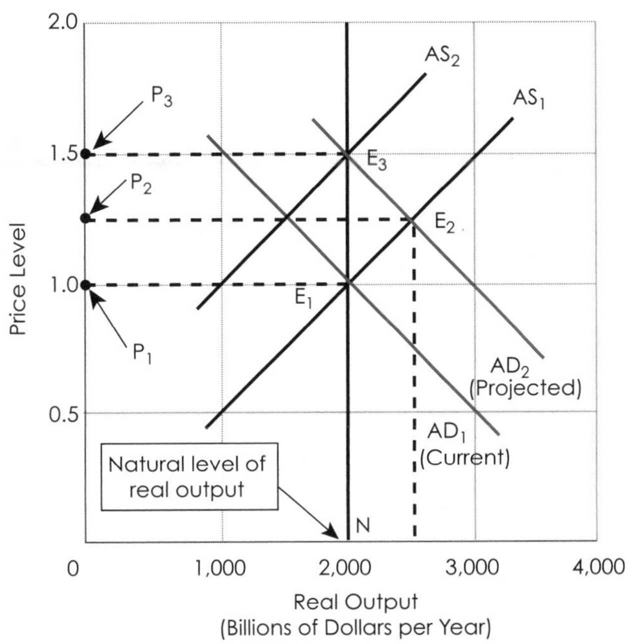

Initially the economy is at E_1. Forecasts show that if no policy changes are made, increases in real private planned expenditure will shift the aggregate demand curve from AD_1 to AD_2, causing the price level to rise as the economy moves to a short-run equilibrium at E_2. In the long run, assuming nothing is done about aggregate demand, the price level would rise still more as the aggregate supply curve shifted upward and the economy moved toward a new long-run equilibrium at E_3. To prevent an increase in the price level, government purchases can be cut or net taxes increased to offset the projected change in private planned expenditure, thus restoring the aggregate demand curve to position AD_1.

Restrictive fiscal policy is one way of warding off the inflation threat. The federal budget for the coming year can be written in such a way as to combine cuts in government purchases and increases in net taxes that will offset the projected increases in private aggregate demand. Suppose that the multiplier is 4, as in our earlier examples. For each $100 by which aggregate demand is projected to shift beyond the level needed to reach the natural level of real output, government purchases can be cut by $25 or net taxes increased by enough to produce the same shift in aggregate demand. The right combination of cuts in government purchases, cuts in transfer payments, and increases in taxes will hold the aggregate demand curve in the desired position at AD_1.

EXPANSIONARY FISCAL POLICY AS A SOURCE OF INFLATION In the preceding example, federal policy makers are the "good guys," crafting a sensible budget designed to restrain inflation. That is the role we would hope for them to play. However, the same diagram could be used to tell a different story, one in which expansionary fiscal policy is the cause of the positive output gap.

In this scenario the economy is in equilibrium at E_1 and forecasters expect it to stay there. However, there is an election coming up. Members of Congress would like to please the voters by boosting federal benefits, cutting taxes, and initiating public works projects. The president, who is also up for reelection, would like to conduct the coming campaign in an atmosphere of rising real output and falling unemployment. Seeing their common interests, Congress and the president craft a strongly expansionary budget for the upcoming election year. When the expansionary budget first goes into effect, the economy moves from E_1 to E_2 in Figure 11.2. As hoped, real output expands and unemployment falls with only a moderate increase in the price level. Voters are pleased, and everyone is reelected.

The next year, however, wages and other input prices begin to rise. As firms adjust their expectations to the new circumstances, not only does inflation of final goods prices continue but real output falls and the unemployment rate rises. The hangover from the election party sets in. This contrast between the relatively benign initial effects of expansionary policy and its less desirable long-run effects is a theme to which we will return several times in later chapters.

Automatic Fiscal Policy

The type of fiscal policy discussed so far—changes in the laws regarding government purchases, taxes, and transfer payments designed to increase or decrease aggregate demand—is known as **discretionary fiscal policy.** The levels of government purchases and net taxes can also change as a result of changing economic conditions even if no discretionary changes are made in the laws governing them. Such changes in government purchases or net taxes, which are known as **automatic fiscal policy,** are most closely associated with changes in real output, the price level, and interest rates.

Discretionary fiscal policy

Changes in the laws regarding government purchases and net taxes.

Automatic fiscal policy

Changes in government purchases or net taxes that are caused by changes in economic conditions given unchanged tax and spending laws.

Changes in the level of real output are one important source of automatic fiscal policy. Real output affects both tax revenues and outlays. An increase in real output increases real revenues from all major tax sources, including income taxes, social security payroll taxes, taxes on corporate profits, and sales taxes. At the same time, an increase in real output cuts real government outlays for transfer payments. This occurs largely because increases in real output are associated with decreases in the unemployment rate. Taking both effects together, an increase in real domestic product tends to reduce the federal budget deficit in both real and nominal terms.

Changes in price level can also affect taxes and government expenditures. With real output held constant, an increase in the price level tends to increase federal tax receipts in nominal terms. At the same time, an increase in the price level tends to increase nominal expenditures. This is partly because most major transfer programs are now indexed so that they can be adjusted for changes in the cost of living and partly because inflation raises the prices of the goods and services that government buys. However, as pointed out before, some elements of government expenditures are fixed in nominal terms. This means that the increase in nominal expenditures will tend to be less than proportional to the increase in the price level.

On balance, nominal taxes rise more than nominal expenditures when the price level increases. Thus, an increase in the price level, other things being equal, tends to reduces the deficit in both real and nominal terms.

Finally, an increase in nominal interest rates raises the nominal cost of financing the national debt. This is only slightly offset by increases in nominal government interest income. Therefore, on balance, an increase in nominal interest rates shifts the budget toward deficit in both nominal and real terms.

In previous chapters, we have seen that when the economy expands real output rises, the price level rises, and unemployment falls. Each of these effects tends to move the government budget toward surplus in real terms, that is, to increase receipts, depress outlays, or both. Whichever side of the budget we look at, automatic fiscal policy operates so as to restrain aggregate demand during an expansion. By the same token, when the economy slows down, the growth rate of real output drops and unemployment rises. The inflation rate slows even if the contraction is not severe enough to cause the price level actually to fall. Thus, during a contraction the real budget swings toward deficit.

Because automatic fiscal policy operates to offset changes in other elements of planned expenditure, such budget components as income taxes and unemployment benefits are known as **automatic stabilizers.** These mechanisms serve to moderate the economy's response to changes in consumption, private planned investment, and net exports.

Automatic stabilizers

Those elements of automatic fiscal policy that move the federal budget toward deficit during an economic contraction and toward surplus during an expansion.

THE BUDGET PROCESS

Our discussion of fiscal policy would be incomplete without at least a brief discussion of how federal officials actually go about making tax and spending decisions. In practice, the decision-making process for fiscal policy often has little to do with the theory of discretionary policy that we have just discussed. Many years ago Herbert Stein, then chairman of the Council of Economic Advisers, wrote that "We have no long-run budget policy—no policy for the size of deficits and for the rate of growth of the public debt over a period of years." Each year, according to Stein, the president and Congress make short-term budgetary decisions that are wholly inconsistent with their declared long-run goals, hoping "that something will happen or be done before the long-run arises, but not yet."[2] What Stein wrote remains very much true today.

The Federal Budgetary System

In discussing the theory of fiscal policy, it is convenient to refer to unnamed "policy makers" who manipulate taxes, transfers, and government purchases. In practice, however, no single agency is responsible for fiscal policy. Budgetary authority is divided between the executive branch, headed by the president, and Congress. Also, budgetary policy must serve many goals, ranging from national security and social equity to simple political ambition, as well as price stability, full employment, and economic growth.

Fiscal year

The federal government's budgetary year, which starts on October 1 of the preceding calendar year.

THE BUDGETARY PROCESS A brief look at the federal budgetary process will indicate where the formal authority for fiscal policy lies. The U.S. government operates on a **fiscal year** that runs from October through September. For example, the fiscal year 2007 runs from October 1, 2006, through September 30, 2007. About 18 months before the beginning of a fiscal year, the executive branch begins preparing the budget. The Office of Management and Budget (OMB) takes the lead in this process. It receives advice from the Council of Economic Advisers (CEA) and the Department of the Treasury. After an outline of the budget has been drawn up, it is sent to the various departments and agencies. Within the executive branch, a period of bargaining ensues in which the Pentagon argues for more defense spending, the Department of Transportation for more highway funds, and so on. During this process the OMB is supposed to act as a restraining force, keeping macroeconomic goals in mind.

By January—nine months before the fiscal year starts—the president must submit the budget to Congress. After the budget has been submitted, Congress assumes the lead in the budgetary process. Its committees and subcommittees look at the president's proposals for the programs and agencies under their jurisdiction. The Congressional Budget Office (CBO) employs a staff of professionals who advise the committees on economic matters, in somewhat the same way that the OMB and CEA advise the president. In May the House and Senate are expected to pass a first budget resolution that sets forth overall spending targets and revenue goals.

Bargaining among committees, between the House and the Senate, and between Congress and the executive branch continues throughout the summer. During this period committees prepare specific spending and tax laws; these are supposed to be guided by the May resolution. Finally, in September, Congress is supposed to pass a second budget resolution that sets binding limits on spending and taxes for the fiscal year beginning October 1. Any bills passed earlier that do not fit within these guidelines are expected to be changed accordingly.

LIMITATIONS OF THE BUDGETARY PROCESS In practice, many things can—and do—go wrong with this process.

The first and most basic problem is that macroeconomic goals—full employment, price stability, and economic growth—carry little weight in the actual budgetary process. Tax and spending decisions are made in dozens of subcommittees, where they are dominated by interest group pressures, vote trading, and the desire of each member of Congress to help the folks at home.

A second problem is that Congress has not always been willing to follow its own rules. The required budget resolutions often are not passed on time; if they are passed, they are not treated as binding. Sometimes the fiscal year starts without a budget. Then agencies must operate on the basis of "continuing resolutions," meaning that they can go on doing whatever they were doing the year before. In 1995, the government shut down for six days in November when Congress failed to pass appropriations bills. According to a document released by the Clinton administration, the government shutdown cost $700–$800 million, including $400 million to furloughed federal employees who were paid, but did not report to work. The Treasury Department reported another $400 million in lost revenue over the four days that the IRS enforcement divisions were closed. More recently in 2003, lawmakers used the threat of a government shutdown to tack provisions on to the needed appropriations bills that benefit their individual districts and states.

Entitlements

Transfer payments governed by long-term laws that are not subject to annual budget review.

Next, there is the problem of so-called mandatory or uncontrollable costs. These include **entitlements**, which are transfer programs governed by long-term laws that are not subject to annual budget review. Examples include social security, military retirement pay, and Medicare. Another major expense that is uncontrollable—for a different reason—is interest on the national debt. Total interest expense is determined by the size of the debt and market interest rates, which, in turn, are beyond the control of fiscal policy. Today well over half of the federal budget is in the "uncontrollable" category. Congress could control most of these costs by passing new laws to replace the current ones, but doing so is not part of the normal budgetary process.

Finally, there are emergency items that cannot be predicted. Modest amounts are included in regular budgets to cover costs of natural disasters such as hurricanes, but some expenses exceed the budgeted emergency allowances. Since 2003, the most glaring example has been spending on the war in Iraq. The Bush administration has not included Iraq war expenditures in its regular budget; instead, it has asked for annual supplemental appropriations to cover the cost of the war. In 2003 through 2006, these totaled some $400 billion dollars. In contrast, aside from just one emergency appropriation, the entire cost of the Vietnam war was financed within the normal budget process.

FISCAL POLICY AND THE FEDERAL DEFICIT

The federal budget deficit has remained a concern for federal and state lawmakers since the large U.S. deficits in the 1980s. Indeed, prior to the Great Depression (1929–1933), one of the primary goals of fiscal policy was to balance the budget. We begin this section by examining the origins of the record deficits of recent years, which lie in both discretionary and automatic elements of fiscal policy. We then turn to the controversy over the effects of the deficit on the economy as a whole.

Figure 11.3 gives two views of the U.S. government budget over time. The first view, the actual budget deficit measures the difference between each year's revenues and outlays. Deficit is the norm. From 1962 through 1997, there was only one small surplus, in 1969. The deficit hit a record of 5.1 percent of GDP in 1985. The economic boom of the 1990s caused revenues to grow faster than outlays, so that by 1998, the budget achieved a surplus. This lasted for four years until recession, tax cuts, and rising defense spending brought the surpluses to an end.

FIGURE 11.3 FEDERAL GOVERNMENT DEFICIT/SURPLUS (BILLIONS OF DOLLARS, 1962–2006)

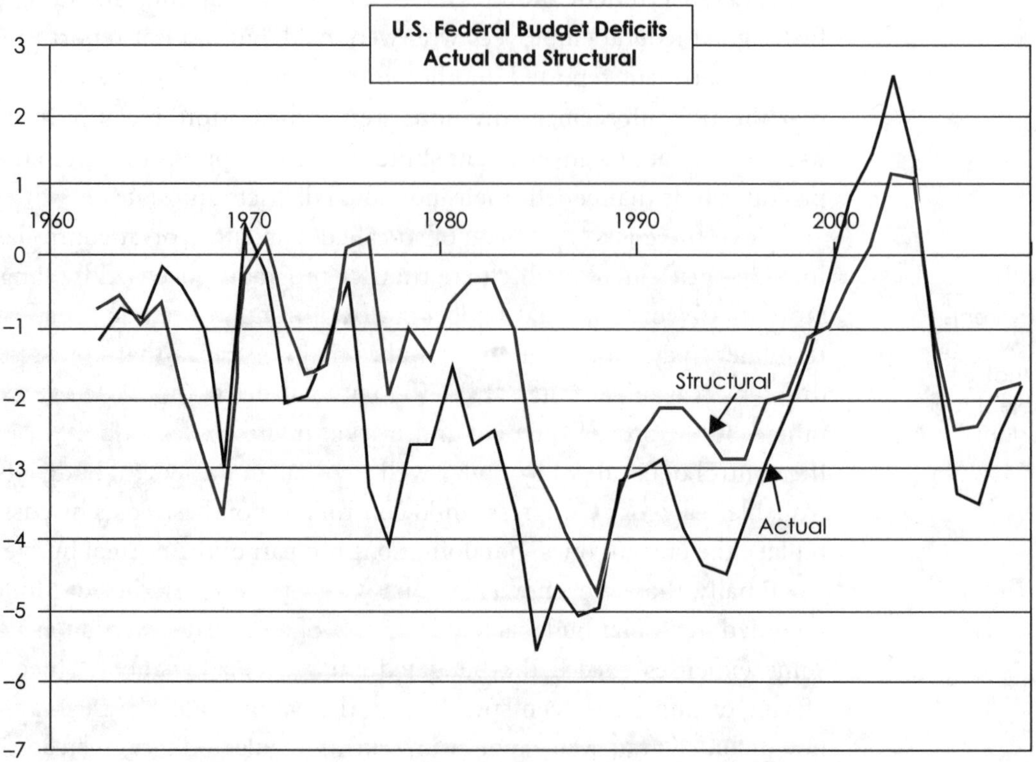

This figure shows two views of the U.S. federal surplus or deficit from 1962 to 2006. The actual surplus or deficit measures the difference between each year's revenues and outlays. The structural deficit is corrected to remove the influence of the business cycle. It can be interpreted as showing what the deficit would have been, given each year's tax and spending laws, if the economy had been at its natural level of GDP in that year.

Source: Congressional Budget Office, *Historical Budget Data, Table E-13 (http://www.cbo.gov/budget/historical.xls)*.

Automatic Fiscal Policy: The Structural Versus Cyclical Deficit

The second view of deficit separates the impact of changes in discretionary policy decisions from the effect of the business cycle. Policymakers do not determine actual levels of government receipts and expenditures. Rather, they pass laws setting tax rates, formulas for transfer payments, and goals for purchases of goods and services. Given these laws, the actual levels of receipts and expenditures depend on the stage of the business cycle. As we have seen, the budget shifts toward deficit when the economy contracts, as tax collections fall and transfer payments rise. Similarly, during expansions the budget shifts toward surplus. As discussed at the beginning of the chapter, the federal government budget is a combination of discretionary fiscal policy decisions and economic conditions.

Structural budget

The budget surplus or deficit that the federal government would incur given current tax and spending laws and unemployment at its natural rate.

Cyclical deficit/surplus

The difference between the structural budget and the actual federal budget. If the actual budget is above the structural budget, there is a cyclical surplus. Likewise, when the actual budget is below the structural budget, there is a cyclical deficit.

The federal budget surplus or deficit that the federal government would run for given tax and spending laws, if there were a zero output gap, that is, if GDP were at its natural, is called the **structural budget**. Changes in the structural budget are interpreted as representing discretionary fiscal policy. The difference between the structural and actual budget is called the **cyclical deficit (or surplus)**. When GDP there is a negative output gap, the cyclical deficit becomes positive because the structural budget exceeds the actual budget. When there is a positive output gap, the structural budget is less than the actual budget, causing a cyclical surplus. Changes in the cyclical deficit or surplus reflect changes in taxes and spending that occur automatically as real output, unemployment, and inflation change over the course of the business cycle.

As Figure 11.3 shows, changes in policy, reflected in the structural deficit, account for the greater part of variations in the actual deficit since 1962. In the early 1980s and early 1990s, when real GDP was below its natural level, the cyclical deficit added to substantial structural deficits. The surpluses of the late 1990s were in part structural, due to increase in taxes relative to outlays, and partly cyclical, due to the economic boom. Similarly, the deficits of the early 2000s were in part cyclical, due to the recession of 2001 and its lingering effects in the next few years, and partly structural, due to the tax cuts and spending increases under the Bush administration. By 2006, real output was close to its natural level. The cyclical deficit was close to zero, and the actual and structural deficits were almost equal.

Economic Priorities

As we have indicated, U.S. federal taxes and spending are the joint result of political decisions reached by the executive branch and Congress. It is hard to judge budget priorities from political rhetoric alone. Both major parties like to provide voters with benefits and promise moderate taxes. Both profess to think that deficits are bad, defending the country is good, and providing income security, especially for the elderly, is sacrosanct. To find which of these priorities has dominated, we need to look at the numbers, as given in Figure 11.4.

Part a of Figure 11.4, which shows separate series for federal revenues and outlays, provides additional insight into the origins of deficits and surpluses. We see that the largest deficits (those of the first Reagan administration in the early 1980s and the George W. Bush administration of the early 2000s) were the result of a combination of tax cuts and increased outlays. In both cases, a significant part of the increased outlays were defense expenditures. Periods of narrowing deficits (the late 1980s) and surpluses (the late 1990s) occurred during periods of rapidly expanding GDP. During such periods, the economy as a whole tends to grow faster than federal spending, so budget outlays decrease as a percentage of GDP without being cut in absolute terms. At the same time, tax laws are written in a way that tends to make total tax revenues increase as a percentage of GDP unless there are changes in tax laws.

FIGURE 11.4 REVENUE AND SPENDING TRENDS FOR THE U.S. FEDERAL GOVERNMENT

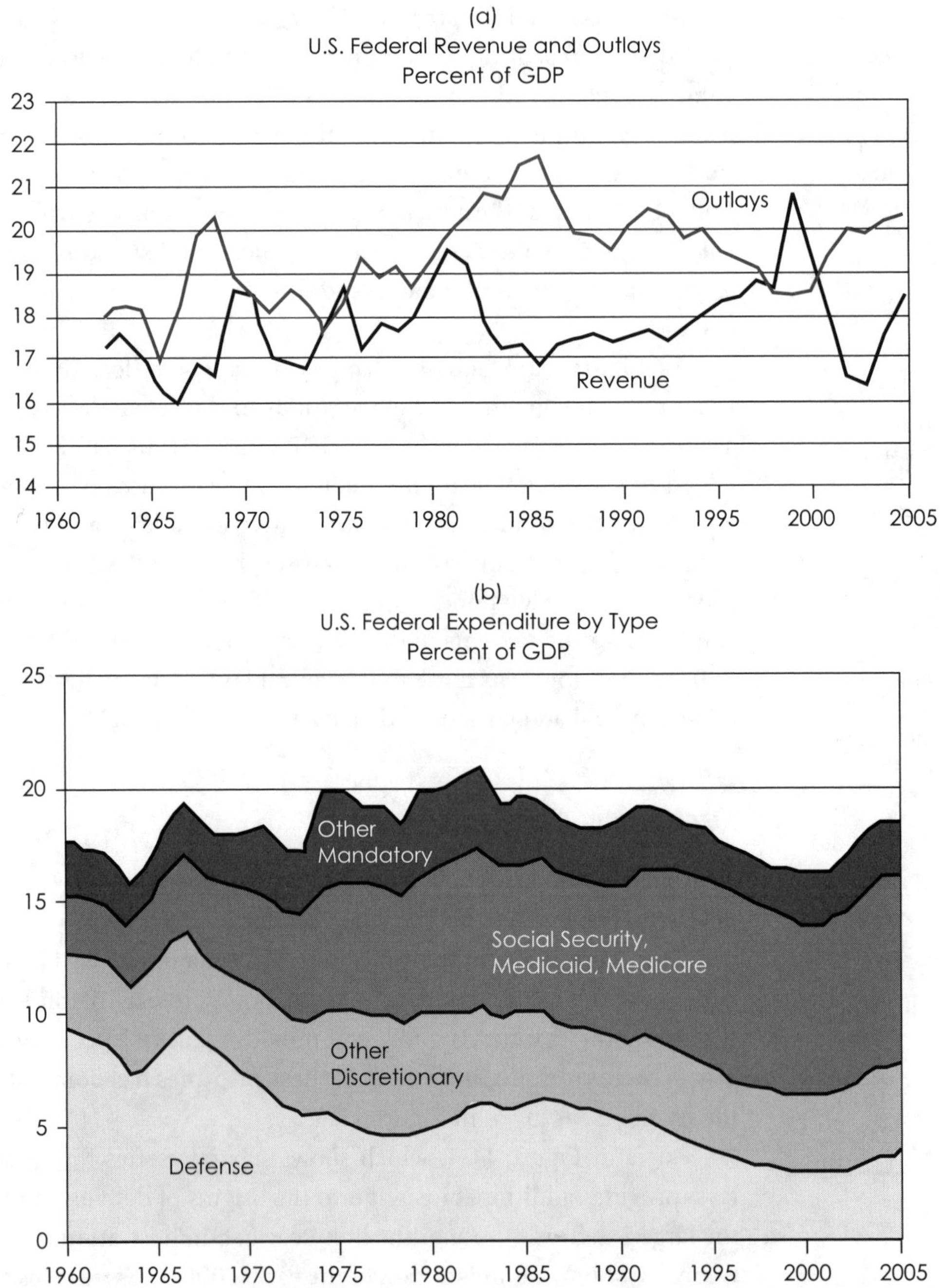

Part a of this figure shows trends in total outlays and revenues as a percent of GDP. They show that the large deficits of the Reagan and George W. Bush administrations were due not solely to tax cuts, but also to spending increases. Part b shows that over the long term, defense spending has decreased as a percentage of GDP while Social Security, Medicare, and Medicaid have increased markedly. Other components of spending, and the total as a percentage of GDP, have varied from year to year around an approximately flat trend.

Source: Congressional Budget Office, Historical Budget Data, Tables E-8 and E-10. (http://www.cbo.gov/budget/historical.xls).

Part b of Figure 11.4 breaks down total outlays into four categories. As can be seen, there has been a long-term decrease in defense spending relative to GDP despite the fact that in absolute terms, the United States today spends about as much on defense as the entire rest of the world put together. In 1999-2001, defense spending as a percent of GDP hit a post-Cold-War low of about 3 percent of GDP. Defense spending is now on the rise again although the conflict in Iraq has not come close to returning it to its level of the Vietnam War.

By far the greatest increase in federal outlays have come in the "entitlements" categories of Social Security, Medicare, and Medicaid. These outlays reflect the increased size and political influence of older people in the U.S. population. The category "other discretionary" spending includes a great variety of programs, ranging from farm subsidies to road building to space exploration. Considering the frequency with which these spending categories make the news, many people are surprised to see that they account for a relatively small part of all spending. Their share relative to GDP has changed little over time. Much the same can be said for the category "other mandatory" spending, which includes items like unemployment compensation and interest on the federal debt.

International Comparisons

Our perspective on government spending in the United States would be incomplete without at least a brief comparison with other countries. To make such a comparison, it is first necessary to shift the focus from the federal government budget to the consolidated government sector, including federal, state, and local branches. The reason is that government spending in the United States is much less centralized than in countries like France or Japan, so that comparisons of central government spending alone would be misleading. As Figure 11.5a shows, spending on direct federal programs in the United States accounted for about 17 percent of GDP as of 1998, and state and local government spending for about 12 percent of GDP. About a quarter of state and local government spending (accounting for about 3 percent of GDP) was financed by federal grants rather than state and local tax revenues.

Part b of Figure 11.5 compares total government spending in the United States with that in other industrialized countries. Government spending in the United States accounts for a smaller share of GDP than in any of the other countries shown. Only Japan comes close in the relatively small size of its government sector. This is especially remarkable when we take into account the fact U.S. defense expenditures account for nearly 4 percent of GDP, compared to 1 to 2 percent in the other countries shown.

The Deficit as a Policy Issue

In recent years, as federal red ink has reached record levels, the deficit has gained prominence as a policy issue. Ordinary people questioned in public opinion polls,

FIGURE 11.5 INTERNATIONAL COMPARISONS OF GOVERNMENT SPENDING

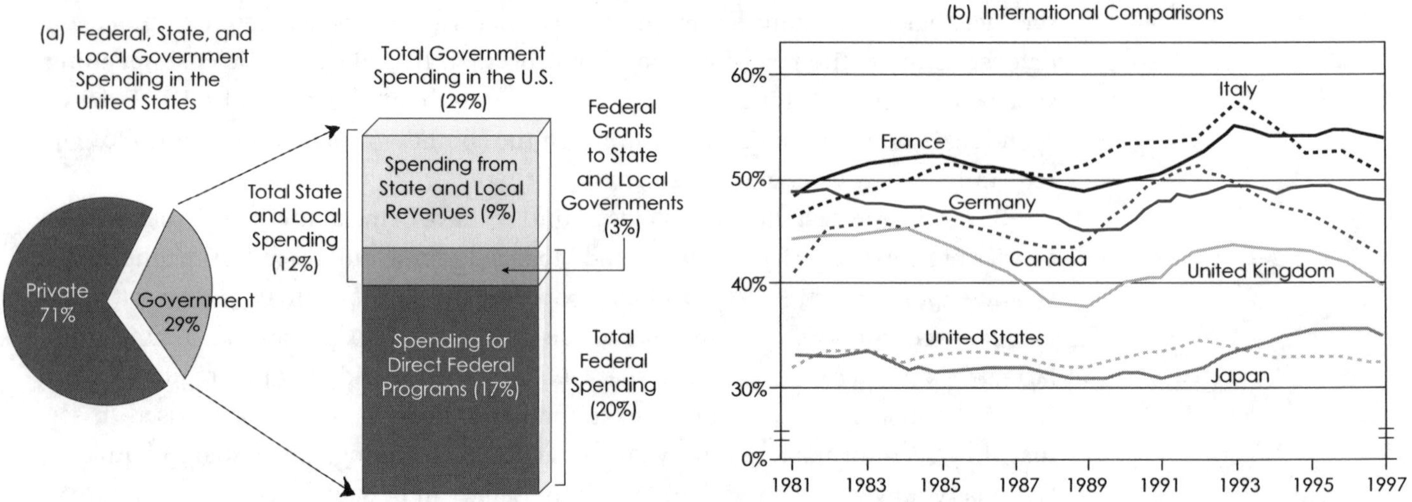

Government spending in the United States is less centralized than in many other countries. As part a shows, direct federal spending on federal programs accounts for just 17 percent of GDP, compared with 29 percent when all levels of government are included. Part b shows that total government spending in the United States accounts for a smaller percentage of GDP than in other high-income countries.

Source: Government Printing Office, GPO Access, Citizen's Guide to the Federal Budget, http://www.gpoaccess.gov/usbudget/fy00/guide01.html#Chart1-2, Charts 1-1 and 1-2.

joined by many professional economists, look on the deficit with foreboding. Can the government go on spending beyond its means forever? Does the deficit place a drag on economic growth? Does it represent a burden on future generations? We will see that there are sound reasons to be concerned. Before examining those reasons, however, we will look at the differing views of economists on the issue.

Reasons Not to Worry About the Deficit

Economists who argue that the federal deficit is not so great a problem begin by making a series of numerical adjustments, which suggest that the federal deficit is not really as large as it seems. We will look at four of these adjustments here.

ADJUSTING FOR THE STATE AND LOCAL SURPLUS The first adjustment is based on the notion that it is not the federal deficit that matters but the combined deficit or surplus of federal, state, and local governments. Although the federal government has been in deficit for all but 4 years since 1970, state and local governments have been in surplus in all but four of those years. The state and local surpluses represent a flow of saving into financial markets that can be used to finance private investment and the federal deficit. For example, when the federal budget deficit hit a record $190 billion in 1986, state and local governments offset more than 10% of that with a $21 billion surplus. The early 2000s were an exception. In 2002 and 2003, as the federal budget again recorded record deficits, combined state and local government budgets were in deficit also. By the end of 2004, state and local government budgets once again returned to surplus.

ADJUSTING FOR THE CYCLICAL COMPONENT When one assesses the impact of fiscal policy on the economy, one should also adjust the federal deficit to remove its cyclical component. The reason is that the cyclical component reflects the state of the economy rather than discretionary policy decisions. Data on the actual and structural deficits were shown earlier in Figure 11.3. For example, in 2004, when the actual deficit was 3.5 percent of GDP, the structural deficit was just 2.4 percent of GDP. It is often argued that the cyclical component of the deficit (1.1 percent of GDP in 2004) is beneficial since it reflects automatic stabilizers that help to moderate the business cycle.

ADJUSTING FOR INFLATION A third adjustment is needed to take the effects of inflation into account. Each year inflation erodes the real value of the federal debt held by the public. For example, if the nominal value of federal debt in the hands of private investors were $1 trillion and the inflation rate were 4 percent, private investors would have to buy almost $40 billion in newly issued government securities just to keep the real value of the total debt constant. This part of the deficit, it is argued, puts no real burden on the rest of the economy because, in real terms, it simply returns investors to the same position they started from. In recent years, as the rate of inflation has fallen, this adjustment is less significant, but it still works to reduce the economic impact of the deficit.

THE DEFICIT AND PRIVATE SAVING Some economists offer another, rather different reason not to worry about the deficit. This is based on the argument that changes in taxes tend to be offset by changes in private saving. If this is true, the public would respond to a tax cut by increasing saving by just the amount needed to buy the extra securities the Treasury would have to sell in order to finance the added deficit. Likewise, a tax increase made to reduce the deficit would decrease saving by the same amount, leaving no additional resources with which to finance private investment. However, recent data suggest that this argument, too, is weaker in the case of recent deficits than in earlier years.

Reasons to Worry About the Deficit

Despite the arguments just given, many economists—probably the majority—still worry about current and projected federal budget deficits. Let's look at some of their concerns.

EFFECTS ON INVESTMENT Earlier in the chapter we saw that when the Treasury borrows to finance a deficit, it adds to total demand for the limited funds made available by private domestic saving, thereby pushing up interest rates. Private borrowers are then crowded out of financial markets. The reduction in private investment is a burden on the economy that slows economic growth and reduces the living standards of future generations. In the early 2000s, as federal budget deficits grew, interest rates remained surprisingly low. As a result, the impact of the deficit on investment was less than it might have been. Whether interest rates will remain low if the budget continues to show a large deficit is a matter of some controversy.

BORROWING FROM ABROAD In defense of deficits it used to be said that the national debt is something "we owe to ourselves." In other words, taxes collected to repay the debt come out of the pockets of some U.S. citizens but go back into the pockets of others, leaving the country as a whole no poorer. However, federal budget deficits push up interest rates in the United States relative to those in the rest of the world. Attracted by the high rates, foreign buyers purchase many of the securities that the Treasury sells to finance the deficit. In addition, because high interest rates on government securities push up the rates on competing private securities, many private U.S. securities also move into foreign hands.[3] Repaying the part of public and private debt owed to foreign investors places a real future burden on the U.S. economy, so the argument that we owe it to ourselves does not apply. As recently as 1993, just 20 percent of the federal debt was owed to foreign investors. Today, the figure is more than half.

THE ENLARGED STRUCTURAL DEFICIT It is widely acknowledged that any cyclical component of a federal deficit is less of a problem than the structural component. What worried many economists in the early 1980s was the way the structural component grew during the 1980s even as the cyclical component fell. The structural deficit was not eliminated until 1999. In the early 2000s, the pattern seems to be repeating itself. By 2004, tax cuts and spending increases not only eliminated the structural surplus (which, arguably, could be seen as a drag on economic growth) but sent the structural deficit back to levels not seen since the 1980s.

THE DANGER OF AN "EXPLODING" DEFICIT The growth of the structural deficit calls attention to still another worry: the increase in the part of the deficit associated with interest payments on the debt.

In the explosive-growth scenario, the amount of borrowing needed just to make interest payments on the debt is so great that the debt grows faster than domestic income even if the rest of the budget remains in balance. As the government borrows more and more each year to make interest payments, it adds to the demand for loanable funds in credit markets. This pushes interest rates higher, making it necessary to borrow even more to make the interest payments. Eventually the deficit "explodes" and threatens to swallow the entire domestic income.[4]

As the point of explosive growth approaches, the government is left with only one way out. It begins to "monetize" the deficit, which in effect means that it finances the deficit by creating new money rather than by borrowing. But financing deficits with newly created money is the classic formula for inflation. Thus, monetization of the deficit converts an explosive deficit into explosive inflation.

Is this scenario too farfetched to be a real threat? Not at all. Creating new money to cover the government deficit is the source of the runaway inflations (at annual rates of 1,000 percent per year and more) that devastated such countries as Bolivia, Argentina, Brazil, and Yugoslavia in the 1980s and 1990s, and Zimbabwe at present. Today inflation is not running out of control in the United States; in fact, it has slowed dramatically from the double-digit rates of the late 1970s and early 1980s. Nevertheless, many economists think that continuing large federal deficits are a potential danger that cannot be ignored. In the next four chapters, we will gain a better understanding of this danger as we look at the mechanisms that are used to create and control money in the U.S. economy.

SUMMARY

1. **How can fiscal policy be used to fight recession and inflation?** *Fiscal policy* means policy that is related to government purchases and net taxes. If a decrease in private planned expenditure threatens to send the economy into a recession, an increase in government purchases or a cut in net taxes can be used to shift the aggregate demand curve to the right, thereby restoring the economy to its natural level of real output. If an excess of private planned expenditure threatens the economy with inflation, a cut in government purchases or an increase in net taxes can shift the aggregate demand curve to the left, thereby restoring stability.

2. **How are government receipts and expenditures affected by changing economic conditions?** Some changes in government receipts and expenditures reflect *discretionary* changes in the laws that govern fiscal policy. However, changes in the levels of these items can also result *automatically* from changes in economic conditions, including real output, unemployment, and the price level. In general, economic expansion tends to raise receipts and restrain expenditures, thereby moving the budget toward surplus. Contraction tends to lower receipts and raise expenditures, thereby moving the budget toward deficit. These automatic changes in receipts and expenditures damp the economy's response to shifts in private planned expenditure and, hence, are known as *automatic stabilizers*.

3. **How does the federal budgetary system work, and what are the limitations of that system?** In the United States authority for fiscal policy is divided between the president and Congress. Each year the president submits a budget plan, which Congress modifies and enacts into law by the beginning of the *fiscal year* on October 1. In practice, macroeconomic goals play a secondary role to political considerations in setting budget priorities.

4. **How is the federal deficit measured, and why has it grown?** The federal deficit can be divided into a cyclical component and a structural component. The *structural deficit* is the estimated level of the deficit, given current tax and spending laws and unemployment at the natural rate. The *cyclical deficit* is the difference between the actual and structural deficits; it tends to increase during a recession and to decrease during an expansion. If unemployment drops below the natural rate at the peak of an expansion, the cyclical deficit becomes negative (that is, there is a cyclical surplus). During the expansion that followed the 1981–1982 recession, the cyclical component of the deficit declined nearly to zero while the structural component grew dramatically. The actual deficit then ballooned during the 1991–1992 recession. Both the actual and structural budgets went into a surplus during the mid- to late-1990s, only to return to deficit in the early 2000s.
5. Are large federal deficits a threat to economic stability? Some economists argue that if the federal deficit is adjusted for state and local government surpluses, the cyclical component of the deficit, capital expenditures, and the effects of inflation, it looks somewhat less threatening. Others claim that the deficit crowds out private investment. They are also concerned about borrowing from abroad to finance the deficit and the possibility that explosive growth of the deficit could ultimately cause severe inflation.

KEY TERMS

Fiscal policy	Fiscal year
Net tax multiplier	Entitlements
Discretional fiscal policy	Structural budget
Automatic fiscal policy	Cyclical deficit/surplus
Automatic stabilizers	

PROBLEMS AND TOPICS FOR DISCUSSION

1. **Discretionary spending.** Suppose that in response to a foreign crisis, the government increases defense spending by $50 billion. Assuming no other changes in government policy and an expenditure multiplier of 4, how would a defense spending increase of that magnitude affect the economy? On the basis of what you have learned in this chapter, what can you say about whether such an increase in defense spending would help or harm the economy?
2. **Applying the multiplier.** Suppose that real output is at its natural level in the current year but forecasts show that if no action is taken, the aggregate demand curve will shift to the left by $500 billion in the coming year. Assuming a multiplier of 2.5, what change in real government purchases will be needed to keep real output at the natural level?
3. **A balanced budget amendment.** From time to time it has been proposed that a law or constitutional amendment be passed that will force the federal government to balance its budget every year Do you think it would be possible to keep the actual budget deficit at zero each year, or should such an amendment aim only to keep the structural deficit at zero? Discuss.
4. **Foreign governments and the federal debt.** In recent years, the biggest buyers of U.S. government securities used to finance the deficit have been foreign governments, especially those of China and Japan. In what ways do foreign government purchases of U.S. securities make the size of the deficit more of a worry than if they had been sold to U.S. investors instead? In what ways do they make the deficit less of a worry?

CASE FOR DISCUSSION

Hungary: The Politics of Fiscal Lies

In September 2006, a wave of political demonstrations exploded in Hungary's capital of Budpapest. Riot police using water cannon battled in the street with crowds that overturned cars and made barriers of burning tires. It was not the image that Hungary, a new and usually well-behaved member of the European Union, was happy to display to the world.

The rioting had an unlikely source: A speech on fiscal policy that Hungarian Prime Minister Ferenc Gyurcsany delivered to a closed meeting of members of his Socialist government. In his speech, Gyurcsany used unusually candid language about the past performance of his government and the tactics his party had used to win a narrow victory in national elections the preceding April. He was quoted as saying, in part, "We screwed up. Not just a bit. A lot... It was perfectly clear that what we were saying wasn't true... You cannot mention a single major government measure we can be proud of... I almost died when I had to pretend that we were actually governing. We lied morning, noon and night."

Unfortunately for Gyurcsany, the speech, intended as a private scolding of party insiders with the intent to improve performance in the future, was leaked to the press. When members of the opposition learned that the prime minister had openly admitted lying to win the election, they took to the streets in protests that soon turned violent.

The specific subject of the lies in question concerned Hungary's government budget. In the run-up to the election, everyone knew that the country had a deficit problem, but government officials tried to assure the nation that the deficit for 2006 would be no more than 4.7 percent of GDP. That would be well above the European Union norm of 3 percent of GDP, but not a disaster. Instead, after the election, it became plain that the deficit for the year would be closer to 10 percent of GDP and that the government had known this all along.

Unfortunately, the steps needed to reduce Hungary's budget deficit are politically painful. These include cutting the number of public employees; cutting costs of an inefficient health system, possibly through partial privatization; reforming a system of social welfare in order to focus payments on the truly poor; and reducing generous transportation subsidies. No one in Hungary even talks about tax increases since taxes are already considered too high.

If all parties could agree to cooperate on a package of reforms, the goal of fiscal consolidation could be achieved. In Hungary, however, each party seems intent on daring the other to bear the political cost of painful expenditure cuts. But any party that actually undertook the needed reforms, without cooperation of the opposition, would surely lose the next election. As Jean-Claude Junker, Prime Minister of Luxembourg, once said, "We all know what to do, we just don't know how to win the election afterwards."

QUESTIONS

1. In recent years, Hungary's economy has been growing at 4 percent or so per year, resulting in GDP that is probably close to its natural level. From such a starting point, what would be the short-term impact on the economy of cutting government spending while taxes remained unchanged? What would be the longer-term impact of the budget cuts? Answer in terms of the economic model presented in this chapter.
2. Hungary has national elections every five years. From a political point of view, taking into account both the short-term and long-term effects of budget cuts, what would be the safest time for a government to attempt policy reforms? What would be the riskiest time?

3. Two of the budget reforms needed in Hungary are a cut in the number of public employees and a reduction in social welfare payments received by those who are not truly poor. From the point of view of the economic model discussed in this chapter, would the same amount saved via payroll reduction or reduction in welfare payments have identical effects on the economy? If not, why not?

END NOTES

1. This example is somewhat simplified in that it assumes that interest rates, planned investment, and exchange rates are unaffected by the fiscal policy change. Chapter 12 will explain how the analysis of fiscal policy needs to be modified to take these factors into effect.
2. Herbert Stein, "After the Ball," *AEI Economist* (December 1984): 2.
3. These effects can also be expressed in terms of concepts that deal with international economic relations: An increase in the federal deficit, other things being equal, tends to move the financial account in the direction of a net financial inflow. This must be offset by a movement of the current account toward deficit. Thus, in an open economy, a federal deficit crowds out net exports as well as domestic investment.
4. The issue of the exploding deficit was raised in Thomas J. Sargent and Neil Wallace, "Some Unpleasant Monetarist Arithmetic," *Federal Reserve Bank of Minneapolis Quarterly Review* (Fall 1981): 1–17. Michael R. Darby refines the argument by showing that the deficit will explode if the real rate of interest (that is, the nominal market rate minus the inflation rate), adjusted for the average tax rate on federal interest payments, exceeds the long-term rate of growth of real GDP. See "Some Pleasant Monetarist Arithmetic," *Federal Reserve Bank of Minneapolis Quarterly Review* (Spring 1984).

CHAPTER 12

An Integrated View of Monetary and Fiscal Policy

After reading this chapter, you will understand:

1. How changes in the money stock affect real output, the price level, and unemployment
2. What is meant by the neutrality of money
3. How fiscal policy affects interest rates and planned investment
4. Keynesian and monetarist views of the Great Depression

Before reading this chapter, make sure you know the meaning of:

1. Elasticity
2. Real and nominal interest rates
3. Natural level of real output
4. Multiplier effect
5. Monetary sector
6. Transmission mechanism

IN CHAPTERS 7, 8, AND 9, we looked at the monetary sector of the economy in isolation. In this chapter we return to the broader themes of inflation, real output, and employment to see how these are shaped by developments in the monetary sector. The goals of high employment, price stability, and economic growth require the president, Congress, and the Federal Reserve to work together. By combining a monetary sector model with the aggregate supply and demand model and the analysis of fiscal policy developed earlier, we will gain a better understanding of why both monetary and fiscal policy play important roles in economic policy, and why the two branches of policy need to be carefully coordinated.

SHORT-RUN EFFECTS OF MONETARY POLICY

Chapter 9 discussed several aspects of the transmission mechanism through which monetary policy affects the economy. The most important of these was the channel acting from monetary policy to planned investment via interest rates. Figure 12.1 shows the interest-investment transmission mechanism at work in the short run in response to a one-time expansion in the money stock.

Initially the monetary sector is in equilibrium at point E_1 in part (a) of the figure. The money supply curve is in the position MS_1, and the money demand curve is at MD_1; thus, the equilibrium interest rate is R_1. Part b of the figure shows a planned investment schedule, which gives a graphical view of the interest-rate transmission mechanism. According to the planned-investment schedule in part (b), interest rate R_1 will result in a level of real planned investment indicated by I_1. This level of planned investment is used as a basis for the aggregate demand curve AD_1 in part (c) along with given conditions regarding consumption, government purchases, and net exports. The initial equilibrium point in part (c) is thus e_1, at the intersection of AD_1 and the aggregate supply curve, AS. Equilibrium real output is Q_1, and the price level is P_1.

Now assume that the Fed uses an open market purchase of securities to inject new reserves into the banking system. As banks compete to make new loans in order put their new reserves to work, the interest rate falls. These effects are shown in Part (a) of the figure as a rightward shift of the money supply curve, accompanied by a decrease in the interest rate.

The falling interest rate lowers the opportunity cost of investment. In response, firms move downward and to the right along the planned-investment schedule shown in part (b). The increase in real planned investment, in turn, causes the aggregate demand curve to shift to the right, as shown in part (c). In response to the boost in demand, real output and the price level both increase and the economy moves upward and to the right along its short-run aggregate supply curve.

As the economy expands, the increase in prices and real output causes nominal domestic income to rise. Bringing the story full circle, the rise in nominal domestic income causes the money demand curve shown in Part (a) of the figure to shift to the right, from MD_1 to MD_2. This limits the fall in the interest rate, but the curve does not shift enough to prevent the interest rate from falling somewhat. The monetary sector comes into equilibrium at point E_2, where the new money supply and demand curves intersect. At the new equilibrium interest rate, R_2, real planned investment is I_2. This level of planned investment, together with the same underlying conditions as before regarding real consumption, government purchases, and net exports, puts the aggregate demand curve in the position AD_2. The new short-run equilibrium for the economy thus is e_2 in part (c), where real domestic product is Q_2 and the price level is P_2.

To summarize, expansionary monetary policy has the following effects in the short run:

FIGURE 12.1 SHORT-RUN EFFECTS OF EXPANSIONARY MONETARY POLICY

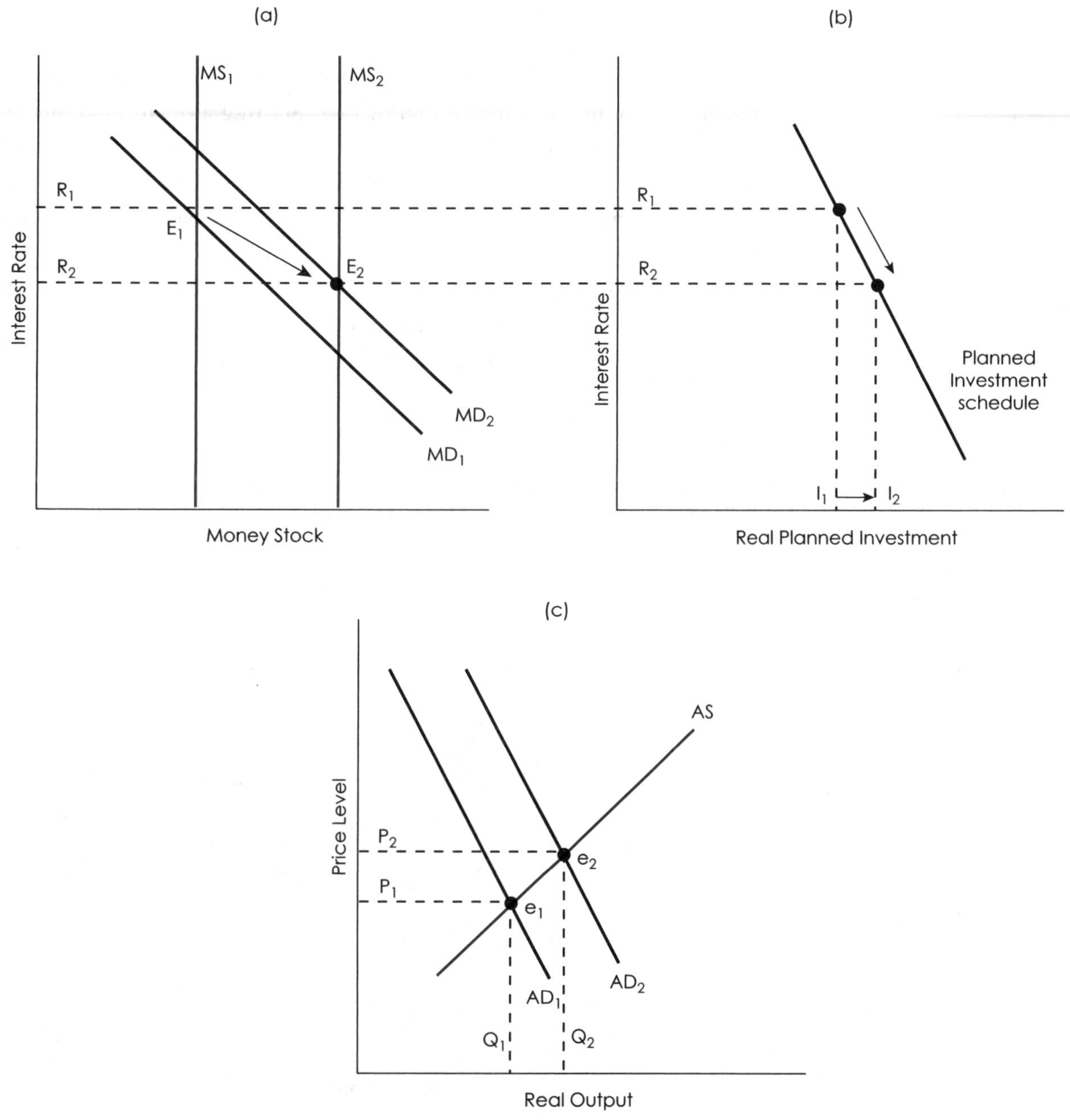

A one-time increase in the money stock shifts the money supply curve from MS_1 to MS_2. The interest rate begins to fall. Real planned investment begins to increase as the economy moves down and to the right along the planned-investment schedule. The increase in planned investment shifts the aggregate demand curve from AD_1 to AD_2, raising real output and the price level. The resulting rise in nominal domestic income shifts the money demand curve to the right from MD_1 to MD_2. This shift is enough to limit the drop in the interest rate but not sufficient to prevent it altogether. In the new short-run equilibrium, the interest rate is lower and real investment, real output, and the price level are all higher than they were initially.

1. A reduction in the interest rate
2. An increase in the level of real output
3. An increase in the price level

Contractionary policy produces an opposite set of short-run effects, as can also be shown using a modification of Figure 12.1. Starting at E_2 in the monetary sector, the Fed tightens monetary policy, shifting the money supply curve to the left. All the arrows are now reversed. A rising interest rate causes a reduction in planned investment. Falling planned investment shifts the aggregate demand curve to the left, causing prices and real output to fall. This, in turn, means that nominal income declines, causing the money demand curve to shift to the left as well, but not enough to prevent some increase in the interest rate. In the new short-run equilibrium, the monetary sector returns to E_1 and the economy as a whole returns to e_1.

FIGURE 12.2 LONG-RUN EFFECTS OF EXPANSIONARY MONETARY POLICY

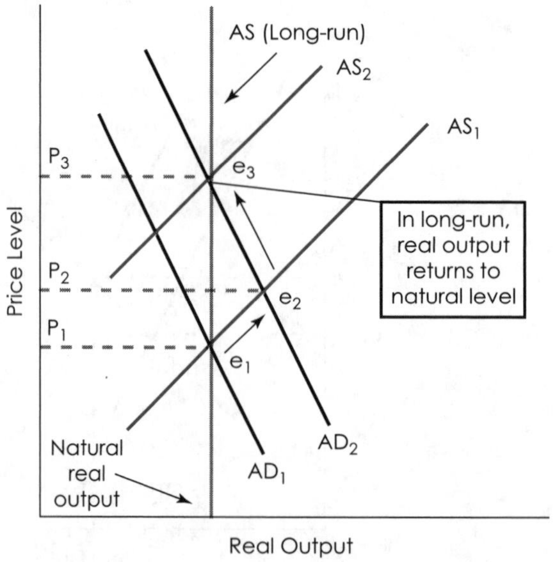

A one-time increase in the money stock causes real output to rise temporarily above its natural level, reaching point e_2. The economy cannot remain at this point indefinitely, however. As expected input prices begin to adjust upward, the aggregate supply curve will shift from AS_1 toward AS_2. The economy will move along aggregate demand curve AD_2 until it reaches a new long-run equilibrium at e_3. As it does so, nominal domestic income will continue to rise, pushing interest rates up until they return to their initial level. Thus, in the long run, a one-time increase in the money stock will only cause a proportional increase in the price level while leaving real output and the interest rate unchanged. This result is known as the *neutrality of money*.

LONG-RUN EFFECTS AND THE NEUTRALITY OF MONEY

In Chapter 10 we explained the distinction between the positively sloped short-run aggregate supply curve and the vertical long-run aggregate supply curve. Movements along the short-run curve are based on firms' expectation that input prices will not change immediately in response to a change in aggregate demand. However, a change in the prices of final goods will eventually affect the level of input prices. As input prices adjust to changes in the prices of final goods, the short-run aggregate supply curve shifts upward until the economy returns to equilibrium at the natural level of real output at a higher point on its long-run aggregate supply curve.

The economy will undergo such a process of long-run adjustment when the money stock changes and then remains at its new level. This process is shown in Figure 12.2.

The process begins with expansionary monetary policy, which lowers interest rates and stimulates aggregate demand. As the aggregate demand curve in Figure 12.2 shifts rightward from AD_1 to AD_2, the economy moves to a new short-run equilibrium at e_2. Now let us see what happens next.

As the economy moves from e_1 to e_2, the average level of final-goods prices increases. Although firms do not expect input prices to increase immediately in proportion to output prices, they will begin to do so in time. As explained in Chapter 10, this happens partly because some goods serve as both inputs and final goods and partly because the rise in the price level raises the cost of living, putting upward pressure on wage rates. Once firms begin to expect increases in input prices, the short-run aggregate supply curve starts to shift upward toward the position AS_2. As it does so, the economy moves up and to the left along aggregate demand curve AD_2 until, eventually, it returns to the natural level of real output at e_3. At that point both final-goods prices and input prices have adjusted upward in proportion to the initial increase in the money stock. For example, if the money stock increases by 10 percent, both final-goods prices and input prices will also increase by 10 percent.

For reasons discussed in Chapter 10, we know that the aggregate demand curve is inelastic. Therefore, as the economy moves up and to the left along the curve, the percentage increase in price is greater than the percentage decrease in real output. This, in turn, means that nominal domestic income and product will increase. In the monetary sector, the increase in nominal domestic income will put upward pressure on real interest rates, eventually pushing them all the way back up to the level they were at before expansionary monetary policy was undertaken. Real planned investment, which had increased while interest rates were lower, decreases again as interest rates rise until investment, too, is back where it started.

The preceding analysis shows that a one-time increase in the money stock has the following long-run effects:

1. An increase in the equilibrium levels of both final-goods and input prices in proportion to the change in the money stock
2. No change in the equilibrium level of real output
3. No change in the equilibrium interest rate

Neutrality of Money

The proposition that in the long run a one-time change in the money stock affects only the price level and not real output, employment, interest rates, or real planned investment.

This set of conclusions is called the principle of the **neutrality of money.** Money is neutral in the sense that one-time changes in its level do not affect the *long-run* equilibrium values of real variables such as real output, real planned investment, employment, or real interest rates. In the long run, a one-time change in the money stock affects only price levels.

The principle of the neutrality of money has a long history in economics. It was stated clearly by Adam Smith's friend David Hume (see *Who Said It? Who Did It? 12.1*). It can also be stated in terms of the equation of exchange. If the terms are rearranged, the equation of exchange can be written in the form P = MV/Q. As we know, the value of velocity depends on the interest rate. Because the long-run equilibrium value of the interest rate is not affected by a one-time change in the money stock, velocity, too, will be unaffected by such a change. Thus, the equation just given tells us that if Q is held constant at its natural level and V is unchanged, a one-time change in the money stock will produce a proportional change in the price level. For example, a doubling of the money stock has the long-run effect of doubling the price level from P_1 to P_3.

WHO SAID IT? WHO DID IT? 12.1

DAVID HUME ON THE NEUTRALITY OF MONEY

David Hume was an early member of the classical school of economics, as well as a noted historian and philosopher. Born in 1711, he was a colleague of Adam Smith at Edinburgh University. He much admired Smith's Wealth of Nations, which was published in 1776, the year Hume died. Although today Smith's contributions to economics overshadow Hume's, many of Hume's writings are regarded as insightful for his time.

Eighteenth-century economists widely agreed that an increase in the money stock—chiefly gold and silver coins at the time—would raise the price level. Price increases had been observed, for example, when the Spanish began bringing gold back to Europe from the New World. A less settled question was whether an increase in the money stock would also "stimulate industry"—that is, cause real output to increase. Today we would say that the issue concerns whether or not money is "neutral."

On that subject, Hume says that although an increase in the price of goods is a "necessary consequence" of an increase in the stock of gold and silver, "it follows not immediately." The change in the money stock does not affect all markets at once: "At first, no alteration is perceived; by degrees the price rises, first of one commodity, then of another; till the whole at last reaches a just proportion with the new quantity of [money]." Agreeing with the modern theory that the stimulus to real output during this phase is only temporary, Hume continues: "In my opinion, it is only in this interval or intermediate situation, between the acquisition of money and the rise of prices, that the increasing quantity of gold and silver is favorable to industry." In Hume's view, there is no long-run effect on real output. In the long run, unlike the short run, money is neutral. A one-time change in the quantity of money has a lasting proportional effect on the price level but on nothing else.

Source: David Hume, "Of Money," in his Writings on Economics, ed. Eugene Rotwein (Madison: University of Wisconsin Press, 1955). Quotations from Hume are taken from Thomas M. Humphrey, "The Early History of the Phillips Curve," *Economic Review* (September–October 1985).

MONEY AND FISCAL POLICY

In Chapter 11, we examined the effects of fiscal policy on planned expenditure and the equilibrium level of real output. We saw that an increase in government purchases or a decrease in net taxes causes an increase in aggregate demand. Now, in this section, we will put our analysis of fiscal policy together with material from earlier chapters to show how changes in fiscal policy interact with developments in the monetary sector.

The Crowding-Out Effect

Figure 12.3 presents the expanded analysis of the effects of fiscal policy, taking the monetary sector into account. Initially the economy is in equilibrium at point e_1 in part (c). Real output is at its natural level, Q_1; the price level is at P_1 and stable. The monetary sector, shown in part (a), is in equilibrium at E_1 with an interest rate of R_1. This interest rate results in real planned investment at the level I_1, as shown in part (b). This level of planned investment, together with consumption, government purchases, and net exports, determines the level of total planned expenditure.

Now the government undertakes expansionary fiscal policy in the form of, say, an increase in real government purchases. (A cut in taxes or an increase in transfer payments would have essentially the same effects.) The result is a rightward shift of the aggregate demand curve. The economy begins to expand. The price level and real output both increase as the economy moves up and to the right along the short-run aggregate supply curve.

Next consider the effects on the monetary sector, shown in part (a) of Figure 12.3. Because both prices and real output are increasing, nominal domestic income must also be rising. The money demand curve therefore shifts to the right. With the money supply curve unchanged, interest rates rise. As they do so, firms move up and to the left along the planned-investment schedule shown in part (b). The level of real planned investment begins to fall, partly offsetting the initial expansionary effect of the decrease in government purchases.

Crowding-out effect

The tendency of expansionary fiscal policy to raise the interest rate and thereby cause a decrease in real planned investment.

This tendency for an increase in government purchases to cause a decrease in real private planned investment is known as the **crowding-out effect.** The crowding out of real investment spending limits the expansion of real output. In Figure 12.3 the economy reaches a new short-run equilibrium at point e_2 in part (c), where real output is at Q_2 and the price level at P_2. This point corresponds to point E_2 in part (a) of the figure. In the new short-run equilibrium, both the price level and real output are lower than they would be if the indirect effect of government purchases on interest rates and investment had not been taken into account.

In an earlier chapter we discussed the effects of fiscal policy in terms of the multiplier effect. Now we see that because of crowding out, a given increase in government purchases shifts the aggregate demand curve by less than the simple multiplier applied to government purchases would imply. Suppose, for example, that

FIGURE 12.3 THE CROWDING-OUT EFFECT

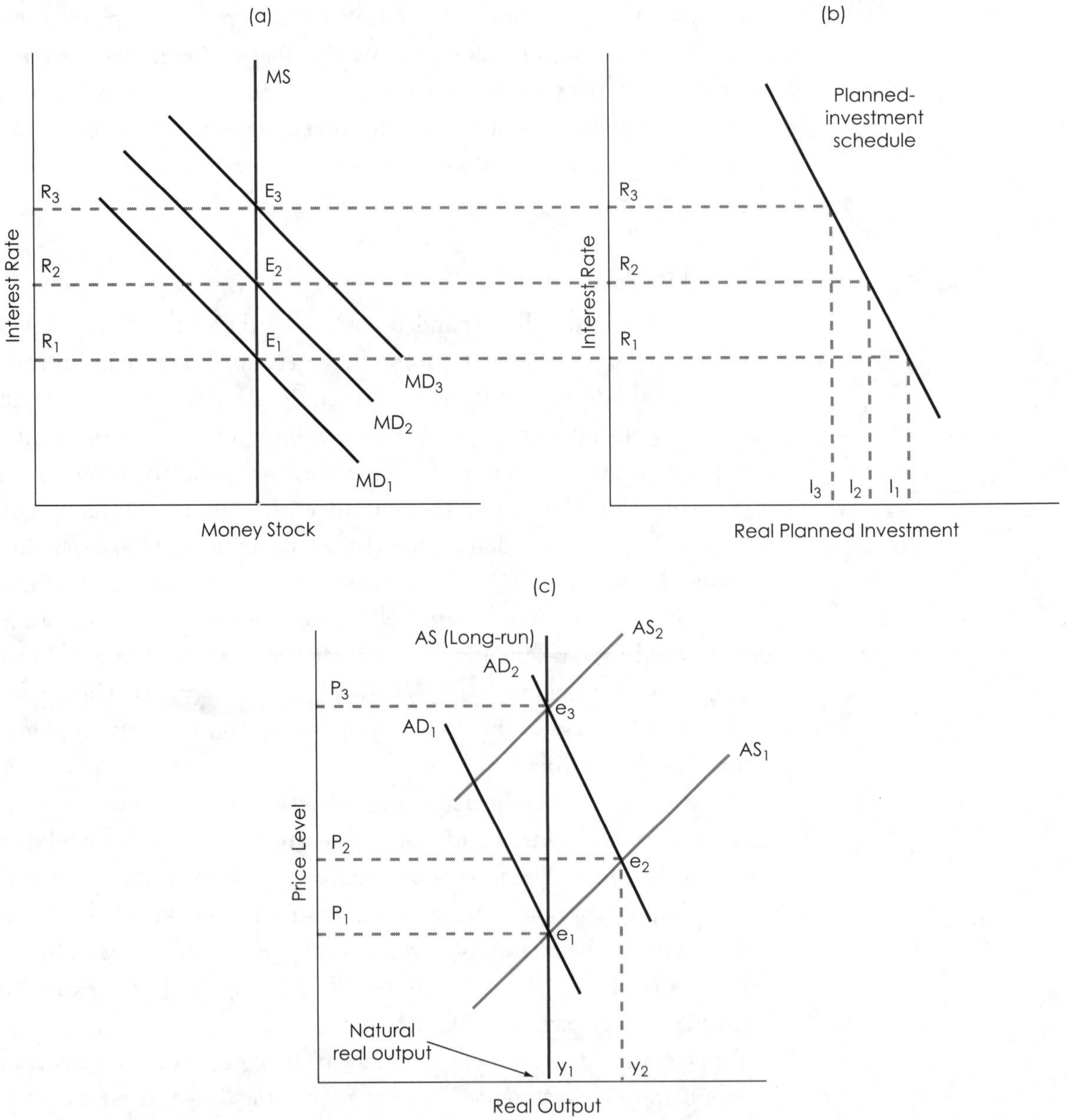

Expansionary fiscal policy shifts the aggregate demand curve to the right from AD_1 to AD_2, as shown in part (c). The resulting increase in nominal domestic income shifts the money demand curve to the right from MD_1 to MD_2, as shown in part (a). As interest rates rise, real planned investment will decrease and the economy will move to the left along the planned-investment schedule shown in part (b). The tendency of expansionary fiscal policy to reduce private planned investment is known as the *crowding-out effect*.

the multiplier is 4 and the change in government purchases is $100 billion. Multiplying these two numbers would lead one to expect a $400 billion shift. But in practice the shift is less because the expansionary effect of the increase in government purchases is partially offset by a decrease in private planned investment.[1]

Fiscal Policy in the Long Run

Fiscal policy is no more able than monetary policy to permanently raise real domestic product above its natural level. Figure 12.4 picks up where Figure 12.3 left off; it shows the long-run effects of expansionary fiscal policy.

Expansionary policy has shifted the aggregate demand curve in part (c) from AD_1 to AD_2, moving the economy to a short-run equilibrium at e_2. Compared with the situation in the initial equilibrium, e_1, real output is above the natural level and the level of final-goods prices has increased. Over time, as the rise in the prices of final goods begins to affect the expected level of input prices, the short-run aggregate supply curve shifts upward. As the economy moves up and to the left along the aggregate demand curve AD_2, prices continue to rise, but real output falls back toward the natural level. A new long-run equilibrium is reached at e_3.

Because the aggregate demand curve is inelastic, nominal domestic income increases in the course of the move from e_2 to e_3. As nominal domestic income rises, the money demand curve must shift farther to the right, from MD_2 to MD_3 in part (a) of Figure 12.4. This causes further crowding out of private planned investment. A continued increase in the interest rate pushes firms farther up and to the left along the planned-investment schedule, as shown in part (b). A new long-run equilibrium is not reached until the expansionary effects of the original fiscal policy action are completely crowded out. The aggregate demand curve remains in its new position, AD_2, but the economy's movement upward and to the left along this curve brings real domestic product all the way back to its natural level.

In one respect, the long-run effects of fiscal policy are similar to those of monetary policy: In both cases there is a higher price level in the new long-run equilibrium but no permanent change in real output. However, there is one important difference. Monetary policy is said to be "neutral" because a one-time increase in the money stock (and perhaps even a lasting change in the rate of money growth) has no long-run effects on any real variables—real output, planned investment, or real interest rates. But fiscal policy is not "neutral" in this sense. Even though expansionary fiscal policy does not change the long-run equilibrium level of real output, it does change the long-run equilibrium values of the interest rates and real planned investment.

The Importance of the Fiscal-Monetary Policy Mix

We have now seen that both fiscal and monetary policy can be used to stimulate aggregate demand and encourage economic expansion, but with opposite effects on interest rates and investment. Other things being equal, expansionary monetary policy tends to lower interest rates and encourage planned investment. On the other hand, tax cuts or increases in government purchases, while also stimulating aggregate demand, do so in a way that raises interest rates and reduces private planned investment—the crowding-out effect. All this suggests that in order to maintain the

FIGURE 12.4 CROWDING OUT IN THE LONG RUN

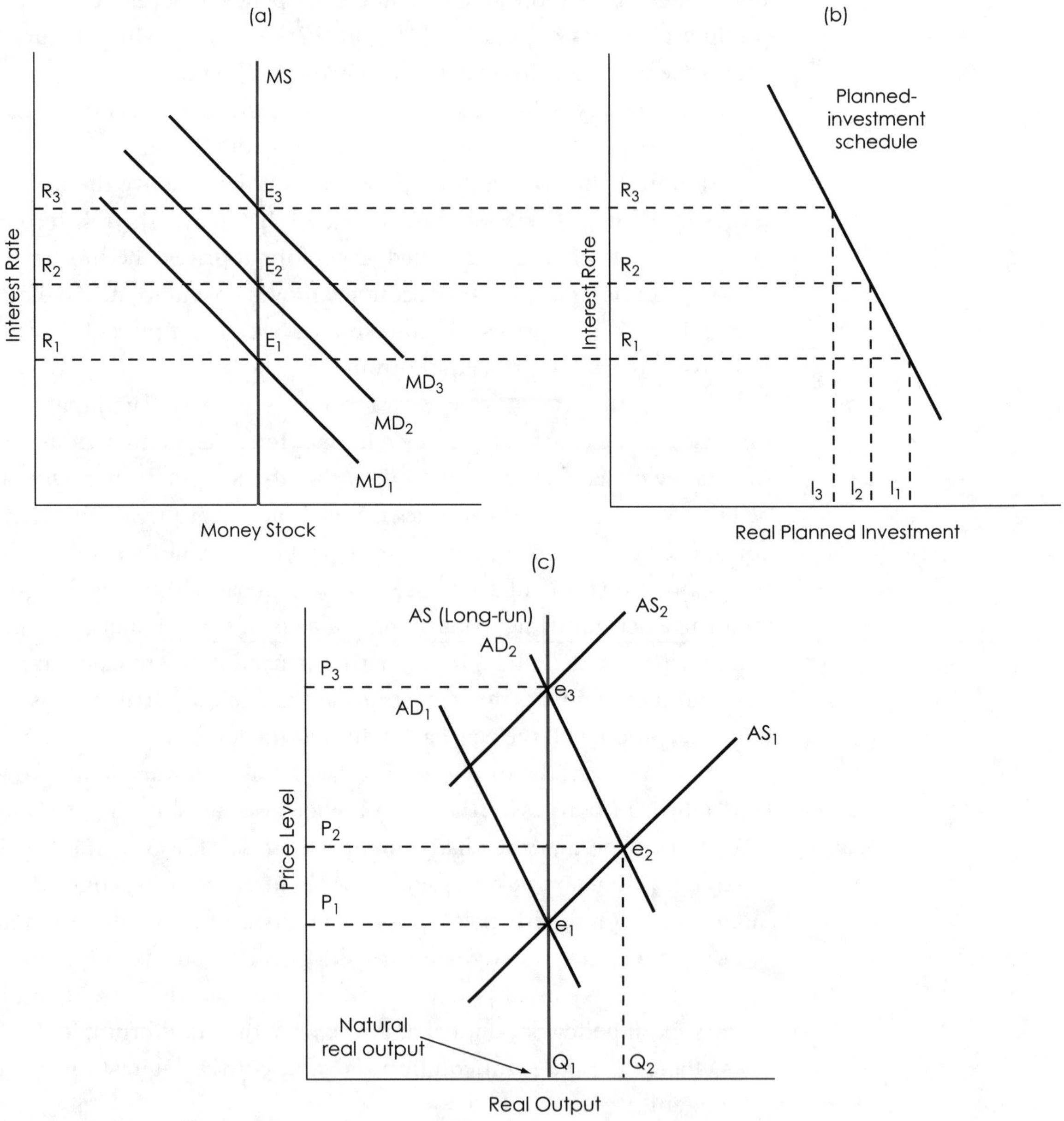

Point e_2 in part (c) of this figure is only a short-run equilibrium. As the aggregate supply curve shifts upward and the economy moves to a new long-run equilibrium at e_3, nominal domestic income continues to rise. The money demand curve shifts farther to the right from MD_2 to MD_3, as shown in part (a). As it does, the economy moves farther to the left along the planned-investment schedule, as shown in part (b). Thus, the crowding-out effect intensifies in the long run as real output returns to its natural level at Q_1.

private investment in machinery, technology, and human resources needed for healthy economic growth in the long run, policy makers must carefully balance the mix of fiscal and monetary policy.

Unfortunately, the natural dynamics of democratic politics make it difficult to maintain the needed monetary-fiscal balance. When economic stimulus is needed, both the president and Congress are quick to suggest a fiscal remedy. After all, lower taxes and higher spending on schools, roads, or social benefits are a form of medicine that is always easy to swallow. The difficulty comes when the fiscal remedy has done its work and the economy is growing again. At that point, unless some fiscal restraint is exercised, monetary policy may be called upon to do too much of the work of slowing the growth of aggregate demand to avoid unwanted inflation. If a clash between excessively expansive fiscal policy and severe tightening of monetary policy does develop, interest rates will be forced up, investment will be discouraged, and the nation's long-term economic health will be threatened.

The issue of fiscal-monetary balance assumed particular importance in 2003–2005. Although strong economic growth usually causes the budget deficit to decrease, it failed to do so during the recovery from the 2001 recession—a recovery that was stimulated, in part, by aggressive tax cuts early in the administration of President George W. Bush. *Economics in the News 12.1* summarizes some of the issues facing policy makers at that time. By 2006, continued economic growth and the action of automatic stabilizers began to moderate the deficit, but the tension between monetary and fiscal policy did not altogether disappear.

Monetarism Versus Keynesianism: A Historical Note

One of the key events in the formation of modern macroeconomics was the Great Depression, which affected the United States from 1929 to 1939. In the first four years of the Depression, real output and prices fell by more than a third and the unemployment rate rose to over a quarter of the labor force. Although there had been serious economic contractions many times during the nineteenth century, there had never been a depression of this magnitude and duration. It forced economists to reexamine their theories from the ground up.

John Maynard Keynes, introduced earlier in *Who Said It? Who Did It? 5.1,* was the most influential theorist of the Depression era. Among other things, he had clear views on the relationship between monetary and fiscal policy. Certainly Keynes recognized that monetary policy could affect interest rates, interest rates planned investment, and planned investment GDP. But he thought these effects would be weak. "There are not many people," he wrote, "who will alter their way of living because the rate of interest has fallen from 5 to 4 percent."[2]

Liquidity trap

A situation in which interest rates near zero lead to accumulation of liquid assets instead of stimulating planned investment.

If interest rates had little effect on investment, Keynes thought, investment might remain inadequate to bring the economy to full employment even if nominal interest rates fell near zero, as they can during a severe contraction. Even if the central bank greatly increased bank reserves and the money supply, people would simply accumulate liquid assets rather than using them to finance investment in plants and equipment. Keynes called this situation a **liquidity trap**. The following chapter will discuss

ECONOMICS IN THE NEWS 12.1
DEALING WITH THE DEFICIT

Testifying before Congress in February 2004, Federal Reserve Chairman Alan Greenspan began by noting that "the most recent indicators suggest that the economy is off to a strong start in 2004, and prospects for sustaining the expansion in the period ahead are good." The economy was growing, inflation was low, and the financial health of businesses had improved. However, he went on to warn, "This favorable short-term outlook for the U.S. economy... is playing out against a backdrop of growing concern about the prospects for the federal budget." More specifically, the federal deficit, which had risen to $375 billion in fiscal year 2003 was projected to rise to a record level of over half a trillion dollars in fiscal year 2004.

Where did this enormous deficit come from? Greenspan noted three sources. First, the Iraq war added tens of billions of dollars to military spending. Second, there were increased expenditures on domestic programs, ranging from agricultural subsidies to education. Greenspan attributed these increases in discretionary spending partly to a weakening of fiscal discipline in Congress as a result of the budget surplus years of the 1990s.

Spending was not the whole story, however. The Bush Administration's tax cuts, which for a time had been helpful in stimulating the recovery from the 2001 recession, were now contributing to the growing budget deficit. Greenspan noted that the ratio of federal debt to GDP—a key indicator of long-term fiscal health—had already begun to edge up after falling during the 1990s. This meant a weakening of the starting point from which lawmakers would have to address future fiscal challenges.

The greatest of these challenges, in Greenspan's view, was the growth in Social Security and Medicare costs as the country prepares for the retirement of the baby-boom generation. He warned "under a range of reasonably plausible assumptions about spending and taxes, we could be in a situation in the decades ahead in which rapid increases in the unified budget deficit set in motion a dynamic in which large deficits result in ever-growing interest payments that augment deficits in future years. The resulting rise in the federal debt could drain funds away from private capital formation and thus over time slow the growth of living standards." In short, he warned of a looming crowding-out effect on an unprecedented scale.

What could be done? As Greenspan pointed out, the alternatives are not terribly attractive. Social Security and Medicare spending, under current law, are expected to rise from 7 percent of GDP in 2004 to 12 percent in 2030. Covering these outlays with increased taxes would not simply mean reversing the Bush tax cuts, but going beyond this to raise the tax burden to a historic high. Greenspan proposed instead slowing the growth of benefits by a combination of increased retirement age and revision of the formula under which retirees are protected against the effects of inflation. That suggestion, however, set off a storm of protest from all corners of the Washington political establishment, where Social Security cuts are regarded as the "third rail" of politics. But doing nothing and letting the deficit grow would force such a severe tightening of monetary policy that interest rates would rise sharply, threatening investment.

"The dimension of the challenge is enormous," Greenspan said in conclusion. "The one certainty is that the resolution of this situation will require difficult choices and that the future performance of the economy will depend on those choices."

Source: Testimony of Chairman Alan Greenspan, Economic outlook and current fiscal issues, before the Committee on the Budget, U.S. House of Representatives, February 25, 2004. Downloaded from www.federalreserve.gov.

the possible relevance of the liquidity trap to low-inflation economies like Japan in the present day.

If a liquidity trap made monetary policy powerless during a severe contraction, what could policy makers do to return the economy to full employment? For Keynes and his followers, the answer was clear: An increase in government purchases should be used to fill the gap between the actual and full-employment aggregate demand. Keynes did not think that monetary policy would always be ineffective. After the economy returned to full employment and interest rates back to or above normal levels, and in times when an overheated economy brought on inflation, monetary policy would play its traditional role. But because of the depression context in which Keynes wrote, the special case of "impotent monetary policy—potent fiscal policy" became the best remembered of his ideas.

After World War II many Keynesian economists forecast a new depression and economic stagnation. They thought that private investment would dry up with the end of wartime government spending. They were wrong: The postwar recovery of the United States and Western Europe was rapid. Central banks in most of the major economies pursued easy monetary policies during those years, and inflation was more widespread than depression. The countries that were able to control inflation did so only by using standard policies of monetary restraint. Economists began to take renewed interest in the role of money in the economy.

Monetarism

A school of economics that emphasizes the importance of changes in the money stock as determinants of changes in real output and the price level.

The new emphasis on money was strongest among a group of economists led by Milton Friedman *(Who Said It? Who Did It? 12.2)*. Friedman's research led him to think that movements in the money supply had a much greater effect on economic events, even under depression conditions, than the early Keynesians had been willing to admit. Because of the emphasis Friedman and his followers placed on monetary policy, their school of thought came to be known as **monetarism**.

WHO SAID IT? WHO DID IT? 12.2
MILTON FRIEDMAN AND MONETARISM

In October 1976, Milton Friedman received the Nobel Memorial Prize in economics, becoming the sixth American to win or share that honor. Few people were surprised. Most people wondered why he had had to wait so long. Perhaps it was because Friedman has built his career outside the economics establishment, challenging almost every major doctrine of that profession.

Friedman was born in New York in 1912, the son of immigrant garment workers. He attended Rutgers University, where he came under the influence of Arthur Burns, then a young assistant professor and later chairman of the Federal Reserve Board. From Burns, Friedman learned the importance of empirical work in economics. Statistical testing of all theory and policy prescriptions became a key feature of Friedman's later work. From Rutgers, Friedman went to the University of Chicago for an M.A. and then east again to Columbia University, where he received his Ph.D. in 1946. He returned to Chicago to teach. There he and his colleagues of the "Chicago school" of economics posed a major challenge to the economists of the "eastern establishment."

If one could single out a recurrent theme in Friedman's work it would be his belief that the market economy works—and that it works best when left alone. This can be seen in his best-known work, *A Monetary History of the United States*. Written with Anna Schwartz, this book attacks two major tenets of Keynesian economics: (1) that the market economy is unstable without the guiding hand of government, and (2) that monetary policy was tried and found useless as a cure for the Great Depression. Friedman and Schwartz found both beliefs to be far from the truth. "The Great Depression," Friedman later wrote, "far from being a sign of the inherent instability of the private enterprise system, is a testament to how much harm can be done by mistakes on the part of a few men when they wield vast power over the monetary system of the country."

Friedman strongly favored a hands-off policy by government in almost every area. In his view, the problem was not that government is evil by nature, but that so many policies end up having the opposite of their intended effects: "The social reformers who seek through politics to do nothing but serve the public interest invariably end up serving some private interest that was not part of their intention to serve. They are led by an invisible hand to serve a private interest." Transport regulation, public education, agricultural subsidies, and housing programs are among the many policy areas in which Friedman believed that the government has done more harm than good and for which a free competitive market would do better.

Friedman's research led to a reinterpretation of the Great Depression. In *A Monetary History of the United States*, Friedman and Anna J. Schwartz explained why what began as a fairly ordinary business contraction in the summer of 1929 turned into a four-year downward spiral from which complete recovery took an entire decade.[3] Their analysis focused on the collapse of the banking system and a precipitous decline in the money stock early in the Depression. In the monetarist view, it was not the inherent impotence of monetary policy that caused the Great Depression, but rather the terrible impact on the economy of serious monetary policy errors. If the Fed had used its available policy instruments—especially open market purchases of securities—more aggressively, the downturn that began in 1929 might never have been more than a brief cyclical contraction.

The debate between monetarists and Keynesians over monetary versus fiscal policy raged throughout the 1960s and 1970s. Some monetarists went so far as to stand Keynes on his head, insisting that the crowding-out effect would be so strong and complete that fiscal policy would be impotent to affect the economy, so that "only money matters." On the other side, some Keynesians advocated using fiscal policy to fine-tune the economy with a degree of short-term precision that now seems implausible. In recent years, the debate has died out or taken other directions than the oversimplified "monetary versus fiscal policy" issue. Mainstream economic policymakers in all countries today acknowledge the importance of prudent management of both monetary and fiscal policy if the goals of long-term economic growth and stability are to be achieved.

SUMMARY

1. **How do changes in the money stock affect real output, the price level, and unemployment?** An increase in the money stock initially lowers interest rates. The resulting increase in real planned investment shifts the aggregate demand curve to the right. As the economy moves up and to the right along the aggregate supply curve, in the short run real output increases, the price level increases, and the unemployment rate falls. A decrease in the money stock has the opposite effects.

2. **What is meant by the neutrality of money?** An increase in the money stock can cause real output to rise above its natural level only in the short run. As input prices rise, the economy returns to the natural level of real output at a higher price level than initially. In the new equilibrium the prices of both final goods and inputs will have changed in proportion to the increase in the money stock, but the values of all real variables—interest rates, planned investment, real output, and employment—will be unaffected. This proposition is known as the *neutrality of money.*

3. **How does fiscal policy affect interest rates and planned investment?** Expansionary fiscal policy shifts the aggregate demand curve to the right. Real output and the price level rise in the short run, as does nominal domestic income. The increase in

nominal domestic income shifts the money demand curve to the right, causing both real and nominal interest rates to increase. This rise in interest rates *crowds out* some real planned investment. As the economy returns to a long-run equilibrium at the natural level of real output, a further rise in the price level causes nominal domestic income to rise still higher, putting additional upward pressure on interest rates. Thus, there is a further depressing effect on real investment, and the crowding-out effect intensifies in the long run.

4. **How did Keynesian and monetarist economists view the relationship of monetary to fiscal policy?** Keynes and his early followers thought that the transmission mechanism from money to GDP via interest rates and investment was weak, especially under depression conditions. They thought that the economy would be unable to recover from a depression on its own and that only expansionary fiscal policy could do the job. After World War II, *monetarists,* led by Milton Friedman, argued that monetary policy is important even under depression conditions. They saw the Fed's policy mistakes following the 1929 crash as a major factor in the length and severity of the Depression. The debate over the relative importance of monetary and fiscal policy continued throughout the 1960s and 1970s. Today most economists see proper management of both monetary and fiscal policy as essential to economic stability and prosperity.

KEY TERMS

Transmission mechanism	Neutrality of money
Planned-investment schedule	Crowding-out effect
	Liquidity trap
	Monetarism

PROBLEMS AND TOPICS FOR DISCUSSION

1. **Update on current policy.** Using government data sources such as the *Economic Report of the President* (http://www.gpoaccess.gov/eop) or cur-rent news sources, determine what has happened to inflation, the unemployment rate, the rate of growth of real GDP, and the federal budget deficit since this chapter was written in early 2007.

2. **Long-run effects of contractionary monetary policy.** Use a set of diagrams similar to Figures 12.1 and 12.2 to trace the long-run effects of a one-time contraction of the money stock beginning from equilibrium at the natural level of real output.

3. **Effects of a tax increase.** Use a set of diagrams similar to Figure 12.4 to trace the effects of a contractionary fiscal policy such as a tax increase. What happens to real output, unemployment, the price level, interest rates, and real planned investment in the short run and in the long run?

4. **Crowding out and the money supply curve.** Use a set of diagrams similar to Figure 12.3 to investigate how the crowding-out effect is influenced by the shape of the money supply curve. First use a positively sloped curve and then a horizontal curve. Discuss the policy implications of your results.

5. **The twin deficits.** Review the discussion of the "twin deficits" in Chapter 5. What is the relevance of the fiscal-monetary policy mix to the "twin deficit" phenomenon? What kind of mix is most likely to produce "twin deficits"?

CASE FOR DISCUSSION

Italy's Budget Woes

For decades following World War II, Italy had a secure place in the European economy as a supplier of well-designed goods produced at reasonable prices by its relatively low-wage labor force. Today, that economic model seems to be broken. Italy faces competition from other countries capable of producing high-quality, low-priced goods. These include not only Asian tigers like China but also the dynamic new Central and Eastern European members of the EU. Faced with this competition, the Italian economy has been performing poorly. As the chart shows, its output gap—the percentage by which real GDP exceeds or falls short of its natural level—has been slipping steadily since 2001 and is expected to remain negative at least through 2008.

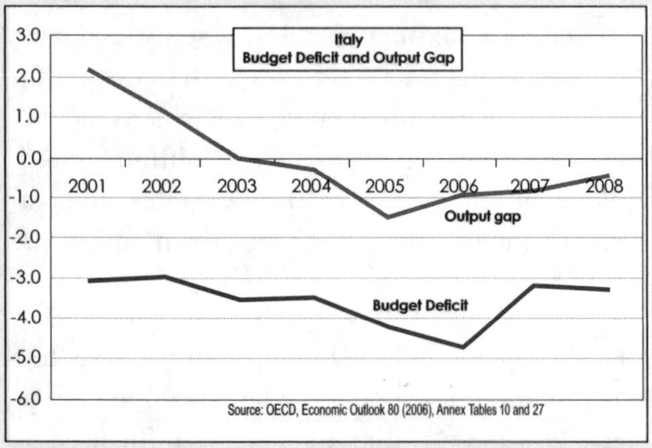

Standard economic models suggest two possible ways to get the Italian economy moving again: Expansionary fiscal policy, in the form of lower taxes or higher government spending, or monetary policy, in the form of faster money growth and lower interest rates. In principle, the right fiscal-monetary policy mix should provide enough of a stimulus to aggregate demand to eliminate the persistent output gap.

Unfortunately, Italy just can't seem to get the policy mix right. On the fiscal policy side, it has run head first into budget rules set by the European Union. Those rules state that a country must not run a budget deficit of more than 3 percent of GDP, subject to potentially large fines. As the chart shows, Italy has failed to meet that limit year after year. The EU also has a rule for total government debt, which is not supposed to exceed 60% of GDP. Italy performs even worse in that category. Its total debt, as of 2006, was 121% percent of GDP, the highest of any country in the EU.

The limits for budget deficits and the debt would be less of a problem for Italy if it could simply switch its policy mix toward tighter fiscal policy combined with an easing of monetary conditions. Doing so, however, lies beyond the power of the Italian government. Since Italy gave up its old currency, the lira, in favor of the euro, there is no way to ease Italian monetary conditions without also easing them for the twelve other countries of the euro area. So far, the European Central Bank has refused to do so.

The reason is inflation. Italy's own inflation is not that bad. In 2006, Italian consumer prices rose by 2.2 percent, exactly the average for the euro area, and the forecast for 2007 was expected to tall to 1.9 percent. Elsewhere in the euro zone, however, things are different. Several other EU countries, including Greece, Spain, and Portugal, have inflation rates that are much farther above the 2 percent target set by the European Central Bank. Any shift toward more expansionary monetary policy for the benefit of Italy would quickly spill over into those countries and push them, and the euro area average, even higher above the 2-percent inflation target.

Is there a way out? Not an easy one. In 2005, the euro area's high-deficit countries, which include Germany and France as well as Italy, reached an uneasy compromise with EU policy makers that will let them continue to violate the deficit ceiling without invoking the feared penalties. But there will be no monetary bale-out, and prospects for Italian growth in 2007 and 2008 don't look much brighter than in preceding years. In the long run, structural reforms of labor markets, tax laws, and an outdated service sector could make the Italian economy flexible enough to start growing again while meeting both deficit and inflation targets. But don't expect that to happen any time soon. After the national elections of 2006, Italy's government held a razor-thin majority in parliament and was hardly in a position to force the needed structural reforms. For the foreseeable future, the tension between fiscal policy, set at the level of country governments, and monetary policy, set for the euro zone as a whole, will surely continue.

QUESTIONS

1. In the days when Italy had its own currency, the lira, how would a switch toward smaller deficits and faster growth of the money stock have affected interest rates? Investment? Aggregate demand? GDP?
2. Some economists think a uniform deficit limit of 3 percent of GDP for all euro zone countries is unrealistic. They say the limit should be higher for countries that are in recession. Explain how an alternative "full employment deficit limit" might be defined and implemented.
3. In the United States, the Fed sets monetary policy for the whole country, but each state has a substantial role in determining taxes and government spending. In what ways do you think the situation of an individual state that grows slower than the U.S. national average is similar to that of Italy within the EU? In what ways does it differ? Discuss.

END NOTES

1. In an earlier chapter we assumed, as a working approximation, that the change in government purchases times the expenditure multiplier would equal the horizontal shift in the aggregate demand curve. Now we can see why this was only an approximation: There would be some crowding out even if the economy moved horizontally to the right on the aggregate supply and demand diagram with the price level unchanged. Even with no change in the price level, there would be some increase in nominal domestic income as a result of the increase in real domestic product. That alone would be enough to shift the money demand curve to the right, although not as far as the shift to MD2 shown in Figure 12.3. Thus, the interest rate would rise somewhat, and there would be some crowding out of private investment. This fixed-price portion of the crowding-out effect keeps the aggregate demand curve from shifting to the right by the full amount of the change in government purchases times the multiplier. However, the amount of the shift can still be thought of as equal to the change in autonomous expenditure times the expenditure multiplier, provided that the change in autonomous expenditure is interpreted as the increase in government purchases minus the change in planned investment resulting from the fixed-price component of crowding out.
2. John Maynard Keynes, *The General Theory of Employment, Interest, and Money* (New York: Harcourt, Brace, and World, 1936), 94.
3. Milton Friedman and Anna Jacobson Schwartz, *A Monetary History of the United States*, 1867–1960 (Princeton, NJ: Princeton University Press, 1963).

CHAPTER 13

Policies for Price Stability

After reading this chapter, you will understand:

1. How inflation or deflation can arise from changes in aggregate demand
2. How inflation or deflation can arise from shifts in the short-run aggregate supply curve
3. What types of policy can be used to achieve price stability

Before reading this chapter, make sure you know the meaning of:

1. Indexation
2. Price level
3. Base year
4. Liquidity trap

If the 1930s were the decade of the Great Depression, the 1970s perhaps should be called the "Great Inflation." Like the Great Depression, the Great Inflation brought lasting changes to economic thought and policy. What went on in that turbulent decade?

The seeds of the Great Inflation were sown in the 1960s. Under President Lyndon Johnson, federal outlays for the Vietnam War rose steadily, but because the war was unpopular at home, Johnson was reluctant to raise taxes. Many economists see the resulting fiscal stimulus as a key factor in the inflation that followed in 1968. The inflation rate rose to 4.2 percent that year and to 5.4 percent the next.[1] In comparison with what was to come, 5.4 percent inflation was moderate—but it was more than three times the 1.7 percent average rate for the decade from 1958 to 1967.

In 1970 and early 1971, the inflation rate continued to creep upward. Then, in August 1971, President Richard Nixon announced a dramatic new economic program. The centerpiece was a 90-day freeze on all prices and wages, followed by further wage and price restraints. This attempt to control prices worked for a time. The inflation rate fell in late 1971 and during 1972. Prices and wages were subject to some degree of control under three presidents for the rest of the decade.

However, in 1973, when the power of wage and price controls to restrain inflation was already waning, the world received a major inflationary shock. In the aftermath of a war with Israel, the Arab members of the Organization of Petroleum Exporting Countries (OPEC) doubled the price of oil—a major U.S. import and a key component of the consumer price index. Inflation accelerated again, with the added complication of retail price controls on gasoline, which led to long waiting lines at gas stations.

In 1974, the inflation rate reached 11 percent and the United States discovered an unpleasant new fact. In the past, inflation had been thought to have a silver lining in the form of low unemployment, but the nation now learned that it could suffer from both high unemployment and high inflation at the same time. In the 1974 to 1975 recession, the unemployment rate rose to nearly 9 percent while the inflation rate fell only slightly. A new concept was born: the "misery index," the sum of the rates of inflation and unemployment. The misery index hit a value of 18 during the 1974 to 1975 recession, and throughout the subsequent recovery it never fell below 13. This was miserable indeed compared with the indexes of 6 or lower to which people had grown accustomed in the 1960s.

Despite the fiscal stimulus of the Vietnam War and the inflationary shock of the oil crisis, the Fed could have curbed inflation by restraining the growth of the money stock. However, just as it had failed to prevent a drop in the money stock from 1929 to 1933, thereby worsening the Great Depression, during the 1970s the Fed failed to prevent rapid growth of the money stock, thus adding fuel to the Great Inflation.

Finally, in October 1979, the Fed put on the brakes and the economy subsequently went through the windshield. In 1980, as the economy entered a brief recession, both inflation and unemployment rose. The misery index soared to an all-time high of 20. On top of this, OPEC chose just that moment to more than double the world oil price for the second time. After a temporary recovery from the 1980 recession, in 1981 the economy entered its most severe downturn since the Great Depression of the 1930s.

Inflation receded during the 1980s, and the misery index returned to single digits. By the mid-1990s, inflation was been brought under control and has remained close to 2 percent since.

In Chapter 12, we saw how Keynesian and monetarist interpretations of the Great Depression had a profound impact on the development of macroeconomic theory. In a similar way, the Great Inflation of the 1970s refocused macroeconomic theory on the problem of inflation. This chapter will look at key elements of macroeconomic theory and policy related to problems of price stability, including not only the problem of inflation but more recent concerns about deflation as well.

INFLATION AND DEFLATION IN THE AGGREGATE SUPPLY AND DEMAND MODEL

Throughout this text we have refined our understanding of sources of shifts in the aggregate demand and supply curves. The sources of such shifts can be summarized as follows:

1. Shifts in the aggregate demand curve may originate in real consumption, planned investment, government purchases, or net exports. Expansionary monetary or fiscal policy shifts the aggregate demand curve to the right; contractionary monetary or fiscal policy shifts it to the left.
2. The long-run aggregate supply curve is a vertical line drawn at the level of natural real output. A change in the level of natural real output shifts the curve.
3. The positively sloped short-run aggregate supply curve is drawn on the assumption that the expected level of input prices adjusts only gradually to changes in aggregate demand and in final goods prices. The height of the intersection of a short-run aggregate supply curve with the long-run aggregate supply curve indicates the expected level of input prices on which that short-run curve is based. An increase in the expected level of input prices shifts the short-run aggregate supply curve upward; a decrease in the expected level of input prices shifts it downward.

We now turn to some of the relationships among inflation, real output, and unemployment that can be derived by applying these principles to specified changes in economic conditions.

Demand-Side Inflation

Demand-side inflation

Inflation caused by an upward shift of the aggregate demand curve while the aggregate supply curve remains fixed or shifts upward at no more than an equal rate.

We begin with the case of **demand-side inflation**, by which we mean inflation caused by an upward shift in the aggregate demand curve while the short-run aggregate supply curve remains fixed or shifts upward at no more than an equal rate. We have already encountered the simplest form of demand-side inflation, which occurs when there is a one-time rightward shift in the aggregate demand curve beginning from an initial state of equilibrium. The response is a movement up and to the right along the short-run aggregate supply curve to a new short-run equilibrium. In the process, real output and the price level of final goods increase while the unemployment rate decreases. After a lag, expectations regarding input prices will adjust and the short-run aggregate supply curve will begin to shift upward. If the aggregate demand curve remains in its new position, the economy will move up and to the left along it to a new long-run equilibrium in which real output returns to its natural level.

However, a one-time expansionary policy action is not the only possibility. Instead, continuing expansionary fiscal or monetary policy may allow aggregate demand to keep growing. In that case, as the short-run aggregate supply curve is driven upward by firms' expectations of ever-higher input prices, the aggregate demand curve keeps pace with it. Real output does not fall back toward its natural level; rather, it is kept above that level by ongoing demand-side inflation. This possibility is illustrated in Figure 13.1, where the economy follows a path from E_1 to E_2 to E_3 and beyond.

The scenario shown in Figure 13.1 has major implications for economic policy. In the short run, starting from a state of long-run equilibrium, an expansionary fiscal or monetary policy is effective in stimulating real economic growth and lower unemployment. The initial cost of such a policy is a small amount of inflation. However, the initial gains in real output can be sustained only at the cost of ongoing demand-side inflation.

Once the initial benefits of the expansion have been realized, policy makers will face a dilemma. One choice is to stop the stimulus. If they do that, inflation will cease but output will fall back to its natural level, and unemployment will rise to its natural rate. The other alternative is to continue the expansionary fiscal or monetary policy. In that case, the positive output gap can be maintained for an extended period. Choosing that path, however, will mean year after year of inflation. Although it is not directly apparent from Figure 13.1, a rate of inflation that is steady in percentage terms from year to year may not be enough to hold unemployment below its natural rate. Under certain plausible assumptions regarding the way expectations of inflation are formed, inflation must accelerate to a higher percentage rate year after year to sustain a positive output gap.

Supply-side inflation

Inflation that is caused by an upward shift in the aggregate supply curve while the aggregate demand curve remains fixed or shifts upward more slowly.

Supply shock

An event, such as an increase in the price of imported oil, a crop failure, or a natural disaster, that raises input prices for all or most firms and pushes up workers' costs of living.

Supply-Side Inflation and Supply Shocks

Demand-side inflation occurs when the aggregate demand curve shifts upward while the aggregate supply curve remains fixed or shifts upward at no more than an equal rate. However, inflation can also occur as a result of an upward shift in the aggregate supply curve while the aggregate demand curve stays in place or shifts upward more slowly. We call this **supply-side inflation.** The upward shifts in the aggregate supply curve are caused by increase in expected input prices, which push up costs of production.

Supply shocks are one source of supply-side inflation. A supply shock is an event independent of changes in aggregate demand that raises the average level of input prices that firms expect. The sudden increases in the cost of imported oil that hit the U.S. economy in 1974, 1979–1980, and 2004–2005 are examples of such events. A

FIGURE 13.1 DEMAND-SIDE INFLATION

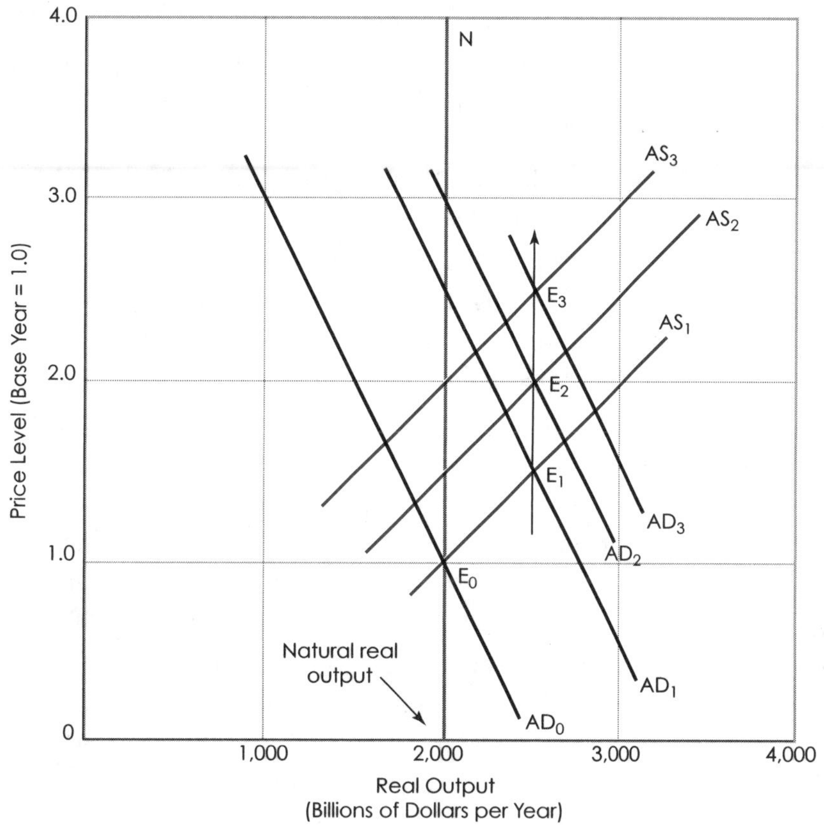

Demand-side inflation begins when a rightward shift in the aggregate demand curve pulls the economy up and to the right along the short-run aggregate supply curve, from E_0 to E_1 in this figure. Subsequently, the short-run aggregate supply curve will begin to shift upward as increases in final-goods prices filter through to cause expected increases in wages and other input prices. If expansionary policy continues to shift the aggregate demand curve upward, as shown here, real output can be kept above its natural level, which corresponds to the long-run aggregate supply curve N, for a sustained period. However, the cost of maintaining this high level of real output is inflation.

rise in the price of oil increases expected input prices through several channels. First, petroleum products themselves are inputs to many production processes in such forms as heating fuel, motor fuel for transportation, and chemical feedstocks. Second, firms anticipate that prices of substitute energy sources, such as natural gas and electric power, will rise when oil prices rise. Finally, firms anticipate that increased prices for oil and other energy sources will affect the cost of living and that nominal wages will sooner or later have to be adjusted to reflect those changes.

Changes in oil prices are particularly dramatic examples of supply shocks, but lesser supply shocks occur frequently. The effects of the weather on farming, construction, and transportation may increase firms' anticipated costs of doing business. Natural disasters, such as earthquakes or hurricanes, raise costs of doing business in the affected areas and may affect input prices in wider areas via changes in demand for such key inputs as construction materials. Finally, changes in the foreign-exchange value of the dollar can affect the prices of inputs that are traded on world markets. A fall in the value of the dollar relative to foreign currencies makes imported inputs (say, imported cotton used by a U.S. textile mill) more expensive; it may also increase demand for U.S. exports of intermediate goods such as chemicals that are traded on the world market, thereby driving up their prices.

Supply shocks can work both ways, however. The increases in world oil prices in the 1970s raised input prices expected by U.S. firms, but the subsequent decreases in oil prices during the early 1980s reduced expected input prices. Similarly, unusually good weather leading to bumper crops or an increase in the foreign-exchange value of the dollar would tend to cause a decrease in expected input prices. During the mid- to late-1990s, the U.S. experienced high economic growth accompanied by low inflation rates. Many economists have explained the decline of inflation in the 1990s in terms of beneficial supply shocks. Americans enjoyed historically low oil prices and technological progress that substantially reduced production costs.

Figure 13.2 illustrates the short-run effects of a supply shock. In the figure the economy begins in long-run equilibrium at E_0. The price level for final goods and the expected level of input prices are equal at 1.0, and real output is at its natural level of $2,000 billion. At this point, something—say a devastating hurricane—causes an increase in the average expected level of input prices. As firms adjust their expectations, the short-run aggregate supply curve shifts upward from AS_0 to AS_1, as shown in Figure 13.2. With the higher expected level of input prices but no matching increase in aggregate demand, firms must revise their plans. They find that it is no longer profitable to produce as much as before. As they cut back their output, each industry moves up and to the left along its industry demand curve. As this happens, the economy as a whole moves upward and to the left along aggregate demand curve AD_0 to E_1.

What happens next depends on what happens to aggregate demand. The supply shock has caused real damage to the economy. Even if people work just as many hours as before, the total quantity of goods and services available for consumption, investment, government purchases, and net exports will be less. If no changes are made in monetary or fiscal policy, so that the aggregate demand curve remains in the position AD_1, the effect of the supply shock will be felt partly in the form of a rise in prices and partly in the form of a reduction in real output, as at point E_1. Instead, policy makers may try to soften the effect on real GDP by using fiscal or monetary policy to shift the aggregate demand curve to the right, to a position like AD_2. In that case, the economy will move toward a point like E_2, where real output is higher but the price level is also higher than at E_1.

Accommodating policy

Expansionary monetary or fiscal policy used to increase aggregate demand in order to moderate the effects of a supply shock on real output.

Expansionary monetary or fiscal policy used to moderate the impact of a supply shock on real output is known as **accommodating policy**. The short-run impact of the supply shock on real output is likely to be less if accommodating policy is used, but the inflationary impact will be greater. Moreover, unless the initial cause of the

FIGURE 13.2 EFFECTS OF A SUPPLY SHOCK

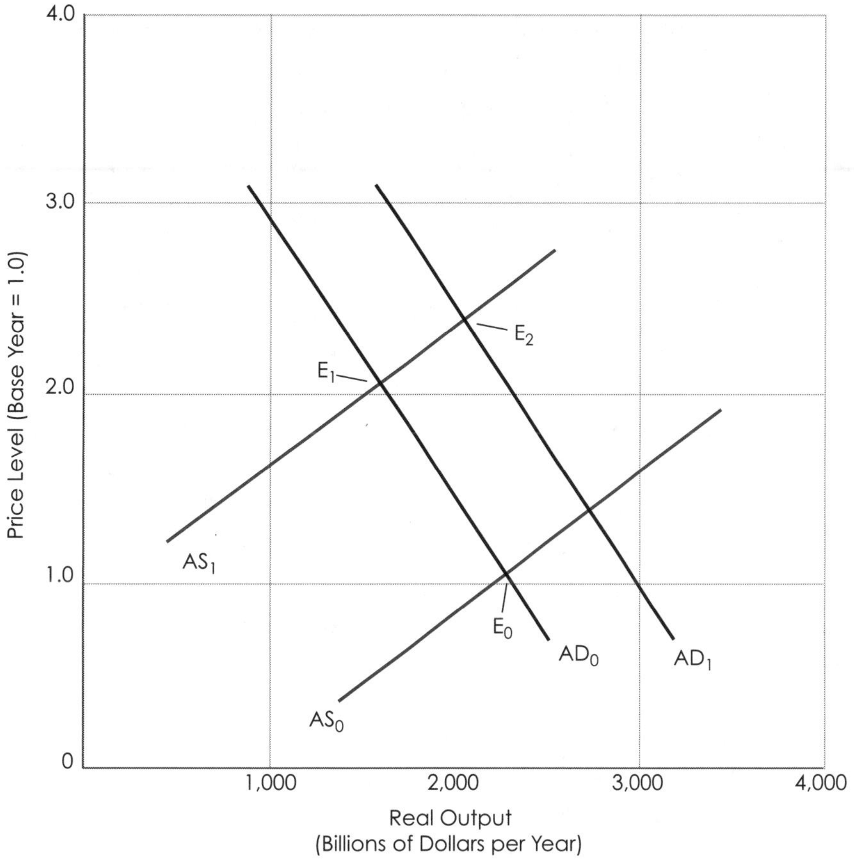

A supply shock is said to occur when an event external to the workings of the domestic economy—say, bad weather or an increase in the price of imports—raises the expected level of input prices. In this figure, a supply shock shifts the short-run aggregate supply curve upward from AS_0 to AS_1 while the aggregate demand curve initially stays at AD_0. The result is a supply-side inflation. The price level rises, real output falls, and the unemployment rate rises.. If accommodating policy is used to shift the aggregate demand curve to AD_1. The economy will move to E_2 . The impact on real output will be smaller, but the inflationary consequences of the supply shock will be greater.

supply shock is quickly reversed, there is a danger that accommodating policy will touch off a prolonged period of demand-side inflation, similar to that shown in Figure 13.1.

Inflationary Expectations and Inflationary Recession

Supply shocks are not the only source of supply-side inflation. Supply-side inflation can also be caused by past experiences of demand-side inflation. To get this result, we must modify our assumptions regarding how firms form their expectations about the level of input prices. Up to this point, we have supposed that firms form their expectations in a backward-looking way. That is they expect input prices in the current year to be at a level equal to that of final goods prices in the previous year. However, when firms have seen inflation in the past, they will expect more inflation in the future and will make their plans accordingly. Under one simple version of this behavior, they might expect wages and other input prices in the coming year to increase by the same percentage as they did the year before.

Figure 13.3 shows what happens when inflationary expectations become established in the economy. We begin from a situation of ongoing demand-side inflation similar to that shown in Figure 13.1. An expansionary fiscal or monetary policy has held output above its natural level for some time. The economy is moving upward along the arrow through E_1 and E_2. After several years of inflation, firms and workers expect more inflation in the future and have adjusted their plans to cope with it as best they can. Their plans are reflected in a series of upward-shifting short-run aggregate supply curves that keep pace with the upward-shifting aggregate demand curve.

What happens now if the government decides to stop inflation by halting the growth of aggregate demand? (We are talking not about reducing the level of aggregate demand but only about stopping its growth.) In terms of Figure 13.3, the effect will be to stop the upward shift of the aggregate demand curve, leaving it in the position AD_2.

FIGURE 13.3 INFLATIONARY RECESSION

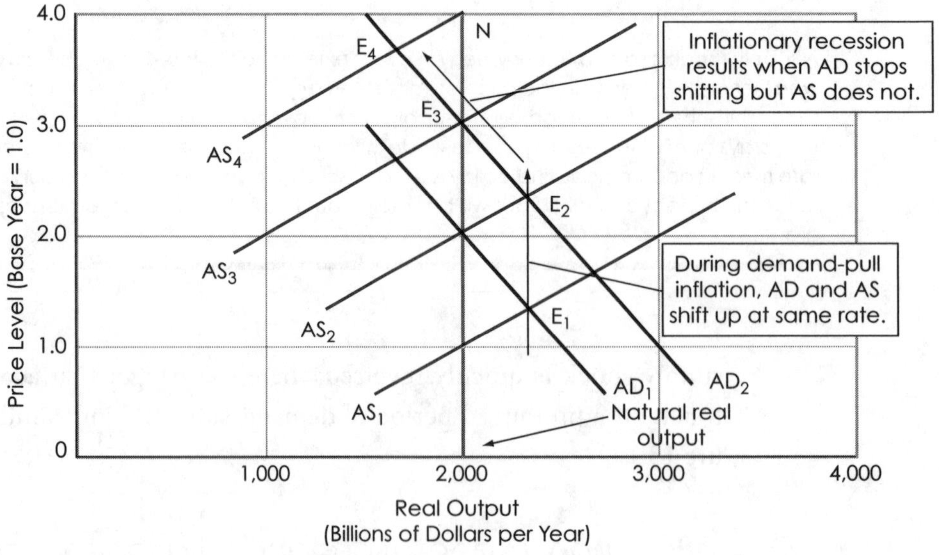

An inflationary recession occurs when aggregate demand slows or stops growing following a period of sustained inflation. In this figure, the aggregate demand curve stops shifting after the economy reaches E_2. Firms expect the level of input prices to continue to rise; thus, the short-run aggregate supply curve moves on up to AS_3 in the next year and to AS_4 in the year after that. As it does, the economy enters a recession during which the price level continues to rise. For a time the inflation rate may actually increase as real output falls.

Halting the growth of aggregate demand will not stop inflation in its tracks. Firms and workers have grown used to inflation and expect it to continue. Workers expect their costs of living to rise further and will have made contracts with their employers giving them offsetting wage increases each year. Firms expect their input prices to rise further and will have become used to passing the increases along to their customers. As long as firms expect their input prices to continue rising and set their prices and output plans on that basis, the short-run aggregate supply curve will continue to shift upward.

With the aggregate supply curve moving upward while the aggregate demand curve stays put, real output starts to fall and unemployment begins to rise. Meanwhile, the price level keeps going up. The economy will soon reach E_3 in Figure 13.3. There real output and unemployment have returned to their natural levels. This is not the end of the story, however. Because firms experienced continued inflation as the economy moved from E_2 to E_3, they are not likely to expect inflation to stop now. As long as firms anticipate a further increase in the prices of final goods, they will continue to expect rising input prices. As a result, the aggregate supply curve will keep drifting upward, as shown by AS_4 in Figure 13.3. As the economy moves along the aggregate demand curve toward E_4, the economy experiences an **inflationary recession**—an episode in which inflation, rising unemployment, and a negative output gap all occur at the same time.[2]

Inflationary recession

An episode in which real output falls toward or below its natural level and unemployment rises toward or above its natural rate while rapid inflation continues.

What can be done to bring the economy out of an inflationary recession? A "cold turkey" approach would be to sit tight and keep the lid on aggregate demand. The negative output gap, reflected in rising unemployment, declining sales, and an unplanned inventory buildup would, in time, cause firms and workers to revise their expectations about the rate of inflation for both inputs and final goods. Prices of raw materials would begin to fall. Workers, seeing first a slowing of the rise in the cost of living, and then an actual decline, would accept lower nominal wages. Lower levels of expected input prices would cause the aggregate supply curve to begin shifting downward. Slowly the economy would slip back down along the aggregate demand curve toward an equilibrium at E_3. But the experience would be a painful one.

A more moderate approach would be to slow the growth of aggregate demand gradually rather than stopping it cold. With luck, this could bring the economy to a "soft landing" at the natural level of real output. It might take longer to slow inflation this way, but a severe recession might be avoided.

In practice, there is a danger that policy makers will overreact to an inflationary recession. Instead of easing the economy to a soft landing, they may first react to pressures to "do something" about inflation (by stopping the growth of aggregate demand altogether) and then react to pressures to "do something" about unemployment by renewing the rapid growth of aggregate demand before inflationary expectations have been broken. Such a "stop-go" policy will result in a highly unstable path for the economy over time.

The truth is that no one knows a quick, painless way to stop inflation once it has become part of public expectations. As we will see, many economists think the best preventative is to keep inflation from getting started in the first place. This is a theme to which we will return in the last section of this chapter.

Deflation and Recession

Deflation

A situation in which the average price level falls for a sustained period of a year or more.

In recent years, as inflation has receded in all but a few countries, economists have become concerned with the possibility of **deflation**—a situation in which the average price level falls for a sustained period. Deflation has not occurred in the United States since the early years of the Great Depression when, between 1929 and 1933, the price level fell by a third. However, other countries, most notably Japan, have experienced deflation in the early twenty-first century. At first it might seem that if inflation is bad, deflation must be good, but that turns out not to be the case. As discussed in *Economics in the News 13.1*, Japan's recent deflation, like the U.S. deflation of the 1930s, was accompanied by high unemployment and a persistent negative output gap. As a result of the Japanese experience, deflation has returned to the attention of policy makers as a risk that all low-inflation countries need to think about.

Deflation is most likely to occur during a recession caused by a decrease in aggregate demand, as illustrated in Figure 13.4. Unlike the situation shown in the preceding figure, where the recession began on a basis of prior inflationary expectations, the situation illustrated in Figure 13.4 begins from a condition in which there is no prior inflation, either actual or expected.

FIGURE 13.4 DEFLATION AND RECESSION

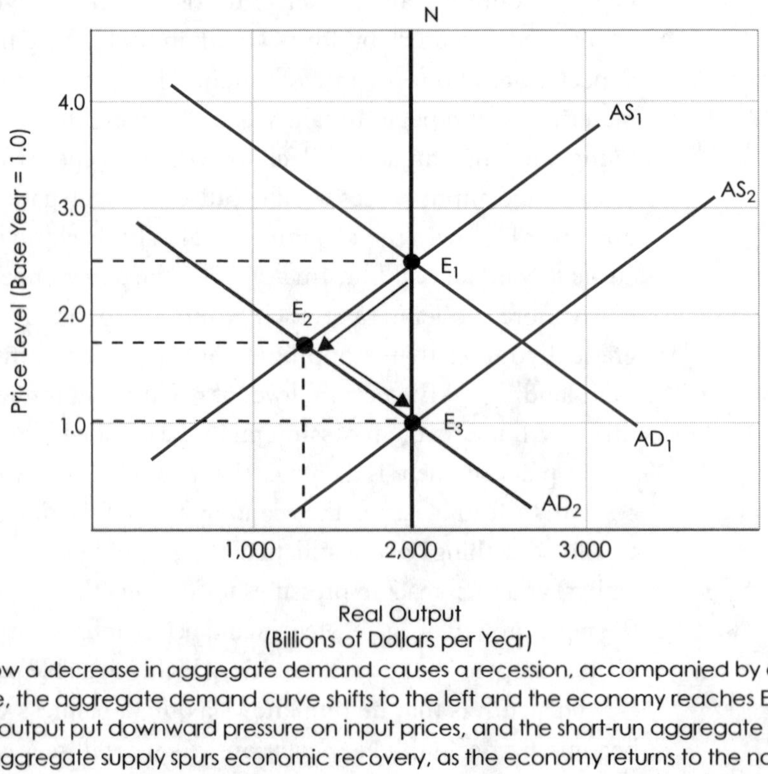

This figure shows how a decrease in aggregate demand causes a recession, accompanied by a deflation (falling prices). In this figure, the aggregate demand curve shifts to the left and the economy reaches E_2. High unemployment and low real output put downward pressure on input prices, and the short-run aggregate supply curve falls to AS_2. The shift in aggregate supply spurs economic recovery, as the economy returns to the natural rate of output at E_3.

ECONOMICS IN THE NEWS 13.1

DEFLATION IN JAPAN

From the 1960s through the 1980s, the Japanese economy was the envy of the world. As Japanese cars, consumer electronics, and industrial goods flooded the world and set new standards of quality, its economy boomed. Japan became the world's second-largest economy, and it became the first Asian country whose living standards were on a par with those of North America and Western Europe. Books with titles like *The Japanese Century* became best sellers.

Then, in the 1990s, all this began to fall apart. One of the first signs of change came from the Consumer Price Index. Japan had never been a high inflation country, but in the early 1990s, inflation slowed sharply from its already moderate rate, as shown here in the left-hand chart. After dipping below zero in 1995 and rising slightly in 1996 through early 1998, the rate of inflation became persistently negative after 1999. Deflation continued for more than six years, until early 2006.

This long period of deflation was accompanied by very poor performance of the real economy. One measure of this is the output gap—positive when real GDP is above its natural level, negative when the economy is performing below potential. The right-hand chart here shows that the Japanese output gap was negative throughout the period of deflation. The chart also shows that unemployment rose substantially during the deflation. Although the unemployment rate remained at moderate levels by the standards of other countries, the weak labor market brought big changes to Japan. Among other effects, it undermined the "jobs for life" tradition that had been a hallmark of the Japanese economy. Although the Japanese unemployment rate has fallen below its peak, some observers think post-deflation official data fail to reveal a substantial amount to hidden unemployment and underemployment.

The damage done by deflation in extended beyond the indicators shown in the charts. Banking and the rest of the financial sector suffered severely. During the post-war boom years, banks had made huge loans secured by mortgages on commercial real estate. As deflation began to undermine both the prices of that real estate and the profits of the companies that owned it, the banks suffered massive losses. Only a permissive and supportive policy by the Bank of Japan (the country's central bank) staved off a financial panic.

To be sure, the Japanese government did not stand idly by. It applied all of the conventional tools of expansionary policy. Beginning in 1993, the government budget, which had been in balance or surplus on average during the 1980s, swung sharply into deficit. Deficits were so large and persistent that net government debt soared from less than 15 percent of GDP in 1991 to nearly 90 percent of GDP by 2006. On the monetary front, policy was also highly expansionary. The central bank lowered short-term interest rates all the way to zero—as low as they could go. However, although expansionary monetary policy led to steady growth of bank reserves, the growing reserves were not translated into new loans. With money so cheap, financial and non-financial companies simply accumulated huge quantities of liquid assets—a classic liquidity trap. In short, conventional monetary and fiscal policy tools were used but were very slow to take effect.

By late 2006, as this is written, the Japanese economy finally seems to have put deflation behind it. Prices finally were rising, unemployment was down, and the output gap, for the first time in years, turned positive. But even if the recovery proves to be lasting, Japan's deflationary decade at the turn of the 21st century stands as a warning to policy makers throughout the world: Deflation is dangerous. Better to prevent it before it starts, because deflation, once entrenched, is hard to fight.

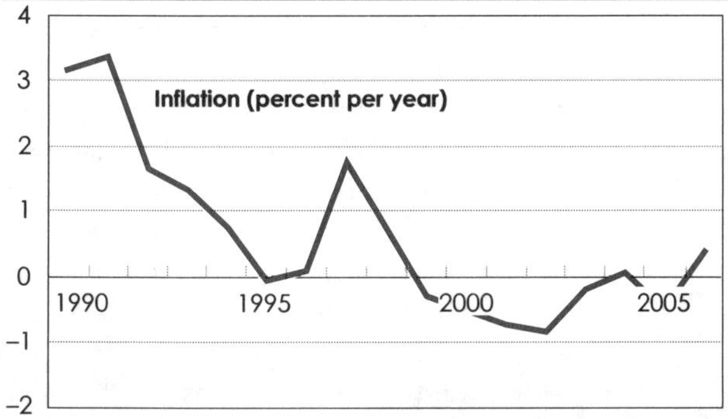

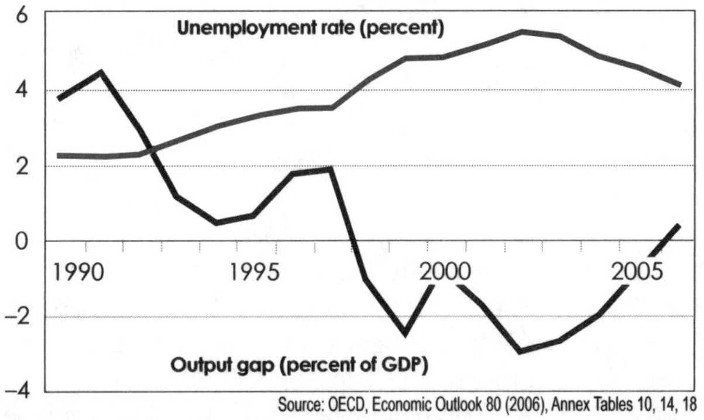

Source: International Monetary Fund, *Deflation: Determinants, Risks and Policy Options*, April 2003, Box 4.3, p. 43.

The deflationary episode begins when a decrease in aggregate demand causes a decrease in real output. The aggregate demand curve falls from AD_1 to AD_2 and the economy's level of output moves to point E_2.

Eventually, the economy's rising unemployment and falling real output will put downward pressure on input prices. To see why, consider how high unemployment affects the wages workers receive. If factory owners see lines of able-bodied workers at their factory gates, they may think they can get away with paying lower wages to their current workers. Workers who are already employed may feel pressured to accept wage cuts for fear of losing their jobs. As the decline in wages begins to affect producers' expected input prices, the AS curve will shift downward (from AS_1 to AS_2), until the economy returns to the natural level of output at E_3.

If recovery via falling wages is possible, then why did the Great Depression last for a full decade and why did Japan's recent stagnation last as long as it did? A number of factors tend to make deflation persist once it gets started. First, firms are likely to find that it is harder to cut nominal wages during deflation than it is to raise them during inflation. Minimum wage laws are one potential barrier to wage decreases. Labor unions are another. A union certainly would not argue with higher wages, but it will probably dispute wage cuts. Even without these institutional barriers, producers may worry that lower wages will damage the motivation and loyalty of workers.

WHO SAID IT? WHO DID IT? 13.1

A. W. H. PHILLIPS AND THE PHILLIPS CURVE

Alban W. H. Phillips, known to his friends as Bill, was an economist whose reputation was based largely on a single paper on the right topic published at the right time. In the late 1950s, the connection between inflation and unemployment was a major unsolved problem of macroeconomic theory. In a famous article published in the journal Economica in 1958, Phillips presented a set of graphs that suggested a stable, inverse relationship between inflation and unemployment. The paper did not contain much by way of a theory to explain the relationship, but his curves became a peg on which all future discussions of the problem would be hung. Every subsequent article on inflation and unemployment discussed the shape of the Phillips curve, the point on the Phillips curve that best served as a policy target, how the Phillips curve could be shifted, and so on. Today the term is so familiar that Phillips' name enjoys a sort of immortality, even though Phillips left further development of the inflation-unemployment relationship to others.

Phillips was born in New Zealand in 1914. He moved to Australia at the age of 16, worked there as an apprentice electrician in a mine, and learned electrical engineering skills. In 1937, he emigrated to Britain. During World War II, he was taken prisoner by the Japanese. After the war, he studied at the London School of Economics and later joined the faculty there. He stayed at LSE until 1967, when he moved to Australian National University.

Phillips's early hands-on electrical training seems to have influenced his approach to economic problems. One of his early projects at LSE was to construct a hydraulic analog computer called the Monetary National Income Automatic Computer (MONIAC), designed to simulate the circular flow of income and product in the economy. By adjusting valves on the computer, flows of water representing saving, taxes, government spending, and other variables could be sent through a series of pipes and tanks. The MONIAC foreshadowed the widespread use of computers in modern economic research. Several copies of Phillips' machine were made, some of which are preserved in working order to this day.

A second set of factors that make deflation hard to reverse centers on monetary policy. As discussed in the previous chapter, interest rates play a key role in transmitting the effects of monetary policy to the real economy via their effects on investment. However, there is a natural lower bound to nominal interest rates: They can go no lower than zero. For a bank to loan money at a negative interest rate—to pay borrowers to take money off its hands—would be an absurdity. Loan demand would be infinite, because borrowers could profit simply by borrowing money and storing it in a safe place. Once a central bank lowers interest rates to zero, the economy risks becoming stuck in a liquidity trap, as seems to have happened in Japan. How to conduct economic policy under conditions of deflation is an issue explored further in the *Case for Discussion* at the end of the chapter.

Finally, there is a danger that deflation can lead to a financial panic. The problem is that banks and other institutions use real estate, business equipment, and even financial assets as collateral for loans. If deflation undermines the value of collateral, borrowers may default on loans, thereby threatening the solvency of financial institutions.

THE PHILLIPS CURVE

At several points, our analysis has suggested an inverse relationship between inflation and unemployment. We have seen that rapidly growing aggregate demand can hold real output above its natural level and unemployment below its natural rate, but at the cost of sustained inflation. We have also seen that deflation tends to bring falling real output and high unemployment. This association between inflation and unemployment can be represented in the form of a graph called a **Phillips curve**, named for A. W. H. Phillips, who first described it in a 1958 paper[3] (see *Who Said It? Who Did It? 13.1*).

Phillips curve

A graph showing the relationship between the inflation rate and the unemployment rate, other things being equal.

The Phillips Curve as a Policy Menu

A representative Phillips curve is drawn in Figure 13.5. During the 1960s, when the Phillips curve first attracted economists' attention, it was viewed as a menu of policy choices. Political liberals sometimes argued that policy makers should choose a point such as L on the Phillips curve; this point would "buy" full employment and prosperity at the price of a modest inflation rate. Conservatives expressed horror at the thought of any degree of inflation and argued for a point such as C, which would achieve price stability at the expense of some jobs.

However, economists soon discovered a problem with viewing the Phillips curve as a policy menu: the choices it offered kept changing while the meal was in progress. As the 1960s unfolded, economists began to notice that inflation-unemployment points for recent years did not fit the curves they had plotted using data from the 1950s. It became common to speak of an upward drift of the Phillips curve: a given level of inflation would "buy" increasingly smaller reductions in unemployment.

FIGURE 13.5 THE PHILLIPS CURVE AS A POLICY MENU

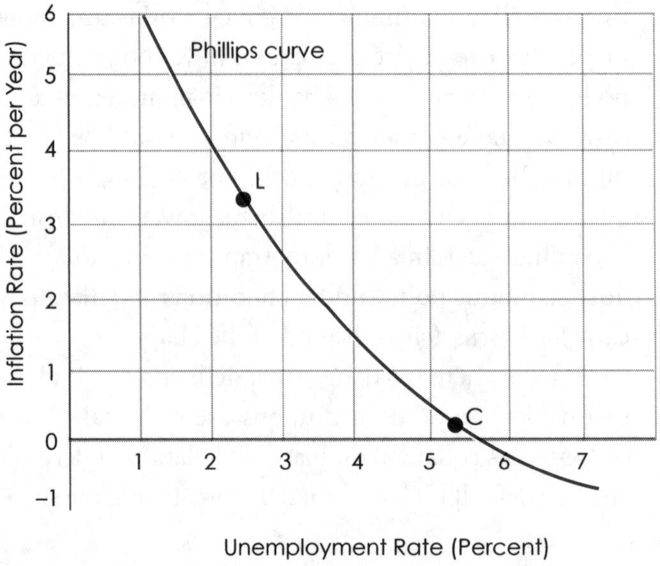

When A. W. H. Phillips first drew attention to the inverse relationship between inflation and unemployment, his "Phillips curve" was treated as a policy menu. Liberals argued that a point such as L should be chosen; this would "buy" a permanent reduction in unemployment at the cost of a little inflation. Conservatives seemed to favor a point such as C, which would offer stable prices at the cost of more joblessness.

Had the upward drift of the Phillips curve been caused by factors outside their control, policy makers could have chosen their preferred point from a new, higher Phillips curve. With the advent of the 1970s, however, perceptions of the Phillips curve started to change. It began to appear that shifts in the Phillips curve were caused by the very policies that had sought to move the economy along the curve.

The Phillips Curve and the Natural Rate of Unemployment

The distinction between the long-run and short-run effects of changes in aggregate demand on prices, output, and unemployment provides the key to this new view of the Phillips curve. A once-and-for-all rise in the level of aggregate demand leads to only a temporary reduction in unemployment. The reason is that the expected levels of wages and other input prices adjust to changes in the level of final-goods prices, thereby pushing up the aggregate supply curve. Thus, real output can rise above its natural level only as long as the short-run aggregate supply curve does not completely catch up with the shifting aggregate demand curve.

Earlier we noted that the natural rate of unemployment corresponds to a state in which the economy is experiencing neither accelerating nor decelerating inflation. We can also say that the natural rate of unemployment is the rate that prevails when the expected inflation rate equals the actual inflation rate. This can happen with real output at its natural level and the expected and actual inflation rates both zero. However, unemployment can also be at its natural rate when the economy is in a moving equilibrium with a constant inflation rate to which everyone has become accustomed.

This modern view of the Phillips curve is illustrated in Figure 13.6. Two short-run Phillips curves are shown, each corresponding to a different expected inflation rate. If no inflation is expected, the Phillips curve takes the position Ph_1. The intersection of this Phillips curve with the horizontal axis indicates the natural rate of unemployment, here taken to be 6 percent. If the actual inflation rate unexpectedly goes up to 2 percent per year, the economy will initially move upward and to the left along this Phillips curve from point A to point B. This will correspond to a movement upward and to the right along the economy's short-run aggregate supply curve; real output and the price level will rise as inflation gets under way and the unemployment rate falls.

If the inflation rate remains at 2 percent per year, people will sooner or later adjust their expectations accordingly. In terms of the diagrams in the chapter on inflation, the rising short-run aggregate supply curve will catch up with the aggregate demand curve. As this happens, real output will return to its natural level and unemployment to its natural rate. From that point, the aggregate demand and short-run aggregate supply curves and their intersection point move upward along the vertical long-run aggregate supply curve at a constant 2 percent rate. In Figure 13.6, this causes an upward shift of the short-run Phillips curve to Ph_2. As a result, the economy moves to point C.

From point C, the economy can move upward or downward along the new short-run Phillips curve, depending on what happens to the actual inflation rate. If inflation

FIGURE 13.6 SHORT-RUN AND LONG-RUN PHILLIPS CURVES

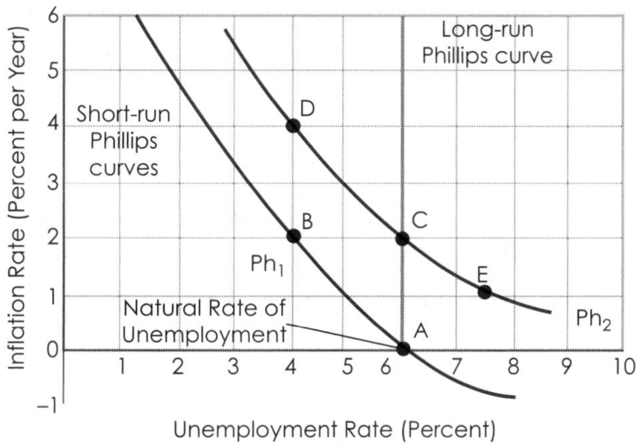

In the modern view of the Phillips curve, there is an inverse relationship between unemployment and inflation only in the short run. Unexpected inflation lowers the unemployment rate, but only until people's expectations adjust to the new inflation rate. Any change in the expected inflation rate shifts the short-run Phillips curve. The long-run Phillips curve is a vertical line drawn at the natural rate of unemployment, here assumed to be 6 percent. The long- and short-run curves intersect at the expected inflation rate for which the short-run curve is drawn.

increases to 4 percent while people expect it to remain at 2 percent, the economy initially will move to point D. If inflation slows to 1 percent while people expect it to remain at 2 percent, the economy at first will move from point C to point E. However, these movements along the short-run Phillips curve will not represent new long-run equilibrium points. As soon as people get used to the new inflation rate, the short-run Phillips curve will shift again.

The Long-Run Phillips Curve

A further implication of the newer view of the Phillips curve is that it must be vertical in the long run. This follows from the notions that unemployment attains its natural rate whenever the actual and expected inflation rates are equal, and that any given steady rate of inflation will be expected to continue. Such a long-run Phillips curve is shown in Figure 13.6 as a vertical line drawn at the natural rate of unemployment. Each short-run Phillips curve intersects the long-run Phillips curve at the expected inflation rate for which the short-run curve is drawn. Thus, unemployment will be at its natural rate only when the actual and expected inflation rates are equal.

The concepts of a vertical long-run Phillips curve and a short-run Phillips curve that shifts upward as inflation accelerates have now become the established view of the relationship between inflation and unemployment. The old view that the Phillips curve could be treated as a policy menu, along which low unemployment could be "purchased" at the expense of a moderate but steady rate of inflation, is no longer accepted. In retrospect, past attempts of policy makers to keep unemployment low by persistently using expansionary monetary and fiscal policy are seen as one of the causes leading to the Great Inflation of the 1970s. *Applying Economic Ideas 13.1* illustrates the consequences of such overly expansionary policy in the United States in the 1960s. In the low-inflation environment of the early twenty-first century, such a strategy seems distinctly unattractive.

STRATEGIES FOR LASTING PRICE STABILITY

In the first section of this chapter, we looked at the mechanisms that get inflation started or cause the economy to slip into deflation. These included both demand-side and supply-side elements. Now we turn to strategies that aim to end inflation or deflation when they occur and, once they are brought under control, to maintain lasting price stability.

What Policy Instruments Are Available?

In the aggregate supply and demand model, changes in the price level can be brought about either by shifts in the AD curve (demand-side inflation) or the AS curve (supply-side inflation). It stands to reason, then, that a complete strategy for price stabi-

APPLYING ECONOMIC IDEAS 13.1

INFLATION IN THE KENNEDY–JOHNSON ERA

John Kennedy came to the presidency in 1960 with the stated intent of getting the country moving again after two recessions in the later years of the Eisenhower administration. Lyndon Johnson, his successor, was equally determined to pursue an expansionary policy. Economists are still debating the relative impact of the tax reductions, heavy defense spending, and accelerating monetary growth that characterized the Kennedy–Johnson years. But there is no doubt that this combination of policies was as expansionary as anyone could have wished. The result was a sustained period of growth and low unemployment.

The accompanying diagram shows the unemployment-inflation record for the economy during the Kennedy–Johnson era. The pattern is just what the theory of the shifting Phillips curve would lead us to expect. At first, the expansionary policy produced major gains in employment with little additional inflation. But starting in 1964, the year of the tax cut, each successive drop in unemployment was accompanied by a bigger jump in prices. By the end of Johnson's term in office, inflation was rising higher and higher each year just to keep unemployment from growing. Although it may have seemed in the first years of this expansionary cycle that the economy was moving upward along a fixed Phillips curve "menu," by the end of the 1960s policy makers were playing catch-up as the Phillips curve shifted steadily upward.

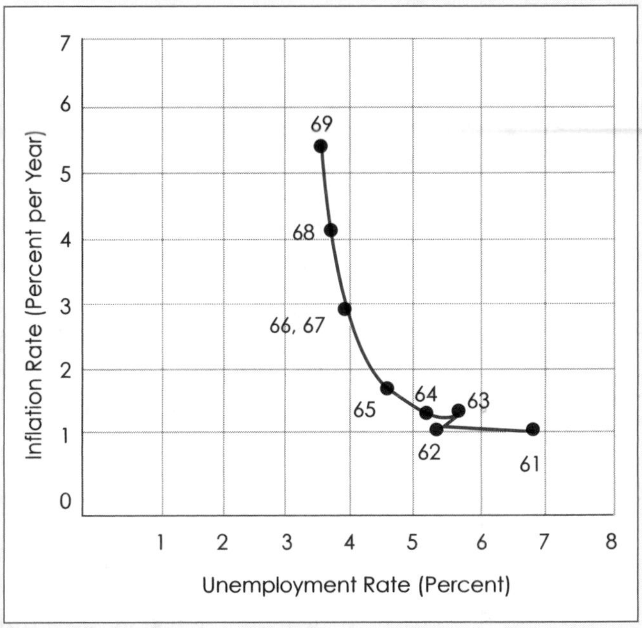

Source: President's Council of Economic Advisers, *Economic Report of the President* (Washington, D.C.: Government Printing Office, 1987), Tables B-35 and B-58. Annual average civilian unemployment rate and percentage change in annual average CPI.

lization should make use of policy instruments that act both on the demand and the supply side of the economy.

We have looked in considerable detail at demand-side policy instruments in earlier chapters. The principal fiscal policy instruments of demand management are changes in government purchases and changes in net taxes. We recall that changes in net taxes can mean either changes in tax rates governing payments to the government, or changes in transfer payments, such as unemployment benefits or Social Security benefits. For monetary policy, we have seen that open market purchases of government securities are the principal policy instrument used by the Federal Reserve to control aggregate demand via changes in the money supply. Supplementary instruments occasionally used by the Fed include changes in the discount rate and, at least in the past, changes in required reserve ratios. Finally, we have noted that intervention in foreign exchange markets via purchases or sales of foreign currencies is a powerful instrument of monetary policy used by central banks in many other countries, although it has not been much used by the Fed in recent years.

Up to this point, we have given less attention to policy instruments that might be used to control shifts in the aggregate supply curve. Our earlier discussion of shifts in the aggregate supply curve emphasized supply shocks like natural disasters or shifts in world commodity prices that lie outside the control of national governments. Policy makers, however, do have some instruments available through which they can influence aggregate supply.

WAGE AND PRICE CONTROLS Direct administrative control over wages and prices has sometimes been used in an attempt to control movements in the aggregate supply curve. It is sometimes argued that wage and price controls can be useful in conjunction with restrictive demand management as a temporary measure to fight an inflationary recession. When policy makers apply the brakes to aggregate demand after a period of rapid inflation, firms and workers may not expect inflation to stop right away. It is possible that workers and firms will see wage and controls as a signal that the government is serious about ending inflation. If so, they may lower their inflationary expectations sooner than they otherwise would.

Any such reduction in expected inflation—if it happens—will remove the supply-side element from the inflationary recession. Knowing that they need not push for higher wages to beat inflation, workers will find their current wages acceptable. Knowing that their input prices will not be rising, firms will be less inclined to reduce output and raise prices. A larger part of the reduction in the growth of nominal GDP will take the form of a slowdown in price increases than would otherwise be the case. The drop in real output and the rise in unemployment will be smaller than they would otherwise be. As a result, the transition to price stability will be quicker and less painful than it would be without controls.

Wage and price controls do not always have the desired effects, however. One problem is that they are often used as a substitute for demand management policy rather than as a supplement to it. The government either tries to use wage and price controls to fight inflation without simultaneously slowing the growth of aggregate demand, or leaves controls in force after the transition is over and a new boom is under way. In that case, wage and price controls will be ineffective or will either be ignored and inflation will return, or they will lead to shortages, rationing, and black markets.

There have been several experiments with wage and price controls in the United States. One took place during World War II. The high level of wartime government spending made it hard to control aggregate demand. Strict price controls were used to suppress inflation. The results were predictable: Rationing was introduced for gasoline, tires, sugar, and many other goods, and widespread black markets emerged.

Another experiment with wage and price controls took place from 1971 to 1974 during the Nixon administration. The Nixon controls were a mixed success at best. They were first introduced when inflation already was falling and may have helped to speed its decline. But they were left in place after prices began to rise again in mid-1972. At that point, they proved useless or worse.

Although wage and price controls can theoretically play a constructive role in managing inflation, they have been used inappropriately so often that they have gone out of fashion among policy makers. As of early 2007, price controls were being used to fight inflation in Venezuela and Zimbabwe, but the number of countries that apply such controls today is much smaller than it was at one time.

CONTROL OF EXCHANGE RATES A second instrument that can be used to influence the aggregate supply curve is the exchange rate of the domestic currency relative to foreign currencies. This instrument is especially powerful in small, relatively open economies. In such economies, the prices of imported goods are an important component of input prices and the prices of imported consumer goods are a key determinant of the cost of living, which in turn affects the level of nominal wages in domestic labor markets. If a central bank that is active in exchange markets allows the domestic currency to appreciate, the prices of imported goods, stated in domestic currency, will decrease. Accordingly, downward pressure is placed on the aggregate supply curve. When the currency depreciates, the aggregate supply curve tends to shift upward. In contrast to wage and price controls, which have fallen out of fashion, the use of exchange rates as an instrument of supply-side macroeconomic policy is actively used in a number of countries. We will return to this topic later in the chapter.

MINOR SUPPLY-SIDE INSTRUMENTS Other minor instruments are sometimes used to affect conditions of aggregate supply. For example, changes in tax rates may have such an effect, to the extent that businesses perceive taxes as an element of cost, or to the extent that tax rates affect workers' wage demands when bargaining with employers. Policies that affect commodity prices can also be used for macroeconomic purposes. An example would be the U.S. strategic petroleum reserve. Releasing supplies of crude oil from the reserve can, in principle, offset the inflationary impact of an increase in world oil prices. These instruments are not likely to have strong, lasting effects on the aggregate price level.

The Importance of Credibility

Regardless of the specific instrument used, it is important to remember that all efforts to affect the position of the aggregate supply curve act through expectations. To the extent that businesses expect wages and other input prices to rise in the future, the aggregate supply curve will shift upward, thwarting efforts to control inflation. To the extent that announced policies to stabilize prices are seen as *credible,* the aggregate supply curve will stabilize and the work of policy makers in slowing inflation or resisting deflation will be easier.

For this reason, policy makers often accompany efforts at price stabilization with aggressive public relations efforts to persuade the public that they are serious in pursuing their announced policy goals. Changing the faces of policy makers sometimes helps. For example, the appointment of Paul Volcker, who was known to be influenced by monetarist ideas, as Chairman of the Federal Reserve in 1979 sent a signal to financial markets that tolerance for inflation was at an end.

Countries that have used exchange rates to control inflation have often reinforced a stabilization campaign by issuing a new currency with a new name. For example, in the 1980s, Israel replaced its old currency, the pound, with a new currency, the shekel. Argentina, as part of a failed attempt to control inflation in the 1980s, changed its peso to the austral and later, in a renewed round of anti-inflation policy, changed it back to the peso. In other cases, policy makers have signaled the seriousness of their attention by making changes in basic laws. For example, a country whose weak, politically subservient central bank has fueled inflation with excessive monetary expansion might announce a new law that makes the central bank independent of political control.

As we turn from a listing of individual instruments to a discussion of the way instruments can be combined into a coherent price stabilization strategy, we will see that the issue of credibility is always of key importance.

Inflation Targeting

Inflation targeting

A strategy for price stability in which policy makers adopt an explicit target range for the rate of inflation over an intermediate time horizon.

One of the most widely used strategies for achieving price stability is known as **inflation targeting**. As the name implies, adopting this strategy means that the central bank, and policy makers in other branches of government as well, adopt an explicit target range for the rate of inflation as the principal aim of macroeconomic policy over an intermediate time horizon.

RELATIONSHIP TO OTHER TARGETS AND GOALS Under an inflation-targeting regime, the target for the rate of inflation occupies an intermediate position between short-term operating targets and long-term policy goals. The price level cannot serve as a short-term operating target for monetary policy because the government's policy instruments affect the price level only indirectly and with a lag. For monetary policy, the transmission mechanism runs from policy instruments that affect the size of the money stock through interest rates and investment to aggregate demand. For fiscal policy, the transmission mechanism runs either through changes in government purchases, which are themselves a component of aggregate demand, or through changes in consumer expenditures caused by changes in tax rates. In either case, shifts in aggregate demand affect the price level, but not immediately. As we have seen, an increase in aggregate demand at first causes real output to increase while causing a moderate rise in prices, and later causes a further increase in prices as the aggregate supply curve shifts upward and real output returns to its natural level.

Because the transmission mechanism from monetary and fiscal policy to prices is long and indirect, inflation-targeting countries cannot expect to keep the rate of inflation exactly on target on a month-to-month basis. Instead, the usual approach is to set a target range for inflation—for example, between 2 and 4 percent—averaged over a one- or two-year time horizon.

The rate of inflation is an intermediate policy target in another sense, as well. Most policy makers view price stability not so much as something that is desirable for its own sake, but as a condition that should be established to facilitate the more fundamental goals of growth in real income and full employment. In particular, as we saw in Chapter 4, low-inflation countries perform consistently better in terms of economic growth. (Figure 4.9 gave data on the relationship between inflation and growth.) Inflation rates well under 10 percent per year appear optimal, although there are a few cases of countries that have done well with inflation in the low double digits. Countries with inflation rates over 100 percent have, on the average, experienced decreasing real GDP.

A too-low a rate of inflation can also be harmful to economic growth. Experience indicates that countries that experience deflation usually have stagnant or falling GDP, as in Japan during the past decade. Germany's recent experience provides another example. In the early 2000s, German inflation was the lowest in the European Union, less than 1 percent per year. At that time, Germany has experienced higher unemployment than its neighbors and virtually no growth of real GDP. To provide a cushion against the danger of falling into deflation, inflation-targeting countries usually aim for a rate of price increase in the low single digits rather than setting a target of zero inflation, which would be needed for complete price stability.

INFLATION TARGETING, EXPECTATIONS, AND CREDIBILITY Earlier we emphasized the importance of credibility to all price stabilization policies. If consumers and businesses expect the government to set reasonable inflation goals and stick to them, the inflationary expectations that shift the aggregate supply curve and destabilize the economy can be kept under control.

No country can avoid some variations in the rate of inflation caused by unpredictable supply shocks or demand disturbances linked to sudden swings in consumer or business confidence. Inflation targeting aims to stabilize expectations when such disturbances occur. Suppose, for example, a country whose inflation has averaged 3 percent per year is hit by a sudden rise in the quarterly inflation rate to 5 percent. In a country where consumers and businesses had low confidence in government policy, they might take actions to protect themselves from more inflation to come. These efforts at self-defense by consumers and businesses would push the aggregate supply curve upward and make the fears of future inflation self-fulfilling. On the other hand, if the country had a well-established inflation target of 2 to 4 percent averaged over a one- or two-year period, private decision makers could be confident that the temporary surge of inflation would be would be reversed by timely use of monetary or fiscal policy. Expecting inflation to fall back within the target range, they would not panic. The resulting stability of the aggregate supply curve would make the job of demand management easier, and in that case, predictions of price stability would be self-fulfilling.

INFLATION TARGETING AND THE FED Inflation targeting is the official policy of the United Kingdom, Canada, Australia, New Zealand, and many emerging market countries. In the United States, however, the Fed has not fully embraced inflation targeting. True, the Fed attaches great importance to keeping inflation low while at the same time avoiding the risk of deflation. It has been highly successful in doing so. Since 1992, the annual inflation rate as measured by the GDP deflator, considered the broadest price-level indicator, has held steady between 1 and 3 percent. Looking at the data alone, an observer might well conclude that the Fed had an inflation target of 2 percent plus or minus 1 percent. Yet the Fed has announced no such target. Instead, it has insisted that an explicit inflation target might limit its flexibility in reacting to unforeseen circumstances.

Some Fed watchers expect this to change. They expect the Fed to announce openly the policy it seems to have been following implicitly. They think doing so will provide an even more stable framework for forward-looking expectations in financial markets than is provided by the excellent record of the Fed's discretionary policy over the past decade.

Exchange-Rate Based Stabilization Policy

Another price stabilization strategy uses the exchange rate of the country's currency, rather than the rate of inflation, as its principle target. This approach is usually called **exchange-rate based stabilization policy (ERB policy).** ERB policy has been used by many emerging market economies, for example by Argentina and Brazil in the 1990s and Ecuador more recently. Several countries undergoing the process of transition from socialist planned economies to a market system have also used ERB policy, including Latvia, Poland, Hungary, and Bulgaria. Some developed countries, for example Denmark, and, before the introduction of the euro. The Netherlands, have also used ERB policy.

Exchange-rate based stabilization policy (ERB)

A policy that uses the exchange rate as the principle operating target for macroeconomic policy.

OPERATING AND INTERMEDIATE TARGETS UNDER ERB POLICY One thing to note about ERB policy is that the exchange rate, unlike the rate of inflation, can be used as an operating target on a day-to-day basis. As we have seen, a country's central bank can control the exchange rate directly through the instrument of buying and selling foreign currency in exchange for its own domestic currency. Sales of foreign currency strengthen the exchange rate of the domestic currency or slow an undesired tendency toward depreciation caused by market forces. Purchases of foreign currency have the opposite effect. In addition, the central bank's use of domestic open market operations to influence interest rates has a strong effect on the exchange rate via their effects on financial inflows or outflows. In fact, interest rates and exchange rates are so closely linked that it is a maxim of central banking that monetary policy can be used either to achieve an operating target for the exchange rate or an operating target for the interest rate, but not for both at once.

Countries that use ERB policy define the operating target for the exchange rate in different ways. Some declare an exactly fixed value of the exchange rate as their target. Others use a target zone, say 10 pesos per dollar plus or minus 2 percent. Still others use an adjustable target, for example, one that includes a steady, planned rate of depreciation of the exchange rate at 5 percent per year. Because the principles involved in meeting any of these targets are similar, we will not take the time to discuss the relative merits of each variant.

In using the exchange rate as an operating target, central banks that use ERB policy also have their eyes on intermediate targets and long-term policy goals. A stable exchange rate makes a very strong contribution to the intermediate target of price stability. This is especially true in relatively small countries that are open to international trade and financial flows. In such countries, a fixed exchange rate is said to provide a "nominal anchor" for price expectations. If the central bank's commitment to the exchange rate target is credible, the stable expectations will provide a good basis for achieving the long-term goals of economic growth and full employment. If the central bank's credibility is weak because of political instability or unfavorable factors in the external economic environment, attempted ERB stabilization may fail.

Hyperinflation

Very rapid inflation.

ERB policy can have an especially powerful effect in a country that suffers from the extremely rapid inflation known as **hyperinflation.** When inflation reaches rates of thousands of percent per year, as it did in countries like Argentina, Brazil, Bolivia, and others in the 1980s and 1990s and in Zimbabwe today, people lose faith almost completely in the value of the local currency. They continue to use it for making day-to-day purchases, but they keep their savings in a safe currency like the dollar or the euro. Contracts for major purchases and often for wages are also made in the foreign rather than the domestic currency. Under these conditions, a credible program to fix the exchange rate of the local currency at a specific value against the dollar or the euro has a powerful effect on expectations. Inflation may end almost overnight as people once again find they can safely use the domestic currency for all their needs. *Applying Economic Ideas 13.2* provides an example of successful use of ERB policy to end the 1996–1997 hyperinflation in Bulgaria.

Problems with ERB Stabilization

Despite the successful use of ERB stabilization policy by many countries, the policy is not without dangers. Some attempts to apply ERB policy without taking potential problems into account have ended in failure.

Conflicts between fiscal and monetary policy are one problem area. Under ERB stabilization, monetary policy must be focused exclusively on maintaining the target exchange rate. The central bank cannot do that and, at the same time, make easy credit available to the government to finance its budget deficit. In fact, excessive growth of the money supply because of central bank lending to finance budget deficits is often the cause of the very hyperinflation that ERB stabilization aims to

APPLYING ECONOMIC IDEAS 13.2
BULGARIA'S SUCCESSFUL EXCHANGE-RATE BASED STABILIZATION

In the early 1990s, during the first years of its transition from Communism to a market system, Bulgaria's economy performed better than the average for countries in Eastern Europe and the former Soviet Union. There was some inflation, but not as severe is in Russia or neighboring Rumania. There was an initial drop in real output, but not as deep a decline as in nearby Ukraine or Georgia.

However, Bulgaria's good start was followed by delays in introducing key economic reforms, especially in the financial sector. In 1996, the economy slowed down and the banking system came close to collapse. In attempting to save the banking system, the Bulgarian central bank pumped money into the economy in a way that brought on rapidly escalating inflation. By the end of 1996, a full-scale inflationary crisis was underway. Protesters took to the streets, the government fell, and a caretaker government took over pending new elections. By early 1997, when the new government set to work, there was a full-fledged inflationary crisis. As the figure shows, prices were rising at a rate of more than 100 percent per month. Clearly, strong medicine was called for.

The new Bulgarian government chose to apply one of the most stringent of all forms of exchange-rate based stabilization policy. In March 1997, it announced that it would introduce a *currency board*—a form of monetary policy that would obligate the central bank to maintain an absolutely fixed exchange rate. Because the European Union was the country's largest trading partner, the Bulgarian lev was pegged to the German mark. Later, when the euro replaced the mark, the peg was transferred to the euro.

As soon as plans for the currency board were announced, an interesting thing happened. As the figure shows, the new policy stopped inflation dead in its tracks—not in July, when it was implemented, but right away in March, as soon as it was announced. Since that time, Bulgaria has enjoyed low inflation and one of the best rates of real economic growth in the region.

The successful Bulgarian experience with ERB stabilization illustrates a point about the importance of credibility to price stabilization policy: If people believe that their government is politically committed to stability and has a technically valid plan for implementing its commitment, then the promise of stabilization becomes self-fulfilling. That, at least, is what seems to have happened in Bulgaria.

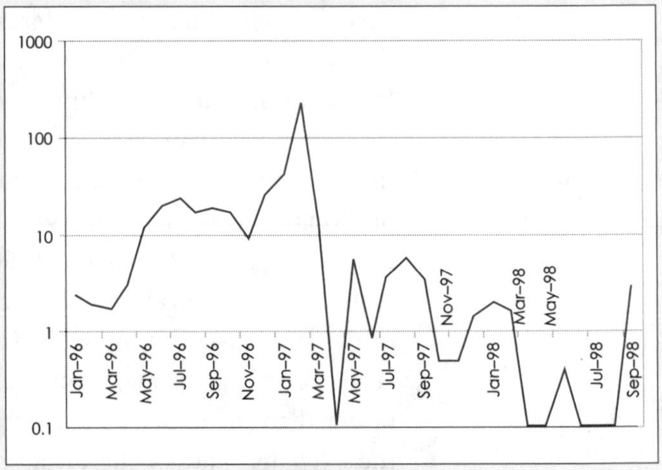

Source: Author's figure based on IFM data.

end. Conflicts arise when a country's central bank tries to implement ERB stabilization while its government does not have the political discipline to control spending and enforce tax collection in order to keep the budget deficit under control. Sooner or later a crisis breaks out in which the government must default on its debt, or the central bank must abandon its exchange rate target, or both. The painful crisis of the Argentine economy at the end of 2001, which included both a default and devaluation, provides a case in point.

Countries that link their currencies to that of a strong partner like the dollar or the euro must consider another potential problem as well. Once a small country links its currency to that of a larger neighbor, the smaller country's economy becomes exposed to all the economic shocks that affect the larger partner. For example, consider the case of Ecuador, which, in 2000, has adopted the U.S. dollar as its currency in a bid to end hyperinflation. If the dollar depreciates relative to the euro or the Japanese yen, Ecuador experiences an increase in the cost of imports, even though it does nothing to cause the depreciation. Similarly, if the U.S. Fed finds it necessary to raise interest rates to resist inflation, Ecuador's interest rates rise as well, potentially harming investment and slowing growth. As of early 2007, Ecuador's new government is considering breaking its currency link to the dollar.

For these reasons, economists advise that ERB stabilization policy is most likely to work if the small country's economy has strong ties to its larger currency partner in other ways besides the exchange rate. It is helpful if a large share of its imports and exports take place with the currency partner. It is helpful if labor and capital markets allow relatively free flow of resources between the two countries. It is helpful if their business cycles are synchronized. And it is helpful if the two countries are similarly affected by shocks like changes in international commodity prices. In all of these respects, conditions were favorable for the successful policy linking the Bulgarian currency to the euro. The same conditions were much less favorable for the linkage of Argentina's peso to the U.S. dollar, helping to explain its ultimate failure.

The preceding cautionary words do not mean that ERB policy can never be used unless initial conditions are ideal. Rather, it means that exchange rate policy should not be applied rigidly without consideration of the context. There are compromises in ERB policy that can help to cushion a country against some of the dangers. For example, in the 1990s Latvia chose to link its currency not to that of a single partner, but to a weighted average of other currencies. In the same period, Poland and Hungary chose to use a pre-announced, gradually slowing rate of depreciation of its currency, rather than an immediate fixed exchange rate, to slow its excessive inflation to the desired level. And in the 1980s, Israel temporarily fixed its exchange rate in order to end an inflationary crisis, but phased out the fixed exchange rate in favor of inflation targeting before a crisis of the Argentine type had a chance to develop. In short, despite some cases of failure, ERB stabilization policy, applied intelligently and flexibly, remains a valuable option in the policy maker's toolkit.

SUMMARY

1. **What are the characteristics of inflation or deflation that arise from shifts in aggregate demand?** Inflation caused by an increase in aggregate demand is known as *demand-side inflation.* In the short run, an increase in aggregate demand will move the economy up and to the right along its short-run aggregate supply curve. As increases in final goods prices come to be reflected in expected input prices, the aggregate supply curve shifts upward. If continued expansionary policy shifts the aggregate demand curve upward at the same rate, the economy can be held above its natural level of real output for an extended period, but at a substantial cost in terms of inflation. During times of economic contraction, a decrease in aggregate demand can move the economy down and to the left along its aggregate supply curve. Prices fall as output contracts, and the economy enters a period of *deflation.*

2. **How can inflation arise from shifts in the short-run aggregate supply curve?** If the short-run aggregate supply curve shifts upward while the aggregate demand curve stays in place or shifts upward more slowly, the economy will experience *supply-side inflation.* Real output will fall, and the economy will enter an *inflationary recession.* One source of supply-side inflation is a *supply shock,* such as an increase in the price of a key input such as petroleum. Another is the momentum of inflationary expectations generated by previous demand-side inflation.

3. **How are inflation and unemployment related?** The short-run relationship between inflation and unemployment is shown by the *Phillips curve,* which shows that for a given expected inflation rate, lower actual inflation rates tend to be linked with higher unemployment rates. The intersection of the short- and long-run Phillips curves corresponds to the expected rate of inflation: an increase in the expected inflation rate tends to shift the short-run Phillips curve upward. The long-run Phillips curve is a vertical line at the natural rate of unemployment. Unemployment will be at its natural rate only when the actual inflation rate equals the expected inflation rate.

4. **What types of policies can be used to achieve lasting price stability?** Lasting price stability requires using the instruments of monetary and fiscal policy to avoid undue swings in aggregate demand. The government's control over aggregate supply is less direct. Instruments like wage and price controls and exchange rate policy can sometimes help, but the most important task is to achieve a degree of credibility that stabilizes expectations. Credibility is enhanced if price stabilization policy conforms to an over all strategy. Two proven stabilization strategies are *inflation targeting and exchange-rate based stabilization policy.*

KEY TERMS

Demand-side inflation
Supply-side inflation
Supply shock
Accommodating policy
Inflationary recession
Deflation
Phillips curve
Inflation targeting
Exchange-rate based stabilization policy
Hyperinflation

PROBLEMS AND TOPICS FOR DISCUSSION

1. **Examining the Great Inflation.** Given the information provided about the "Great Inflation" in the case at the beginning of this chapter, would you describe the nature of that inflation as demand-side, supply-side, or a mixture of the two? Discuss.

2. **Expected input prices.** Three aggregate supply curves are shown in Figure 13.1. What is the expected level of input prices associated with each?

3. **Favorable supply shocks.** Supply shocks are not always bad. Use aggregate supply and demand curves to explain the short-run and long-run effects of a favorable supply shock, such as a decline in world oil prices. Could a supply shock ever cause deflation?

4. **Price expectations and real output.** Use the aggregate supply and demand model to show that real output can be above its natural level only when the current level of final-goods prices is above the level of expected input prices. Show too that real output can be below its natural level only when the current level of final-goods prices is below the level of expected input prices.

5. **Publicity and policy changes.** Assume that the economy has been going through a long period of demand-side inflation. The government decides to try to stop the inflation by means of restrictive monetary and fiscal policies. Should it make the required policy changes with as little fanfare as possible, or should it publicize them widely? Will it make any difference? Why or why not?

6. **Forecasting inflation.** What do you expect the inflation rate to be next year? Do you know what it was last year? Last month? On what sources do you rely for information about past and present inflation and for forming your expectations about the future? Do you think this course will affect your ability to forecast inflation in the future? Discuss.

7. **The current rate of inflation.** Inflation data given in this chapter refer to year-to-year percentage changes in the consumer price index. Use the most recent *Economic Report of the President* (available online at www.gpoaccess.gov/eop/) to determine the rate of inflation for the most recent years available. Has inflation remained relatively steady—in the 1 to 3 percent range experienced throughout the later 1990s and early 2000s? If not, can you suggest any reason for the change based on the theories presented in this chapter?

CASE FOR DISCUSSION

Deflation—Could It Happen in the United States?

Slowing inflation in the early 21st century has made deflation seem more of a possibility for the United States than at any time since the 1930s. In early May of 2003 the Federal Reserve signaled its concern about what it called the risk, still seen as a minor one, that the 1 percent inflation prevailing at that time could turn to lead to a period of falling prices. Testifying before Congress later in the month, Fed Chairman Alan Greenspan reiterated that concern. And in late 2003, he told a group of world bankers that while the development of deflationary forces was a low probability event, the Fed would lean over backward to make certain they are contained.

Why the Concern About Deflation?

The combination of weak demand for goods and services and competitive pressures from an overhang of excess capacity can squeeze profit margins and force price discounts. The accompanying slack demand for labor then tends to slow the pace of money wage in-creases and lead to further price weakness. This is how recessions and sluggish recoveries painfully bring down the rate of inflation. And when inflation is already low, prices can actually begin falling.

Falling prices and the expectation of further declines can, in turn, make demand still weaker.

Consumers may delay some purchases in hopes of getting better prices. Potential home buyers and business investors are discouraged from borrowing for fear they will have to repay their debts out of earnings and revenues diminished by the decline in prices. A reduction in interest rates could overcome this barrier to investment. But, since interest rates can't fall below zero, many of those who worry about deflation fear that the Federal Reserve would have little power left to support demand and fight deflation if interest rates were already low when deflation began.

What Can Be Done?

Despite a breathless tone of some of the media discussion about deflation, most economists did not want to exaggerate the danger. There are a number of monetary and fiscal tools available to stimulate demand and fight deflation, even after the short-term interest rate targeted by the Fed has been pushed down to zero (it was at 1 1/4 percent in 2003). Fed governor (now Chairman) Ben Bernanke discussed some of these tools in a November, 2002 speech. For example, he noted, the Fed could act to push down the interest rates not just of Federal Funds, but also on on longer-term government securities. That would promote lower rates on private loans and bonds, which are usually higher than short-term rates even when short-term rates are near zero. One powerful way to do this, Bernanke suggested, would be for the Fed to announce that it stood ready to make unlimited purchases of medium or even long-term Treasury securities at a price that would achieve some targeted low interest yield. Bernanke also suggested that, among other measures, the Fed could make interest-free loans to banks, accepting private debt as collateral and, if it became necessary, could ask the Congress for authority to buy private debt itself.

If such monetary policy measures were not enough, the Federal government could generate additional demand with a large, temporary stimulus of tax relief and spending measures. Since households are likely to spend a smaller fraction of a temporary than a permanent tax cut, the size of the reduction should be calibrated accordingly. As Bernanke suggested, the addition to the deficit created by the stimulus could be financed by direct Fed purchases of Treasury securities, so as to prevent the added deficit from raising interest rates and to avoid a large in-crease in the publicly held federal debt.

While likely harmful in a prosperous or rapidly recovering economy, these measures could be safe and highly useful in an economy with low inflation or deflation and plagued with chronically weak demand.

Is Japan a Model of What Inflation Can Do?

Japan's decade-long stagnation was accompanied by falling prices, but Japan is not necessarily an example of what inevitably follows from a modest deflation. In the first place, as economist Adam Posen has pointed out, Japan did not use the full range of monetary tools available to fight deflation. With respect to fiscal policy, the Japanese were reluctant to undertake aggressive stimulus, on grounds that their debt had already grown sharply relative to GDP. But this objection could be overcome by having the Bank of Japan buy the government securities needed to finance the stimulus—as suggested above for the U.S.

Japan also has some deep structural problems that are slowing the growth of investment that is desperately needed to help end stagnation. While Japan has developed a number of world-class export industries, a 2000 study by the McKinsey Global Institute showed that a substantial fraction of domestic output was produced by firms with productivity far below those in corresponding U.S. industries. The study documented the regulations, restrictions, land policies, subsidies, and tax incentives that have provided an anti-competitive shelter for inefficient business practices and firms. The potential for modernizing "catch-up" investment in a wide range of domestically oriented industries has been inhibited by this web of protective devices, and political opposition has kept the pace of liberalization slow.

Furthermore, following the bursting of its 1980s real estate bubble, the Japanese banking system became saddled with a massive volume of bad loans. Successive efforts to get the bad loans off the books and re-capitalize the banks were frustrated or watered down by entrenched interests within the Japanese Diet, because such a process might force many protected "zombie" firms into bankruptcy. It is difficult to determine the extent to which productive new investments have been deterred by an inability to get bank financing, rather than by the combined effects of stagnant aggregate demand and the protections afforded to existing business establishments. But it's probably much more the latter than the former.

Conclusion

Deflation, while not a likely forecast for the U.S., needs to be recognized as a downside risk, and the Fed is right to do so. This should, however, be kept in perspective. In particular, what has happened to Japan is not a model. The U.S. financial system is not hamstrung with a debilitating burden of bad loans. Compared to Japan, it shelters many fewer sectors from competition and imposes smaller barriers to investments that challenge existing industry structures. From a macroeconomic standpoint, the Federal Reserve has made explicit its intent to move promptly to counteract faltering demand, and its willingness to adopt innovative monetary tools should short-term interest rates fall to zero. Most important, it seems quite likely that the appearance of deflationary forces would lead to a substantial further economic stimulus. Indeed, in the current political climate, the main concern is not that the response would be insufficient, but that it would go beyond the needed temporary stimulus, providing yet another permanent tax cut and loading more debt burdens on future generations.

Source: Based in part on Charles L. Schultz, "How Much Should We Worry about a U.S. Deflation?" Brookings Institution, June 4, 2003.

QUESTIONS

1. Why is it important for U.S. policy makers to avoid a deflation?
2. If an economy were suffering from a fall in aggregate demand that caused deflation, and if the central bank refused to provide the stimulus needed to raise aggregate demand, what other actions could the government take to bring the economy out of its slump?
3. Suppose that an economy is suffering from a deflation and that the central bank has already cut short-term nominal interest rates to zero. What would the real short-term interest rate be if the price level was falling by 2 percent per year? 5 percent per year? Which would be more important as an influence on investment decisions, real or nominal rates? Why?

END NOTES

1. All figures for inflation given here are year-to-year percentage changes in the consumer price index.
2. This situation is sometimes called *stagflation*, but the term is not apt. The term *stagflation*—a combination of "stagnation" and "inflation"—was coined in the 1970s to describe a situation of slow or zero growth in real output, high inflation, and unemployment in excess of its natural rate. The term *inflationary recession* is more suitable for periods that combine high inflation rates with actual drops in real output. The 1974 to 1975 and 1980 recessions were inflationary recessions in this sense.
3. A. W. H. Phillips, "The Relationship between Unemployment and the Rate of Change of Money Wage Rages in the United Kingdom, 1861–1957," *Economica*, new series, 25 (November 1958): 283–299.

CHAPTER 14

Economic Growth, Productivity, and Saving

After reading this chapter, you will understand:

1. How the economy can grow while maintaining price stability
2. How insufficient growth of aggregate demand can cause growth with deflation
3. How expansion of aggregate demand at a faster rate than natural real output can cause inflation
4. Trends in U.S. productivity growth
5. What policies are available to promote economic growth

Before reading this chapter, make sure you know the meaning of:

1. Total factor productivity
2. Leakages and injections
3. Cyclical and structural deficits
4. Crowding-out effect
5. Inflation targeting

AN INCREASINGLY COMPETITIVE world economy is putting pressure on industry, agriculture, and service providers in the United States. The response varies. Some firms disappear as jobs are moved abroad. Some survive by turning to low-cost sources of labor, including both legal and illegal immigrants. But if the U.S. economy is to maintain and improve its high living standards over the long run, it must do what the orange growers of Immokalee, Florida did, as discussed in *Economics in the News 14.1.* That is to increase productivity both by investment in new equipment and by training workers to perform higher paying, high-skill jobs.

In this chapter, we will look at the issue of productivity using the same aggregate supply and demand tools that we applied in the chapter on inflation. We will begin by discussing the policies required for long-run economic growth without excessive

ECONOMICS IN THE NEWS 14.1

MECHANIZATION REDRAWS PROFILE OF AMERICAN AGRICULTURE

IMMOKALEE, Fla.—Chugging down a row of trees, the pair of canopy shakers in Paul Meador's orange grove here seem like a cross between a bulldozer and a hairbrush, their hungry steel bristles working through the tree crowns as if untangling colossal heads of hair. In under 15 minutes, the machines shake loose 36,000 pounds of oranges from 100 trees, catch the fruit, and drop it into a large storage car. "This would have taken four pickers all day long," Mr. Meador said.

Canopy shakers are still an unusual sight in Florida's orange groves. Most of the crop is harvested by hand, mainly by illegal Mexican immigrants. Nylon sacks slung across their backs, perched atop 16-foot ladders, they pluck oranges at a rate of 70 to 90 cents per 90-pound box, or less than $75 a day.

But as globalization creeps into the groves, it is threatening to displace the workers. Facing increased competition from Brazil and a glut of oranges on world markets, alarmed growers here have been turning to labor-saving technology as their best hope for survival.

"The Florida industry has to reduce costs to stay in business," said Everett Loukonen, agribusiness manager for the Barron Collier Company, which uses shakers to harvest about half of the 40.5 million pounds of oranges reaped annually from its 10,000 acres in southwestern Florida.

The spread of mechanization could redraw the profile of Immokalee, which today is a rather typical American farming town. Seventy-one percent of the population of 20,000 is Latino—with much of the balance coming from Haiti—and 46 percent of the residents are foreign born, according to the 2000 census. About 40 percent of the residents live under the poverty line, and the median family income is below $23,000—less than half that of the United States as a whole. Philip Martin, an economist at U.C. Davis, points to the poverty as an argument in favor of labor-saving technology. He estimates that about 10 percent of immigrant farm workers leave the fields every year to seek better jobs. Rather than push more farmhands out of work, he contends, introducing machines will simply reduce the demand for new workers to replenish the labor pool.

And there are some beneficiaries among workers: those lucky enough to operate the new gear. Perched in the air-conditioned booth of Mr. Meador's canopy shaker, a jumpy ranchera tune crackling from the radio, Felix Real, a former picker, said he can make up to $120 a day driving the contraption down the rows, about twice as much as he used to make.

Yet many Immokalee workers are nervous. "They are using the machines on the good groves and leaving us with the scraggly ones," said Venancio Torres, an immigrant from Mexico's coastal state of Veracruz, who has been picking oranges in Florida for three years.

Source: Eduardo Porter, "In Florida Groves, Cheap Labor Means Machines," *The New York Times*, March 22, 2004.

inflation. Next we will look at the record of productivity growth in the U.S. economy and likely future trends. Finally, we will discuss policies for promoting economic growth.

This chapter represents a return to the theme of long-run economic growth, with which led off our exploration of macroeconomics in Chapter 4. Now we will take advantage of the tools we have developed in the meantime to take a closer look at issues of growth and productivity. We will begin by discussing how monetary and fiscal policy can be used to manage aggregate demand in a way that maintains price stability and full employment during periods of economic growth. Next we will look at the record of productivity growth in the U.S. economy and likely future trends. Finally, we will discuss policies for promoting economic growth.

ECONOMIC GROWTH AND DEMAND MANAGEMENT

In Chapter 4, we saw that the sources of economic growth include both increases in the total quantity of inputs and increases in total factor productivity. Although much of this chapter will be concerned with issues of productivity, we will begin by looking at monetary and fiscal policy in an economy where increases in quantities of inputs with unchanged technology and skills are the only source of economic growth.

Demand Management as Inputs Grow

Figure 14.1 uses the aggregate supply and demand model to show the effects of growth of natural real output that arises from a steady, proportional increase in inputs of labor, capital, and natural resources. The economy starts out in equilibrium at E_0 with a natural real output of $1,500 billion per year, represented by the long-run aggregate supply curve N_0. Over time, as investment increases the stock of capital and population growth enlarges the labor force, the long-run aggregate supply curve shifts to the right to N_1.

As natural real output grows, the economy does not move up along its short-run aggregate supply curve as it does when aggregate demand shifts while natural output remains constant. Instead, the short-run aggregate supply curve shifts to the right along with the long-run curve. For the moment, we are assuming that growth results from increasing the quantity of labor and capital with no changes in technology or quality of inputs of the type that would change costs per unit of output. We also assume that there is no change in the expected level of productivity-adjusted input

FIGURE 14.1 GROWTH WITH STABLE PRICES

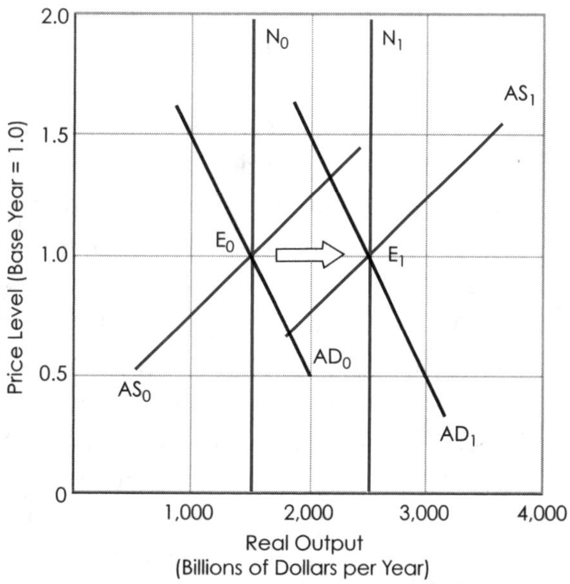

Over time, investment and growth of the labor force cause natural real output to rise with no change in productivity or costs per unit of output. As an increase in natural real output shifts the long-run aggregate supply curve from N_0 to N_1, the short-run aggregate supply curve also shifts to the right. If aggregate demand is allowed to grow at the same rate, the economy will move smoothly from its initial equilibrium at E_0 to a new equilibrium at E_1. Prices will be stable, and unemployment will remain at its natural rate.

prices. For these reasons, the intersection of the long-run and short-run curves will remain at the same price level, 1.0 in this case.

In Figure 14.1, the economy at first is able to produce $1,500 billion of goods and services at a price level of 1.0. The shift in natural real output means that the economy can now potentially produce $2,500 billion of goods and services at the same price level. In order to actually achieve this, however, there must be appropriate growth of aggregate demand. If, as shown in the figure, the aggregate demand curve shifts to the right by the same amount as natural real output, firms will be able to sell all the output produced at the new natural level without cutting their prices. Under these conditions the economy will move smoothly from E_0 to E_1. At these points, as well as all points in between, the economy will remain in long-run equilibrium. Prices will be stable; productivity-adjusted input prices will remain at the level expected by business managers; real output will keep up with its rising natural level; and unemployment will be steady at its natural rate.

GROWTH RECESSION Figure 14.1 shows the ideal condition of steady economic growth with no inflation or excessive unemployment. However, the economy does not always run smoothly. One danger is that fiscal and monetary policy may be mismanaged in a way that disturbs the smooth growth of the economy. Figure 14.2 shows what happens when aggregate demand fails to keep up with natural real output.

As before, the economy starts from equilibrium at E_0. Natural real output then rises from $1,500 billion to $2,500 billion, as shown by the shift of the long-run aggregate supply curve from N_0 to N_1. The short-run aggregate supply curve also shifts rightward, to AS_1. This time, however, tight monetary and fiscal policies restrain the growth of aggregate demand. With the aggregate demand curve stuck at AD_0, the economy cannot reach the intersection of AS_1 with N_1.

What will happen? If real output initially increases in line with the increases in inputs while aggregate demand remains unchanged, unplanned inventory buildup will take place. Firms' managers are disappointed; they are producing more than before, but they cannot sell all their output at the prices that prevailed previously. To keep stocks of unsold goods from building up, firms cut their prices, hoping to boost sales. At the same time, they cut back their production plans. They increase output a little, but not by as much as the growth of natural real output. Thus, as the long-run aggregate supply curve shifts from N_0 to N_1 and the short-run aggregate supply curve shifts with it, firms' price and output cuts are moving them downward and to the left along the new aggregate supply curve, AS_1. The economy thus moves to E_1, where the aggregate demand curve AD_0, which has not moved from its original position, intersects AS_1. Given the increased inputs of capital and labor, the economy could produce $2,500 billion in real output; but at E_1, output is only about $1,800 billion. The feeble growth in real output means that not enough jobs will be created to absorb all the new workers entering the labor force. Thus, the unemployment rate will rise. If workers resist cuts in nominal wages even though the prices of goods they buy are falling, adjustment will be even slower.

FIGURE 14.2 GROWTH RECESSION

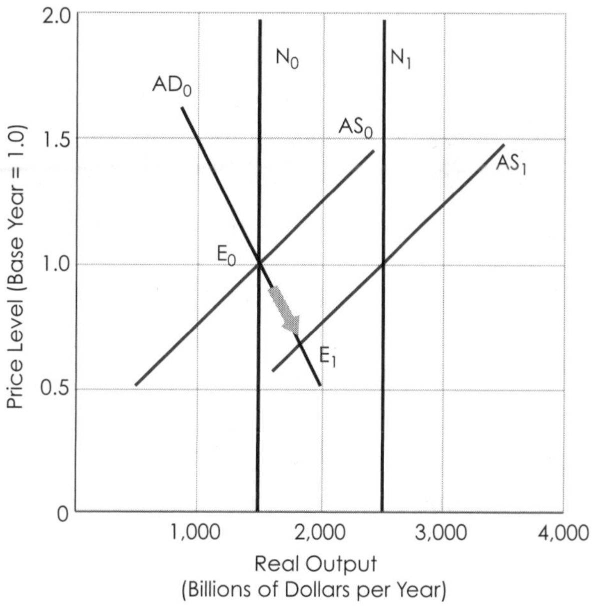

In the case shown here, natural real output grows while aggregate demand remains fixed. Thus, as the long- and short-run aggregate supply curves shift to the right, the aggregate demand curve remains unchanged. The economy moves down and to the right along the aggregate demand curve and at the same time moves down and to the left along the new short-run aggregate supply curve, AS_1, as it shifts to the right. The economy experiences falling prices and ends up at E_1, where unemployment is higher than its natural rate even though real output has grown. This is sometimes called a growth recession.

A situation in which real output grows, but not by enough to keep the price level from falling or unemployment from rising above its natural rate, is a form of deflation. Unlike the Japanese deflation examined in the preceding chapter, real output does not actually fall, but it does not grow enough to keep up with potential real output. Because this situation combines rising output with rising unemployment, it is sometimes called a **growth recession.**

Growth recession

A situation in which real output grows, but not quickly enough to keep unemployment from rising.

GROWTH WITH INFLATION Growth with deflation results from overly cautious economic policy. The economy has the capacity to grow, but policy makers do not give it the room it needs. In the United States, however, policy makers have more often made the opposite mistake: They have pushed the economy beyond the ability of natural real output to grow. The result has been growth with inflation.

The situation of growth with inflation is another form of the demand-side inflation discussed in Chapter 13. The difference, as Figure 14.3 shows, is that growth of natural real output is now shifting the long-run aggregate supply curve to the right. As it does so, the short-run aggregate supply curve shifts with it. While natural real output grows from $1,000 billion to $2,000 billion, expansionary monetary or fiscal policy boosts the level of aggregate demand even more forcefully. The new aggregate demand curve, AD_1, intersects the new short-run aggregate supply curve, AS_1, at E_1. The actual level of real output rises above its natural level and unemployment falls below its natural rate.

The inflation experienced as the economy moves from E_0 to E_1, the economy experiences demand-pull inflation, which will affect expectations in the following period. When the expected level of input prices rises, the short-run aggregate supply curve will be pushed upward at the same time that growth in natural real output carries both the short- and long-run aggregate supply curves farther to the right. On balance, the short-run curve will end up in the position AS_2. To keep real output above its natural level by the same amount, the aggregate demand curve would have to shift to a position such as AD_2. In moving from E_1 to E_2, output would stay exactly the same distance above its natural level, keeping unemployment steady at a value somewhat below its natural rate. However, prices will rise by more than they did during the move from E_0 to E_1. Over time, inflation could get out of control, accelerating to a point at which it could not easily be stopped without a painful inflationary recession.

FIGURE 14.3 GROWTH WITH INFLATION

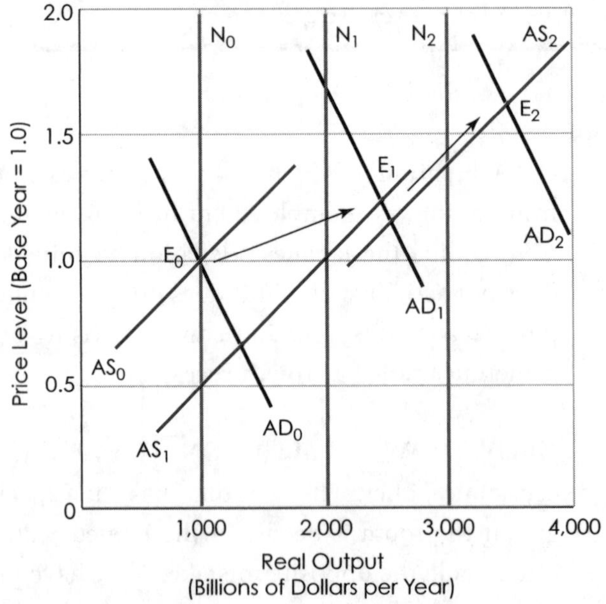

In this example, aggregate demand is allowed to grow more rapidly than natural real output. As the economy grows, it also experiences demand-side inflation. As the economy moves from E_0 to E_1, the unemployment rate falls and there is only mild inflation. If aggregate demand is expanded aggressively to try to keep unemployment below its natural rate, inflation will accelerate.

Demand Management and Productivity Growth

Up to this point, we have looked only at growth resulting from increased inputs, with no changes in unit costs or productivity. In reality, increases in total factor productivity are a very important source of economic growth. Figure 14.4 shows how the problem of demand management is affected when productivity change is introduced.

As in our earlier examples, we assume that the economy begins from a position of equilibrium at E_0, where real output is at its natural level of Q_0 and the price level is P_0. Over time, the natural level of real output increases, the long-run aggregate supply curve shifts rightward from N_0 to N_1. This time, at least part of the growth is caused by improvements in skills or technology. The resulting increase in total factor productivity means that if input prices are expected to remain unchanged, the expected cost of production per unit of output will decrease. In the figure, this is reflected in a downward shift of the short-run aggregate supply curve from AS_0 to AS_1.

How should policy makers respond to the growth in productivity? One option would be to follow an inflation-targeting strategy. To maintain complete price stability, the central bank would need to allow aggregate demand to increase as shown by

FIGURE 14.4 ECONOMIC GROWTH WITH PRODUCTIVITY CHANGE

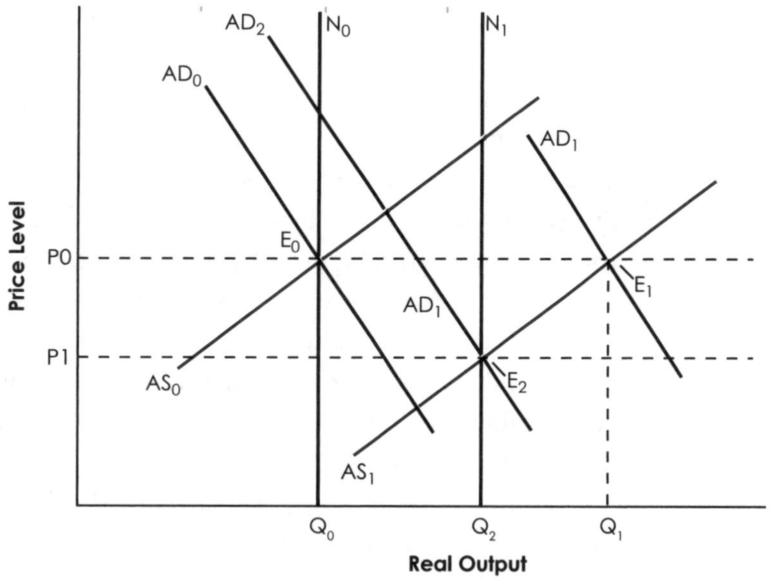

As productivity increases, the long-run aggregate supply curve shifts rightward to N_1. At the same time, decreased unit costs shift the short-run aggregate supply curve downward to AS_1. With an inflation-targeting strategy, aggregate demand would have to be increased to AD_1 to hold the price level at P_0, and a positive output gap would develop. Alternatively, increasing aggregate demand only to AD_2 would allow the price level to fall to P_1 while holding real output at its new natural level and avoiding any distortions associated with an output gap.

the curve AD_1, or a little more if the target rate of inflation were slightly above zero. AD_1 intersects the new aggregate supply curve AS_1 at E_1, where the level of real output is significantly higher than the new natural level of real output shown by N_2.

Alternatively, policy makers could aim at a slower rate of growth of aggregate demand, just enough to keep up with the growth of natural real output. To accomplish this, the aggregate demand curve would need to shift only to AD_2. The new point of equilibrium would be E_2. Real output would just reach its new natural level, and the price level would fall to P_1.

Which of these two policies is better? As discussed in Chapter 13, the first alternative, inflation targeting, is a popular one. It is the official policy today of many central banks around the world. Others that have not officially adopted inflation targeting, including the Federal Reserve and the European Central Bank, in practice place a high priority on controlling inflation. Those who favor inflation targeting argue that an expectation of low inflation provides a stable climate for business planning and best serves the goals of stability and prosperity in the long run.

On the other hand, inflation targeting during a period of rapid productivity growth has some potential drawbacks. As shown in Figure 14.4, the reduction in labor and other inputs required per unit of output causes the short-run aggregate supply curve to move downward. In order to keep output prices from falling, the central bank must reduce interest rates below the level that would allow real GDP just to keep up with growth of its natural level. As the aggregate demand curve shifts to a position like AD_1, a positive output gap develops and unemployment falls below its natural level.

Over time, the combination of low unemployment and tight industrial capacity will put upward pressure on wages and other input prices. As this happens, the short-run aggregate supply curve begins to shift upward from the position AS_1. Now the central bank must again adjust its monetary policy. If it were to maintain policy at the expansionary level shown by AD_1, inflation would develop, somewhat like the scenario shown earlier in Figure 14.3. Instead, it can raise its target interest rate to shift the aggregate demand curve to a position intermediate between AD_1 and AD_2. Ideally, the end result would be a situation where the short-run aggregate supply and aggregate demand curves intersect at the new natural level of output Q_2, with the price level remaining at or close to P_0 throughout the adjustment.

As long ago as the 1930s, the Austrian economist Frederick Hayek expressed concern about the kind of policy we have described. Hayek argued that trying to keep inflation at zero or a little higher during a period of rapid productivity growth would destabilize the economy. First the central bank would have to push interest rates to an abnormally low level in order to keep prices from falling in the face of reduced output costs. Then, as low unemployment and capacity constraints forced wages and other input prices upward, interest rates would have to be raised higher than normal to restrain inflation. During the period of low interest rates, businesses would be induced to make excessive investments in projects with long payback periods. When interest rates rose these investments would turn out to be unprofitable. A wave of business failures would cause a collapse of demand. Instead of coming to rest at the new level of natural real output, the economy would overshoot its equilibrium and enter a boom-and-bust cycle. Hayek saw the Great Depression as just such a bust, coming, as it did, after a long period of price stability and rapid productivity growth in the 1920s.

For many years, Hayek's analysis was overshadowed, first by Keynesian prescriptions for getting the economy out of the Depression and then by Keynesian-Monetarist controversies during the inflationary 1960s and 1970s. Recently, however, economists have showed renewed interest in many of the issues central to Hayek's earlier work. In particular, many economists have become concerned with the problem of **asset bubbles**. Asset bubbles are rapid increases in the price of assets like stocks, housing, or commercial real-estate that appear to be out of line with prevailing, moderate, increases in prices of final goods. Recent examples of asset bubbles in the United States are the rapid increase in "dot.com" technology stocks in the 1990s, and the boom in residential real estate in the early 2000s. The dot.com boom, which occurred during a period of rapid productivity growth, low inflation, and falling unemployment, was followed by the recession of 2001. Some economists interpret this as a modern Hayekian episode. As this is written in early 2007, some also fear that the end of the recent housing boom will be followed by a new recession.

Asset bubbles

A rapid increase in the price of assets, like stocks or housing, that is out of line with the prevailing rate of inflation.

Economists who are concerned about this kind of boom-and-bust cycle argue that central banks should tighten monetary policy more quickly when asset bubbles begin to develop. Doing so might require allowing inflation to fall below the rates of 1-3 percent usually proposed by inflation-targeting advocates, perhaps even allowing periods of moderate deflation. Such deflation need not have the full range of negative side effects seen, for example, in Japan in the 1990s. In particular, when productivity growth is rapidly increasing output per labor hour, moderate deflation of output prices is not incompatible with moderate increases in workers' real and nominal wages.

All of this remains an area in which macroeconomic theory and policy is still developing. At present, there is no clear consensus as to exactly how central bankers should deal with asset bubbles or whether moderate deflation is sometimes beneficial during periods of rapid productivity growth.

RECENT TRENDS IN ECONOMIC GROWTH AND PRODUCTIVITY

In this section, we will consider where gains in productivity come from. As we did in Chapter 4, we will break the sources of growth of natural real output into two components: the growth of total labor inputs, on the one hand, and the growth of output per unit of labor, or *labor productivity*, on the other.

The growth of total labor inputs tends to be determined by social and demographic factors that differ from one country to another, but that do not change rapidly within any one country. Taking all factors into account, total hours worked in the U.S. economy have grown at a steady but moderate pace in recent decades. In contrast, as Figure 14.5 shows, growth of labor productivity has varied substantially over the past half century. Setting aside substantial short-term cyclical variations, productivity trends can be broken into three longer periods. From 1960 to 1973, productivity grew at an average rate of about 2.8 percent, continuing a trend that had begun at the end of World War II. Then, from 1974 to 1991, productivity growth fell by more than half, to an average annual rate of just 1.5 percent. Since the early 1990s, the productivity slowdown has been reversed, growing at a 2.7 percent annual rate from 1995 through 2000 and even faster, at 3.1 percent, from 2000 to 2005.

Explaining the Productivity Slowdown and Its Reversals

The productivity slowdown of the 1970s and 1980s and the more recent productivity boom have been the subject of extensive study. The following factors are among those most often cited as contributing to varying productivity trends:

- **Changes in the labor force.** Many analyses of the earlier productivity slowdown point to the entry of millions of women and young people into the labor force during the 1970s. These new workers were, on the whole, capable and motivated, but they tended to have less experience than those who

FIGURE 14.5 U.S. PRODUCTIVITY GROWTH

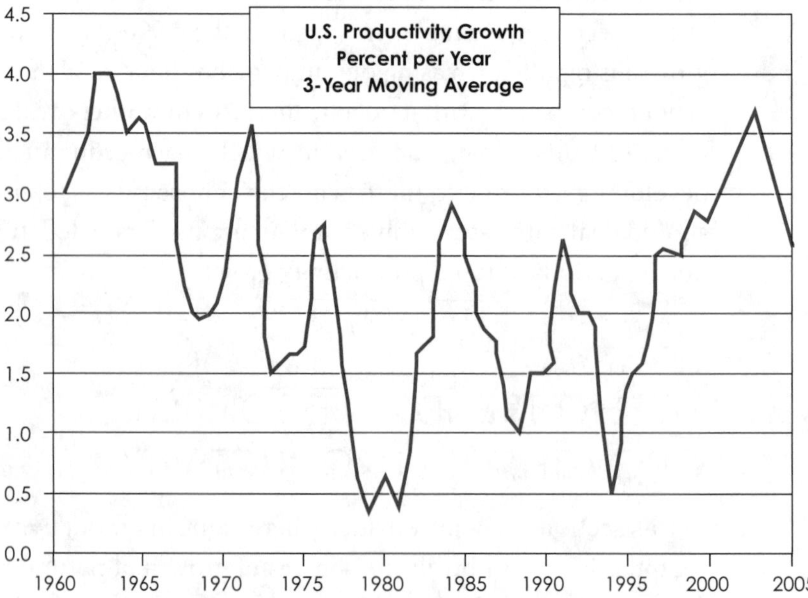

From 1960 through 1973, productivity grew at an average annual rate of 3.1 percent. From 1974 to 1991, productivity growth slowed substantially, to an average of just 1.5 percent per year. Since the mid-1990s, productivity growth has recovered.

Source: *Economic Report of the President*, 2007, table B-50.

already held jobs. At the same time, by their sheer number they pulled down the ratio of capital to labor. By the 1990s, these demographic changes had worked their way through, allowing historic productivity trends to resume.

- **Supply shocks.** Some economists believe that the oil price shocks of the 1970s contributed to the productivity slowdown by rendering much of the economy's capital stock obsolete. Many inefficient older trucks, planes, furnaces, generators, and so on had to be retired or placed on standby because high oil prices made them too costly to operate. The effect was almost the same as if the equipment had been destroyed by fire or flood. Moreover, it is argued, the oil price shocks made it necessary to rechannel much investment into finding ways to get by with less oil—either through the design of more energy-efficient equipment or through the production of substitute energy sources—rather than into other productivity-enhancing areas of research. By the end of the 1980s, the effects of these supply shocks had run their course, leaving a leaner, more efficient capital stock as a basis for further growth.
- **Research and technology.** During the 1970s, research and development spending fell from a high of 3 percent of GDP to a low of 2.2 percent in 1977. Some economists have seen the R&D slowdown as a major culprit in the stagnation of productivity. In the 1980s and even more in the 1990s, these trends were reversed and replaced by a technology boom, as businesses made huge investments in computers and communications technology. At first the impact of these on economy-wide productivity was disappointing, but after a period of learning and organizational change the new technologies began to pay off in a big way. Some economists see the spurt of productivity in the early 2000s as a delayed result of technology investments of the preceding decade.
- **Inflation.** As we saw in the preceding chapter, inflation is an enemy of economic growth. The productivity slowdown of the 1970s occurred at the same time as the speedup of inflation. Inflation disrupted business planning and labor-management relations, and distorted the impact of taxes on business and investment income. This not only reduced total investment but also tended to channel investment toward uses that did little to enhance productivity, such as housing and tax shelters, and away from more productive projects. Since 1992, inflation has returned to the moderate range of 1 to 3 percent. Many economists think it is not coincidental that the moderation of inflation coincided with the revival of productivity growth.

International Productivity Trends

The United States was not the only country to experience a productivity slowdown in the 1970s. Instead, the slowdown affected most of the major industrialized countries. For example, the rate of increase in output per worker-hour in manufacturing, one frequently cited measure of productivity, fell from 3.2 percent per year in the period from 1960 to 1973 and to 1.4 percent per year in the period from 1973 to 1979 in the United States. However, over the same period the annual rate of growth of manufacturing output per worker-hour fell from 10.3 percent to 5.5 percent in Japan; from 6.4 to 4.6 percent in France; from 6.4 to 2.6 percent in Sweden; and from 4.2 to 1.2 percent in the United Kingdom.[1]

On the other hand, the revival of productivity growth in the United States has not been duplicated in many other advanced countries. Productivity growth has continued to lag in the European Union, a development that some observers blame on overly rigid central regulation and insufficiently flexible labor markets. And, as discussed in *Economics in the News 14.2,* Japan, which used to be seen as a world productivity leader, has fallen behind.

Measurement Problems

A major reason that productivity is so hard to understand is that the whole field is plagued by serious measurement problems. Productivity numbers attempt to measure output per unit of input. That is simple enough when the output is a standardized good for which quality does not change over time, such as coal or lumber; but much of the economy does not fit this pattern.

For one thing, an increasing portion of the economy is devoted to producing goods for which quality changes are more important than quantity changes. Computers are the classic example, but quality changes in such areas as pharmaceuticals, aircraft, and even automobiles are hardly less striking. National income statisticians try to capture some of these quality changes in their measures of output, but their efforts are not fully successful. Economist John Kendrick of Georgetown University, a leading expert on productivity, thinks that failure to adjust fully for quality changes leads to a 0.36 percentage point understatement in the annual rate of growth of real GDP.[2] This, in turn, reduces estimates of productivity growth.

Moreover, the measurement problems get worse when we turn from goods-producing industries to services, which now account for some two-thirds of GDP. After 1973, official measures of productivity in the service sector fell to nearly zero, and according to some data, even became negative. But what do the numbers pertaining to service-industry productivity actually mean?

In the opinion of a growing number of economists, they mean very little. The basic problem is the impossibility of measuring the output of services in quantity terms. Suppose, for example, that an insurance company raises its premiums without changing the numbers of people it employs or types of policies that it offers. Perhaps the increase reflects the need to cover increases in the risks to which policyholders are exposed, say, a rising crime rate. In that case, it could be argued that the increased revenue reflects greater service to customers, and hence, an increase in productivity. But perhaps the premium increase simply reflects higher costs. In that case, output

ECONOMICS IN THE NEWS 14.2

TALE OF TWO ECONOMIES

One of the most remarkable developments of the last 10 years was the dual reversal of fortune by the world's two largest economies—the simultaneous economic ascendance of the United States and decline of Japan. Fiscal and monetary policies certainly contributed in both instances. However, new research shows that microeconomic factors, especially the different organization and strategies of the two countries' information technology sectors, may have been more important.

Information technology may matter less than "New Economy" promoters once claimed, but the strength and length of the 1990s U.S. boom clearly owed much to IT. According to first-rate analysis by the Commerce Department, IT companies, while constituting less than 8 percent of the GDP, accounted for nearly 30 percent of U.S. economic growth from 1995 to 2000. Harvard's Dale Jorgenson and the Fed's Kevin Stiroh trace more than three-fourths of increased U.S. productivity growth to IT advances and strong business investment to deploy those advances.

Throughout the '80s, many Americans envied Japan its technological prowess, but there is a strong case that Japan's IT weakness magnified its slow growth and weak productivity gains in the '90s. One of Japan's top economists, Rizaburo Nezu of the Fujitsu Research Institute, has recently documented the various and complex ways in which, less than a generation after Japanese firms pioneered the miniaturization and marketing of electronics, Japan has "disappeared from world IT competition."

Today, the world's 10 largest IT companies include six American firms but only one Japanese company, the mobile phone and ISP giant NTT DoCoMo. Japan's domestic macroeconomic troubles cannot explain this. IT companies draw on global markets and technologies. For the last decade, companies could borrow money in Tokyo to develop or buy IT technologies more cheaply than in New York. And since 1990, Japanese firms have invested in R & D and in IT hardware at higher rates than their U.S. counterparts.

Yet the '90s saw Japanese IT fail spectacularly, market segment by market segment. The main culprits were the flawed strategies and organization of Japanese IT companies. The semiconductor industry is, in many ways, the very heart of IT development. Twelve years ago, U.S. and Japanese firms each controlled more than 40 percent of the world market. Over the next decade, their corporate strategies diverged; by 2000, American chip makers accounted for 55 percent of global semiconductor sales, and Japanese companies were left with just 25 percent. Leading chip makers in Japan (and Europe) tried to produce all kinds of chips. This strategy required them to diffuse their R & D resources. As they fell behind technologically, their market share eroded. Their counterparts in America (and Korea) concentrated on a few, select classes of chips and vastly expanded their market share.

American firms today control two-thirds of the world PC market and 80 percent of global server sales. In each case, Japanese producers account for less than 5 percent. Again, contrasting production strategies may explain the Japanese's also-ran status. The American companies that have come to dominate PC and server sales—Dell, IBM, Sun Microsystems, Compaq, and HP—concentrate on procurement, logistics, and after-sales service and leave most of the computer design and production to firms like Taiwan's Quanta and Acer. Japan's once-great computer makers—Fujitsu, Toshiba, and Sony—have persisted in doing almost everything at home and for themselves, an increasingly improvident strategy in an era of globalization.

Source: Robert Shapiro, "The IT Split," *Slate*, August 21, 2002 (abbreviated from original article).

per worker is unchanged. Not knowing how to measure output, the government reports no productivity figures for the insurance industry at all.

No productivity figures are reported for health care, real estate, or stock brokerage services, either. In all, figures are reported for industries employing only 30 percent of all service workers. In some of those for which figures are reported, the data are tainted by measurement problems. For example, in banking, output is counted in terms of the number of trust accounts maintained and number of checks cleared, with no adjustment for the dollar volume of each transaction. Nor is there any attempt to measure the improvement in quality resulting from the many new services banks have added in recent years.

Small wonder that a productivity expert like Michael Darby, formerly chief economist at the Commerce Department, says frankly, "At our current state of knowledge, we don't really know what's happening to service-sector productivity. It could well be growing faster than manufacturing productivity, instead of much slower."[3]

POLICIES FOR PROMOTING ECONOMIC GROWTH AND SAVING

Throughout this book, we have listed growth of real output as one of the fundamental goals of macroeconomic policy. Economists from a variety of schools of thought, who disagree on many other things, see growth as important both to improvement in material welfare and to maintenance of national security. Accordingly, a variety of policies designed to promote growth have been advanced.

One element of growth policy commands widespread agreement: As we saw in the first section of this chapter, policy makers must allow a rate of growth of aggregate demand that will at least roughly match that of natural real output. If demand is permitted to grow too rapidly, inflation will be higher. Rapid inflation, as we have seen, may have been one of the villains of the productivity slowdown of the 1970s. On the other hand, if demand grows too slowly, the economy may slip into a deflationary contraction.

In addition to policies designed to match the growth of actual and natural real output, policies have been proposed that are intended to promote the growth of natural real output itself. First we will consider the use of conventional monetary and fiscal policy tools to promote such growth. We then consider policies that aim to increase the economy's growth potential by encouraging saving and investment.

Economic Growth and the Fiscal-Monetary Policy Mix

There is more than one way to achieve a given level or rate of growth of aggregate demand. But although a mix of expansionary fiscal policy and tight monetary policy might produce the same growth rate of aggregate demand as a mix of tight fiscal policy and expansionary monetary policy, the two policy mixes have different effects on interest rates. Our basic macroeconomic model suggests that an easy monetary/tight fiscal policy mix leads to lower real and nominal interest rates than a tight monetary/easy fiscal policy mix. Because the easy monetary/tight fiscal policy mix yields lower real interest rates, it also results in more real investment.

The economists President Kennedy brought to Washington in the early 1960s relied in part on this principle to help fulfill Kennedy's campaign pledge to "get the country moving again." They saw no problem with federal budget deficits as a means of pulling the economy out of a recession, but they firmly believed that the deficit should disappear as the economy approached its natural level of real output. If it did not, the deficit would crowd out private investment and slow economic growth.

In the 1990s, the idea of shifting the policy mix toward tighter fiscal and easier monetary policies to promote growth again became popular. In one form or another, the concept was endorsed by all three major candidates in the 1992 presidential elections. For example, the first President Bush declared that "the primary economic goal of my Administration is to achieve the highest possible rate of economic growth." He announced a plan to promote growth through a combination of spending cuts to eliminate the federal budget deficit, combined with tax incentives to further stimulate investment. Victorious candidate Bill Clinton also pledged deficit reduction as a key to faster growth, taking the political risk of stating that cutting the deficit would require tax increases. This strategy paid off. As we saw in earlier chapters, the U.S. federal budget returned to surplus in the 1990s for the first time in a generation. The surpluses reversed the crowding-out effect of deficits and helped finance the technology investments that have since boosted productivity growth.

The budget surpluses of the 1990s disappeared in the first decade of the twenty-first century, however. President George W. Bush used expansionary fiscal policy, in the form of broad tax cuts, to speed recovery from the 2001 recession. Later, a sharp rise in federal spending, including both the enormous cost of financing the Iraq war and growth in domestic spending, pushed deficits to record levels. By 2004, the federal budget deficit had reached an all-time record, and the Federal Reserve was once again warning that the fiscal-monetary policy mix was seriously out of balance.

Growth and Saving

As noted in earlier chapters, investment must be financed either by saving that takes place within the country, or by inflows of capital from abroad. Accordingly, economists concerned with growth have noted with alarm a sharp decline in net national saving in the United States. Net national saving is a broad measure that combines business and household saving with the government surplus (saving) or deficit (dissaving). As shown in Figure 14.6, net national saving has trended downward in recent decades. The only major exception to the trend was a brief recovery around the turn of the century that coincided with the unusual federal budget surpluses of that time. In the early twenty-first century, net national saving has reached record lows. This reflected both a return of large budget deficits and exceptionally low personal saving.

Private and government savings are also important in terms of trade and borrowing from abroad. Recall the relationship between private savings (S), investment (I), the government budget (T – G), and the current account surplus or deficit, (EX – IM):

$$(EX - IM) = (T - G) + (S - I)$$

FIGURE 14.6 NET NATIONAL SAVING

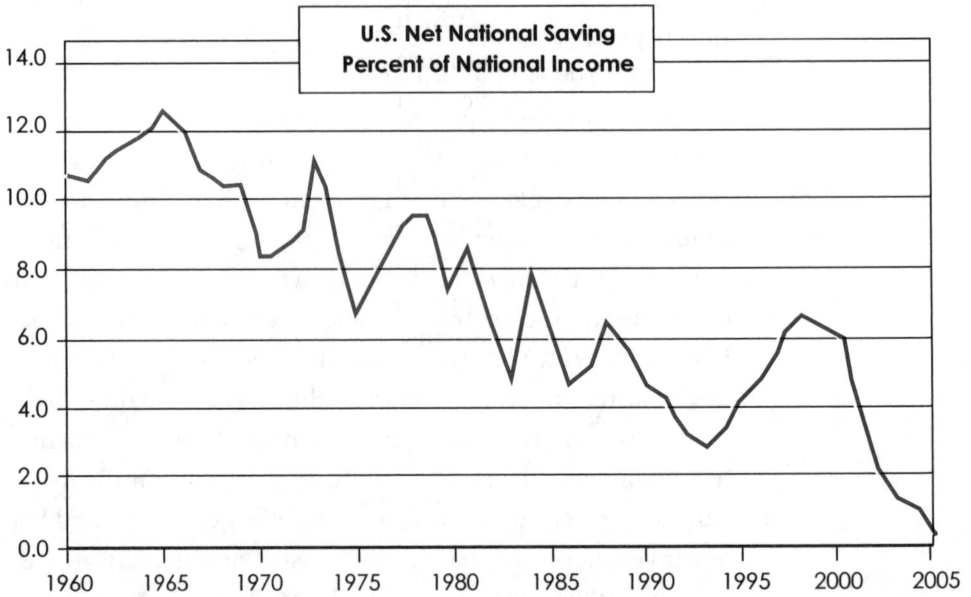

As the chart shows, U.S. net national savings has been on a downward trend in recent decades. The only substantial exception was the brief period of budget surpluses around the turn of the century. Since that time, budget deficits have returned, and in 2005 net national saving fell to a new low.

Source: *Economic Report of the President*, 2007, Table B-32.

Other things being equal, budget deficits have a negative effect on the current account. If the U.S. runs a federal budget deficit, then (T – G) is negative, causing a movement toward deficit in the current account (EX – IM). The current account also represents net capital flows. An excess of imports over exports must be financed by a net capital inflow into the U.S.—that is, by net borrowing from abroad plus net sales of assets to foreign buyers—so that the value of the current account deficit and the value of capital inflows are equal. As we saw in earlier chapters, the record federal budget deficits of the early 2000s have been financed largely by financial inflows in the form of purchases of U.S. government securities by Asian central banks.

Government policy makers and independent economists have recommended a variety of policies to promote saving. Some emphasize increasing the rate of return on saving, for example, by making income from savings wholly or partially tax exempt. Tax-deferred Individual Retirement Accounts are an example of such a policy.

How Much Saving Is Enough?

In the debate over the saving shortfall and policies to deal with it, one question is almost never asked: How much saving is enough? Participants in the debate almost universally agree that more saving is better. What is more, they do not always limit themselves to positive economic arguments regarding the effects of saving on capital accumulation and growth. Many commentators are given to sweeping normative declarations to the effect that low savings "cheat the future" and to condemnations of a culture that allegedly "bombards us with messages to buy things—not save." In short, a low saving rate is perceived as a sign of moral weakness.

But there are counterarguments to these claims. First, the primary reason saving is valued is that it promotes more rapid economic growth. Yet there is a long tradition in economics that questions the unlimited desirability of economic growth itself. (See Who Said It? Who Did It? 4.1 for an example.) This anti-growth tradition is manifested today in certain parts of the environmental movement that identify excessive growth of material output, combined with inadequate attention to nonmaterial sources of human welfare, as the root of many current problems from the extinction of species to global warming.

Second, the welfare of future generations is constantly evoked in the debate over saving. But as long as growth of per capita real income does not come to a stop altogether (and it has not done so), future generations will be richer than our own. Saving thus is a transfer from the relatively poor present to the relatively rich future. Why is such a transfer desirable, considering that most people favor transfers from the rich to the poor rather than from the poor to the rich within any given generation? This question is never asked or answered by proponents of a higher saving rate.

Finally, why should the private component of national saving be a matter of public policy in the first place? After all, personal and business saving are not the result of decisions reached in some big town meeting—they are the outcome of millions of individual decisions by households and business managers. In the case of households, we are willing to leave people free to choose whether to buy better food (consumption) or buy a better house (saving) and free to choose how much of their lifetime income to enjoy themselves and how much to leave to their children. In the case of firms, we are content to leave stockholders, acting through their agents in corporate management, free to choose between reinvestment of earnings and distribution of dividends. If we are content to leave all these microlevel choices up to individuals, why should we not be content with whatever national saving rate results from adding together their outcomes?

The debate over the saving shortfall would be more enlightening if the question of how much saving is enough were at least considered.

SUMMARY

1. **How can the economy grow while maintaining price stability?** As growth of natural real output shifts the long-run aggregate supply curve to the right, the short-run aggregate supply curve will shift with it, provided there is no change in the expected level of productivity-adjusted input prices. If aggregate demand is allowed to grow at the same rate as natural real output, the aggregate demand curve will shift along with the others. Under these conditions output will grow smoothly, final-goods prices will be stable, and unemployment will remain at its natural rate.

2. **How can insufficient growth of aggregate demand lead to growth combined with deflation?** If aggregate demand does not keep up with the growth of natural real output, firms will be unable to sell all the output they are able to produce. Unplanned inventory buildup will put downward pressure on prices and cause the actual level of real output to grow more slowly than the natural level. The result is growth with deflation, or a *growth recession,* during which real output grows but the unemployment rate rises. However, if improvements in productivity cause downward movement of the aggregate real supply curve, moderate deflation may be consistent with a policy of maintaining full employment and a zero output gap.

3. **How can expansion of aggregate demand at a faster rate than natural real output cause inflation?** If aggregate demand grows faster than natural real output, demand-pull inflation will result.-If inflation targeting is used to hold price increases to a moderate rate, lasting prosperity is possible. However, if growth of aggregate demand is excessive, inflation will accelerate. This condition may be difficult to reverse without triggering an inflationary recession.

4. **What factors explain substantial swings in the rate of U.S. productivity growth over the past half century?** From the end of World War II until the early 1970s, productivity growth averaged 2.8 percent per year. From 1973 to 1991, it fell to about half of that, before recovering during the later 1990s. Explanations for these fluctuations include changes in the age and gender composition of the labor force, supply shocks caused by oil price increases, inflation, changes in spending on research and development, and trends in technology. No one of these factors seems to fully explain the swings in productivity. Problems in measuring productivity, especially in the service sector, add to the difficulties of fully understanding productivity trends.

5. **What policies are available to promote economic growth?** According to our basic macroeconomic model, growth will be promoted by a policy mix that includes a structurally balanced budget and a monetary policy leading to relatively low interest rates. Economic growth can be promoted by other policies encouraging saving and investment, as well. In addition, growth could potentially be stimulated by tax policies designed to encourage saving and investment.

KEY TERMS

Growth recession   Asset bubbles

PROBLEMS AND TOPICS FOR DISCUSSION

1. **Productivity in the orange grove.** Review *Economics in the News 14.1.* How do improvements in technology increase the rate of economic growth? What adjustment of monetary and fiscal

policy is needed when technology investments cause the growth of natural real output to accelerate? What are the possible sources of saving needed to finance investments in technology? Who gains, and who loses when technological change occurs?

2. **Personal saving.** Most people have negative saving when they are young (that is, they consume more than their income), have positive saving during their prime working years, and then have negative saving again in retirement. Do you expect your own saving to follow this pattern? Why or why not?

3. **Latest productivity data.** The latest data on productivity in the United States are available online from the Bureau of Labor Statistics (http://www.bls.gov/lpc/home.htm). How do the latest data compare with those reported in Figure 14.5? Looking at the details of the BLS reports, in what sectors is productivity growing fastest? Slowest?

CASE FOR DISCUSSION

The Great American Savings Shortfall

At the turn of the twenty-first century, American consumers helped to keep the economy afloat through a relatively short recession in 2001and speed the following recovery. Tax cuts and low interest rates encouraged people to borrow and spend. Low saving, however, leaves us in a quandary: Don't we need to save now to afford the coming surge in retirements from the baby boom generation? The personal savings rate in the U.S. at 2% or less. How do policy makers boost saving without threatening economic recovery?

There is little agreement regarding what to do about the saving rate. Some advocate traditional economic incentives, including a cut in capital gains taxes (such as those implemented by President George W. Bush), tax-favored family savings plans, and reforms to Social Security. Others recommend alternatives such as investment tax credits to encourage business saving. Frank Levy of the University of Maryland and Richard C. Michel of the Urban Institute maintain that the problem is less about tax incentives than about culture—a culture, they say, that "bombards us with messages to buy things—not save—every day." In this context, they see the key to increased saving as "a change in national outlook."*

Levy and Michel suggest that we think of under saving as cholesterol. "Both are the byproduct of immediate gratification, neither involves short-run cost, both accrue slowly with real dangers for the future." If policymakers are serious about the saving shortfall, they say, they should talk as plainly about it as doctors talk about cholesterol. Why not publish national guidelines on what people ought to save—a simple schedule that relates annual savings to family income and age? "In a word, with guidelines on everything from salt intake to safe sex, a problem without guidelines is not seen as a problem," Levy and Michel conclude.

*Frank Levy and Richard C. Michel, "Why America Won't Save," *The Washington Post*, February 4, 1990, p. C1.

QUESTIONS

1. How would you define "under saving"? Are you yourself under saving? Is the country as a whole? How would you go about determining the ideal rate of national saving? Or is more saving always better, without limit?
2. The article suggests that saving, like eating a healthy diet, involves a trade-off between present and future gratification. Use a production possibility frontier to illustrate this trade-off. Label the horizontal axis "saving" and the vertical axis "consumption." First draw a frontier that is based

on a fixed current income. Mark a point A on the frontier that represents a relatively low saving rate and a point B that represents a relatively high rate. Next draw two frontiers that represent future income levels—one based on saving rate A and the other on saving rate B. Why will the two future frontiers not be the same? Is it possible to draw the frontiers in such a way that the higher current saving rate will permit both higher saving and higher consumption in the future?

3. Do you think Levy's and Michel's proposal for national saving guidelines would have a significant impact on the national saving rate? How would you go about determining the proper guidelines? Would you favor voluntary guidelines, compulsory guidelines, or none at all? Discuss.

END NOTES

1. U.S. Department of Labor, Bureau of Labor Statistics, "International Comparisons of Manufacturing Productivity and Labor Cost Trends," USDL 89–322, June 30, 1989, Table 1.
2. "Are GNP Estimates Understated?" *The Margin* (January–February 1990): 13.
3. As quoted in Alfred L. Malabre, Jr., and Linkley H. Clark, Jr., "Productivity Statistics for the Service Sector May Understate Gains," *The Wall Street Journal*, August 12, 1992.

GLOSSARY

Accommodating policy   Expansionary monetary or fiscal policy used to increase aggregate demand in order to moderate the effects of a supply shock on real output

Aggregate demand   Total real planned expenditure

Aggregate demand curve   A graph showing the relationship between aggregate demand and the aggregate price level

Aggregate supply   Total real output of final goods and services (real GDP)

Aggregate supply curve   A graph showing the relationship between real output (real domestic product) and the average price level of final goods

Appreciate   Increase in value — such as the value of one country's currency increasing relative to the currency of another country

Assets   All the things that the firm or household owns or to which it holds a legal claim

Automatic fiscal policy   Changes in government purchases or net taxes caused by changes in economic conditions given unchanged tax and spending laws

Automatic stabilizers   Those elements of automatic fiscal policy that move the federal budget toward deficit during an economic contraction and toward surplus during an expansion

Autonomous   In the context of the income-expenditure model, refers to an expenditure that is independent of the level of real domestic income

Autonomous consumption   The part of total real consumption expenditure that is independent of the level of real disposable income. For any given consumption schedule, real autonomous consumption equals the level of real consumption associated with zero real disposable income

Autonomous net taxes   Taxes or transfer payments that do not vary with the level of domestic income

Average propensity to consume   Total consumption for any income level divided by total disposable income

Balance sheet A financial statement showing what a firm or household owns and what it owes

Base year The year that is chosen as a basis for comparison in calculating a price index or price level

Bond A certificate that represents a promise, in return for borrowed funds, to repay the loan over a period of years, with interest, according to an agreed-upon schedule

Business cycle Pattern of irregular but repeated expansion and contraction of aggregate economic activity

Capital All means of production that are created by people, including tools, industrial equipment, and structures

Central bank A government agency responsible for regulating a country's banking system and carrying out monetary policy

Change in demand A change in the quantity of a good that buyers are willing and able to purchase that results from a change in some condition other than the price of that good; shown by a shift in the demand curve

Change in quantity demanded A change in the quantity of a good that buyers are willing and able to purchase that results from a change in the good's price, other things being equal; shown by a movement from one point to another along a demand curve

Change in quantity supplied A change in the quantity of a good that suppliers are willing and able to sell that results from a change in the good's price, other things being equal; shown by a movement along a supply curve

Change in supply A change in the quantity of a good that suppliers are willing and able to sell that results from a change in some condition other than the good's price; shown by a shift in the supply curve

Circular flow of income and product The flow of goods and services between households and firms, balanced by the flow of payments made in exchange for goods and services

Closed economy An economy that has no links to the rest of the world

Commercial banks Financial intermediaries that provide a broad range of banking services, including accepting demand deposits and making commercial loans

Common stock Certificate of shared ownership in a corporation that gives the owner a vote in the selection of the firm's management and the right to a share in its profits

Comparative advantage Ability to produce a good or service at a relatively lower opportunity cost than someone else

Complementary goods Pair of goods for which an increase in the price of one results in a decrease in demand for the other

Conditional forecast Prediction of future economic events in the form "If A, then B, other things being equal"

Consumer Price Index (CPI) Average of the prices of a market basket of goods and services purchased by a typical urban household

Consumption All purchases of goods and services by households for the purpose of immediate use

Consumption schedule (consumption function) Graph that shows how real consumption expenditure varies as real disposable income changes, other things being equal

Cross-elasticity of demand The ratio of the percentage change in the quantity of a good demanded to a given percentage change in the price of some other good, other things being equal

Crowding-out effect Tendency of expansionary fiscal policy to raise the interest rate and thereby cause a decrease in real planned investment

Currency Coins and paper money

Current account The section of a country's international accounts that consists of imports and exports of goods and services and unilateral transfers

Current account balance The value of a country's exports of goods and services minus the value of its imports of goods and services plus its net transfer receipts from foreign sources

Cyclical deficit/surplus The difference between the structural budget and the actual federal budget—if the actual budget is above the structural budget, there is a cyclical surplus. Likewise, when the actual budget is below the structural budget, there is a cyclical deficit

Cyclical unemployment The difference between the observed rate of unemployment at a given point in the business cycle and the natural rate of unemployment

Demand The willingness and ability of buyers to purchase goods

Demand curve A graphical representation of the relationship between the price of a good and the quantity of that good that buyers demand

Demand-side inflation Inflation caused by an upward shift of the aggregate demand curve while the aggregate supply curve remains fixed or shifts upward at no more than an equal rate

Deposit multiplier The quantity of total deposits that can be created for each dollar of total reserves in a simple banking system where deposits are the only form of money, equal to 1/Reserve ratio

Depository institutions Financial intermediaries, including commercial banks and thrift institutions, which accept deposits from the public

Depreciate Decrease in value of a currency is said to depreciate relative to the value of the currency of another country

Direct relationship A relationship between two variables in which an increase in the value of one variable is associated with an increase in the value of the other

Discount rate The interest rate charged by the Fed on loans of reserves to banks

Discount window The department through which the Federal Reserve lends reserves to banks

Discouraged worker A person who would work if a suitable job were available but has given up looking for such a job

Discretionary fiscal policy Changes in the laws regarding government purchases and net taxes

Disposable personal income (disposable income) Income minus taxes

Domestic income The total income of all types, including wages, rents, interest payments, and profits, paid in return for factors of production used in producing domestic product

Domestic product The total value of all goods and services produced annually in a given country

Econometrics The statistical analysis of empirical economic data

Economic efficiency A state of affairs in which it is impossible to make any change that satisfies one person's wants more fully without causing some other person's wants to be satisfied less fully

Economics The social science that seeks to understand the choices people make in using scarce resources to meet their wants

Efficiency in distribution A situation in which it is not possible, by redistributing existing supplies of goods, to satisfy one person's wants more fully without causing some other person's wants to be satisfied less fully

Efficiency in production A situation in which it is not possible, given available knowledge and productive resources, to produce more of one good without forgoing the opportunity to produce some of another good

Elastic demand A situation in which quantity demanded changes by a larger percentage than price, so that total revenue increases as price decreases

Elasticity A measure of the response of one variable to a change in another, stated as a ratio of the percentage change in one variable to the associated percentage change in another variable

Empirical Based on experience or observation

Employed A term used to refer to a person who is working at least 1 hour a week for pay or at least 15 hours per week as an unpaid worker in a family business

Employment-population ratio The percentage of the noninstitutional adult population that is employed

Endogenous Term applied to any variable that is determined by other variables included in an economic model

Entitlements Transfer payments governed by long-term laws that are not subject to annual budget review

Entrepreneurship The process of looking for new possibilities—making use of new ways of doing things, being alert to new opportunities, and overcoming old limits

Equation of exchange An equation that shows the relationship among the money stock (M), the income velocity of money (V), the price level (P), and real domestic product (Q); written as MV = PQ

Equilibrium A condition in which buyers' and sellers' plans exactly mesh in the marketplace, so that the quantity supplied exactly equals the quantity demanded at a given price

Excess quantity demanded (shortage) A condition in which the quantity of a good demanded at a given price exceeds the quantity supplied

Excess quantity supplied (surplus) A condition in which the quantity of a good supplied at a given price exceeds the quantity demanded

Excess reserves The difference between the amount of reserve a bank actually holds and the minimum required by regulations

Exchange controls Restrictions on the freedom of firms and individuals to exchange the domestic currency for foreign currencies at market rates

Exchange-rate based stabilization policy A policy that uses the exchange rate as the principle operating target for macroeconomic policy

Exogenous Term applied to any variable that is determined by non-economic considerations, or by economic considerations that lie outside the scope of a given model

Expenditure multiplier The ratio of the resultant shift in real aggregate demand to an initial shift in one of the components of aggregate demand

Factors of production The basic inputs of labor, capital, and natural resources used in producing all goods and services

Federal funds market A market in which banks lend reserves to one another for periods as short as 24 hours

Federal funds rate The interest rate on overnight loans of reserves from one bank to another

Federal funds target The Fed's target for the federal funds rate, announced by the Federal Open Market Committee (FOMC)

Final goods and services Goods and services that are sold to or ready for sale to parties that will use them for consumption, investment, government purchases, or export

Financial account The section of a country's international accounts that consists of purchases and sales of assets and international borrowing and lending—also known as *capital account* or *capital* and *financial account*

Financial inflow Purchases of domestic assets by foreign buyers and borrowing from foreign lenders; also often called capital inflows

Financial intermediaries A group of firms, including banks, insurance companies, pension funds, and mutual funds, that gather funds from net savers and lend them to net borrowers

Financial markets A set of market institutions whose function is to channel the flow of funds from net savers to net borrowers

Financial outflow Purchases of foreign assets by domestic residents or loans by domestic lenders to foreign borrowers; also often called capital outflows

Fiscal policy Policy that is concerned with government purchases, taxes, and transfer payments

Fiscal year The federal government's budgetary year, which starts on October 1 of the preceding calendar year

Fixed investment Purchases of newly produced capital goods

Flow A process that occurs continuously through time, measured in units per time period

Foreign-exchange market A market in which the currency of one country is traded for that of another

Frictional unemployment The portion of unemployment that is accounted for by the short periods of unemployment needed for matching jobs with job seekers

GDP deflator A weighted average of the prices of all final goods and services produced in the economy

Government expenditures Government purchases of goods and services plus transfer payments

Government purchases of goods and services (government purchases) Purchases of goods by all levels of government plus purchases of services from contractors and wages of government employees

Gross domestic product (GDP) The value at current market prices of all final goods and services produced annually in a given country

Gross national product (GNP) The dollar value at current market prices of all final goods and services produced annually by factors of production owned by residents of a given country, regardless of where those factors are located

Growth recession A situation in which real output grows, but not quickly enough to keep unemployment from rising

Hierarchy A way of achieving coordination in which individual actions are guided by instructions from a central authority

Hyperinflation Very rapid inflation

Income elasticity of demand The ratio of the percentage change in the quantity of a good demanded to a given percentage change in consumer incomes, other things being equal

Income-expenditure model A model in which the equilibrium level of real domestic income is determined by treating real planned expenditure and real domestic product as functions of the level of real domestic income

Income-product line A graph showing the level of real domestic product (aggregate supply) associated with each level of real domestic income

Inconvertibility (of a currency) A situation in which a country's currency can be exchanged for foreign currency only through a government agency or with a government permit

Indexation A policy of automatically adjusting a value or payment in proportion to changes in the average price level

Inelastic demand A situation in which quantity demanded changes by a smaller percentage than price, so that total revenue decreases as price decreases

Inferior good A good for which an increase in consumer incomes results in a decrease in demand

Inflation Sustained increase in the average level of prices of all goods and services

Inflationary recession An episode in which real output falls below its natural level and unemployment rises above its natural rate while inflation continues

Inflation targeting A strategy for price stability in which policy makers adopt an explicit target range for the rate of inflation over an intermediate time horizon

Injections The government purchase, investment, and net export components of the circular flow

Input prices A measure of the average prices of labor, raw materials, and other inputs that firms use to produce goods and services

Inventory A stock of a finished good awaiting sale or use

Inventory investment Changes in stocks of finished goods ready for sale, raw materials, and partially completed goods in process of production

Inverse relationship A relationship between two variables in which an increase in the value of one variable is associated with a decrease in the value of the other

Investment The sum of fixed investment and inventory investment

Labor The contributions to production made by people working with their minds and muscles

Labor force The sum of all individuals who are employed and all individuals who are unemployed

Labor productivity A measure of how much workers produce in a given period of time, usually measured as output per hour of work

Law of demand The principle that an inverse relationship exists between the price of a good and the quantity of that good that buyers demand, other things being equal

Leakages The saving, net tax, and import components of the circular flow

Liabilities All the legal claims against a firm by nonowners or against a household by nonmember

Liquidity An asset's ability to be used directly as a means of payment, or to be readily converted into one, while retaining a fixed nominal value

Liquidity trap A situation in which interest rates near zero lead to accumulation of liquid assets instead of stimulating planned investment

M1 A measure of the money supply that includes currency and transaction deposits

M2 A measure of the money supply that include M1 plus retail money market mutual fund shares, money market deposit accounts, and saving deposits

Macroeconomics The branch of economics that studies large-scale economic phenomena, particularly inflation, unemployment, and economic growth

Marginal propensity to consume The proportion of each added dollar of real disposable income that households devote to consumption

Marginal propensity to import The percentage of each added dollar of real disposable income that is devoted to real consumption of imported goods and services

Marginal tax rate The percentage of each added dollar of real domestic income that must be paid in taxes

Market Any arrangement people have for trading with one another

Merchandise balance The value of a country's merchandise exports minus the value of its merchandise imports

Microeconomics The branch of economics that studies the choices of individuals, including households, business firms, and government agencies

Model In economics, synonym for theory, often applied to theories that are stated in graphical or mathematical form

Monetarism School of economics that emphasizes the importance of changes in the money stock as determinants of changes in real output and the price level

Money Asset that serves as a means of payment, a store of purchasing power, and a unit of account

Monetary base The sum of currency and reserve deposits, the monetary liabilities of the central bank

Money multiplier The total quantity of money that can be created for each dollar of the monetary base

Multiplier effect The tendency of a given exogenous change in planned expenditure to increase equilibrium GDP by a greater amount

National income The total income earned by a country's residents, including wages, rents, interest payments, and profits

National income accounts Set of official government statistics on aggregate economic activity

Natural level of real output The trend of real GDP growth over time, also known as potential real output

Natural rate of unemployment The sum of frictional and structural unemployment; the rate of unemployment that persists when the economy is experiencing neither accelerating nor decelerating inflation

Natural resources Anything that can be used as a productive input in its natural state, such as farmland, building sites, forests, and mineral deposits

Negative slope A slope having a value less than zero

Net domestic product (NDP) Gross domestic product minus an allowance (called the capital consumption allowance) that represents the value of capital equipment used up in the production process

Net exports Exports minus imports of goods and services

Net taxes Tax revenue minus transfer payments

Net tax multiplier The ratio of an induced change in real aggregate demand to a given change in real net taxes

Net worth The firm's or household's assets minus its liabilities

Neutrality of Money The proposition that in the long run a one-time change in the money stock affects only the price level and not real output, employment, interest rates, or real planned investment

Nominal In economics, a term that refers to data that have not been adjusted for the effects of inflation

Nominal exchange rate The exchange rate expressed in the usual way: in terms of current units of foreign currency per current dollar

Nominal interest rate The interest rate expressed in the usual way: in terms of current dollars without adjustment for inflation

Normal good A good for which an increase in consumer incomes results in an increase in demand

Normative economics The area of economics that is devoted to judgments about whether economic policies or conditions are good or bad

Open economy An economy that is linked to the outside world by imports, exports, and financial transactions

Open market operation Purchase (sale) by the Fed of government securities from (to) the public

Operating target A financial variable for which the Fed sets a short-term target, which it then uses as a guide in the day-to-day conduct of open market operations

Opportunity cost The cost of a good or service measured in terms of the forgone opportunity to pursue the best possible alternative activity with the same time or resources

Output gap The economy's current level of real output minus its natural level of real output, stated as a percentage of the natural level

Perfectly elastic demand A situation in which the demand curve is a horizontal line

Perfectly inelastic demand A situation in which the demand curve is a vertical line

Personal income The total income received by households, including earned income and transfer payments

Phillips curve A graph showing the relationship between the inflation rate and the unemployment rate, other things being equal

Planned expenditure The sum of consumption, government purchases, net exports, and planned investment

Planned-expenditure schedule A graph showing the level of total real planned expenditure associated with each level of real domestic income

Planned inventory investment Changes in the level of inventory made on purpose, as part of a firm's business plan

Planned investment The sum of fixed investment and planned inventory investment

Planned investment schedule A graph showing the relationship between the total quantity of real planned investment expenditure and the real interest rate

Positive economics The area of economics that is concerned with facts and the relationships among them

Positive slope A slope having a value greater than zero

Price elasticity of demand The ratio of the percentage change in the quantity of a good demanded to a given percentage change in its price, other things being equal

Price elasticity of supply The ratio of the percentage change in the quantity of a good supplied to a given percentage change in its price, other things being equal

Price index A weighted average of the prices of goods and services expressed in relation to a base year value of 100

Price level A weighted average of the prices of goods and services expressed in relation to a base year value of 1.0

Price stability A situation in which the rate of inflation is low enough so that it is not a significant factor in business and individual decision making

Producer price index (PPI) A price index based on a sample of goods and services bought by business firms

Production possibility frontier A graph that shows possible combinations of goods that can be produced by an economy given available knowledge and factors of production

Purchasing power parity A situation in which a given sum of money will buy the same market basket of goods and services when converted from one currency to another at prevailing exchange rates

Real In economics, a term that refers to data that have been adjusted for the effects of inflation

Real exchange rate The nominal exchange rate adjusted for changes in the price levels of both countries relative to a chosen base year

Real interest rate The nominal interest rate minus the rate of inflation

Realized expenditure The sum of all planned and unplanned expenditures

Realized investment The sum of planned and unplanned investment

Real output A synonym for real gross domestic product

Recession A cyclical economic contraction that lasts six months or more

Reserve ratio The quantity of reserves held by banks, stated as a percentage of deposits

Required reserves The minimum amount of reserves that the Fed requires depository institutions to hold

Reserves Cash in bank vaults and banks' non-interest-bearing deposits with the Federal Reserve System

Revenue Price multiplied by quantity sold

Saving The part of household income that is not used to buy goods and services or to pay taxes

Savings deposit A deposit at a bank that can be fully redeemed at any time, but from which checks cannot be written

Scarcity A situation in which there is not enough of a resource to meet all of everyone's wants

Securities A collective term for common stocks, bonds, and other financial instruments

Slope For a straight line, the ratio of the change in the y value to the change in the x value between any two points on the line

Spontaneous order A way of achieving coordination in which individuals adjust their actions in response to cues from their immediate environment

Stock A quantity that exists at a given point in time, measured in terms of units only

Structural budget The budget surplus or deficit that the federal government would incur given current tax and spending laws and unemployment at its natural rate

Structural budget deficit The deficit that would prevail in any year given that year's tax and spending laws, assuming real GDP to be at its natural level

Structural unemployment The portion of unemployment that is accounted for by people who are out of work for long periods because their skills do not match those required for available jobs

Substitute goods A pair of goods for which an increase in the price of one causes an increase in demand for the other

Supply The willingness and ability of sellers to provide goods for sale in a market

Supply curve A graphical representation of the relationship between the price of a good and the quantity of that good that sellers are willing to supply

Supply-side inflation Inflation that is caused by an upward shift in the aggregate supply curve while the aggregate demand curve remains fixed or shifts upward more slowly

Supply shock An event, such as an increase in the price of imported oil, a crop failure, or a natural disaster, that raises input prices for all or most firms and pushes up workers' costs of living

Target reserve ratio The minimum amount of reserves a bank needs to hold that is consistent with regulations and safe banking practices

Tangent A straight line that touches a curve at a given point without intersecting it

Tax incidence The distribution of the economic burden of a tax

Tax revenue The total value of all taxes collected by government

Theory A representation of the way in which facts are related to one another

Thrift institutions (thrifts) A group of financial intermediaries that operate much like commercial banks, including savings and loan associations, savings banks, and credit unions

Time deposit A deposit at a bank or thrift institution from which funds can be withdrawn without payment of a penalty only at the end of an agreed-upon period

Total Factor Productivity A measurement of improvements in technology and organization that allow increases in the output produced by given quantities of labor and capital

Transaction deposit A deposit from which funds can be freely withdrawn by check or electronic transfer to make payments to third parties

Transfer payments Payment by government to individuals not made in return for services currently performed, for example, unemployment compensation and pensions

Transmission mechanism The set of channels through which monetary policy affects planned expenditure

Unemployed A term used to refer to a person who is not employed but is actively looking for work

Unemployment rate The percentage of the labor force that is unemployed

Unit elastic demand A situation in which price and quantity demanded change by the same percentage, so that total revenue remains unchanged as price changes

Unplanned inventory investment Changes in the level of inventory arising from a difference between planned and actual sales

Value added The dollar value of an industry's sales less the value of intermediate goods purchased for use in production

Velocity (income velocity of money) The ratio of nominal domestic income to the money stock; a measure of the average number of times each dollar of the money stock is used each year to purchase final goods and services of the kind that enter into GDP

INDEX

T

U

V

W